WINNICOTT

Also by F. Robert Rodman

NOT DYING
A Memoir

KEEPING HOPE ALIVE
On Becoming a Psychotherapist

THE SPONTANEOUS GESTURE
Selected Letters of D. W. Winnicott (Editor)

WINNICOTT

LIFE AND WORK

F. Robert Rodman, M.D.

A Merloyd Lawrence Book

PERSEUS PUBLISHING
A Member of the Perseus Books Group

Library of Congress Control Number: 2003102146
ISBN 0-7382-0397-1

Perseus Publishing is a Member of the Perseus Books Group.
Find us on the World Wide Web at http://www.perseuspublishing.com.
Perseus Publishing books are available at special discounts for bulk purchases in the U.S. by corporations, institutions, and other organizations. For more information, please contact the Special Markets Department at the Perseus Books Group, 11 Cambridge Center, Cambridge, MA 02142, or call (800) 255-1514 or (617) 252-5298, or e-mail j.mccrary@perseusbooks.com.

Text design by Reginald Thompson
Set in 10-point Palatino by the Perseus Books Group

First printing, April 2003

1 2 3 4 5 6 7 8 9 10—06 05 04 03

For Nick Rodman

Acknowledgments

I had no book in mind when Donald Winnicott replied to my request for his opinion of papers I had written in the 1960s, but those replies turned out to be the root of this biography. Out of this correspondence came my request to his widow, Clare Winnicott, that I collect and edit a volume of his letters. She allowed that project to come to fruition and gave me access to many letters and documents that are the matrix of information from which I have derived this book. After Mrs. Winnicott's death in 1984, Madeleine Davis, a member of the Winnicott Board of Editors, supported my editorial work and then agreed to collaborate with me on a biography. Since she knew far more than I, it was my great good fortune to work as her co-author. Her husband, the distinguished pediatrician John Davis, a colleague of Winnicott's, now Professor Emeritus at Cambridge, was a cordial and knowledgeable presence then and through subsequent years.

In 1988 Madeleine arranged a group of interviews which we conducted, the start of our joint work proper. Soon after that she was diagnosed with breast cancer and died in 1991. We had communicated often through letters and phone calls, and I came to cherish the brilliant and humane insights of which she seemed always capable.

I would not have continued with the book except for a proposal from Arthur Rosenthal, formerly director of the Harvard University Press. I eventually presented the project to the redoubtable Merloyd Lawrence at Perseus Books. She was well acquainted with Winnicott, having edited collections of his essays. She has made graceful and coherent much in my writing that was awkward and confusing. All infelicities and errors, are, of course, my own.

I wish Marion Milner were alive to receive my gratitude for the warmth and insight she afforded me on the several occasions on which we talked at her home in Chalk Farm. I am grateful to Nina and Musa Farhi for their friendship and intelligence, to Christopher Bollas for providing me with shelter for a week in 1988 when Madeleine and I set out on our interviewing rounds, and to members of the Squiggle Foundation. I well remember wandering into a meeting being chaired by Alexander Newman, with Marion seated in the front row and Nina Farhi taking the podium at one point with her particularly explicit, powerful, and eloquent speaking style. The poetry of William Blake was often quoted. Above all, this concentrated and serious attention to Winnicott, outside of an analytic Institute, was more than enlivening. It was electrifying.

I would like to express my gratitude to those many individuals in southwest England who responded to my inquiries with generous replies. Their letters enriched this book beyond measure. Hannah ("Queen") Henry, a dear friend of Donald, Alice, and, later, Clare Winnicott, supplied me with all the memories and memorabilia in her possession, an unparalleled treasure. I received many letters from individuals who reached out to me on the basis of a small insert in the Plymouth newspaper. They are Elspeth Mills, Stewart Watts-Wills, Mrs. B. I. Tweddle, Mr. Ken Fenn, S. Brown, Mrs. P. M. Sharp, Mrs. Mary Gamble, Mrs. Judith Etherton, Mr. Alfred M. Palmer, Mrs. Aimee Fewings, P. M. Wingett, Miss V. A. Brown, J. Eldrey, Mr. C. Pearn, Mrs. M. M. Gibbs, Mr. A. W. J. Hallett, Mr. S. Moore, Inez Warren, Mrs. W. Coombes, Betty M. E. Brant, Mrs. K. M. Ayres, Mrs. Lilla Johns, Mrs. Margery Draper, Reg Collicott, Mrs. Vera Spear, G. A. Bennett, Mrs. Lilian Widdicombe, Mrs. Phyllis Turner, Mrs. M. Griffiths, Edith M. Urch, Mrs. D. Hughes, Michael Byatt, Caroline Nash, Edna Wallis, D. E. and E. G. Howard, G. R. Palmer, Mr. C. May, Mrs. Doris V. B. Lyon, Mr. J. J. Cammann, Dorothy Siewruck, George Rowe, Jenny Cardew, Pamela Phillips, Crispin Gill, and Ann M. Lewis. I want to give special recognition to the work of Barry Poland, whose research was of great use, and Victor Barton, whose yeoman work and assiduous devotion to the unearthing of early material about the Winnicotts, up to recent times, immeasurably enhanced this undertaking. I was the recipient of a completely spontaneous outpouring of help from the citizens of Plymouth, whose memories helped to reconstruct something of the early life of Donald Winnicott and his family. I thank them all.

Madeleine and I interviewed Jimmy Ede, Winnicott's friend from his schooldays, in Edinburgh in 1988, and Mr. Ede's daughters as well. We talked with Rosa Taylor, the second wife of Alice Winnicott's brother Jim. Peter Woolland, the grandson of Winnicott's uncle Richard Winnicott, provided recollections and valuable photographs. Margaret Little talked about Donald then and was a continuing and generous correspondent from then until her death a few years later. I interviewed Enid Balint in 1988 and again at a UCLA conference. Martin James recollected Donald for me in 1988. I am grateful to have known all of these people and to have benefited from their willingness to pass on what they knew about Donald Winnicott. Toward the end of my work, I learned further from Drs. Judith Issroff and James Hood. Professor John Turner deepened my understanding of Winnicott's relationship to the Romantics and the role of illusion in his thinking. Brooke Hopkins called my attention to Winnicott's value in relation to the Jesus myth and other religious subjects. I am greatly indebted to my fellow psychoanalyst and biographer Linda Hopkins for innumerable helpful comments and her particular knowledge of Masud Khan. Georges Borchardt, my agent, shepherded me through the many turns this project took.

Dr. Jennifer Johns, who is in charge of the Winnicott Trust, has been a kind and generous colleague, and I have greatly benefited from her encouragement. I met her late father, Dr. Thomas Main, in 1963, and like to think of continuities with his reflections in my own, even if they are sometimes tenuous ones. I fondly recall having spent a month at St. Mary's Hospital Medical School in 1958, close by Paddington Green, even if what I was studying then was vascular surgery and I had not yet heard the name of Donald Winnicott.

I feel indebted to people senior to me who recognized something extraordinary about Donald Winnicott, chief among them my teachers Drs. Anna Kulka and Norbert Rieger. Dr. Rieger ran the children's division of the Camarillo State Hospital in California, where he worked with the most severely disabled of children with unstinting effort and constant reflection on the subject of what could be done on their behalf.

Foremost among those who have helped me to understand the mind, and to revise that understanding in the light of growing knowledge, is Dr. Leo Rangell, my friend and mentor of 37 years.

Two audiences over the years gave me leave to express myself and therefore to learn about my preoccupations. One was, from 1976 to 1981, a group in Gothenberg, Sweden: the child therapists of that city and others who studied and worked in the Psychological Institute of the University there. Professor Knut Larsson and Birgitta Steg, my longstanding colleagues and dear friends were responsible for those many unforgettable occasions. The other audience was at the University of São Paulo, Brazil, where, on the basis of my edition of Winnicott's selected letters, I was invited to lecture by Professora Ivonise Fernandes da Motta. At this writing I have done so on three occasions, each time with groups at all levels of psychoanalytic experience, always to my benefit. I heartily thank my Swedish and Brazilian friends.

My family have seen me through years and years of my preoccupation with this book and have put up with my silent absorption at the dining room table in front of the laptop every weekend since what seems like time immemorial. They have borne a sacrifice imposed by me in the high value I placed on completing this book. I cannot repay them for that. The 1985 trip to England that my wife, Kathy, and I took with our eighteen-month-old daughter, Sarah, when I was given stacks of material by Madeleine Davis, stands out as one of the brightest of times. Little did we know how many years of work would follow.

Chronology

1945   Continues series of original papers that will be a feature
         of his work for the rest of his life
1948   Father dies
1949   Suffers two coronaries; separates from Alice
1950   Suffers a third coronary after a patient commits suicide
1951   Writes and presents paper on transitional objects
1952   Refuses to contribute the paper to a book in honor of
         Melanie Klein; marries Clare Britton and moves into 87,
         Chester Square, Belgravia
1958   Publishes *Through Paediatrics to Psycho-Analysis*, a collec-
         tion of professional papers; previously published other
         books for lay audiences.
1960   Death of Melanie Klein
1961   Publishes *The Maturational Processes and the Facilitating
         Environment*
1968   "Use of an Object" given in New York; life-threatening
         illness follows
1971   Dies in London

WINNICOTT

PART ONE

I learnt from him, that Poetry, even that of the loftiest, and seemingly, that of the wildest odes, had a logic of its own, as severe as that of science; and more difficult, because more subtle, more complex, and dependent on more and more fugitive causes.

—S. T. Coleridge
Biographia Literaria (1817)

— 1 —

"The Introductory Chapter to a Book"

Donald Winnicott was forty-nine when he addressed the British Psycho-Analytical Society on the evening of November 28, 1945. The country, depleted of blood and resources by World War II, was essentially bankrupt. Much of London was reduced to leftover walls and rubble-strewn bombscapes. Poverty and food shortages were widespread; but nonetheless the war was finally over, and there was therefore a measure of hope that the work of reconstruction might begin. That was the spirit that animated Winnicott's presentation. The paper he gave that evening, "Primitive Emotional Development," began: "It will be clear at once from my title that I have chosen a very wide subject. All I can attempt to do is to make a preliminary personal statement, as if writing the introductory chapter to a book. I shall not first give an historical survey and show the development of my ideas from the theories of others, because my mind does not work that way. What happens is that I gather this and that, here and there, settle down to clinical experience, form my own theories and then, last of all, interest myself in looking to see where I stole what. Perhaps this is as good a method as any." Unlike Samuel Taylor Coleridge, another student of the imagination, who was disheartened to be accused of plagiarism, as most authors would be, Winnicott, with his bold use of the word "stole," displays a sense of the free play of his mind, of which he was proud.

He goes on: "About primitive emotional development there is a good deal that is not known or properly understood, at least by me, and it could well be argued that this discussion ought to be postponed five or ten years. Against this there is the fact that misunderstandings constantly recur in the Society's scientific meetings, and perhaps we shall find that we do know enough already to prevent some of these misunderstandings by a discussion of these primitive emotional states."

The resounding importance of Winnicott's subject and the boldness of his insights were belied by his appearance and presentation. He was relatively short in stature, five foot seven. His voice was somewhat high-pitched, with very precise enunciation, and his childhood origins in Devon were evident in the regional accent with which he spoke enthusiastically. He had a good deal of experience by then of giving papers, and had published quite a few in the pediatric literature, many of them included in a 1931 book, *Clinical Notes on Disorders of Childhood*.

He continues: "Primarily interested in the child patient, and the infant, I decided that I must study psychosis in analysis. I have had about a dozen psychotic adult patients, and half of these have rather extensively been analysed. This happened in the war and I might say that I hardly noticed the blitz, being all the time engaged in analysis of psychotic patients who are notoriously and maddeningly oblivious of bombs, earthquakes, and floods."[1] Already he implies a close identification of himself as the analyst with his psychotic patients. And yet, in spite of "hardly noticing the blitz," it was he who, during one of their meetings, called the attention of the members of the society to the fact that bombs happened to be falling.

"As a result of this work," he goes on, "I have a great deal to communicate and to bring into alignment with current theories, and perhaps this paper may be taken as a beginning. By listening to what I have to say, and criticizing, you help me to take my next step, which is the study of the sources of my ideas, both in clinical work and in the published writings of analysts. It has in fact been extremely difficult to keep clinical material out of this paper, which I wished nevertheless to keep short so that there might be plenty of time for discussion."

Winnicott started his own analysis in 1923, when he was twenty-seven years old. He had become aware of Freud's theories while in medical school, but did not seek out analysis for himself until the year of his marriage to Alice Taylor, which was also the year of his appointment as a children's doctor to three hospitals and the year when he started his private practice. He sought help for personal problems from Ernest Jones, the founder of British psychoanalysis, and was given a list of analysts from which to choose, but he could not make a choice. He was then referred to James Strachey, himself recently back from Vienna, where he and his wife had undergone analysis with Freud.

A few years later, Winnicott became one of the first candidates[2] in the British Society. He was not yet knowledgeable enough to have developed a point of view about the issues of the day; but eventually his own temperament and growing stock of observations drove him into a deep, lifelong absorption with basic questions of human psychology. He became one of the most original of psychological and philosophical thinkers, and was a clinician of extraordinary skill.

His independence of mind can best be appreciated against the background of controversy that had been a part of the history of psychoanalysis from its beginnings and then took a particular turn in the British Society in the late 1930s and early 1940s. The well-known schisms between the young Freud and his associates Carl Jung and Alfred Adler had marked the field. Other breaks with Wilhelm Stekel, Wilhelm Reich, Otto Rank, and Sándor Ferenczi followed. An older Freud, now afflicted with cancer of the jaw, oversaw but kept a degree of distance from the conflict that arose between his daughter Anna and Melanie Klein. Their disagreements are central to an understanding of the history of child analysis, and to the individual development of Donald Winnicott.

Psychoanalysis in Great Britain had begun with Ernest Jones's enthusiastic response to the writings of Sigmund Freud, whom he first met in Vienna in 1908.[3] Jones was a Welsh neurologist who became one of Freud's closest colleagues and most energetic champions. He founded the London Psycho-Analytical Society in 1913; but, faced with the preference of one member for the theories of Jung over Freud, he disbanded the organization and, in 1919, tried again, this time under the rubric the British Psycho-Analytical Society. This was a small group (twenty members, six of whom were women), which, with its primarily Anglo-Saxon composition, differed from the mostly Jewish societies on the European continent. The pragmatic, empiricist English character was fundamental to its distinct contributions to psychoanalysis.[4]

An attempt to foster understanding between the British and the European societies was part of the background that brought the forty-four-year-old Melanie Klein to England in 1926.[5] She had been analyzed by two of Freud's associates, Sándor Ferenczi in Budapest and then Karl Abraham in Berlin. During this period she had begun to observe her own children through a psychoanalytic lens. Her findings, and what she made of them, were the first hints of an original and powerful theory of the earliest development of mind, an area previously neglected by Freud. The British analysts, under Jones's direction, invited her to give a series of lectures, after which, partly in response to Jones's wish that she analyze his wife and his two children, she emigrated to England. For her, this was a welcome change from conditions in Berlin, where, after the death of Karl Abraham, she was treated badly by the Hungarian analysts Sándor Rado and Franz Alexander.

Klein prospered in the receptive atmosphere of the British Society throughout the remainder of the 1920s and well into the 1930s. As the menace of Nazism intensified and the whole of European life was torn asunder, psychoanalysts, like everyone else, sought places of safety. Most of those who could emigrated to countries in the West.[6] Sigmund Freud and his family settled in London, through the intervention of Ernest Jones and Princess Marie Bonaparte, herself a psychoanalyst. Other analysts went to the United States, Canada, and South America.[7]

Anna Freud, born in 1895, was the youngest child of Sigmund and Martha Freud. Having been trained as an elementary school teacher and analyzed by her father, she contributed a viewpoint to the nascent field of child analysis sharply at odds with Klein's.[8] Anna Freud, whose work was primarily with school-age youngsters, thought that children in general were not capable of developing transferences the way adults could. She emphasized the importance of forming a supportive bond with a child who needed analysis, her thought being that since children were still under the influence of their parents, the internal structure of the mind had not yet solidified in a way that would allow that structure to be reactivated toward a psychoanalyst. This was rather different from Klein's no-nonsense interpretive approach, which was based on the belief that children's play was the equivalent of an adult's free associations and a child was fully capable of forming transferences. She dated the development of the structure of the mind to a much earlier stage than did either Sigmund or Anna Freud.

With Anna Freud's arrival in London and her entry into the British Society, the stage was set for controversy.[9] The large number of European analysts taken into the British Society altered the balance drastically and permanently, some lining up as allies of Klein, others with Anna Freud. The primarily Jewish emigrants began to outnumber the original members of the society. There was a sense of competition between Anna Freud and Melanie Klein for the title of most legitimate heir of Sigmund Freud. Anna was his daughter and had been analyzed by her father, but Klein believed that her own theory followed much more directly and powerfully in Freud's tradition.

During World War II, many members of the society served in the military,[10] but a substantial group of those who remained in London managed to attend a long series of what came to be known as the "Extraordinary Meetings," in which the differences of opinion between followers of Klein and those of Anna Freud were aired. The impetus for those meetings came originally from a number of public attacks on Klein launched by her analyst daughter Melitta Schmideberg, in league with Schmideberg's analyst, the prominent Edward Glover. Glover, second in command to Jones in the British hierarchy, had started out as a Klein enthusiast. The meetings were an attempt to tame the reckless assaults on Klein.[11] The atmosphere of controversy, fueled by the uncertainties of war and the disorientation experienced by those on both sides who were working with colleagues from a different culture, rose to a fever pitch in the early 1940s.[12]

The so-called Controversial Discussions drew many interested participants as members tried to puzzle out their differences and arrive at a method of working together in spite of them. The proceedings led to a compromise that was a tribute to British civility. It took some years before the settlement of those differences, in the form of a permanent splitting of training into program A (led by Melanie Klein) and program B (led by Anna Freud), was put in place. Between these two was the "Middle Group" made up of analysts who wished not to be allied with either of the other two; they were diverse in background and belief. Donald Winnicott had been regarded as a follower of Melanie Klein. He was thirty-eight when he graduated from the British Institute for Psychoanalysis in 1934, and soon after qualified as a child analyst. Klein had provided a good deal of supervision of his child cases between 1935 and 1940[13] and had selected him to analyze one of her own children. Although he was on excellent terms with Klein and her followers, and continued to have great respect for her point of view and herself personally, it was gradually becoming apparent that his viewpoint was taking a divergent path.[14] At the heart of their growing disagreements was Winnicott's conviction that the mother as an actual, external figure was crucial to the development of the psyche of the child. Klein, by contrast, emphasized the indigenous elements in the conception of the mother in the mind of the child. It was thus the child's fantasy life that, in essence, determined the sort of mother a child had, with all the ramifications flowing therefrom. Winnicott, a pediatrician who conducted a clinic for children and their mothers for most of his working life, saw it otherwise.

At the time he presented "Primitive Emotional Development," Winnicott was having a romance with Clare Britton, who would eventually become his second wife. She was a psychiatric social worker with whom he supervised in Oxfordshire the care of evacuated children during the war. During this relationship, which would continue for the rest of his life, he became an entirely new kind of thinker and writer about the psychoanalytic understanding of human life. The immanence of the personal element in Winnicott's writing ("my mind does not work that way"), and, presumably, in his highly disciplined therapeutic work as well, constantly colored his thinking, leading him to acknowledge that it was always a human being who was conducting an analysis, and that the process was not simply a systematic application of objectivity and science.

It may seem obvious that a psychoanalyst is always a person, but the culture of science, pretensions to science, and the writings of those who wish to be taken seriously as scientists do tend to generate poses and styles that are intended to imply that observations, and reflections on those observations, are the work of completely unemotional, which is to say, completely "objective" instruments.[15] The psychoanalytic literature is no exception. Winnicott consistently presented himself as a real person, and therefore closer to what he would eventually call a True Self, than all other psychoanalytic writers.

When Clare entered his life, Donald had been married for twenty years to a rather disturbed woman, the former Alice Taylor. He had given generously of his caretaking self, but the marriage had been fruitless in several ways. There was no sex, and of course no children, but perhaps neither partner wished it otherwise.

Winnicott's development as a person and as a psychoanalytic thinker depended greatly on his unceasing self-analysis. This effort to realize his capacities personally and professionally led him toward the late achievement of a fully sexual relationship with Clare. This personal transformation was accompanied by a vast output of papers and books that gradually influenced large numbers of fellow analysts as well as many others in related fields and the public in general.

Winnicott's idea that his paper on primitive emotional development could be considered the "introductory chapter to a book" indicates his sense of a beginning—not only the new postwar beginning of Britain as a whole, but a *personal* beginning as well, signified by his relationship to his newly found love, Clare Britton. His bold presentation of a personal approach to producing papers carried an implied expectation that this would appeal to his audience. Did he have prior experience with that audience that made this a reasonable expectation, or was he simply "being himself," finally, as he had in earlier years, especially within the warm and appreciative context of his own family? He was, I think, "assuming" the audience into family-mindedness, coaching them, as a result of his own transference needs, to play this role in his internal/external personal drama. He would in time influence a very wide circle of readers in this way by according them a certain respect as participants in an unfolding story or theory.

When Winnicott speaks of how, "last of all," he interests himself "in looking to see where [he] stole what," he might be comparing himself to those evacuated children who had developed "the antisocial tendency." He and Clare had studied such children in Oxfordshire. His paper on the antisocial tendency would outline a theory of how, for children with an initially satisfactory relationship to their parents, who were then subjected to deprivation, the antisocial reaction was an expression of their sense of being entitled to whatever they stole. He called such symptoms signs of the child's hope that observing adults might take note and provide what was needed for the sake of continuing development. Winnicott's identification with these children is expressed in his characterization of himself as one who steals, too.

"Stealing" and actions that express excited hatred seem to have been required, in Winnicott's thinking, for transcending "goodness," "niceness," "conformity." What he called "stealing" and hating was the indispensable key to instinctually driven behavior, including everything connected to the expression of the True Self and sexuality. Here he was reaching deep into himself for the conditions that would enable him to behave transgressively, to allow indigenous energies to burst forth despite the expectations of others. Noncompliance became one of the great themes of his life and work.[16] Sexual experience feels real, he would later say, to the extent that it incorporates aggression.

Winnicott admits that "there is a good deal that is not known or properly understood, at least by me," but goes on to say that his attempt is worthwhile anyway. Again he makes room for his imperfect grasp. And, as in his comment about the introduction to a book, he speaks of "this paper. . . . as a beginning." He then mentions his relationship to his audience, which he needs in order that he may "take [his] next step, which is a study of the sources of [his] ideas." He reverses the usual requirement that the writer must already have studied the sources of his ideas before he sits down to write. Thus, his conception of what is required for himself, as a unique contributor, is an audience that can facilitate his grasp of where his ideas come from. At a later phase of his career,[17] he would express further thoughts on what a contributor requires of his listeners, who, at their best, constitute a "facilitating environment" to meet the contributor's "maturational processes." In his theorizing and in his presentation of his own mental state, he makes adequate room for the state of continuous dependency that characterizes human life.

Altogether, these few paragraphs demonstrate a sense of confidence that trenches upon defiance, a willingness to stand in the limelight in order to be criticized and appreciated, not only for the ideas he intends to express, but also for the personal style with which he expresses them. A philosophy of psychoanalytic science is being promulgated by example, one that would have profound appeal to many, but would prove as well to be far ahead of what his audience was prepared to imagine in the twenty-five years of life that lay ahead of him, and in the years after. His close colleague Marion Milner's description of her first impression of him as a Catherine wheel, the twirling firework that throws off sparks in all directions,[18] captures his dazzling play of thought, fantasy, and speculation, his capacity to envision what no one had previously seen.

— 2 —

Origins and Early Life

D onald Woods Winnicott was born on April 7, 1896, "to a merchant's wife in England's damp but beautiful west country."[1] The woman defined in those late Victorian days by the occupation of her husband would become, in the long development of Winnicott's appreciation, that guardian of human development, "the good-enough mother," while the father, the "merchant," faded into an occasionally acknowledged but rather two-dimensional presence—until close to the end of his life, that is, when he finally wrote something essential about the father, "the first whole person" the child encounters.

Clare Britton Winnicott's memoir[2] provides the principal source of information about her husband's early life. Her description of an idyllic turn-of-the-century English provincial childhood supports the notion of Winnicott as a man with deep roots in a nurturing environment, leading logically to the good-natured and clever pediatrician-psychoanalyst who understood children, mothers, and deeply disturbed patients. Although she is careful to tell us that all was not perfect ("He often found life hard and could be despondent and depressed and angry"), her "Reflection" does not examine the sources of conflict in his early life in any depth. She once told me that, unlike so many others, she did *not* idealize her husband.[3] In the memoir her intention was, in any case, to focus on the playful aspects of his way of being, not to provide a biography.

His "merchant" father was the forty-year-old John Frederick Winnicott, his mother, Elizabeth Martha Woods Winnicott, thirty-four. The Westcountry town was Plymouth, Devon. J. Frederick Winnicott was an enterprising businessman who, with his older brother, Richard Weeks Winnicott, operated a wholesale and retail hardware business in Frankfort Street. Their Wesleyan ancestors had "come down out of the Midlands" in the eighteenth century.[4]

Westcountry England was a center of non-Anglican faiths of all sorts, ranging from those, such as Wesleyanism, which fostered independence of mind, to the Plymouth Brethren, a Quaker sect of the same era, which fostered subservience to a fixed view of man, and is described by Edmund Gosse in his celebrated autobiography *Father and Son*.[5] Gosse's father was one of many who could not manage a transition from traditional religious teachings about man's origin to the new ideas promulgated by Darwin,[6] but Frederick Winnicott seems not to have participated in this widespread spiritual crisis. Donald, under no paternal pressure to adhere to a specific view in the matter, would embrace Darwin's ideas enthusiastically, just as Freud had. They eventually contributed to his early absorption with psychoanalysis.

According to Clare Winnicott, Donald's father taught him to read the Bible and find in it whatever he could as a personal guide. This encouragement would seem to have led easily to the freedom that he would one day celebrate in his own brand of thought, so startlingly different from other concepts in analytic currency. Yet the development of that precious independence can hardly have been as easy as it seems. Winnicott was to be preoccupied with achieving it throughout his life.

His mother, Elizabeth, an Anglican before she married,[7] was born on January 1, 1862, the daughter of William Woods, a chemist, and his wife, Anne Woods, née White. Her brother worked in their father's business.[8] Her marriage took place on January 26, 1887, when she was twenty-four, in the parish church of St. Andrews in Plymouth.

These were patriarchal times. The husband had authority over the wife, father over children, brother over sister.[9] Although Bessie Winnicott was not the actual legal property of her husband, she had escaped that status by only three years, for it was not until 1884 that "a wife was not liable for prison if she refused to return to the conjugal home, and soon afterwards legislation removed from the husband the right to confine her in the event of such behaviour. So the wife ceased to be the property of the husband."[10] Donald's personal growth and ultimate social influence took place at a time when changes in the status of women were well under way.

In a 1900 photograph taken of the Winnicott family at their large Victorian home, Rockville,[11] formerly called Rock Villa,[12] we can see a slim-waisted, full-bosomed young woman peeking out from behind her proud and composed husband, who holds a top hat in his hand, as if to indicate his prepossessing status. In two photographs taken more than twenty years later, we see a much heavier woman; in one she wears a serious, perhaps even timid expression, and in the other a jolly smile. The latter was taken at a regatta. She stands next to her husband, who holds a cigarette, and is still slim, and smiling.

In an interview Donald's close friend from boarding school days, Stanley Ede, often called "Jim" or "Jimmy," remembered Mrs. Winnicott[13] coming down the large staircase in the morning clapping her hands, as if to strike a pleasant note for the day.[14] She was said to be a loving woman who tolerated the boys' habit of moving the furniture, including a grand piano, around in the drawing room. Jimmy eventually became a distinguished interior designer, and Donald was himself deeply concerned with space — the real, external space within which people dwelt and also with what he conceptualized as the transitional space in the mind. Toward the end of his life, and among many of his followers, the term "potential space" became identified with Donald. He would characteristically rearrange the parts of his papers on his way to a final version of them,[15] and he delighted in challenging the accepted notions of how things were, through both his often unpredictable behavior and his psychoanalytic ideas. Perhaps his habit of rearrangement, which included unpredictable comical pratfalls in adult life, was intended to enliven his mother first of all, and all the others who followed, and to produce novelty as an antidote for sameness, boredom, or perhaps depression, something like what his mother may have been trying to do when she clapped her hands. Or, alternatively, perhaps it simply revealed an aesthetic cast of mind, a celebration of infinite possibility.

From a poem written by Donald late in his life called "The Tree,"[16] we discern strong evidence that Bessie Winnicott was a depressed woman and that Donald took it as his task to provide her with relief. This poem tells of his mother's depression and the effect of his conviction that it was up to him to bring her back to life. It is the most powerful surviving evidence of his struggle. Donald's mother was clearly a background figure to her husband, whose career was brilliant and public. In 1887, at a party at the Plymouth Mechanics' Institute to celebrate the marriage of their newly chosen honorary secretary, the hope was expressed "that his Rosalind would not stand between Orlando and his endeavours to promote the success and prosperity of the Institute."[17] She did not.

We thus know a good deal about the activities of Donald's father but very little about his mother. Besides "The Tree," there are a few telling scraps that attest to his understanding of her, as well as the testimony of a lifetime of study and devotion to understanding mothers and babies. Marion Milner[18] told me that Donald had said he was weaned early because his mother could not stand her own excitement during breast feeding. In 1996 she showed me a well-known drawing by Winnicott of mother and infant with an emphatically drawn backbone form within the figure of the mother. She wondered whether this represented his mother's father's "forbidding penis" which stood between herself and Donald, that is, if it was a stricture originating in the attitude of her father that had led to a conflict when she found herself stimulated by her son's feeding.

It is unlikely that the work with his second analyst, Joan Riviere, would have fostered Winnicott's idea that his mother had had so much influence in his life. The Kleinians emphasized the child's fantasy life over and above any influence by the mother. This became Winnicott's complaint, stated and restated in terms that contributed to his decision to go his own way. James Strachey, his first analyst, may have raised the subject; the letters between Strachey and his wife that refer to his patient include remarks about very early life. But it is most likely that this comment to Marion Milner came out of his self-analysis. Winnicott himself, the scholar of his own origins, was almost certainly the sole witness. It seems to explain a number of aspects of his life. And it is consistent with his mother's habit of clapping her hands as she came down the staircase in the morning. If she was in fact a woman who stayed shy of sexual excitement, she might have required methods of coping, resulting in a sort of deadness. The evidence does indicate that she was depressed. Here, however, one becomes aware of a chain of reasoning, a hypothetical arrangement, bits and pieces of which extend well into the world of the biographer's constructions. The idea of her father, as represented in the drawing by the backbone separating mother and baby, as the figure that prohibited her excitement during breast feeding, may represent a level of speculation that tries the reader's patience, but I record what I was told nonetheless.[19]

Frederick Winnicott was born in Devonport on September 8, 1855, the son of Richard R. and Caroline Winnicott. Richard, a "furnishing and general ironmonger, plumber and gas fitter," had an interest in politics that influenced his son, who would eventually become mayor of Plymouth and receive a knighthood. A concern with civic affairs was part of family life. By 1880, probably following the death of his father, Frederick's much-enlarged hardware business had become known as "Winnicott Brothers."[20]

In a newspaper interview on his ninety-first birthday, in 1946,[21] Frederick's reminiscences of childhood demonstrate a certain playfulness of attitude, even though the weight of civic honors, and the obvious pleasure he took in receiving them, would tend to suggest a very formal, hardworking, and not especially humorous person. This impression is reinforced in the dominant tone of his letters to Donald, as well as by his decision to send Donald to boarding school at age fourteen because he was getting into bad company.

Libraries seem to have held considerable interest for Frederick. He became treasurer of the Devon and Cornwall Literary Society at the Athenaeum when it acquired the books belonging to the Mechanics' Institute, and was later chairman of the Plymouth Library Committee. In 1925 he gave to the building that housed the library a large stained-glass window dedicated to the memory of his wife, who had died the previous year. At ninety-one, he was reading two newspapers a day and keeping abreast of new biographies and travel books, which "he prefers to fiction."[22]

His list of public duties is a lengthy one.[23] He was twice elected mayor of Plymouth, 1906–7 and 1921–22. (His brother Richard was mayor in 1904–5 and again in 1924–5.) By the time he received his knighthood, in 1924, the British peerage was no longer the sole preserve of the aristocracy. In response to the news that he had been knighted, Sir Frederick was moved to remember his roots, partly to indicate that his origins in Devonport, a poor area, were more humble than a knighthood would imply.[24] In her memoir Clare quotes from Donald's autobiographical notebook: "[My father] was sensitive about his lack of education (he had had learning difficulties) and he always said that because of this he had not aspired to Parliament, but had kept to local politics."[25] Thus, in spite of the honor bestowed, and the wealth that sustained a comfortable life, to the extent that Frederick Winnicott could be called a shopkeeper, the Winnicotts would have been perceived as a lower-middle-class family.[26] Like his ancestors, Frederick was a deeply religious man who supported church work throughout his life.[27] His thriving business and religious commitments, however, left little time for his family.[28]

At the time of Donald's birth in 1896, the family lived at 17 Gordon Terrace,[29] but by 1899 they had moved into their grand home, Rockville, in Seymour Road, Mannamead.[30] This was undoubtedly the fruit of the prosperity of Winnicott Brothers. By 1903 the family of Donald's brother Richard was also listed as living at Rockville, and remained there until 1910, when Richard purchased a large home of his own, "Hyperion," also in Seymour Road. This was an eventful period in which the brothers were elected in succession mayor of Plymouth. It seems that for at least seven years, from the time Donald was seven until he was fourteen, and left home for boarding school, the two families shared a roof. Richard and his wife, Annie, had two daughters[31] and three sons.[32] Altogether there were eight children and four adults living at Rockville, a large family indeed.

Clare makes no mention of this living arrangement, nor does Donald. I infer it from the fact that the brothers' addresses were identical from 1903 to 1910. If true, it raises interest in the simultaneity of Donald's departure for boarding school, in 1910, and the move of his uncle's family. Perhaps the change in the boy's arrangements resulted from more than Donald's getting into bad company. Might there have been influences by one or more of his cousins that led to some sort of turmoil?

Frederick's "head of the family" posture in the 1900 photograph would seem to have been earned. Jimmy Ede remembered him seventy-five years later as always overdressed.[33] His waxed mustaches are in evidence in all his photographs. Ede found it difficult to imagine Frederick and Donald as father and son, though he grudgingly supposed that Donald loved his father. One might think that Frederick himself was an egregiously "good" person whose example was felt to be constricting young Donald, and that the decision to send him away to boarding school was instigated by Donald himself to help him break free of the bonds of his father's all too compelling example. The survival of so much documentation of Frederick's good deeds and personal prominence suggests that he was an overpowering, narcissistic presence for his son.[34]

In the photograph, Donald, the youngest of Frederick and Bessie's three children, sits at the very center, the son born after two girls. Violet, six years older, already wears glasses. She was recalled by Jim Ede as having been a bit less accessible than Kathleen, who was just a year younger than she, and more capable, he said, of "taking a joke." Kathleen may have been engaged once, but neither would ever marry. In his letters to his sisters, as in those to his parents in the early years, Winnicott wrote in a spirit of humor and irony, characteristics that emerge on occasion in his letters to others, though never so fully. In the high-spirited and loving letters to "V & K," one catches the flavor of the privileged younger brother speaking in nearly paternal tones—brother as quasi-father. While Donald went out into the wider world, both of his sisters remained spinsters, devoted to their parents, and then, after 1925, when their mother died, to their father alone. In later life they were said to be "saintly." They had little or no idea of the significance of their brother's contribution to our knowledge of human psychology, and remained deeply provincial to the end.[35]

Rockville was a commodious home with a multi-level garden, which included a tennis court, pond, croquet lawn, orchard, and vegetable garden, and a large octagonal gazebo,[36] all enclosed by high trees. In an advertisement for its sale, much later,[37] it was said to "boast not only five large bedrooms, but two bathrooms, a shower room, a magnificent billiards room with barrel-vaulted ceiling and a deep walk in pantry and utility room with a . . . cast iron range. The drawing room . . . is the piece-de-resistance of the entire house, particularly because of its magnificent intricately carved fireplace surrounded with its elaborately mirrored and shelved overmantel, carved side panels and upholstered seats." There was a huge orangery just off the kitchen[38] and quarters for the resident staff to the rear. Elspeth Mills, who was employed there between 1929 and 1935, after Mrs. Winnicott's death, wrote me that "there was a large glass frontage book case in the breakfast room at Rockville filled with very old books. Whether any got read its [sic] not for me to say but there [sic] main reading . . . was there [sic] bible & we had prayers each day. Also they had the Western Morning News; the Daily Telegraph; The Weekly Methodist Recorder + the Christian Herald."

Donald Winnicott was born in 1896, the year after Oscar Wilde was sent to Reading Gaol and the year before Queen Victoria celebrated sixty years on the throne. The British Empire constituted one fourth of the landmass of the earth and had a population of 450 million. It was from Plymouth harbor that "the great fleets of the medieval and Elizabethan eras set sail, including Drake's." Plymouth was the home of Sir Walter Raleigh, and the gathering place for the Pilgrims, who fled England for the New World in the early seventeenth century. (Indeed it was Frederick Winnicott who dedicated the monument to their embarcation, and contributed the stonework which housed the plaque.)[39] An expedition that departed Plymouth for Virginia (headed by Richard Strachey, an ancestor of Winnicott's first analyst, James Strachey) only to be shipwrecked on Bermuda became the background for Shakespeare's play *The Tempest*. Napoleon had appeared in Plymouth Sound in 1811.

In the early years of the twentieth century, Plymouth offered amusements appealing to a young boy, including[40] "Punch and Judy shows and barrel organs playing in the streets, with gaily-dressed monkeys trained to take pennies from the willing crowds." There were "dancing bears and German bands" as well. On Good Friday morning "boys would go round the streets ringing handbells and selling hot-cross buns for a ha'penny each, or seven for tuppence. They were straight from the oven and [undoubtedly] tasted delicious."

When Donald was five, in 1901, Queen Victoria died. Edward VII was crowned the following year, the same year that saw the end of the Boer War. (Frederick had helped to raise funds for armaments in the British cause.) There were no telephones at the time of his birth in that part of England. The first one was installed in 1909, a year before he left for school. Although the first electric tram made its appearance in Plymouth in 1899, there were no motorcars to speak of until 1904, when there were eight thousand in the whole of England. Frederick retained the key he used for the first tram ride in the combined tramways of the three towns of Plymouth, Stonehouse, and Devonport, which were amalgamated into Greater Plymouth.[41] One imagines the young Donald Winnicott within easy reach of these scenes and events, holding the hand of his father or mother and soaking up a multitude of impressions. The novelty of cars gave people great delight, of which we get an inkling in the description of the notorious Mr. Toad in *The Wind and the Willows*,[42] published in 1908, and this delight remained with Winnicott almost throughout his life. People often remembered him for the tricks he performed in driving his cars, such as standing up in the driver's seat, head out the roof, while steering with a stick. One thinks of him as a sort of psychoanalytic Mr. Toad, inveterately fun-loving and irrepressible.[43]

It was a time of change. Robert Steven Smyth Baden-Powell founded the Boy Scouts early in the new century (he once visited Donald's home for a ceremonial occasion), and one resident of Plymouth recalls in 1910 waving "to General William Booth, founder of the Salvation Army, as he drove down Albert Road in an open landau, his white beard whipped by the wind."[44] At the time of Winnicott's childhood it was still possible to rejoice in the new technology that was beginning to transform Western society, and the comforts of wealth could shield a family from the filth and disease rampant among the lower classes. Not yet did the society in which he was raised have to confront the wholesale slaughter of the Great War, in which a total of 7 million were to die: 9 percent of English men between twenty and forty-five would be killed in battle.

Frederick Winnicott's civic devotion served as a model for his son, for Donald showed, throughout his life a preoccupation with social issues. He took for granted that he had a responsibility to make his views known in the larger society of which he was a part. While living up to his father's example, he would nonetheless be driven to seek ways to unburden himself of an expressive, artistic temperament, harnessed, as it came to be, to a scientific intent. His papers are rife with evidence for this. They show the marriage of art and science in his thought, and the transcendence of whatever characteristics of each had led historically to their segregation. The appeal to the reader is based on the possibility of personal wholeness.

A late interview with Clare Winnicott discloses that at the age of nine, Donald looked in the mirror and decided that he was "too nice." This judgment was followed by a period of bad behavior and low grades in school.[45] In 1965, Winnicott is reported by the historian Paul Roazen[46] to have said that he had had "a disturbed adolescence" and had lost his ability to recall his dreams when he was nine.[47] Besides implying a child who was precociously aware of dreaming and the recollection of dreams, this makes nine a very significant age for Winnicott and suggests that the misbehavior that prompted his father to send him away may have originated in his decision to alter his demeanor, to do away somehow with being "too nice." We do not know why exactly he came to that conclusion

just then. Given other commentary about his childhood living arrangements, with "too many mothers"[48] forever present, it seems possible that
he was calling his father's attention to himself as a way of emerging from
a "niceness" that was hindering his development.

We look back into these early years for clues to the emotional climate surrounding Donald's development. A sexless first marriage, two sisters
who probably remained virginal throughout their lives: these data imply
a non-sexual or, more probably, an anti-sexual childhood. Certainly the
impression given in Clare's "personal reflection" is that the Winnicotts
were a remarkably happy family. But the cost of this happiness must
have included severe strictures on disruptive behavior. Donald's intolerance of such conditions was demonstrated in the smashing of a doll
about which he was teased by his father at age three, in doing poorly in
school at the age of nine after realizing that he was "too nice," and then
getting into bad company at twelve, as evidenced by his use of the word
"drat." This, we are told, is what led to his father's decision to send him
away to boarding school. Was it his father, then, who insisted that he be
"nice"? If so, was this insistence simply another example of the attitude
that led to his early weaning because his enthusiasm produced too much
excitement in his mother?

In a 1967 description of his childhood,[49] Donald said that, what with
his mother and two sisters and a nanny, he probably had too much mothering and "things never quite righted themselves." In sending him away,
Frederick took up the opposition to that excessive mothering, for which
Donald was eventually grateful, since it showed that his father was
"there to kill and be killed," an essential feature of fathering for a son.[50]
Yet even this affirmative statement about his father's assumption of a
masculine role in his life is not convincing.

The study of Winnicott evokes the very definite sense that something was drastically wrong in his relationship to his father, yet he never
makes any such disclosure himself. Nevertheless, fathers are mainly left
out of his clinical preoccupations. He was unable to tell his father that he
did not wish to follow in his footsteps as a businessman but preferred to
become a doctor instead, and thirty-five years later he was unable—or
unwilling—to tell him of his marital problems and decision to divorce.
The unpredictable truths of Donald's life, the very freedom which he
prized so highly, had to be kept secret. And of course, by the time of his

divorce, his father was a very old man. Although Winnicott did not tell his father about his intention to study medicine, nor, later, his decision to divorce, he nevertheless *acted*.

There are quarrels about money in the correspondence with his father,[51] with Donald, at forty-four, protesting about not being sufficiently trusted to look after his own financial affairs (at which he did not, in fact, do well). At the time of Frederick's death, Donald decided not to accept any more money than he already had.[52] Perhaps his father's method of coping is revealed in the fact that in all the surviving letters from Frederick to Donald there is not a single mention of a memory or an association to Bessie, who had died in 1925. This is possibly a sign of the same sort of stoicism and a consequent silence that excludes unpleasant emotion. Violet and Kathleen seem to have substituted for their mother and are frequently cited for their good cheer and selflessness. We can wonder whether Bessie's depression was caused or intensified by alienation from a husband whose self-absorbed habit of mind excluded attention to such a condition. Indeed, lacking evidence, we can also wonder whether she shared in the same spirit of abnegation.

Jim Ede said of Mrs. Winnicott that she was extremely kind, though she did not recognize, for example, the inappropriateness of making a gift of a magnificent embroidered tablecloth to a boy—himself in this case. Here is a single detail from which one might infer that Donald's mother was not in close touch with the differences between male and female, and therefore might have caused or added to any gender confusion Donald may have had about himself.[53] Could she have thought of Donald as female? Not so far-fetched a suggestion in view of his motherly disposition, his womanly voice, and his identification on occasion with female characters, such as Cathy in *Wuthering Heights*.[54]

That the idealization of the sexless woman[55] prevalent in Winnicott's childhood was maintained so long suggests the magnitude of social forces intended to keep women in a state of subservience akin to enslavement. Woman as mother, and the relationship of her baby to herself, would become the subject most identified with Winnicott. He brought forth a newly comprehensive grasp of the mother's importance in the rearing of healthy children, but did not include in his study due acknowledgment of the role of her sexuality. It wasn't so much woman as an individual being as woman as the bearer and nurturer of children that preoccupied him. Does this represent a limitation on his otherwise relent-less delving into the psychology of the mother? There is a blank spot in his theorizing, not only about fathers but also about the sexual aspect of mothers, which is perhaps a sign of respect for his mother's inhibited sexuality.[56] The emphasis was on the child's ruthless demand for feeding and uninhibited self-expression at the breast, from which other uninhibited self-expression would follow, but he would leave out of the equation the mother's sexual stimulation by the nursing infant.

Although Winnicott does not warrant criticism for what he did not contribute, particularly in view of all he did, it is nonetheless interesting to consider how his own sexual problems affected his psychoanalytic meditations. For each contributor has his or her own life as a basis for the imaginative construction of those of others.

— 3 —

Boarding School

Donald entered the Leys School in 1910, when he was fourteen. The school, located in Cambridge, was founded in the aftermath of the 1867 report of the Taunton Commission on endowed schools: "We need schools that shall provide good instruction for the whole of the lowest portion of what is commonly called the middle class, and we cannot overstate our sense of the importance of the need. These are schools that we have called Schools of the Third Grade." Their function was to supply "the essential material, namely disciplined faculties and sound elementary knowledge in the learners, for a subsequent technical education where this was required or appropriate." The commissioners believed that "many of the farmers, many of the richer shopkeepers, many professional men, all but the wealthier gentry, would probably wish to have their sons educated in schools of this sort, if the education were thoroughly good of its kind."[1]

Another factor, perhaps more important, in the choice of the Leys for young Donald was that "it has long been a complaint that the sons of Methodists in passing through the Universities become alienated from the Church of their fathers." There were, however, "a few honourable exceptions. In the altered circumstances of the Universities it is the duty of the Methodist Connexion to take steps to remedy this evil."[2] The spirit of these sentences would seem consistent with Frederick Winnicott's wish to reform a son who said "drat," an utterance that may have symbolized an urge in Donald to distance himself from his father. This would, of course, be typical of an adolescent, but Donald's subsequent career, featuring the absence of the father in his extensive theorizing about childhood, leads us to believe that whatever comes down to us anecdotally in the form of "drat" constituted a deeper and more enduring issue than the passing phase of adolescence.

The Leys was the first Methodist public school. It is the school described in James Hilton's novel *Goodbye Mr. Chips*.[3] The master on whom Mr. Chips was based, W. H. Balgarnie (an expert on "Fives"), was teaching at the school in those days. Balgarnie represented a whole side of the Leys that was encouraging to its students. It was not a place characterized by the same sort of bullying that typified other public schools. "For Leysian and non-Leysian alike 'Mr. Chips' is the nostalgic personification of the most agreeable aspects of public school life. The combination of an eccentric academic individuality and the warm humanity of the housemaster, set in the context of spacious tradition and lifelong devotion, is inevitably appealing, but the lasting quality and attraction derives from the fidelity with which Hilton recreated and high-lighted aspects of the Cambridge scene he knew so well."[4]

In one letter home (November 30, 1913), Donald mentions that bruises on his face had prompted Mr. Balgarnie to say that "he will give me [a penalty] for fighting," demonstrating how far he had come from being "too nice" as a nine-year-old. Winnicott recalled in late life that "at school [my] chief interest was running the mile."[5]

Our primary sources about Donald's years at the Leys are limited to his own letters, since no records about pupils were kept until 1934. Brett Kahr's *Biographical Portrait* of Winnicott provides a sketch of Leysian life in Edwardian times; it makes no mention of any kind of hardship.[6] This echoes the tone of Clare Winnicott's reflections. Winnicott claimed in his 1965 interview with Paul Roazen that he had had "a disturbed adolescence,"[7] but we have no evidence to throw light on his particular struggles. In fact there are no primary data from the first three years of his boarding school career, unless a note quoted by Clare in her memoir, addressed to his mother on Mother's Day, is from that period. It has more of the flavor of a younger boy than the three that can be dated to his fourth year and after.

In spite of an avowedly unhappy time,[8] which could simply be the archetypical unhappy time of all adolescents, it does seem that Donald thrived at the Leys. This was the wider world, beyond the comforts and constrictions of Rockville and Plymouth. As he later said, he was encountering cultural life for the first time, something missing from his earlier life except for the effects of "an evangelical religion."[9] The school archivist, G. C. Houghton, in a 1992 review of what was known about Donald's student years,[10] wrote: "You will see what a wide range of the school life he was involved in: A member of the school football [Rugby] Team—but not an exceptional player; a Fives and Tennis player; a boy who took part in public debates and who also wrote short stories; a musician playing at concerts and good enough to give an 'oration' at Speech Day." Among the mentions he found of Donald's name are these: "D. W. Winnicott allowed himself to be carried away into a detailed description of the Palace of Peace, the point of which was somewhat doubtful" (Debating Society) and "Small and not clever, but runs hard and defends well" (football team). A red leather copy of Kipling's *Second Jungle Book* was awarded to Donald in June 1913 as a prize for music (general ability). The plate glued to the inside cover is signed "W. J. A. Barber, Head Master." The seal of the school is emblazoned on its cover, along with a gold embossed figure of an elephant, with an ancient Eastern symbol between the elephant's eyes, the swastika.[11]

Brett Kahr gives us some sense of life at the Leys during Donald's days:[12]

The Headmaster, Dr. William Fiddian Moulton, had created an environment in which scholarship, religion, and athletics could be pursued simultaneously. Virtually all the boys had come from proud, successful, gentrified families, and many had followed their fathers or elder brothers or cousins to the Leys School. Winnicott lodged in North House "B," one of the rather large and spartan residential halls. His young Housemaster, James Edgar (Jesse) Mellor was a devoted alumnus, a classicist trained at Jesus College, Cambridge, and immersed in all aspects of school life. He was tremendously popular among the boys. He was Captain of "Mr. Mellor's XV" rugby football team. The School Clubs included "The Leys Fortnightly" Committee, the Literary and Debating Society Committee, the Natural History Society Committee, the Bicycle Club Committee, and the Games

Committee. All the pupils were required to attend chapel twice daily for compulsory prayers. In the spring of 1911, Winnicott entered the Half Mile Handicap race for boys under sixteen years of age and the school newspaper reported that "Winnicott ran excellently." Besides track events, Winnicott played football, and joined the cricket team for a time. Later he joined the choir and became a member of the School Scouts.[13]

The *Fortnightly* for October 3, 1913, contains an essay titled "Smith" by "Housing Enthusiast. D. W. W." It concerns an encounter with Schmidt, a town planning official for the German city of Essen, who has total control over the uses to which land is put and has fashioned quite a beautiful town for the benefit of all its citizens. Their freedom to do as they like with their land is virtually nonexistent, but this does not seem to matter very much. The people love their beautiful town. The piece ends with a declaration that Germany can be content with Schmidt and his like, but the English are happier with the more disorderly arrangement that individual freedom engenders: "In England, private feuds would take the place of beautiful buildings, and civil war would be fought in the vast parks. . . . Englishmen, taken as a whole, . . . would never stand so officious an official for one fortnight." In another of his essays, "The Best Remedy," Donald observes: "Only quite recently have the towns in Germany begun to allow the people to play on the grass in the parks; and now that after the English custom the authorities do allow it, more than surprising is the difficulty of getting even the youngsters to overstep the miniature railings, let alone the impossibility of accustoming the older gravel-pathed generation to walk in the grass."

By this time Donald had given a good deal of thought to the relationship between the individual, society, and culture, and in particular to how morality enters into the structure of society and therefore the shaping of individuals within that society. He could view the German character with ironic objectivity just on the brink of the Great War and draw the line in favor of English values. These two pieces are remarkably perceptive for a seventeen-year-old.

From the evidence of three letters to his family,[14] we can conclude that by this age Donald had become an ebullient, forthright, and extraordinarily entertaining young man with wide-ranging intellectual interests. On November 3, 1913, he wrote:

The missing one is coming back soon! Only two more Fridays, two more Saturdays and two more Sundays. . . . Now let me see! What have I to thank you for, this week. How can people deny the existance [sic] of the science of telepathy? How did Mother know that a few weeks ago I possessed not a farthing, except that telepathy played a leading part? Aha. Never mind how! *I got my 5/-*. HA! . . .

Yes, well I am longing to get home now. It seems very wonderful that the time is going so quickly. I am having a wonderfully good time here, too good did I hear some one say? Well that may be. I hope not. I am starting another sheet, but I shall not have time to fill it, I am afraid. I am sitting at the back of the hall, and a chap to the right has very dexterously taken off his coat, unhinged his collar and waistecoat [sic] back. . . and put on his coat again. This was done without his being spotted, but now he looks exactly like a parson and is doing all manner of antics, imitating the Head, the Bursar and anyone who occurs to his mind. He is really a rather humorous lad.

On December 23, 1913(?), he reported:

The impossible has happened. It really seemed impossible that I should play again for the 1st XV. But yesterday, greatly to my joyful surprise, I was picked to play 7/8ths again in the most important match of the season, against Dundle. This was the first opportunity I had had for playing 7/8ths for the 1st, and you can imagine how I enjoyed it. *N. B.* This *by no means* means I am going to get my first colours. I came out of the fray quite safe, except that I had hurt my foot, had had a kick in the back, and a blow on my right side of my head, which has made the upper lip and cheek all round the eye and underneath, utterly senseless and dead to this moment. It is really awfully funny. I can't tickle it, but on the other hand it can't itch.

And on May 9, 1914, he described his train trip back to Cambridge in great detail.

Punctually in time we arrived at Paddington in a kind of ground fog, neither thick nor extending far round London. It was like a large local cloud. However I found my way without the sun to Praed Street Station, and entrained at King's Cross. I had under my arms a

waste-paper basket full of books, oranges and other articles of furniture, a . . . bag, a waterproof coat, a couple of pictures, a walking stick.
In this plight was I, feeling only glad I had left my tennis racquet behind. When standing on the platform I found Annie [H]ilton. We
greeted one another, and I came to the conclusion that her voice in
only an hour would not put me off her at all. I like her, except when
she says yes.

Young Donald played the piano, sang in chorus, was a leader of the
Boy Scouts and a determined helper of poor children in Cambridge. In
his letters he proudly displays a dispassionate, manly, or perhaps even a
detached attitude toward himself, as shown in his descriptions of the
blows he takes as a rugby player, and also toward biological matters,
such as the cut-up pieces of an animal heart that kept on beating, which,
far from disturbing him, made a deep impression, and perhaps even
gave him a thrill. In that letter, his associations flow beyond the present,
toward the dissection of a frog, on the basis of which his teacher was
going to write to the manager of the Plymouth Aquarium to ask if Donald could "look around etc." He goes on: "Topping of him I think. I dare
say Father could have got me in, but it would be much more profitable to
get an intro from a co-scientist and biologist." Donald was proud to have
earned access to the local aquarium by himself. Indeed he balances repeated expressions of gratitude with barrages of words that tell of his adventures, or barrages of adventurous words. One can imagine the young
man, probably dressed in tweeds, with crinkled blue eyes and blond hair,
so full of good humor, brightly connected with the world around him,
chattering away about the life he was leading.

Donald shows, if only by the two thousand–word length of the May
9, 1914, letter, a propulsive wish to let his life be known, to put it into
words for his family's amusement, but also—and here we see a foreshadowing of his later career as a writer for larger audiences—for the sake of
the readers of certain English newspapers. He is the self-appointed historian of King Edward VII's visit to the Leys. He can take for granted that
the audience for his letter, his family, will be interested in everything he
has to say, at whatever length he chooses to say it. In the writing life to
follow, as a psychoanalyst, he will continue to be prolific. The description of the king's visit can be grouped with a description of his train journey from Plymouth to Cambridge, and with an account in a later letter,

from medical school, of an enjoyable struggle in the streets of London between students at Bart's (St. Bartholomew's Hospital, where he studied
medicine) and their counterparts at University College Hospital. Notable
as well is a long letter from Cambridge to his mother in which he tells of
the staging of a cowboys-and-Indians skit by the Scouts he oversees. All
of these topics are closely observed, rife with humor, and full of the fundamental pleasure of being a witness to humanity in action.

The drawings that accompany the letters show that words could not
contain him, were not adequate to the urgency of his wish to be known.
His language, so full of feeling, has the quality of gesture that is supplemented by what he draws. For example, he illustrates his rugby injury
for his parents thus:

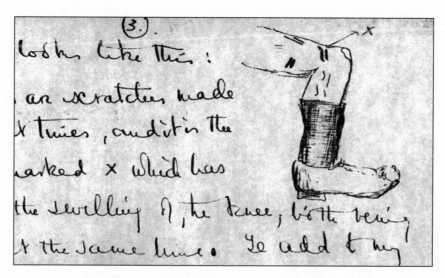

He sketches the telegrams he sends to newspapers offering his account of the King's visit for publication. He wants to be entertaining, and
makes backhanded, ironic comments, thus taking a stand against senti-
mentality of any kind, a pose that makes it possible for him to express
love and caring: "I don't think I had better waste much more time over
you, so unwillingly am I doing it too."

He was a great reader, a lover of words, as he would always be. As of
November 30, 1913, he was reading Stephenson's "Essays of Travel," was
midway through "the life of the Brontes," but "mainly [he was] reading
"Marshall's The Frog," and he hoped to read "Bateson's Principles of
Mendelism (or Mendelianism)." For Christmas, besides money, he

wanted books: "The Minerals of the World," "Life of Huxley," "Poems of Oscar Wilde," "More Poems of Oscar Wilde," and "the last three volumes of the Everyman Encyclopaedia." He makes a couple of references in his letters to his friend Stanley Ede. In one he asks his own family to send any interesting parts of his letter on to Stanley, who, he is sure, will return them. In another he says that Stanley has had "scarcely a decent letter."

Clare published in her memoir a letter Donald wrote to his mother on the occasion of Mother's Day.[15] In it there is a fine little expression of his love for her, a quiet, virtually private statement, as if put down by accident or overheard: "Less than four weeks now and I shall be home at this time having our Sunday supper. I do like our Sunday supper at Rockville, although I don't know why. I perhaps do not like it so much at the time, only it is a nice meal to look back upon." It is almost a haunting statement, the reflective young man noticing the difference between the experience of the moment and the re-experience looking back. "So cool," he says, "with mint sauce and cold meat." And so reminiscent in tone of Frederick's association of cold mutton with "our inland past."[16] Here is a possible trace of identification with a father who reflects on the connection between the past and the present, a state of mind so relevant to the work of the psychoanalyst.

Frederick reflected upon his origins at the time of receiving his knighthood, and showed a consciousness of the past in many other ways, for example, by retaining mementos of notable events and by sponsoring the memorial to the Pilgrims who set sail from Plymouth for the New World. The leap from one world into another is paralleled by Frederick's success as a businessman and civic leader (in spite of a learning impediment and lack of education), as it is in Donald's boarding school liberation from provincial Plymouth life and his subsequent experiences as a psychoanalyst, starting with his daily visits to Bloomsbury for his personal analysis. We can also reach all the way ahead to the last years of his life, when, as a celebrated figure, he crossed the Atlantic in 1968 to bring his own original word from Britain to the New York Psychoanalytic Society. By then, he was something of a Pilgrim himself.

In an anecdote from his adult life, Donald and his first wife's brother, Jim Taylor, a doctor, were in a railroad station. Noticing the engineer, Jim asked Donald if he thought the engineer was happy. Donald replied, "He looks like he is, but he doesn't know it."[17]

— 4 —

Cambridge

Winnicott's account of how he decided to become a doctor begins with a fractured clavicle during his schooldays.[1] While recuperating, he thought to himself that he would have to depend on doctors for help with physical problems unless he became one himself. How being a doctor would enable a person to take care of his own fractured clavicle need not be explained, since this is only a statement of fantasy. Probably what he meant was that he did not want to be dependent on a doctor if he got sick. Doctors often start out by "identifying with the aggressor," to use Anna Freud's concept.[2] They overcome their fear by appropriating the power of the person who frightened them. Winnicott also claimed that he had never wanted to be anything but a doctor, which probably takes the ambition back to an even earlier time than that of his broken collar bone.

He entered Jesus College, Cambridge, as a pre-medical student in 1914, having declared his intentions to his father through the good offices of Jimmy Ede.[3] It is a strange fact that it was Jimmy who wrote to Frederick to tell him that Donald did not want to work in the family business but preferred to study medicine. Jimmy was precisely a year older than Donald (they had the same birthday, April 7), a kind of senior twin in that respect, but it says something about Donald's diffidence or fearfulness with respect to his father that he would have his friend represent him in this deeply personal matter. He apparently needed the support of another male figure in making room for his own development. And, of course, Donald's mother is not even mentioned in this context, the crucial person being his father and his father only, just as it was when the decision was made to send him away to school. Donald's decision left his father without a successor. Eventually, it would be his brother Richard's sons, Harold and Victor, who would come into the business. Did Donald feel hostility to his father that threatened to show through in the revealing of the simple fact that he wanted to be a doctor? Was it the news: "I am not like you are, Father"? And was it also: "Look, Father, I can't face you with this, can't bear your hurt. Nothing between us has prepared us for this moment of parting"?

In 1988, Jim Ede only grudgingly acknowledged that, by nature, Frederick and Donald could be seen as father and son; his emphasis was on the vast gulf that separated them as people. And just as his father was left alone with no one to carry on his business, so, eventually, would Donald himself be alone, a childless figure without a son to imaginatively kill and succeed him. The testimony of a former employee of Sir Frederick's that pay was low and raises had to be requested in person suggests a certain lack of generosity that may have contributed to Donald's fear of a direct confrontation with his father—a fear, perhaps, that his father's opposition could endanger the decision itself.

Donald studied biology in preparation for medical school proper, which would come after three years. He spoke later of the coldness of his pre-medical work,[4] the emotionlessly, objective study of living tissue, something that many a medical psychoanalyst comments upon, when looking back. There is much for an analyst to undo in the training of a physician. In Donald's letters from the Leys School, we see him nearly boasting of his own objectivity (the dissected heart tissue that continues to beat, which he calls "a fine sight"), and this is probably the manly proto-physician speaking, toughening himself up for the tasks of the doctor who does not shrink from what would repel or paralyze others. He is also differentiating himself here from females, whom he saw as more tender-hearted, writing of skulls and bones on his bookcase ". . . to strike awe into the hearts of ladies."

Donald's university degree was an ordinary and undistinguished third-class bachelor of arts. He later received an M.A., routinely granted without additional study.[5] He was not an outstanding student. Perhaps his fun-loving nature took precedence over arduous devotion to course work. He loved music; he had a piano in his suite, sang in a tenor voice, and was frequently a center of attention at social gatherings.

Three letters from Cambridge survive, and one from the ship on which he served as surgeon-probationer.[6] In the first letter (September 10, 1916), to his mother, he introduces a section with "two commands and one answer," with the same tone of authority he uses with his sisters—evidence of male ascendancy, even with respect to his mother. He questions his mother's memory: "When you first asked me [for certain names] I sat straight down and wrote you a post card with the names and descriptions of the lads on it. This I sent off, and whether you have never received it or whether you have simply forgotten will probably remain a mystery." (Her forgetfulness may have been a symptom of depression.) He then speaks of having forgotten something himself, having left his sponge "at the Dennisons," who sent him "a lovely one, slightly bigger than my own and much softer." He mentions, too, having accepted an assignment to put on some sort of a show with his Scout troop in spite of the fact that "Father told me that I must learn to decline a bad offer." In other words, he stands up to his father. Here, through the veil of his associations, we see his mental condition: to some extent he is like his mother, or perhaps unable to differentiate from her, and at the same time sharply differentiated from his father, who is perhaps disqualified as one who could support his differentiation from his mother. He then goes on to describe his adventure in organizing the Scouts for a cowboys-and-Indians skit, with all sorts of amusing asides to give it life and color. He seems to have been enjoying life in a way his father could not.

Donald then introduces the observation that "I am afraid I am boring you with this, but it was so infinitely better than a book to me, and such a revelation of the powers of the imagination of the boys that I shall never forget the day." Why does he make this point? Obviously he is preoccupied with what brings him pleasure, rank-ordering the causes. In this case the human imagination in action prevails even over the contents of books, which also rank high, as evidenced in his many references to his reading. And books were the emblems of Winnicott's intellectual development, the means by which his lively mind could thrive, and by which the great world might take up residence in his own two hands. Of the Scouts he says, "Each one was absolutely different from the others, and half the charm lay there."

The letter refers to his devoted efforts on behalf of the Scouts in a way that would become familiar throughout his life. His devotion to certain kinds of patients would also require extraordinary effort, which he was prepared to make, as we see in a second, undated letter:

> *Scout funds* are doing well. I have extracted two half sovereigns within a week, one from a lady called Miss Pratt and another from Mrs. J. H. S. McArthur, Hon Pres. of Leys School Camb etc. Also a Weslyan [sic] draper gave us 5/-. And if the boys bring their pennies regularly we should get 2/- a week or £5 a year from that alone. So you see we shall probably be able to get along fine now. We have cleared our debt with a surplus. One of the poorest (also one of the best) of the scouts has been ill and cannot afford very easily the emulsion which the doctor would like him to have to build up his strength again. In fact he would have—most likely—to go without this altogether if we can't do something in the matter. So the chemist is supplying him at a slightly reduced fee since he said it would cost me a lot if I was doing it myself alone. So I have it sent him every fortnight and the cost is 1/2 per fortnight. I have paid this week and I propose asking a few of my near relations, and a few friends up here to send me a few pence towards the next few 1/2's. I could tell you a lot about the wonderful Mother of this boy. Both the boy and his brother are in the troop and are clean and respectable altho' the conditions are about the least promising financially than those of all the other scouts. The Father has a paralysis and a degenerating brain. Every time a new piece goes he gets fits. This will go on till he dies. The older of the two boys—only children, is the only one old enough to work, and he has been ill and can only take a job which will give him a more or less open life, and consequently which brings in the infinitessimal [sic] amounts of money at first. The woman is the brightest of all the scouts' Mothers and always has a smile on her worn face. She knocked herself up a while ago by staying up all night two nights a week so as to be able to earn money for the children in the day, and do washing and ironing and mending after her work. On the whole I feel that Mother deserves a little help. And this is a way that I can help without hurting any feelings.

From this loving letter to his mother a reader would not guess at the depths of conflict that affected his relationship to her, especially without the evidence contained in his poem "The Tree." Yet "The Tree" would not be written for another forty-seven years. Donald's adult realizations about his mother were not yet formed at the time of this letter. In the pre-analytic adolescent, fathoms below this love lay a reef of interconnected associations and conflicts that would form a foundation for otherwise in-explicable decisions and actions. Only gradually would he explore that reef. "I wonder when you will really be called up," he says. This appears to be a slip in which he substitutes his mother for himself, for it is Donald who is going to be "called up," that is, for military service, more evidence of his condition of mind.

An energetic, ebullient letter to "my dears" is dated just before Christmas, December 9, 1916. He is longing to come home, he says, but sorry that he will spend no more winters in Cambridge. He describes the "annual bust up in my rooms, this year surpassing all others in row and hilarity. It was simply fine." In a portrait of the life he now understands is fast disappearing, the letter reports:

We sang songs, did acrobatics, played rugger—polo—golf—soccer—hockey with walking sticks and my old top hat (that I bought for 2/-). Also we made awful noises, and owing to the beautiful arrangement of my rooms no damage was done. If I had had burnished tables, glazed pictures, and Turkey carpets we should have done about £7 worth damage. But as it was we did none. And yet my room looks quite nice. A lot of people tell me they like it.

I have bought a Planisphere or map of the Stars, which goes very well along side Baden Powell—the blackboard, Beethoven and the map of Cambridge. I have also hung over the chimney piece a skele-ton of a chicken. Poor little thing, it was imprisoned in a wall while some painting was being done, and it was found starved to death. I was doing experiments on it, to find out how long it will take to de-compose right away by being hung up with a pin.

V. & K. ought to feel very proud to be hung up next to Baden Powell (an article by which I enclose), or vice versa. They are going to be framed when I get the £5 gratuity from the War Office. I have al-most spent it already—at least—well no I haven't really. But you know.

People like looking at my bookcases because of the variety of the books therein. Greek Testament, German Dict., "Plant Animals" Sainte Bible. "Rocks" Chaucer. Darwin, or again, "Fishes," Holy Bible, Wild Animals I Have Known, & Pathology—etc. All sorts you know. I like mixtures. HA! In my bedroom I have inked in life-size silhouettes of various friends., This gives infinite pleasure and merriment. Behind the piano are sacks, empty, and full of paper, and various cooking utensils for camp. Life is very sweet. Who would think of war to hear me talking. And yet I may as well enjoy myself, even in war time.

To enjoy himself under all circumstances was his principal goal.

Even without any formal medical training, he was pressed into service by the exigencies of war. In the temporary hospitals set up at Cambridge, Donald became a medical trainee and was thus not obliged to enter active military service. As of his letter of December 9, he wore a uniform. Many of his classmates saw battle, and many died. According to Clare, they haunted him all his life.[7] He felt that his own spared life should stand in for theirs. Here we can speculate that the sense of being a substitute, as with so many memories and ideas, may well have served a "screen" function. It was his task to carry the burden of living for those who (in fact, or possibly in fantasy as well, as with never-born male siblings) could not.

Clare noted that "one of the patients, who became a lifelong friend, remembers Donald in those days: 'The first time I saw him was in hospital in Cambridge in 1916 in the first war; he was a medical student who liked to sing a comic song on Saturday evenings in the ward—and sang "Apple Dumplings" and cheered us all up.'"[8]

In 1917, Donald enrolled in the Royal Navy and was accepted as a surgeon-probationer with duty as a medical officer on a destroyer, HMS *Lucifer*. Not having had any formal medical training, he must have picked up enough of the rudiments to at least act as an impostor. It was fortunate that an experienced orderly was also on the destroyer to which he was assigned, someone to teach him a bit of practical medical lore. Donald was there, he said, "to reassure the sailors' mothers that their boys had a doctor on board."[9]

During his military service Donald read the novels of Henry James and George Meredith—not medical books to sharpen his thinking about patients, but works of fiction. This gives some indication of his preferences, which is supported by the tone of the one surviving letter from the HMS *Lucifer*. In his choice of fiction we see, too, a different cast of mind from that of his father. The imaginative element in fiction, which is the world of the dream, appealed to him in a way that it did not appeal to Frederick Winnicott.

— 5 —

Medical School

D onald entered St. Bartholomew's Hospital Medical College (Bart's) in the fall of 1917.[1] This is at odds with Clare's dating of his clinical work as beginning after the war, which ended in November 1918. She tells us that he was fully committed to his medical studies, and the evidence of his later life supports her statement: "Donald had some great teachers at the hospital, and he always said that it was Lord Horder who taught him the importance of taking a careful case history, and to listen to what the patient said, rather than simply to ask questions."

The emphasis that Dr. Thomas Horder (later Lord Horder) placed on listening carefully to the patient for an understanding of the disease that lay behind the symptoms was apparently not a common one. Donald would one day say that psychoanalysis was actually only an extension of this process of history taking. His absorption of Lord Horder's humanitarian and scientific lessons was undoubtedly the outcome of his prior life and temperament, so well demonstrated in the letters extant from his school and university days. He was in need of one or more idealized figures to serve as guides to his future. This would have been true whether or not his relationship to his own father was strong, but was all the more so in view of the distance that separated them emotionally.

The vagueness of Donald's romantic attachments is well indicated by Clare's comment, "It is difficult to give any dates in relation to Donald's girl friends, but he had quite close attachments to friends of his sisters and later to others he met through his Cambridge friends," the latter probably including Alice Taylor, whom he eventually married. That "he came close to marriage on several occasions" is unsupported by specifics. Jimmy Ede dismissed the suggestion that his sister Fiona and Donald were a serious couple. We know little of Donald's social life except for Clare's listing of "singing, sprees, dancing, occasional skiing holidays, and hurrying off at the last minute to hear operas for the first time, where he usually stood in his slippers at the back of the 'Gods.'"

Clare noted, too, that "during the training Donald became ill with what turned out to be an abscess in the lung and was a patient in Bart's for three months. A friend who visited him there remembers it in these words: 'It was a gigantic old ward with a high ceiling dwarfing the serried ranks of beds, patients and visitors. He was *intensely* amused and interested at being lost in a crowd and said 'I am convinced that every doctor ought to have been once in his life in a hospital bed as a patient.'" There is no suggestion here of the potentially serious condition of a lung abscess of three months' duration.

Winnicott later told the story of his discovery of Freud, which dated from this period of his life. He had "ceased to be able to recall his dreams."[2] He called in at Lewis's and asked the librarian for a book that might enable him to make a recovery. He was given a copy of one of Bergson's works, which he found quite irrelevant. He returned the book and was given instead a work by the Swiss parson, Oskar Pfister.[3] This led him to *The Interpretation of Dreams* (1900). Winnicott had a profound sense that psychoanalysis would be a part of his life's work.

It is a matter of some interest that Winnicott gives, as the condition that led to his discovery of Freud, that he had "ceased to be able to recall his dreams." If it is true, as we learn from Roazen, that this began when he was nine years old,[4] one would have to infer that he had closely monitored his internal life, and that access to his dreams was therefore taken for granted, so much so that losing that access constituted for Winnicott a kind of a symptom. Was this the literal event, or was it simply the focus, while some other, deeper symptom, some other loss of access, was more definitively troubling?

It is possible that his dream life represented contact with his mother, that the impact of a breakthrough of rage at his mother was the root of the struggle. What was within and on which he drew would stand for what he had taken in from his mother. Could he therefore live as one who could hate successfully and yet stay in touch with his own inner resources? Could he love and hate at the same time, starting with his mother and continuing after that with a particular woman, a mate?

Winnicott graduated in 1920, continuing thereafter to work as house physician under Professor Francis Fraser. "In the same year he qualified as a Member of the Royal College of Surgeons (MRCS) and as a Licentiate of the Royal College of Physicians (LRCP),"[5] which enabled him to practice in Britain. It seems that he never took, or certainly never passed, his third MB in surgery, midwifery, and gynecology, but by 1920 he was a qualified doctor specializing in children's medicine. This meant that he did not have the higher degree of Doctor of Medicine, although he became a full member of the Royal College of Physicians (MRCP) in 1922. The publication in the United States, in 1958, of his *Collected Papers: Through Paediatrics to Psycho-Analysis* raised the question of his status. He was identified by his publisher as an M.D., to which he at first objected, but then acceded since this was the only proper designation in America for a practicing physician.[6]

The fact that he chose to specialize in children's medicine (the word "pediatrician" was not in common use at that time), a field then so much at variance with an interest in mental or emotional problems, unlike psychiatry and neurology, is not so odd when we think of the devotion to children he had already demonstrated in his work with Scouts in Cambridge. He took great delight in their behavior and appearance and capacities and was dedicated to their welfare in extraordinary ways. His own capacity for enthusiasm, seen in all of his letters, betokens the survival into adulthood of an attribute often associated with early life.

He had always shared with his sisters what was regarded as a family talent for getting on with children, and throughout his training he had been interested in children's problems. "Donald Winnicott had the most astonishing powers with children," his colleague the pediatrician Peter Tizard would write in his obituary. "To say that he understood children would to me sound false and vaguely patronizing: it was rather that children understood him."[7]

As an example of Donald's expressive presence, and of his first explicit absorption with and impressive grasp of fundamental psychoanalytic principles, there is the letter, dated November 5, 1919, written to his sister Violet in his last year of medical school. His return address, in Paddington, foreshadows the long association he would eventually have with the Paddington Green Children's Hospital, where he practiced pediatrics and child psychiatry, and with the nearby St. Mary's Hospital Medical School, with which it was eventually associated. The letter contains a passing reference to his lonely bed, a brief discussion of Mrs. Astor and politics,[8] a lyrical description of a nine-mile autumn walk, and then an extensive account of the rivalry between students at Bart's and University College Hospital in the streets of London.[9] This is the fun-loving Donald again, now at twenty-three. The letter is distinguished, however, by his attempt to tell Violet about psychoanalysis, his first reference to the subject that would preoccupy him for the rest of his life:

Psychotherapy progresses.[10] Do not trouble to read further as (at your invitation) I am going to explain a little about it.

First a few definitions. Therapy means treatment. Psychotherapy means the treatment of disorders of the mind apart from those depending on disease of the brain. The Brain is the mass of grey and white matter which lies hidden in the skull, whereas the mind is that part of a person which stores memories, thinks and wills (if it does will at all). The brain is unlike the mind as a nerve is unlike the impulse that travels down it [i.e., the brain is a thing; the mind is action].

Suggestion is the active principle of almost all medicine; it is that by which a doctor ensures that a medicine will act. It is the influence of a man's personality and way of putting things over the progress of the patient. Everyone knows how effective and necessary suggestion is in affecting a cure. Hypnotism is a method of giving a concentrated dose of suggestion.

Now then we come to Psychoanalysis. This long word denotes a method developed by Freud by which mind disorders can be cured without the aid of Hypnosis, and with a lasting result as opposed to the temporary cure sometimes produced under Hypnosis. Psychoanalysis is superior to hypnosis and must supersede it, but it is only very slow in being taken up by English physicians because it requires hard work and prolonged study (also great sympathy) none of which are needed for Hypnosis. Only yesterday I saw a man suffering from shell shock put under Hypnosis by the man who looks after mental diseases at Bart's. This man could never do Psychoanalysis because it needs patience and sympathy and other properties which he does not possess.

The discharged soldier was helped a little, perhaps, by the Hypnosis, but he will not be cured because Hypnosis only treats one or two of the symptoms: whereas Psychoanalysis cuts right at the root of the matter.

May I explain to you a little about this method which Freud has so cleverly devised for the cure of mind disorders? If there is anything which is not completely simple for anyone to understand I want you to tell me because I am now practising so that one day I shall be able to help introduce the subject to English people so that who runs may read.

The subject is such an enormous one that I must ask you to assume some astoundingly controversial axioms. For instance we will take it for granted that there is a division of the Mind into the conscious and a subconscious, and that in the latter are stored all impressions received since birth (and possibly before). We can have a diagram in which a man's mind is represented as a pyramid in subconsciousness with just the tip above the border line. For memory we devise all manner of weird methods for diving into the subconscious. Between one thought and the next there is always some connection or other whether it be a logical connection of ideas, a pun on two words or some other link which turns consciousness into an uninterrupted sequence of events.

I must turn right away now to the instincts. No matter how many there are, but anyhow these are natural directions in which the something which we call the life force must travel outwards.

Again I must go across and state boldly that an idea or an abnormal tendency, so long as it is in the conscious mind or completely understood by the conscious mind, can definitely be controlled by the will in a human being who is not out of his mind. But it is equally true that an instinct repressed along abnormal paths is liable to be shoved down deep into the subconscious and there act as a foreign body: this "foreign body" may remain in the subconscious for a whole lifetime and completely control the life of the individual who has no control over this curious tendency since it is not known to him even to exist.

In short Psychonalysis is a method by which, simply by making one back step after another the patient is led to trace back his dreams and obsessions to their origin which has often been harboured since infancy or childhood. The patient is amazed to find his curious behavior explained and the cause brought up into consciousness. He is then able to bring his own will into the battle and his will is given a fair chance.

Hypnosis you see depends on a patient borrowing will from the physician. Psychoanalysis only gives a man a fair chance to bring his own will against the situation in question. And as a person's will is always sufficient against a realised tendency (as a rough rule) there is great hope for the future.

I shall probably be accused of blasphemy if I say that Christ was a leading psychotherapist. (I don't know why, but Violet is fond of saying that what I say is blasphemy, when there is no connexion whatever between what I have said and the term.) It is no less true that extreme acts and religious rituals and obsessions are an exact counterpart of these mind disorders, and by psychotherapy, many fanatics or extremists in religion can be brought (if treated early) to a real understanding of religion with its use in setting a high ethical standard. Thus they are brought from being a nuisance to the community and a centre of religious contagion to normal, useful and social members, in a position from which to develop along their own individual lines.

So now you know a little about a very vast subject which has the great charm of being really useful. It remains for me to put what I am

learning to the test. Even if I do not take up any subject which allows
of psychotherapy in my work, the knowledge will always be useful
as a hobby.

In addition to the central importance of its documenting Donald's
enthusiasm and understanding of psychoanalysis at age twenty-three in
1919 (the year in which Ernest Jones reorganized the British Psycho-
Analytic Society), this letter also contains a few bold speculative forays at
the very inception of what might be deemed his entrance into the field.
First, Winnicott questions whether there is such a thing as "will" (even
though he goes on to elaborate on the role of will in human psychology);
second, he poses the possibility that memories may extend back to the
period before birth (a subject he would explore at length in the years
ahead); and third, he already thinks of himself as a pioneer among English physicians when he writes, "I am now practising so that one day I
shall be able to help introduce the subject to English people so that who
runs may read." His audacity is undercut by the use of the word
"hobby," as if he caught himself overdoing it and wanted to retrench.

Special note should be taken of the clarity of language in this very
early letter. This was unusual—even rare—then as always among psychoanalytic writers, and it distinguishes Winnicott, who undertook the description of so many phenomena that were outside the realm of the written
or spoken word until he came to grips with them and found the words that
enlarged our consciousness.

Another piece of writing is a poem that appeared in the April 1920
number of the *St. Bartholomew's Hospital Journal*. It was the month of his
twenty-fourth birthday.

A SHROPSHIRE SURGEON

Vide *"A Shropshire Lad," No. VIII.*

Farewell, trephine and stomach-pump!
Farewell! to ruddy gore;
Herbert, watch my latest jump,
For I shall jump no more.

The clock strikes in the cold grey square,
By now he may have died
Who yesterday was wake and ware,—
Whose head I opened wide.

The Sister thinks me long away,
'Tis time my fast were broke:
We watched him sleep till rising day—
Maybe he'll not be woke.

O! here's a bloody hand to shake,
And O man, here's good bye;
No more we'll cut for cutting's sake,
My bloody hands and I.

D. W. W.

This is his farewell to medical school, the renunciation of cutting instruments. Soon he would approach the brain/mind through the medium of speech rather than instruments. As a children's doctor, Winnicott would start out examining his patients as well as listening to them, until one day the trappings of the physician would disappear and only the observing person would be there, in a high state of playful attentiveness, representing all that he had learned up to that point.

— 6 —

Hospital Work

After his graduation from "Barts" in 1920, Donald worked in hospitals as a house physician, gaining intensive experience with physically ill patients. The Professor of Medicine at St. Bartholomew's in Winnicott's time was Sir Archibald Garrod, "and his deputy, and then successor, was Professor Francis Fraser. Winnicott was Fraser's third house physician." Winnicott claimed that "he got the job because he had asked for it just when nobody else wanted to work with this 'outsider from Scotland.' Actually, by the time that his application was being considered, there were already many other candidates for the post, but Professor Fraser stuck to his promise. Winnicott got his Membership a year later, but . . . he explains this as being inevitable since he had been hearing one of the country's best physicians over a period of a year discussing just those questions which he was asked in Membership. He said he would never have got it if he had had to work for it."[1] "As a casualty officer (emergency room physician), he "worked almost all day and night but he would not have missed the experience for the world. It contained the challenge of the unexpected and provided the stimulation that he reveled in."[2]

Whether any of this time was devoted entirely to work with children is not clear, even though both of Winnicott's appointments in 1923 involved the care of children. There was no pediatric residency then, and he did not have a psychiatric residency either, so it could not truthfully be said that he was either a psychiatrist, a child psychiatrist, or a pediatrician at the time. In later life, with a massive experience in children's health in all its physical and emotional aspects, he could write about child psychiatry as an authority, but at the start of his clinical work he was still putting together, out of his own intense interest, a variety of experiences with children into a kind of expertise. This would eventually (in 1931) result in *Clinical Notes on Disorders of Childhood*, a work intended for general practitioners, in which he describes his experiences as a young physician. The book is concerned mainly with common disorders. Many of the articles had already been published in the medical literature. He wrote of it in a short summary of his career: "This book was one of the first in which there was a fusing of the two aspects of paediatrics, that of medical care and that of child psychiatry."[3] In 1971 his successor at Paddington Green, Dr. Susanna Isaacs, wrote that the book

> is still fascinating and stimulating. His crystal-clear style of writing was developing, so that the book would still be shocking to some physically-minded colleagues. Shocking because D. W. W.'s perception of the ubiquitous importance of emotion is revealed so succinctly, his conclusions and his evidence were ineluctable. Even when writing this early work he acted on his knowledge that "it is just as much a symptom of anxiety to try to force children to know as to try to keep them from finding out." This refers to providing children with the physical facts about human sexuality. But one of Winnicott's strengths was that he could see the overall pattern of response underlying an individual occurrence. So he knew that you could only disturb people by trying to force knowledge on them.[4]

One review was distinctly hostile. Winnicott had written in chapter 1, "In fact, in the case of a sick child, it is usually possible to guess with reasonable certainty why health has not been maintained, for the causes of disease are few." The reviewer's acid comment was: "Physicians who rely upon guessing are somewhat dangerous."[5]

In the introduction to his book, Winnicott wrote:

> The newly-qualified practitioner of medicine becomes a houseman at his hospital and, as is well known, receives shock after shock. He has

to spend much of his time seeing and rejecting cases that are "not interesting" in order to find a sufficient number of cases about which he knows something to keep his ward full. Fortunately for him there is an extreme shortage of hospital beds in most towns, certainly in London, and with any luck he can during his six months' tenure of office keep out of the beds that are under his care most cases that are not "cases."

The experience has, however, disturbed his equanimity, and his medical education has begun.

He now perhaps takes a post of casualty officer in a busy children's hospital, and before his time is up he regrets what he has done. For a huge percentage of his cases "have nothing wrong with them," have catarrh, are "neurotic," have quite severe physical illness with no physical signs, and so on, and but for meeting an occasional case of intussusception, volvulus, pneumonia "with beautiful bronchial breathing" and perhaps scurvy—he would lose interest.

His education continues.

Soon he is in general practice, and as he must not only earn his living but also feel that he is justifying his existence, he now finds every case interesting. Moreover, in practice, he never sees a case of intussusception, pyloric stenosis he finds to be much more rare than projectile vomiting, and he feels lucky if a case of scurvy crosses his path in ten years. He now complains: Why was I not taught about the common disorders and symptoms at my teaching hospital?

Winnicott goes on to conclude: "Someone must write a book for him and this book may be taken to be an attempt in that direction."

In his 1949 paper on birth trauma ("Birth Memories, Birth Trauma, and Anxiety"), Winnicott described the case of a fifty-year-old woman whom he treated during his tenure as a house physician. The patient in question, Miss H., a shorthand-typist, suffered from a severe neurosis, which included bouts of extreme constipation of an intensity that Winnicott had not previously encountered. Miss H. also struggled with acute attacks of anxiety. On the basis of quite rudimentary knowledge derived from reading, he facilitated a basic cathartic treatment in which the patient "would lie and sleep, and then suddenly wake in a nightmare. I would help her to wake by repeating over and over again the words that she had shouted out in the acute anxiety attack. By this means when she wakened I was able to keep her in touch with the anxiety situation and to get her to remember all sorts of traumatic incidents from her very event-ful early childhood." Hannah Henry, a close friend of Winnicott's tells of a patient, probably different from the one just described, whom he helped in a similar way (see chapter 8).

He made reference in the 1950s to a patient encountered during this same period. It was a "case of compulsive over-breathing which came my way when I was a House Physician in 1922; this went on for many hours and was leading to serious physical effects, but it disappeared when in the history-taking I and the patient discovered that it started during intercourse and as part of a phobia of intercourse."[6] He was by this time clearly preoccupied with the principles of psychoanalysis, and was trying out his early powers.

In a late retrospective talk about his training,[7] he spoke of "mistakes that I hate to think about. Once, before the days of insulin, I drowned a diabetic patient in a stupid and ignorant attempt to apply instructions from above. The fact that the man would have died anyway does not make me feel better. And I have done worse things. Happy is the young doctor who does not get exposed as ignorant before he has built up some position among colleagues that will see him through disasters." It is typi-cal of him that he would present a balanced portrayal of success and fail-ure, primarily out of loyalty to empirical fact, and to neutralize any idealization that might creep into recollections of the past. He referred again to this sense of failure shortly before he died, citing the case of the diabetic man then too.[8]

Winnicott flourished in his work as a pediatrician, often dealing with some very difficult cases. His practice included the treatment of children who had become afflicted with polio or extreme summer diar-rhea in the course of epidemics. At this time antibiotic remedies had not yet become available, and as Winnicott later recalled, "our wards were full of children with pus in the lungs or the bones or the meninges."[9] The discovery of antibiotics would not come until 1928, when, in his corner office at St. Mary's Hospital Medical School, close by Paddington Green, Alexander Fleming noticed an area in a petri dish culture that was clear of bacteria, just adjacent to an area contaminated by a fungus that had floated in through his open window. He had the presence of mind and in-tellectual brilliance to make an inference, and shortly thereafter, what we have come to know as penicillin was identified. It was the product of the mold called *Penicillium Notatum*.[10]

In the meantime, Clare recalled, Donald, having discovered psycho-analysis, decided "that he must . . . stay in London to undergo analysis." She notes that "after taking his Membership examination, [he] set up as a Consultant in Children's Medicine (there was no specialty in pediatrics in those days)."[11] In 1923, "he received an appointment as House Physician at the Hospital for Sick Children at Great Ormond Street in London, in order to study an anticipated epidemic of summer diarrhoea. But a full-scale epidemic did not develop as predicted, and so Winnicott did not actually assume the appointment."[12]

In the same year he obtained two other hospital appointments, at the Queen's Hospital for Children and at Paddington Green Children's Hospital. At the Queen's Hospital for Children, known fondly as "the Queen's," he also worked for three sessions each week as physician in charge of the London County Council Rheumatism Supervisory Centre, treating patients with rheumatic fever and subsequent rheumatic heart disease, a common affliction at that time. Winnicott also had to deal with patients suffering from chorea. He resigned from "the Queen's" in 1934 but continued to run the rheumatism clinic there. His practice as consultant at Paddington Green became the core of his clinical experience. He would remain there for forty years, retiring reluctantly in 1963.[13] He referred to his clinic at the Paddington Green Children's Hospital as his "Psychiatric Snack Bar," a place where large numbers of patients could receive a little psychological sustenance. This designation came from the "Peanuts" cartoon series, drawn by Charles Schulz.

In *Human Nature*[14] (1988, written in 1952) Winnicott writes: "I would like to mention [Dr. Leonard George] Guthrie, author of *Functional Nervous Disorders in Childhood* [1907], not because he reached great heights but because he was a pioneer to whom I owe the special climate at Paddington Green Children's Hospital which made my appointment there in 1923 possible. After Guthrie's tragic death I was to carry on the work of his department, and I was not aware at the time that it was because of my own leanings towards the psychological in paediatrics that I was appointed to the consulting staff of the hospital."

Starting early in his practice, Winnicott published numerous papers on pediatric subjects, including "Varicella Encephalitis and Vaccinia Encephalitis" (1926), "Short Communication on Enuresis" (1930), "Pathological Sleeping" (1930), "Pre-systolic Murmur, Possibly Not Due to Mitral Stenosis" (1931), and "Papular Urticaria and the Dynamics of Skin

Sensation" (1934)." In 1928, he wrote "The Only Child," on "Fidgetiness" in 1931, "The Difficult Child" in 1934.

Although the special climate at the Paddington Green Children's Hospital nurtured Winnicott's blossoming interest in the psychological aspects of pediatrics, most of his colleagues in the 1920s had little patience for exploring the emotional components of children's illnesses. Donald Winnicott's "ideas were on the whole rejected by his contemporaries in paediatrics and . . . he suffered a real, though unintended, persecution at their hands."[15]

Many years later William Gillespie would make these comments during the British Psycho-Analytical Society's Memorial Meeting in honor of Winnicott:

> A quality that underlay his ability to be original was courage, which was combined, I should say, with a certain ruthlessness—a strange thing to say about such a gentle person as DW. The earliest manifestation of these qualities that I myself know of was the stand he took about "growing pains" and rheumatism. After all, by maintaining that children suffering in this way were not rheumatic and did not require prolonged bed rest, he was not only risking his own professional reputation, and career—he was also putting the children's lives at risk, unless one assumes, as perhaps one must, that W felt absolutely sure that *he* was right and all the rest of the profession wrong. I have also heard him say that children would have been better off bombed than evacuated; and his attitude about a patient's right to take his own life, with the implication that no one should try too hard to stop him, is well known. That is what I mean by W's occasional ruthlessness, and I believe that without it he would have made a great deal less impact than he did. Nevertheless, "His life was gentle, and the elements so mixed in him that this very quality was turned to noble ends, for he was a man full of love and tenderness as well."[16]

— 7 —

Alice Taylor

Clare writes that Donald "came to the brink of marriage more than once but did not actually marry (for the first time) until the age of twenty-eight." Donald was married on July 7, 1923. He was twenty-seven. The wedding took place in the parish church at Frensham, Surrey.[1]

The woman he married was thirty-one-year-old Alice Buxton Taylor, the daughter of John W. Taylor, a deeply religious Wesleyan Methodist (who eventually converted to the Anglican religion, as did Donald), a poet, and a gynecologist. In 1904 Taylor became president of the British Gynaecological Society, "of which he had been a Fellow since its inception. His 'Inaugural Address' gave him the opportunity of speaking out very strongly on a subject about which for some years he had been greatly disquieted—the decline of the birth-rate, not only in England, but in the whole of Western Europe. 'His outspoken denunciation of the evils which underlie this great social fact made a remarkable impression on the thoughtful laity.'"[2]

Alice, born in Birmingham in 1892, was the second child, after Mary, who would one day marry a famous architect. She was followed by another sister, Pauline, who never married, a brother, and then another brother, Jim, who became a doctor and a good friend of Donald Winnicott. Rosa Taylor, Jim's second wife, a member of the Shaumberg family of St. Petersburg, a gynecologist, told Madeleine Davis and me in 1988 that Alice's father was "one of those people who thought you only have sex when you want a baby. He was a saint, idealized by his children, but he almost never played with them because he was so busy." A highly successful, busy Wesleyan with little time for his children: this could equally describe Donald's father.

John Taylor died in 1910, when Alice was eighteen. She attended Cambridge and eventually worked in the National Physical Laboratory at Teddington. We do not know what she did in a place devoted to science. She herself was a deeply artistic person, who, during her marriage, painted, potted, sculpted, and played music. Her beliefs in the supernatural, evidenced by the notion that Lawrence of Arabia was communicating with her through a parrot, further suggest that at the very least, she was not accustomed to the rigors of scientific thought. She may have met Donald at Cambridge, as Hannah Henry, a friend of both, speculates. This is the more likely because Donald's old friend Jimmy Ede was at Cambridge with Alice. The other possibility is that they were introduced while Alice was working at Teddington by David Bentley, who was employed there as well. Donald had met Bentley and his wife, Lilian, sometime before he and Alice were married in 1923.

Hannah Henry[3] tells the story, as told to her by Lilian Bentley, that one day, Donald knocked on the Bentleys' door "to ask if he could have a room for the weekend (before he was married and coming to see Alice). When Lilian opened the door and said Hello, Donald stammered out 'Oh, I'm sorry I thought this was a cottage,' to which Lilian burst out laughing and said, well it is. It was obvious she was not a working class Cottager, with her cultured voice. Her father was a Solicitor and quite well off and she with an Oxford B.A. Donald was most embarrassed but they remained marvellous friends for life and saw a lot of each other, living only 10 minutes away." This must have been in the early 1920s. His comment "I thought this was a cottage" calls to mind his later, famous declaration, "There is no such thing as a baby," in the sense that he finds himself willing, on the spur of the moment, to contravene an obvious fact, to play with reality rather than submit to it, or, rather, to submit to a reality that he accidentally invents.

Hannah and her husband became friends of the newlywed Winnicotts. They'd met while camping in Sussex in August 1926. Along with the Bentleys—David, Lilian, and their children—they all grew close and saw one another on the weekends.

When business required that the Henrys live closer to town, they moved to a flat on the far side of Hampstead Heath. They continued to meet Alice and Donald quite often, mostly on the weekends. Donald liked to walk. On one occasion Hannah recalled, "they were looking after a dog for a friend, a Great Dane, and I met Donald. When he saw me he started to run this dog on a lead [and] simply flew."

The Winnicott home, Sydney House, 7 Pilgrims Lane, "was only two minutes walk to the Heath, one of the loveliest bits of London, more country than parts of supposedly real country.[4] [I]t had 5 ponds, with wild life and one where one could swim. In the summer there were sheep and a real shepherd. But this didn't suit Alice. She said Donald had said she could always live in the country and she never let up on this, always resented this and that he would not be an ordinary G.P. like her father[5] and brother. She hated his new career, said it was killing him, and in this I had to agree, when I lived with them . . . in the war."

Hannah stayed with the Winnicotts for a period of six months near the beginning of World War II, when she had to evacuate her home in Suffolk. She remembers that Donald "would see people at the house, in the evenings, after a busy day, and after a long session, he was drained, he gave everything. But Alice had no sympathy." Hannah remembered Alice saying that flowers died more quickly in the city than in the country, perhaps a reference to human life as well, or the fragile nature of beauty, and certainly an expression of her own feelings of resentment.

After Donald had served for a period looking after the children at "the Queens" in a very impoverished part of London, he opened an office in Queen Anne Street. He then bought a home in Hampstead, North London. Kahr[6] tells us that Donald actually opened his first office in 1924 at 33, Weymouth Street, after which he moved to 44, Queen Anne Street, and then 47. Clare writes that "At the beginning he found Harley Street formidable because he had few patients, so in order to impress the very dignified porter who opened the door to patients for all the doctors in the house, he tells how he used to pay the fares of some of his hospital mothers and children so that they could visit him in Harley Street. Of course the procedure was not entirely on behalf of the porter, because he selected cases in which he was particularly interested and to which he wanted to give more time so that he could begin to explore the psychological aspects of illness."[7]

By the time of the move to Hampstead, Donald had not only begun a private practice but also was in daily psychoanalysis with James Strachey, whom he saw at 41 Gordon Square, Bloomsbury.[8] This would have made it quite impractical for him to have continued to live in the country. Clearly, shaping his career was going to take precedence over all else. Hannah Henry knew nothing of this, nor of the subject of psychoanalysis. She writes: "I was completely out of touch [with him] educationally. Maybe this put me at a disadvantage with Donald or so I thought, but on the other hand I could have been relaxed in contrast to his more formal work. Certainly I knew nothing of a medical life and especially of this 'new thing' as it was then thought of publicly and especially in my own husband. I know he thought it was crazy. . . . I did not feel this, but hadn't a clue as to what it was all about. It didn't really matter, we were great friends and I was very fond of him and I'm sure he me." There is much evidence for this.

Hannah describes the Winnicotts' home:

Sydney House was charming, laid well back from the road, Pilgrims Lane, leading out from Hampstead Village High Street and running onto the Heath. [There was a] nice front garden [with a] slight incline to the front door, three steps up. Large hall, quite imposing stairs up. On the right the dining room, with left down to semi-basement kitchen, the windows of which were above ground. Two hall windows in the dining room looking out [of] French windows, with old fashioned shutters. This is where Polyphemus lived [a parrot Alice inherited from her mother] with his shouts of Alice, God Bless the King and God Save Old Polyopkins. Alice said it would never say Donald. It was covered up at night and me being up first would take the cover off and it always crawled up the side of the cage and whispered Kiss Cookie, Kiss Cookie. So I Imagine the cook always did what I was doing.

There was a door from the hall, and behind the dining room the lounge, although they referred to it as the studio, [a] lovely room. [It had a] large oval window looking out onto a rambling garden, [with] a church beyond their boundary. Donald's grand [piano] was there, some lovely pictures, some dreadful ones [by] Alice, a bust of [T. E.]

Lawrence which was very good. Sofas, chairs, knick knacks, a very comfortable room. Both these rooms had Adams fireplaces and Adams wallpapers. . . Alice and Donald loved it all. Over the dining room [was] their bedroom with the same charming French windows leading out to a small balcony and shutters and a marvellous view over the Heath. [There were] four other bedrooms higher up, I went right up top. The view all over London was spectacular but for the first few weeks of the Blitz we all slept and almost lived all the time in the shored-up kitchen—under the table. But I got little sleep so in the end decided to go up top again, having seen the result of bombing. I said I'll come down on top, rather than be buried alive, but we were lucky, it never happened.

Below stairs, before the war, lived the maids. "When [Donald] introduced me to them, away we went downstairs. He knocked on the door before he was invited in and to sit down. They weren't just servants, they were friends. We were offered a cup of tea to show it was their home. I liked that. And Donald had learned [a] habit from Cook. If her tea was too hot to drink, she would pour some in the saucer to cool it, and drink it afterwards. With Donald with our own tea drinking, he would say 'Let's go down to the kitchen' and we would do the same. This is why I always felt he was so child-like, in simple things, and of course we would laugh over it."

Alice, she writes, "was very sweet, [with] an angelic face, I always thought Christ-like, long face, beautiful blue eyes, fair hair, parted in the middle with a gentle wave, no makeup ever, natural complexion, very slow in her movements. I never saw her hurry." (Marion Milner thought Alice nice-looking, but she seemed too large, Donald being so small, only five foot seven.)[9] "Alice dabbled in art, painted sometimes ghastly things, made pottery and sculpted," recalled Hannah. "She had a kiln at No. 7. These pots too [were] awful, one large room was full of pots. Goodness knows what happened to them." Two of her landscapes that I saw in Rosa Taylor's home were very slightly reminiscent of Cézanne. She signed her paintings and pottery "Claverdon," the name of the village of her family home, near Broadway. She "sang like an angel, was unconventional, fey." "Fey" was the word used by Marion Milner. It was also sometimes used to describe Donald, for example, by Ursula Bowlby. But she thought that "people were being kind about the first Mrs. Winnicott, to call her fey (which is not a critical adjective). I only met her once or twice, but would call her dotty. She was perfectly amiable and nice, but the archetypical shapeless form in baggy tweeds—I think she may have had a loom and made them herself—and a long string of beads, which she may also have made."[10]

Hannah recollects that "according to Lilian Bentley, the marriage was never consummated. Lilian was the most honest person. . . and I know Donald confided in her." Lilian, with whom he discussed his and Alice's sexual situation and, later on, the fact that his love with Clare was in fact consummated,[11] "must have acted like a Mother to him, perhaps more so, as one might not be able to discuss such a personal subject with one's Mother." Along with Michael Balint, Rosa Taylor worked with a group of virgin wives. It is not clear whether Alice was a member of this group. Some of the women were able to respond to suggestions (for example, that they put a finger in their vagina, then two), while others, too neurotic or psychotic, could not. They had all chosen men who were "kind," said Dr. Taylor, which always meant "impotent." Probably pertinent is her observation that whenever Alice's artwork was progressing—a painting, for example—she would have to put a stop to it. This conflict about creative endeavor might well reflect a similar attitude toward the consummation of love, yet both she and Donald were deeply committed to self-expression, probably working against ingrained conflict. In his theory of the True Self, Donald would one day make a point of saying that it wants to remain hidden, wants not to be found.

"Alice had some nice ways and I never heard a cross word between them," writes Hannah Henry of the Winnicotts' marriage. The two of them "had a lot in common. They were [both] very musical, both in the Madrigal Society, both played the recorder, Donald the piano. It was lovely the way they picked up their recorders in the evenings, Alice harmonising to Donald's tune, and how they enjoyed it. It helped I'm sure to relax any tension."

Certainly Alice was either emotionally disturbed, neurologically impaired, or some combination of both. According to Lilian Bentley, Hannah writes, Alice "had had a bang on the head while working at the Lab (one nasty person said it wasn't hard enough) and there was some damage, and this caused her to fall asleep. She was certainly often in a dreamlike state," and "she'd fall into a brown study." Alice also "wasn't often keen on hygiene and this nauseated me and I wondered if it had the same effect on Donald."[12]

While she lived with the Winnicotts during the war, Hannah recalls, "on the very first raid [of the Blitz], on a beautiful September afternoon (Saturday), we heard this huge drone, looked up and saw dozens of planes, way up so high like great silver fishes. No warning had gone off but later there were bangs in the distance. Donald and I went on the Heath and up Parliament Hill, quite the highest spot around London. One could see for miles, the whole of London and beyond St. Paul's. It looked as if the whole of London was on fire. We sat on seats and Donald was in despair. He said, 'Queen, those poor poor people.'" It turned out that things were not as bad as they looked; the bombs were aimed at Battersea Power Stations in the East End of London, where so many of Donald's patients lived.

The Winnicotts "both took on the role of Wardens in their road when raids occurred, donning their tin hats and out. One of the garages they turned into a first aid post, fully equipped for any casualties. Alice took it all so seriously, she bought a nurse's uniform, or rather the nearest she could, which was an old fashioned maid's print dress, white apron, and a head piece and small cape. She certainly looked the part. What would have happened if she had to deal with a patient I don't know. On one evening off they went out at the sound of the siren and after about two hours Donald came in and I said 'Where's Alice?' 'Oh! She's plying for hire,'—terrific laughter. 'Oh Queen what have I said?' Then we had coffee." What a relief it must have been for Donald to be able to laugh about his burden and joke, in this case, that his virgin wife was a prostitute.

On one occasion during the war, "Donald's father was doing something in connection with his Will and it needed Alice's signature which meant her going to Plymouth. Couldn't be trusted by Post because of bombing, etc. I can't tell you how long it took to get her in the mood to go: weeks and weeks. At last she decided. Donald got her a ticket, entrusted me with it and to see her on the train, four o'clock in the afternoon on a train that would take her without a change. He made arrangements for us to stop half way to the station and have tea with the Matron at Paddington Green Hospital. Eventually I got her on the train I never thought I'd make." Following Donald's instructions, Hannah phoned him as soon as Alice was safely away. "He said 'Thank God Queen, let's do something, where shall we go? Come along home.' So we saw a film, something Alice would never have seen. Afterwards a meal and home and what a relief! She was away a week. So Donald had to live with that. The strain must have been enormous."

That strain was put into words during the times Donald drove Marion Milner home from lectures.[13] This may have been after 1945, or possibly earlier, during the war. When he drove, he said, "that means I'm less deprived." Also, during the years of Marion's analysis with Donald, which took place in her own consulting room (for "geographical reasons"), he left behind "a beautiful crucifix out of matches—with a rubber band—Christ's head leaning forward." She thought, "He must have been trying to communicate something of his state of mind before the divorce."[14] His metaphor comparing himself with Christ is seen dramatically in his 1963 poem "The Tree," sent to Jim Taylor, which makes the connection to his relationship with his mother. This poem was written during his successful second marriage, fifteen years after his divorce from Alice, at a time of continuing self-analysis which was attaining profound proportions.

During the war, Martin James's wife, Lydia, rode on the bus with Alice from Mill Hill, where the Maudsley Hospital had been evacuated.[15] (I do not know whether she had a job there or was undergoing diagnostic testing or treatment, or was in analysis with Clifford Scott, who may have been working there.) Lydia thought that Alice was mad, and Dr. James told me in 1988 that Jim Taylor had pleaded with Donald not to marry her because she was mad. By contrast, Marion Milner reports that Jim said that even though Alice heard messages in birdsongs, she was *not* mad. She was never in a mental hospital and, according to Rosa Taylor, was "not the kind you hospitalize."

During the war, Hannah wrote, Alice "bought a[n] old established pottery works in Kent. The . . . old boy who owned it, stayed on and managed and turned out some lovely stuff. We would go there once a week, for Alice to attend to the business side. This meant crossing London north to south, and she would not make an early start, say 10 o'clock, so they could get back home before Black Out (when the bombs would start). I would keep on and on, Alice come on, but come on she would not, never starting till lunch time. I would have to wait, food packed up, until she decided to leave." Alice would then drive across London. "She knew the way, and then I would take over and really move. On more than one occasion she fell asleep at the wheel and [would] go over red lights and when I shrieked, she would say quite calmly, 'Don't shout Queen.' I told Donald she wasn't safe and I was worried about her. He said 'Queen, I know, but I can't worry, there's nothing I can do about it.' So there we were down at this factory, and leaving so late, arriving always at the outskirts of London in the dark, blackout, no lights except side and bombs falling. I was not a patient person but I stuck it out."

Joyce Coles, who became Donald's secretary in October 1948, tells a similar story from the period about eight years later.[16] Donald asked: "'Would you go with Alice in her car, take her, take a whole day? I'd like you to go because if she goes alone she's apt to fall asleep.' I didn't believe it. She had a big Humber. It couldn't get into third gear, you had to go from second to fourth. She started to drive, at 70 miles per hour in Kent, she fell asleep, the car veered off the road. I yelled at her: 'You must let me drive.' He sent me again another time. I wanted to drive that time and had to run into the road to stop her. She nodded off in the house too."

Hannah Henry said: "She had been used to running a home, they always had a couple of maids, but of course . . . [the maids] had to leave for war work, so I was a great help. But she chipped in now and again. We shared the cooking and I saw that Donald had clean shirts and hankies and shoes. At that early stage there were no laundries functioning. He and I always had breakfast together, Alice arriving late, never looking as if she had washed or bathed and while eating could fall asleep. Donald said once, 'Have you ever seen anyone sleep and eat at the same time?' (with a smile). There definitely was something wrong with her."

Alice had "crushes," at least one in addition to her strange romantic preoccupation with T. E. Lawrence. Hannah, who thought that these "fancified lovers" were the result of a lack of sexual satisfaction, lived before the war in a house called Theberton, formerly Church Farm, which was located on an estate belonging to the Doughty family. One of the sons was Charles Doughty, who became famous for his book *Arabia Deserta*. He had lived with wild tribes and became the inspiration for Lawrence of Arabia, whom he met on several occasions. Alice knew the connection with Doughty. When the Winnicotts visited Hannah, Donald teased, "How lovely Queen is at Theberton, right next door to Neill's School," with Alice replying, "Yes, and she's living next door to Doughty's old home." Donald was referring to the famous Summerhill school of A. S. Neill, known locally as the "do-as-you-like" school, in which he took a great interest.

Hannah writes: "Theberton, although on the East Coast, had the earliest spring, and the wild flowers are wonderful, still are [as of 1993]. One could always have snowdrops and aconite . . . in the third week of January. They grew beside the road, the woods were full. There was nowhere in England like it. The Doughtys were great naturalists, and large notices were put up on the trees: 'Please do not pick the flowers.' Alice had a passion for flowers and the countryside, so every spring I sent her a box of these flowers and she would take some and place them on the plaque in St. Paul's Cathedral in memory of Lawrence of Arabia." Lawrence's mother once asked where they came from.[17]

Alice's first knowledge of Lawrence may have come through Jim Ede, who studied at Cambridge in the same period as she. Jim, a "great friend of Lawrence," according to Hannah, had many letters. "He let Alice read them (I too read them). This was just after [Lawrence's] tragic death. Alice was devastated. She had previously done a bust of him and it really was very good. She referred to him as a spiritual contact. . . . Lawrence signed his letters T. E. S. He had joined the RAF and called himself T. E. Shaw." Alice swore that the spirit of Lawrence was in her parrot, which was calling out "TES."

Of Donald, Hannah recalled: "He was always involved with the poor people. So many couldn't pay him but now and again he was paid in kind, like a Barrow boy giving him a box of oranges. I know of at least three families he helped—not with money, but in one case arranging for milk and butter to be supplied to under nourished children, another he paid for dancing lessons for a young girl." He sometimes would ask Hannah to take a patient under her wing. She remembered one, "a lovely girl about 18 years, on the stage who was involved with a much older wealthy man. She had been quite ill, and Donald wanted to get her away for a rest without the man pest[er]ing her, so he rang up: 'Queen will you take this girl and be a friend.' I did of course, but this man followed her here."

Another patient, Tommy Tudor Hart, "with his Nannie," stayed with Hannah several times. His parents great friends of Donald's, the Father a doctor, Mother involved with Medicine, Tommy autistic, the youngest of 5 children, Father studying under Donald. The Nanny, so I understand, was Donald's first interest in analysis. She was a patient at St. Mary's Hackney Road where Donald was "walking the Wards." She was admitted and no one could get a word out of her. Donald made the habit of sitting on the bed and talking and one day she spoke and from there he learned her history, and he thought— this works. She was of Asian descent by her appearance, [a] tiny little thing, and really so ugly. Obviously Donald kept in touch and when he was involved with Tommy, [there was]. . . Nellie (although she gave herself the name of "Primrose"—less like that pretty little flower as you can imagine.) So I had them both for several long holidays and later the family took a house for them to live as a family. It worked well, and Tommy improved, he joined the Scouts, went to Church and loved Nellie. He must have been about 7 or 8 when Nellie became involved. I lost touch for a while personally, but Donald kept me informed. I loved Tommy too, he looked like an Angel and when they came in from their walks, he would tear along to my room, sometimes kitchen, and put his face right into mine and say "Sing" and we would both bellow out "Onward Christian Soldiers," the only thing he knew and he had learned by his Church going. The last time I saw Donald on my way through London. . . I found out that Nellie had died and Tommy too at the age of 19 years, so Donald did a good job there.

One of the things in the war that saddened him was the evacuation of children out of London to the country away from family and friends. He said how wrong this was. Whatever happened, families should stay together. How right he was as history has shown. We even had them here [in Aldeburgh] in the first few weeks of the war and then we too were pushed out expecting invasion from just across the water. When he knew I was going through a traumatic time with my husband, he said "Queen you were never so happy as when you were walking around the garden in 'Holmlea,' West Horsley big with child." On one of their visits (I was very overdue with [my son]) Donald had just bought a second hand Rolls—2 seater, it was like a chariot, he said "Come on, I'll bump you around the countryside and get you moving." Well of course it didn't, one feels nothing in a Rolls, but it was a lovely experience and how he enjoyed that car.

He had a passion for Golden Syrup for his breakfast toast, not the usual English Marmalade and we were rationed, so I would send him my coupons. On Sundays breakfast was a real treat, relaxed, reading the papers and Donald eating the whole of his Butter ration in one go. I think 1 ounce. In so many ways he was child like enjoying simple pleasures, and enjoying them so much. Once arriving for a visit, he opened the door to me, and said "Queen how nice—I almost kissed you."[18]

He could be so funny. I have wondered if you were connected with Donald's interests many years ago, because he had friends in USA and visited them, I knew not where, but they gave me vivid descriptions of the families, I likened them to the Kennedys. They were wealthy, had an Island, and in the holidays had re-unions with other branches—like a clan. They would arrive by sea-plane and go on marvellous pic-nics. I saw scads of all this, they seemed a fascinating crowd. I had post cards from other places too, one in the Hotel they were staying on the 40th floor I think. . . , a thrill for both, and perhaps you know something of this, or could you be one of the family? [She may be referring to the family of Malcolm Forbes. In 1937, Donald and Alice sailed from Naushon Island to Martha's Vineyard with the Forbeses, where they had a memorable picnic.]

On another of his visits to me, again recovering from heart trouble rather a serious one (spring, 1949), I was then living in a lovely house about 4 miles from here, Snape, now the home of our Aldeburgh Music Festival. [It was] founded by Benjamin Britten & Peter Pears. I had taken a friend as partner in my Guest House business and started taking in elderly gentlefolk—disastrous, both with partner and clients, the house designed by Luytens, beautiful. It was peaceful and Donald loved it, Alice too, but in a different way. We were about 20 miles from a small market town that Donald wanted to visit, so he asked me if I would take him, Alice didn't want to go, it was connected with his work—and that was that. We arrived to find a beautiful Elizabethan house owned by Sir Cedric Morris, artist, professional flower grower and art school.[19] Donald had put a patient there as a pupil—and paid. It was an unusual place, the students were scattered about the garden doing any old thing. Donald wandered off after introducing me to the owner, charming man, who put me in the hands of his manservant—a regular "Jeeves'" dressed in semi-evening clothes, but obviously by his accent a gentleman.[20] He made tea for me in a lovely alcove setting, it was a most unusual setting and I was happy to be alone and sap it all up. So Donald met the lady who was his patient and had tea with her, he seemed happy with her and the benefit she actually was getting in the surroundings. The owner Sir Cedric specialised in irises and there were beds of them, huge bearded ones, beautiful colours. He had shown them all over the world, and won many awards, some from our own Royal Horticultural Society.[21]

How I wonder did Donald know of these places especially here in the wilds of Suffolk. Certainly he grew to like Suffolk, it has a charm of its own, it appealed to me when I first found it in 1933, it is not like so many of our other counties in England all trim, hedges cut—gardens planted like regimental soldiers. The hedges by the road side are rampant, with rambling wild roses, honeysuckle, what I call a semi wild beauty, and the sea perhaps. Donald likened it to Devon his home which he loved passionately but Suffolk was more accessible. That's why after the breakup with Alice he went home to be nursed by sisters Kathleen and Violet, who I knew so well, lovely people. They always came to see me in the early days when Donald and Alice lived in Thames Ditton. We kept in touch by phone and at the end when only one [was] left and went blind, she would phone almost every night, and [she was] a lively person to the end—over 90.

Throughout these years, Donald and Alice remained close to his public school friend Jim Ede and his wife, and loved their two daughters, Elizabeth and Mary. In Edinburgh, in 1988,[22] the sisters remembered being cared for by the Winnicotts for over a year at least while Jim and his wife traveled abroad. They had great fun always, with Donald quacking like Donald Duck, as they called him, leaping up steps, and driving them in his car. One time he was standing on the seat, leaning over the wheel to steer. He explained the seriousness of his patients' problems, talked about them with great enthusiasm—probably, they now think, because he did not have a sympathetic audience in his wife. He told them not to be concerned if they were ever very angry with their parents, who were strict, tidy, and controlling. Mrs. Ede herself was controlled by her husband, who made all the choices in the home, though he was away often. The girls loved what Donald had to say. He brought a breath of freedom into their lives.

Donald and Alice were, for them, like surrogate parents. The girls were, in a sense, the closest thing to children of their own that they ever had. Jim told me and Madeleine Davis that Donald wrote him a letter asking if he could be a guardian to his children. He seemed to be asking to adopt them, and Jim took exception to this. Why should Donald think, he wondered, that they would want to give them up?

Beginning early in the war and lasting for seven years—until, that is, Donald and Alice actually separated—they took into their home a girl named Susan, who is the subject of Marion Milner's book *The Hands of the Living God*. (Donald is Doctor X.) They also took in a delinquent boy in the late 1940s, just prior to their separation. He was the subject of "Hate in the Countertransference" (1947). I surmise that Alice chose to take in this boy as well, and that these substitutes for their own children were intended to supplement their ever-less-satisfying marriage.

Elizabeth and Mary recalled that Alice became "even more dotty" as the girls got into their teens, and she seemed ten years older than Donald by the end. They knew that she communed with T. E. Lawrence through her parrot. As children, they couldn't understand why Donald left her, though they could in time. Elizabeth believes that Donald left Alice because of his heart attack.

In 1944, Donald's affair with Clare Britton began in secret, during their Oxfordshire work with evacuated children. By 1948 at the latest, he had decided to divorce Alice, but felt it necessary to wait for his father's death, which occurred on December 31 of that year. Marion recalled that she met Donald sometime after he had a heart attack in the spring of 1947.[23] After it "recurred," in her words, she saw him in 1948 (more probably 1949) and this was when he told her about Clare. Her recollection that it "recurred" suggests that Winnicott's February 1949 heart attack was not his first. This doubt is consistent with the fact that he misrepresented the number of cardiac events he suffered. Milner was afraid that he would die if he didn't leave Alice and told him so. Rosa Taylor said that when he had his heart attack, Alice recommended to her brother Jim, a doctor, that Donald put Detto drops (a disinfectant) in his nose.

Margaret Little, a physician and the patient who was placed in the art school in Suffolk, herself a friend of Marion Milner (who had treated her for a short period before Little came to Winnicott), recalled her session the day of Donald's 1949 heart attack. He wasn't feeling well and he told her that he had laryngitis, but she knew his problem was cardiac, and in ten minutes he agreed that it was serious and excused her. According to his secretary Joyce Coles, he had his first coronary at Queen Anne Street in about October 1949 (though this was at least his second, possibly even his third), soon after she started to work for him.[24] It was evening before he admitted he was ill. He went home to bed in Pilgrim's Lane for five weeks. It was not long after this that he left Alice. "He knew he couldn't stand the strain of Alice anymore," said Coles.

One day in 1949, Joyce Coles "came back from lunch to find Alice sitting in her room in floods of tears. He [Donald] had taken her out for lunch, which was very unusual. She said 'He's left me'—it was 1:30 in the afternoon—I said: 'Are you sure?' 'Yes,' she said, 'he told me over the luncheon table—he's not going back home.' From then on Donald slept in Queen Anne Street in his consulting room. He stayed with Clare on the weekends, in her apartment in Redcliffe Gardens, Chelsea." Mrs. Coles recalls being treated rudely by Alice when she came for his mail, late, at Donald's request, in 1949, a few months after she'd started to work for him. And there were complications relating to ration books. Coles had to collect his weekly rations from shops in Hampstead and bring them to Queen Anne Street. He would then take them to Clare's for the weekend. Coles resented being burdened with this task. He would say: "I haven't got time—would you be willing to?" Sometimes she would be about to refuse, but then other feelings would prompt her to give in. He would also leave his breakfast dishes for her to wash after he had slept at Queen Anne Street.[25]

Donald was remembered at this period by the wife of his second cousin Peter Woolland[26] (a grandson of Donald's uncle Richard): "It is 1949. He is curled up alone on a chair in the living room in front of the fireplace, observing and reading *Alice in Wonderland*." He had just separated from Alice. He must have retired to Rockville to be nursed by his sisters in the aftermath of this event, or possibly in the aftermath of the coronary that followed. He returned to Rockville on other occasions, certain as he was of the ancient and enduring love of his sisters, within a context of family and continuity.

Hannah Henry has preserved a moving letter written by Donald on October 30, 1950. Donald's error in addressing this letter to his friend at Claverdon, Alice's ancestral village, rather than her own home in Suffolk can be a subject of speculation, as can the emended sentence in which he makes sure that Hannah knows that it is "certain dominating trains of thought *in Alice"* to which he refers, not such trends in himself. Clearly he must have been in an emotionally and physically exhausted condition. The letter is postmarked "31 Oct 1950, 3:45 PM":

Mrs. Queen Henry
Claverdon
63 Craig Path
Aldeburgh
  Suffolk
Welbeck 5050   47, Queen Anne Street   W. 1

                                                        30 X 50

Dear Queen

It was good to hear from you. So there you are now at Aldeburgh complete with old women who are so happy with you, according to their capacity to be happy anywhere.

Do you know I've been ill again? Had a second attack 8 wks ago, and have only now been able to get back here from Plymouth. Sisters nursed me back to health. I've a few weeks now for convalescence, and its suiting me to be here.

I had meant to write & tell you the sad news that I've abandoned Alice. The Winnicott firm has dissolved. It came to that. I'm not trying to get out of the fact that I'm just being horrid.

It seemed to me clear that we were doing each other harm, & that the future held nothing better for us in our relationship, only worse. This is awful when one remembers how much Alice & I have experienced together, and have as common memories. Nevertheless, when two people live together, either the body warms or cools[27] when there is contact, and for me there had come a feeling of strain that is indescribable. For Alice too I'm sure there should eventually be relief.

There is a third person, someone who has a different effect on me, but I don't really believe I'd have allowed this to mark things up if I had not been bothered by certain dominating trains of thought in Alice that wrecked my relation to Alice. The strange thing is that I'm awfully fond of Alice, deeply attached, always shall be, but can't bear the idea of a return to actually living with her.

I think you ought to know these things, as I believe you are fond of *both* of us, and many of our friends are deeply distressed to find

I'm not the ideal dear boy they thought I was. I wouldn't like you to hear about it by chance.

Sorry this is all about me, or us—I'm sorry too that you won't ever be visited again by Alice-and-Donald. I think each of us will continue to be very fond of you in our separate ways.

My love to you.
Donald

Alice is still at No. 7 yet, when not at New Quay.
Remember the war visits? Sleep on kitchen floor etc.?

He refers here to his "second attack," but it was at least his third (two were documented in 1949) or possibly even his fourth, if Milner's 1947 recollection is accurate.

After their separation, Alice moved to Wales to be with her sister Pauline. "She spoke the language of course," recalled Hannah. "They are a great singing nation and she lived in her youth on the borders. With Pauline [and her other sister] they [had] formed a trio. She played the violin, they gave classical concerts to schools mostly. . . . Pauline never married and after the war farmed with a friend in Wales, breeding an almost extinct breed of Dexter Cattle—miniature. I wrote to her on Alice's death, but she never replied—did she connect me too much with Donald? She [Alice] was left very comfortably off, but of course [their separation and divorce] was something she had thought never could happen, a great shock. Donald continued to support her. Some of his friends thought she was still alive at the time of his death in 1971. Rosa Taylor believed Alice loved him to the end: "She attended his funeral and cried and cried." Yet, according to research conducted by Brett Kahr,[28] Alice died in 1969 and could not have been at the funeral.

Marion Milner, who told me that Clare burned all of Alice's letters to Donald (seven have survived), compares Alice and Clare this way: "elderflour fritters versus beefsteak." She thought that Alice had given Donald a "reception for life" but no holding, which he needed, especially after his heart attack. He needed a chance at more reality, to be held by reality, and when he got it, it enabled him to soar. Virginal Alice was afraid of fruition, and she held him back when that was what he yearned for. As we shall see, Clare regarded herself as tough and gave the impression of being so, much in contrast to the fey, disabled Alice. And yet for twenty-seven years Donald-and-Alice had constituted "a firm." In the first flush of his love affair with Clare, six years earlier, he was determined to preserve his home. But six more years of Alice, at least two heart attacks, the liberating death of his elderly father, and the continuing intimate tie with Clare led him to a definitive moment of separation and then divorce. Having worked to harness his hate,[29] he did finally allow himself to behave in a "horrid" way, to not be the "ideal dear boy" people thought he was. In dissolving the Winnicott "firm," he was probably demonstrating a capacity to separate himself from the mother figure that Alice must, to some extent, have been. Since nobody was ever going to possess all of him,[30] nor possess all of Clare either, he had arrived at a moment that combined love and personal differentiation, and a condition of mind in which he could, to quote Marion Milner, finally "soar."

— 8 —

Analysis and Marriage

In 1923, soon after his marriage to Alice, Donald consulted Ernest Jones in the search for an analyst with whom he could have the experience of being a patient. That he describes himself as "an inhibited young man"[1] shows that he knew this work was required for more than academic reasons. He needed help.[2] We know now that his marriage was marked by an absence of sexual relations. To what extent this was the result of Donald's impotence or Alice's reluctance or a combination of the two we can only guess. According to Rosa Taylor, the two problems always went together.

After having been unable to choose from a list of possible analysts provided to him by Jones, Donald was given the name of James Strachey. Their work together, which included Strachey's supervision of Donald's work with his own patients, continued to about 1933. Paul Roazen, historian of psychoanalysis, writes "I could not . . . understand how Winnicott had lain on Strachey's couch for so many years; Winnicott was so full of his own ideas as probably to have been relatively impervious to an uncomprehending analyst."[3]

James Strachey was a member of a famous Bloomsbury family. He and his wife, Alix, had been analysands of Freud. Alix was, at the time of James's analysis of Winnicott, in Berlin receiving analytic help from Karl

Abraham, as was Melanie Klein, with whom she became friendly. A book of correspondence between the Stracheys[4] documents the period, and enlarges our understanding of the intimate connections between the Stracheys and the psychoanalytic life in Berlin from which Melanie Klein extracted herself for transplantation to England. This volume includes a number of comments about Winnicott's analysis, largely in the spirit of the correspondence, which is one of relentless gossip-mongering. We see no sense of the respect and confidentiality that are supposed to be the inviolate condition between analyst and analysand. But, then, these highly literate people, charged with translating important works into English and suddenly authorized by Freud to consider themselves psychoanalysts, had begun their own analyses only four years prior (James on October 4, 1920), and were no doubt preoccupied with being "in the know," that is, in touch with insights that would escape the notice of ordinary people. Their analyses with Freud qualified them, in their eyes, for access to special knowledge, possibly adding to a class-based attitude of superiority. And they had each other for colleagues, so there was a sense of privacy between them. And within that sense of privacy, we glimpse the underside of respect, the intensely ambivalent attitude that an analyst may have toward a patient, much, as Winnicott eventually taught, as a mother may have toward a baby. Winnicott himself would eventually blow open the subject in 1947 with "Hate in the Counter-Transference."

Strachey was nine years older than Winnicott. His father was knighted shortly after the start of their work together, as Winnicott's father would be as well. Both had been directed into psychoanalysis by Ernest Jones, who, seeking the respectability of medicine for English psychoanalysts, had advised Strachey to go to medical school, an endeavor that lasted all of three weeks. As a doctor, Winnicott had an important credential that Strachey lacked.[5] It is interesting to consider two excerpts from the Stracheys' correspondence: In one, Alix, pondering how James's practice could be closed up with patients still in the midst of analysis, writes, "Perhaps fresh data will turn up—Mrs. D[isher] will solve all, or Mr. W[innicott] will die or f—ck his wife all of a sudden . . ." In the other, written ten years earlier (January 23, 1914), James wrote to his brother Lytton, "Fact is that even now that I've grown cosmopolitan & a beard, I could *never* succeed in convincing anyone that I'd fucked a woman."[6] Here we read a hint of a condition in Strachey's life that resonated with Winnicott's impotence. He is known to have had homosexual affairs as a young man.[7] Perhaps more relevant is the fact that Strachey considered himself incompletely analyzed[8] and wondered, by 1925, whether he was simply "sinking into melancholia" or possibly even "dementia praecox," and sought further work with James Glover.[9]

Among the subjects found worthy of comment by Strachey is his patient's slowness in paying bills: Donald ignored them. On one occasion, preoccupied with forgetting names, he forgot to sign his check. Strachey even suspected him of lying. He thinks Donald altered his writing when trying to sell stock to pay his fees. In this way, he could have delayed payment of his fees still further.[10] There is no speculation on the transference meaning of this behavior, that is, on why he wouldn't seem to want to pay his bills.

In his letters from school and college Donald had been so detailed in his account of spending, one might think he would be prudent and precise. But this was not the case and would be an issue in his second analysis as well, when Joan Riviere felt she had been misled as to his financial state. In fact, he was careless with regard to money and invested at abysmally low interest rates.[11]

We learn from Strachey that Donald loved to urinate into the sea, and that he thought he might have urinated on his mother just after birth. Strachey adds that perhaps he did so while still in utero. This was probably intended as an ironic, competitive outdoing of Donald's willingness to speculate. But here is an inkling of the reach of Donald's imagination, already evident in his description of psychoanalysis in the letter to his sister Violet, which he would one day use to elaborate the idea of the intrauterine influence in human development. He believed in a time of innocence before the infant encounters the mother, a time of pre- pre-ruth. Nothing was going to be out of bounds for consideration.

Furthermore, and interestingly, we learn about Donald's notion of the mother as castrator. There are two dreams recounted here, in one of which his mother is disguised in a bear (bare) skin. Her penis pops out and castrates him. This contrasts with an "affectionate passage" with his father in another dream, in which no such event occurs. Strachey thought that Donald was in retreat from his "murderous anti-dad impulses," and that his normal Oedipal conflict was more deeply repressed than in the inverted version.[12]

One wonders in what way Strachey's homosexual past might have affected his work, either in his comfort with homosexual themes, which could have made it easier for his patients to express themselves in this area, or in leading him to identify such material.[13] Marion Milner told me that Winnicott once reminisced to her about a time "when I was young and beautiful," but she believed that there was no sign that he was a homosexual. On another occasion she said, "The homosexual idea never came to Donald." Yet he was a maternal person with a womanly voice. The separating of the male and female elements from questions of object choice would later become a focus of his thinking in the 1960s.

In his 1969 obituary of Strachey, Winnicott wrote, "I knew nothing of Strachey as a man, of course, till 1933, when I stopped my ten-year analysis with him. Then I slowly discovered that he was just about as shy as I was. I longed to get to know him but always I had the awful feeling that he was nothing if not erudite and sophisticated, which I was not. He was at home in an area which I had discovered too late, since I had not met the cultural life (except in the form of an evangelical religion) until I was at public school. Strachey had grown up in it, in this third area of living, the area of cultural experience. Strachey's familiarity with literature, music and ballet filled me with envy and made me feel somewhat boorish when in his company."[14]

It is relevant, I think, that he includes the following notation: "What I noticed about this shy man was his unaggressive nature, yet there is no need to think he had no aggressive feelings, and in any case he could be stubborn." It is relevant because of Winnicott's preoccupation with his own aggression or lack thereof (being "too nice" at age nine), and his cultivation of what he enjoyed calling his hate. In addition, his theory of infant development placed greatest emphasis on the origin and vicissitudes of aggression, resulting ultimately in its indispensable role in the experience of reality.

Looking back from 1952 in a letter to Melanie Klein, Donald comments about both of his analyses, from which he got so much, but not what he wished: a reception for his gestures. This seemed to be fundamental to his needs, a lifelong pursuit. He speaks in his 1967 talk to the 1952 Club of the unremembered dreams of his analyses, leading to papers that would, he must have always hoped, be received as gifts worthy of serious attention, if not admiration. To what extent this has sexual meaning is not clear. On the mother level, it would seem pre-sexual—the wish, in Kleinian terms, for reparation—as if he could take comfort in being regarded as a genuine contributor. This is certainly the plaint in his letter to Joan Riviere[15] in which he cites her (and Klein's) belief that he has nothing to contribute to the psychology of early development. One might also ask if his impotence was related to the sense that what he had to offer was going to be insufficient, and if so, whether it was based on his anti-father impulses, that is, whether his father was the depreciated model for his own inadequacy.

The phrase "if Winnie cracks up" appears in a letter from Strachey, and suggests at least a degree of concern for Winnicott's stability. Yet perhaps this is a common enough concern with many patients. One wonders, given (see chapter 1) Donald's likening himself to psychotics, what there is to it, until we remember that he also said, "We are poor indeed if we are only sane."[16]

Winnicott's analytic training as a candidate did not begin until 1927. In his later writings he discusses two of his early cases from this period. The first, from "The Antisocial Tendency," (1956), reads:

> For my first child analysis I chose a delinquent. This boy attended regularly for a year and the treatment stopped because of the disturbance that the boy caused in the clinic. I could say that the analysis was going well, and its cessation caused distress both to the boy and to myself in spite of the fact that on several occasions I got badly bitten on the buttocks.[17] The boy got out on the roof and also he spilt so much water that the basement became flooded. He broke into my locked car and drove it away in bottom gear on the self-starter. The clinic ordered termination of the treatment for the sake of the other patients. He went to an approved school.
>
> I may say that he is now 35, and he has been able to earn his living in a job that caters for his restlessness. He is married, with several children. Nevertheless I am afraid to follow up his case for fear that I should become involved again with a psychopath, and I prefer that society should continue to take the burden of his management.
>
> It can easily be seen that the treatment of this boy should have been not psycho-analysis but placement. Psycho-analysis only made sense if added after placement. Since this time I have watched analysts of all kinds fail in the psycho-analysis of antisocial children.

Winnicott subsequently wrote, in "A Personal View of the Kleinian Contribution" (1962):

In my second child training case in the early thirties I was lucky in that I had a girl of three who had started her illness (anorexia) on her first birthday. The material of the analysis was Oedipal, with reactions to the primal scene, and the child was in no way psychotic. Moreover she got well and she is now married happily and rearing her own family. But her Oedipus conflict started on her first birthday when she for the first time sat at table with her two parents. The child, who had shown no symptoms previously, reached out for food, solemnly looked at her two parents, and withdrew her hand. Thus started a severe anorexia, at exactly one year. In the material of the analysis the primal scene appeared as a meal, and sometimes the parents ate the child, whereas at other times the child upset the table (bed) and destroyed the whole set-up. Her analysis was finished in time for her to have a genital Oedipus complex before the onset of the latency period.

Elsewhere he added:[18] "Gradually identification with each of the two parents gave relief. Incidentally, as a mother she was sadistic towards her incontinent dolls, and also she was sadistic as a teacher, though her parents were very tolerant, and she herself had had no problems in regard to dryness and cleanliness." He concludes: "This child, because she was normal, nearly employed the real parents in place of more primitive superego elements at the age of 12 months, and with my analytic help and support she quickly, at 2 1/2 to 3 1/2, became able to defy and overthrow, and to identify, and even to obey. She now has two healthy children, born in holy wedlock!"

Donald's fellow candidates during his training were Susan Isaacs[19] and Nina Searl. He graduated in 1935, having terminated his analysis two years earlier. His membership paper, "The Manic Defence" (1935), showed the influence of Melanie Klein, whom he must have learned from during his training. The following year, he became a qualified child analyst, and around the same time started a new analysis, with Joan Riviere. One wonders whether he thought of his own first analysis as not having succeeded and therefore felt that he required someone who knew a great deal about deep resistances. Although, in a letter to Ernest Jones (July 17, 1952), Winnicott says that Strachey's technique with him was "cold-blooded," Strachey comes across as loose, and at one point Winnicott said (not in reference to his analysis) that Strachey was lazy.[20]

Klein's paper "A Contribution to the Genesis of Manic-Depressive States," given at the International Psychoanalytic Association's Lucerne Congress in 1934, had caused some of those previously well disposed toward her to withdraw their backing, among them Edward Glover.[21] This must have been a dividing line in the build-up of allegiances. Winnicott came down on the side of Klein and her adherent, Joan Riviere, for the time being.

— 9 —

Joan Riviere

In the final years of the 1930s Winnicott was conducting his private practice, learning child analysis under the supervision of Melanie Klein, and living in Hampstead with Alice. The dark foreshadowing of war was becoming ever more evident, but life went on. The Winnicotts had a sailing vacation in 1937, off the east coast of the United States in the company of Malcom Forbes. Winnicott was also analyzing Melanie Klein's son Eric.

At the end of 1936, when he resumed analysis, this time with Joan Riviere, his training was complete, and he had been admitted into membership in the British Psycho-Analytical Society. Melanie Klein, from whom he had learned so much as his supervisor, was said to have been his first choice as an analyst.[1] But because she wanted him to analyze her son, she did not accept him for analysis.[2] It is possible that, as his supervisor, she believed that he needed more analysis in order to understand her own thinking better. A suggestion from Klein that Donald consult Riviere was broached by Riviere in her first letter to him. Riviere was a close supporter of Klein and her theories from the early 1920s, and she became Klein's most cogent explicator, succeeded in later years by Hanna Segal. She was also one of the founding members of the British Psycho-Analytical Society.

Riviere was born in Sussex in 1883, a year after the death of her parents' first baby, a boy. She was therefore what has come to be known as a "substitute child." She had a younger sister and brother, and was quite close to her father, Hugh John Verrall, who was a solicitor with an interest in matters of public import. Her mother was more domestically inclined and had worked as a governess for six years prior to her marriage. She was a severe, punitive woman and there was some distance between her and Joan, who looked down on her "because she came from a lower social and intellectual class than her father."[3]

At seventeen Joan was sent to Germany for a year to learn the language, which would equip her to become Freud's translator two decades later. She did not go to university, although her uncle, the Cambridge classicist A. W. Verrall, introduced her to the academic world. James Strachey recalled meeting her at her uncle's house and described her as a "tall, strikingly handsome, distinguished-looking" woman. At twenty-three, she married the barrister Evelyn Riviere. They had one child.

Joan had a breakdown after the death of her father in 1909 and was in a sanatorium for a while, either at that point or later on. There were other periods of disability and episodes of tuberculosis in the years that followed and during her analysis with Ernest Jones which occurred from 1916 to 1921. Jones treated her in a way that encouraged a positive, probably an erotic transference, with the inevitable disappointment that he did not live up to what she took to be expressions of affection or love for her. He lent her his house more than once and she cared for his dog and communicated with him more as a friend than an analysand. They may have had an affair.[4] Stymied by the intensity of her transference, he eventually referred her to Freud, who was impressed with her, but, instead of treating her as a patient first and foremost, thought of asking her to be his translator. This was the period—in the early 1920s—when he assigned James Strachey the same task. To Jones, Freud wrote in a cynical way that Riviere was "a real power and can be put to work by a slight expenditure of kindness and 'recognition.'"[5] Later on, Herbert Rosenfeld, one of her supervisees, reported that she told him she resented being "put to use" as a translator by Freud before her difficulties had been addressed and resolved.

Riviere was the first lay analyst in England. "She belonged in the English tradition of the gifted amateur who pursued her interests with a seeming casualness that concealed real passion."[6] Athol Hughes, who has published a sketch of Riviere's life along with her collected papers, a volume on which this chapter heavily depends,[7] reported that "her letters to Jones of 1918 and 1919 showed . . . a deep sense of despair and a search for someone on whom she could rely absolutely." This theme, this search, would have resonated with Winnicott's later notion of "regression to dependency" for certain patients, quite possibly people like Riviere. Yet in a contradictory way, Riviere seems to have sustained a psychoanalytic attitude that would probably not confront such a regression in any way but through interpretation. This is likely the substance of Winnicott's later complaint that neither Strachey nor Riviere was able or willing to see value in his "gestures."

Riviere's most notable paper, on the negative therapeutic reaction, deals with narcissistic patients who are inaccessible because they expect analysis to push them toward despair or possibly suicide by compromising their preoccupation with restoring to life their destroyed internal objects.[8] The first priority for such patients is total dedication to the destroyed objects out of guilt and out of love, ultimately, for them. These patients function with the manic defense in the forefront, a means by which they give the illusion of omnipotent control of their objects. They also avoid the intrusion of any notion that may open them up to depressive anxiety, with its attendant harrowing feelings about the condition of the loved and hated internal objects. She writes: "To my mind it is the [patient's] love for his internal objects which lies behind and produces the unbearable guilt and pain, the need to sacrifice his life for theirs, and so the prospect of death, that makes this resistance so stubborn. And we can counter this resistance only by unearthing this love and so the guilt with it. To these patients if not to all, the analyst represents an internal object. So it is the positive transference in the patient that we must bring to realization; and this is what they resist beyond all, although they know how well to parade a substitute 'friendliness,' which they declare to be normal and appropriate and claim ought to satisfy us as 'not neurotic.'"[9]

There is no case material in this paper, which is written in an authoritative and disciplined way. Even the discussion of the usefulness of positive transference comes through without any recommendations about how to achieve it. It is easy to think that here she is speaking of herself and her work with Freud, whose own writing on those wrecked by success is the principal literature on the subject.[10] Freud discussed people whose lives come to ruin in the aftermath of success. Patients who deteriorate in response to insights that are ordinarily helpful to others are in a similar category. Riviere's paper corrects his misapprehensions as to the cause and treatment of such patients.

More recently, Anton Kris has discussed Freud's account of the treatment of a narcissistic patient, who is easily identified as Joan Riviere. Kris comments on the necessity for interventions by the analyst that foster love in the patient. How that is to be achieved is not made clear. We are in an area that might be called controversial or even dangerous, given the traditional requirement that the analyst present himself as a scientist, one who is objective, and a doctor, kindly perhaps, but in some sense removed, not, above all, one who cures through love. Kris writes:

> The idea that the outcome may depend on the extent to which the personality of the analyst allows the patient to put him in the place of the ego ideal—that is, whether the analyst's more tolerant judgment can replace the patient's punitive self-criticism—may very well refer to the difference between Freud's relative success and Jones's impasse with Riviere. How far Freud went along the path of temptation, the reader must be left to judge. Freud would surely have insisted that he only went as far as was necessary to permit analysis to work, rather than to produce a cure by love alone. I believe love is the force of greater strength needed to oppose punitive, unconscious self-criticism, as did Freud. In his discussion of the treatment of "the exceptions," he had written that, "the doctor, in his educative work, makes use of one of the components of love. . . . Side by side with the exigencies of life, love is the great educator."[11] The task, from the point of view of technique, is to foster the analytic process in such a way that love is permitted to develop.[12]

Kris's comment that "love is the force of greater strength" probably refers to the patient's love, but there is an element of ambiguity that allows for speculation that he is also speaking of love in the analyst. This is consistent with Riviere's awareness of the necessity for the positive to be genuinely appreciated and recognized by the patient as part of the transference, which is an interesting point of view rather in opposition to her emphasis always on the internal as opposed to the external. Kris is saying that the behavior of the analyst, above and beyond the informational value of his interpretations, is a crucial factor in the treatment of patients with narcissistic personality disorders, taking off, I think, from his own thinking as well as from Riviere's passing remarks. Athol Hughes reports that John Bowlby, one of Riviere's analysands, said that she "held strong views that psychoanalysis was in no way concerned with external events," and Winnicott reported that when he said he was going to prepare a classification of the environment, she would not accept it, and this delayed his development for some years.[13]

Riviere's early life was probably marked by the effects of having a cold mother.[14] The fact of her emotional breakdowns tends to support that possibility. What we see in her, in a later letter to Winnicott about one of his candidates, is a demonstration of coldness, or possibly coldheartedness, which suggests another way of coping with early suffering: a hard shell. I have the impression that without such a shell, which might be called a Kleinian shell, she would have faced inner collapse, based on the intensity of her lifelong need for love.

Riviere's paper on the negative therapeutic reaction was read to the British Psycho-Analytic Society in 1935 and Donald Winnicott's membership paper, "The Manic Defence," was read that same year. Since Klein's paper on manic-depressive states had been given at the Lucerne Congress in 1934,[15] there was a concatenation of interests that probably contributed to his decision to consult her in 1936.

It is of great interest that Riviere's disciplined, Kleinian emphasis on the internal at the expense of the external should have yielded an idea that may have had to do with the behavior of the analyst apart from making interpretations. At the very end of her paper she writes: "A false and treacherous transference in our patients is such a blow to our narcissism, and so poisons and paralyzes our instrument for good (our understanding of the patient's unconscious mind), that it tends to rouse strong depressive anxieties in ourselves. So the patient's falseness often enough meets with denial by us and remains unseen and unanalysed by us too." Here the student of Winnicott begins to recognize the roots of the idea that analysis can seem to progress but never get anywhere because of a collaboration that is accepted between the analyst and the patient's False Self.

Letters from Joan Riviere to Winnicott[16] give something of the flavor of their interaction during the period of his analysis, together with a few relevant facts. The first letter is dated December 30, 1936:

Dear Dr. Winnicott

I know that you are not very satisfied with the analysis you have so far had with me. I think this may not only arise from the usual phantasy & transference sources, but may be partly due also to the actual circumstances in this special instance.

Your analysis with me is in a different category from the usual private patient one undertakes, & I think that fact affects us both in a way we have not sufficiently taken into account. When there is a preliminary interview, as with an ordinary case, the patient gives the analyst at any rate one view of himself & his reasons for wanting analysis; and this gives the analyst on his side an opportunity to put certain points of view before the patient. I think the fact that circumstances enabled you & me to dispense with this preliminary mutual explanation has actually had an unfortunate influence both on your position & on mine. Apart from your telephone conversation about dates & fee, we came to no mutual agreement about what we were going to undertake, & I fancy we may really be working at cross-purposes.

In any case, I feel very uncertain whether or how much you are wanting this analysis, or what you expect of it—in other words, what your motives for undertaking it were. I am not even quite clear whether the whole stimulus to it came from Mrs. Klein. If so, that is another unfavourable factor.

As far as my own position in the matter, I feel that that also has been left too vague. I think it would have been better for me to have explained to you in the traditional way what in my opinion analysis can do and what it cannot, & also what the necessary conditions for it are. In my belief it rests upon a co-operation between patient & analyst which is maintained by various motives in each of them. Among the analyst's motives, his need to make a livelihood plays a part. I should probably have told you that my regular fee is 2 guineas; as you know, this is less by a third or half than other front rank analysts (doctors) in London ask, although in the opinion of good judges I am regarded as second to no one here in ability.

What I want to say now is that I am doubtful whether we should continue on the present basis. I feel uncertain whether you realize the difficulties of the position; therefore it seems to me much fairer both to myself & to you to put an end to the present tacit assumption on which we have been proceeding, & to let us have a frank & open understanding about what we both feel able to do.

We can talk more about it when I see you again. From my own side I would only say further here that, as regards the fee, I can & will continue your analysis at one guinea if necessary but that from what I now know of your circumstances it does not, without further explanation, seem to be either necessary or desirable to do so. So I could suggest that that point should be reconsidered along with the general question of the analysis as a whole.

I don't want you to be at all upset by my writing this. I want to do everything I can for you and not to make anything more difficult for you, even if this should appear to do so in some ways. So far I don't think we have gained by ignoring real difficulties. But whatever you feel, please don't feel that I am not wishing to help you as much as I possibly can.

Yours very sincerely,

Joan Riviere

A number of complicating elements are discussed in this apparently sincere effort to improve the conditions of Donald's analysis. That she does not want him "to be at all upset by my writing this" might well indicate that she is under the sway of a countertransference attitude, which we see in many of Donald's friends and associates, in which he is regarded as more fragile than he realizes and therefore requiring the protection of others. She is here attempting to clarify and strengthen the conditions for his analysis, with which he has tampered through misrepresenting his financial situation, and at the same time she shows concern about his reaction to her challenge. With his misleading account of his finances, and the consequent low fee, we have a third example of what might be called his symptom around fees. He forgot to pay Ernest Jones's consultation fee when he first sought an analyst, and he made a problem out of paying James Strachey. There was an accompanying generosity as to time off and vacations and special arrangements, but, as with his father, the stinginess was there. It seems astonishing that he would actually, consciously bargain for a low fee when he could have afforded to pay in full, so Strachey's suspicion that he simply lied about financial matters may have been accurate.

A second letter is dated "Jan. 4. 1936" (actually 1937):

Dear Dr. Winnicott

Thank you for your letter & cheque. I am very sorry if my letter perturbed you. But I think it was best for both of us to try to find a foothold of everyday fact & reality on which your analysis can be securely based, as every analysis must be. In your case, being a full analyst yourself, my task is much more difficult than usual, & my liabilities much greater. If it proves that you value your analysis with me (and not merely value "me") it will be easier for me. As I said before, the supposition that I don't want to continue would be absolutely imaginary.

It is because it has become clear that you undervalue my work that I think it right to ask if you can pay my full fee. In any case, there is no question of my taking more than my usual fee, nor of your paying any more for the past months; so I return your 16 guineas. I want to start fresh now.

The question of fees is indeed not all, but the other things will arise in their own time.

I am well now, though influenza has had its full way in the household these 10 days. But I shall be free again & well as usual by the 11th.

With all my good wishes for 1937.

There are three themes that characterize the next several letters: (1) Riviere's recurrent, severe respiratory illnesses, which laid her low and interfered with the analysis; (2) the disruptive effects of World War II; and (3) Riviere and Winnicott's attempt to maintain some degree of continuity of analysis. It is easy to imagine that Riviere's illnesses would have inhibited Winnicott from engaging fully in analysis. He would have been dealing with a physically fragile woman, possibly reminiscent of his depressed mother. Provision would have to be made for her illnesses, and besides, and in a contradictory way, she presented herself as a severe taskmaster (in her writings, as a follower of Klein, and as described by others). These letters do not demonstrate the severe side of her, however, but show only the ill person trying to do her best. The first is written from an address in Wales, dated "Sep. 8. 1937":

I hope you have had a very good time in America & enjoyed it all. I shall be glad to know how it went off. I was very glad to have your letter before you left & interested in your dream. . . .

I have enjoyed this most beautiful country immensely. I knew parts of walks both north & south of here, but not these estuaries, & they are magical & most romantic. [She discloses her "romantic" reaction to her analysand. Does she have a romantic inclination toward Winnicott? Is there an echo here of her erotic transference to Jones?]

Hoping to hear that all is well with you.

Yours very sincerely

Joan Riviere

On January 11, 1939, she wrote to say that she was sorry Winnicott had been "attacked by the wretched germ." She was still sick in bed herself, after four weeks. She expresses concern: "I hope you are letting yourself be well looked after, & won't be too omnipotent about your recovery—& I do so hope you aren't being uncomfortable or in any pain."

From Sussex on January 25, 1939, she writes more about their schedule as affected by her illness: "I enjoyed getting down here immensely—in spite of 4 most inhospitable days since—nothing but lashing rain & gales, though yesterday was a marvellous interlude. Hot sun & cloudless sky in which I basked." Another letter on February 2 tells about her recovery and the weather.

There were no copies of correspondence in Winnicott's files for the early part of 1939. Probably analytic work proceeded as scheduled. But everything changed on September 1, 1939, when World War II began in Europe. Riviere wrote the following day:

Sandhills

Christchurch

Hants.

Dear Dr. Winnicott

I have just heard you rang up at home. I had been wondering whether I should hear from you & where you were—& was going to write to you this weekend. I am very sorry I am not there to see you. I have no patients who will be in London now except possibly you, & no doubt you don't know yet where you will be working.

We shall stay here with these friends (where we came for August) till we know where my husband is likely to be sent, that is if he can do any legal work, either for the gov't or for younger men.

I have been wondering what you were feeling & how you were. I am glad that the people of this country are ready to stand up & resist madness & that we can hope to save what this lovely England stands for & that the trainloads of children [i.e., the children being evacuated to the countryside] may yet one day carry it on.

I shall be here till I let you know my new address. Please write & tell me what is happening to you.

> With all my best wishes for you—Your friend
> Joan Riviere

"Your friend" announces the sudden change that war brought, as in other bits of correspondence, representing, as it doubtless did, a general condition in which the usual formalities were set aside and feelings of affection were allowed expression.

From the same address on September 13 Riviere wrote:

I was glad to hear again from you. I can imagine how trying it is in London now with nothing much to do. I have heard the same from other doctors. I am quite ready to do anything I can to help by letter—but it's a question what can be done that way—still I am sure something can.

I am glad to hear your news. It is very bad about Freud.[17] I wish I were certain he would be spared all suffering—I know it is difficult for doctors—perhaps they are more humane than they were.

I don't expect you are serious about the Navy or the Ministry of Information. The latter I would veto outright—the Navy only if you must, but it would be an apostasy from what you are specially equipped & gifted for: the psychological healing. You will be needed if you can wait a bit.—I am very sorry about Alice. I wonder what Scott is doing. I haven't heard.[18]

Things are in the greatest confusion with me & it seems impossible to make plans & decisions. As soon as one gets something arranged, it breaks down. Nobody keeps their word or sticks to what they arranged. We may know more in a week or two about what the Law Courts & the Bar will do; I am trying to find somewhere where we can afford to live out of London between London & Oxford, as we shall be dependent on my husband's earnings & (as you say) have all our rents, etc. It seems the Courts will work partly in London & partly Oxford.

Do you know where your hospital will be? I don't suppose distance & time & petrol ration would enable you to get to me for analysis once war gets really going.

I am writing letters about 8 hours a day & have been for about 3 weeks or more. It is maddening to be in this exquisite place & unable to have the pleasure of it. Still it is no good coming back to London till one can do something definite. If you write & I don't reply at once, you will know it is simply because I am making about seeing rooms in the country etc. & trying to make decisions & have not time for any letters but business ones. But I am very glad to get your letters & hear all you are doing & thinking.

With all good wishes

One letter indicates that they are to resume their work in January 1940. Another from the Isle of Wight on May 17 reads, "I shall see you on Monday as usual." And from Chichester on August 21, 1940:

I am glad to hear you are well & going to have a week away. I will expect to see you again on Monday, Sep. 2 as usual.

It has been lovely weather here and a good change really, though the war news is always so absorbing & nothing outweighs it. Last week there were plenty of night raids & sirens 5 times a day—dog-fights overhead—planes down all round about & there are still time bombs about & people have had to leave their houses. However of course as usual one sees very little of anything directly. Actually I was on top of the Downs during most of activity & saw & heard very little—just too far north.

I am glad you have got a new & interesting patient. It is a great pity about Scott having to go and I am afraid it will be difficult for you & very unfortunate. [interrupting Alice's analysis]

One good thing is that the fear of internment for analysts [of non-British origin] can now probably be considered over.

On September 2, 1941, Riviere wrote: "I am expecting to be back on Monday & hope to see you at 3.15 if that will suit you." Except for the next letter, which has no year, this is the last extant reference to analytic appointments.

March 28, Little Chalfont

Thank you for your letters. I am so glad you are reading & enjoying it. Yes, I agree about thumb-sucking. I don't share your demand for everything to be spontaneous in the sense of inspired, perhaps because I have not so much horror of what has been "carefully" handled and worked over. In other words, perhaps, I do believe human beings can sometimes make something good & not that it always has to be God doing it! But I think human beings have to be careful, or they make such mistakes. . . .

I am expecting you on Monday next.

The early letters stop at this point, but Riviere continued to be a presence in Donald's life. Their later relationship will be considered in due course.

Riviere's encouragement of his reading with pleasure may refer to an inhibition that has disappeared, for the time being at least. (Winnicott refers to a problem reading Freud in a letter to James Strachey in 1951.)[19] Her mention of his supposed insistence that everything must come from inspiration, which means it is God that is the ultimate source, is an extreme one. Nonetheless, his confidence in the power of internal sources, the value of the spontaneous gesture (which he would ultimately say is the True Self in action), is by this time very great. It is his belief that, under certain circumstances, people reach the point of risking the expression of what is deep within them, that much good comes of this, or at least that, in the context of a relationship (mother-child to start with), the person allows himself to be known in this way. This is an utterly different idea from the concept of expression as a result of the conscious handling and working over of a problem, though the two are not incompatible if one sets out to combine them. They must be a complementary series. Riviere's is a casual statement, however, and as such it sketches out two different attitudes with wide implications. In a theoretical context one could say that they mark a fundamental difference between the Kleinian and the Winnicottian views of human existence.

— 10 —

Clare Britton

During World War II, Donald Winnicott was engaged as a consultant in Oxfordshire, where difficult children were housed in staffed hostels as part of the evacuation scheme for their protection. Clare Britton, a social worker, was also a consultant there. Every Friday she met with Winnicott to discuss the issues that preoccupied the staff.

Clare was a graduate of the mental health course at the London School of Economics.[1] She is quoted by Joel Kanter, a social worker who has written extensively about her, as having said that she was told by her boss that "there's a difficult doctor. . . comes down once a week. He doesn't believe in social work because he likes to do it all himself. But its really in quite a mess and you must go and straighten the whole thing up."[2] As it turned out, Clare was more than willing to straighten things up with the "difficult doctor." Kanter quotes a friend and colleague of Clare's who said it "soon became clear that Friday had become a 'red-letter day.'"[3]

Clare Britton was born in 1906 in Scarborough, a town in the North of England.* The eldest of four children, she was the daughter of a Baptist minister who himself was the son of a charismatic Baptist minister. Clare's father, who increased the membership of whatever church he

* Most of the information on Clare's background was obtained in a 1981 interview I conducted with her.

preached in, was often concerned with social issues. The family moved several times during her childhood, eventually arriving at Southend-on-Sea, where Clare graduated from high school. She never associated herself with any church organization as an adult and, like Winnicott, was fiercely independent of ideology of any kind. She had two brothers, James (Jimmy) and Karl, and a sister, Elizabeth. Jimmy became a specialist in language use in children, Karl in philosophy. (One of Karl's teachers was Ludwig Wittgenstein.) Elizabeth taught art in a high school.

Clare trained as a social worker at the London School of Economics (LSE) in 1937, and worked after that in Wales with children and teenagers. In 1940, back at LSE, she completed the mental health course. During the war, she worked with evacuees in the area of Reading, then moved to the Midlands, and finally to Oxfordshire, where she met Donald Winnicott. A measure of his importance to her may be gleaned from a May 25, 1944, diary entry in which her brother Karl wrote that she had discussed with him a job offer to work with refugee children, but was concerned that moving would disrupt her relationship with Dr. Winnicott.

Seventy-four letters (there may be more) from Clare to Donald[4] document some of their experiences in Oxfordshire during 1943 and 1944. They were in charge of dealing with the arrangements for 110 evacuated children, separated from their families for their physical and often psychological safety. These were children who had not adjusted well to wartime conditions. There were five homes, or hostels,[5] which housed the children, who were deemed unsuitable for placement with families. Staff problems as well as behavioral problems of the children preoccupied them. It was a frustrating kind of work, out of which grew Donald's idea of the delinquent act as a sign of deprivation, the child's gesture to anyone who could decipher it that, having been adequately cared for originally, he or she was now without what he or she had a right to and needed.

Most of the letters discuss in some detail the work they were doing, almost always including personal remarks. Clare often complains about her job and her life. Sometimes, she says, she feels dead, or like an outsider who is kept from having direct contact with the children but is simply moving them about. Hovering in the background is her preoccupation with her future. Will she ever get married? Should she take another job? She becomes a commentator on Donald's ideas, offering her own criticisms and revisions. Eventually they combined forces to write an article for a periodical called *The New Era*.[6]

As their relationship grew into a love affair, it brought permanent changes into the lives of both—documented in the letters. Clare drops her salutation "Dr. Winnicott" in favor of none at all or, in one notable case, "My Dear." The fact that "Donald" never appears, even in the love letters written at the end of 1944, suggests some sense of her difficulty in transforming herself from co-worker and assistant to lover. In one letter she writes: "There is nothing to say to you—except that *I* shall never be fundamentally disappointed in you—because you've helped me to find myself—to be really feminine & know I could have a baby & that I want one & *don't* want a job! All *very* painful—but *very* important—in fact the most important thing that's happened to me. I think you would have made a *lovely* missionary—& I might have been one too—& we might have met in a jungle somewhere & it would have been *wonderful!*"

Donald traveled to Oxford on Fridays, while maintaining his practice and clinic at Paddington Green (as long as it was functioning) the rest of the week.[7] Dr. Barbara Woodhead, whom Winnicott had analyzed, worked with him as a consultant and Norma Williams, who had no formal training, was a trusted assistant to whom he referred patients privately.[8] For various reasons related to work considerations, he sometimes slept in the environs of Oxford on a Thursday or a Friday night.

Clare's lengthy discussions of Donald's ideas illustrate the changing nature of their relationship, in which Clare, though not an analyst herself, nor even a therapist (though she wanted to be one), puts forth what she *does* know, or *does* feel, or *has* thought about. This is Clare showing her assertive capacities and her intelligence, and Donald, in need of a strong woman, received her as such. In their correspondence Donald's voice is not heard directly, thought he is sensed as a listener through Clare's changing locution and tone over time. From that period there also exist two incisive reports of his on their work, and here we encounter a powerful, confident voice. He is full of conviction and verbal grace, while Clare is seen, in the light of these documents, as much the more diffident character, if efficient and insightful. These typewritten statements do not support her contention, in a few instances, that he is uncertain, indecisive, and to her therefore exasperating. This side of him is not visible in his written work or in letters to others, certainly not in his responses to various colleagues who gave papers. Yet in a 1946 letter to Clare he says "When I am cut off from you I feel paralysed for all action and originality,"[9] which suggests the degree to which his dependency had by then become a part of their relationship—and the fear of which may have led earlier to his marriage to Alice, a person on whom he could not depend. He must have anticipated that if he allowed himself to become ever more intimate with Clare, this aspect of him would emerge.

In her letters Clare is clearly full of admiration for Donald's capabilities. She asks him for reading material (in one instance specifically on depression, for which he recommends Melanie Klein's *Love, Hate, and Reparation*).[10] She wanted desperately to develop personally. At one point she urges him to "be a man," meaning, with reference to a movie she had seen called *Lady in the Dark*,[11] that as a woman she would thereby be relieved of the necessity to play the man's role. While explicitly leaving him out of this discussion as a reference point, she was making a plea for Donald to be more masculine and decisive. She wished to be instructed on precisely what he wanted from her. Here she was addressing the deeper, wholly personal matter of Donald's capacity, or lack thereof, to make a romantic move in her direction. To her, indecisiveness probably meant faint-heartedness. She wanted him to take the developmental step that would make a passionate tie between them truly possible. But the urging itself took on a certain toughness. She felt that she had to be tough in order, eventually, to relinquish that role to him.

This aspect of their relationship is illustrated by a letter of February 17, 1943, in which she is critical of Winnicott for having "gone back on the Lashbrook idea," whatever that was, which was his own idea in the first place: "Now, I don't feel that by going back on what you originally said—that you have let me down—so to speak—in a personal way (I hope I could stand that!) but I *do* feel—& have felt a hundred times in this job—rather dismayed by your uncertainty. Simply from the job point of view—it is *hard for me to* cope *with*—however well I may understand it. Forgive me for saying this—I don't mean to be critical—simply to point out one of my difficulties to you. (Possibly I am trying to find in you the certainty I lack in myself & must find eventually in myself—in the meantime its dreadfully hard going!)"

That last, parenthetical sentence in which Clare shows her introspective courage would have been appealing to Donald. And her disavowal of the sense of being let down "in a personal way" is probably an instance of negation as Freud understood it. As subsequent events would prove, she was more personally involved than she either knew consciously or was willing to disclose to him.

Later in the letter she considers whether it was true, as he had said, that she was "growing on the job," and this leads her to the question of whether this was the right job for her:

> Do you realise that it is an inch by inch battle with [her co-workers] Helen as well as Gurney—& I am very much aware of the cost to Helen—as well as to myself. Inevitably this has been a struggle—as I was thrown in on top of them—when neither of them was really prepared to relinquish their positions. This, I believe, is really true whatever they may say. The Committee gave me a job *on paper*—but do you realise that I've had almost no backing from any quarter in putting it into effect. The trouble is that fighting does not come natural to me! Sometimes I think that I am *too* aware of other people's desires & needs—& can therefore never really hurt people—or perhaps quite simply, I haven't enough male hormones!—or perhaps you can think of another reason? You say, I should be given *time* to grow—but don't forget that I need *room* as well—& *not merely on paper*. Perhaps this isn't the kind of job I should *try* to grow into? I am very much wondering. Can you help me about this. . . .
>
> Do forgive this letter.

In pointing out that she needs "room" to grow, and "not merely on paper," she is demanding something more concrete than a title or even a job. She wants a place of her own, the secure place that is required for her development.

In another (undated) letter, written "in the office—simply frightfully bored," and "written for my own interest & possibly yours?" she takes up a political subject, the Liberal Party, essentially challenging Donald's views, which she regards as impractically idealistic. She herself is, by contrast, realistic and pragmatic, willing to recognize the self-centered element behind personal motivation, while he seems, as implied in the letter at least, not willing to do so: "You are asking them [the Liberal Party] to stop thinking so much—& 'feel' instead (or as well)—but *what* are they to feel about?—they now comprise a section of the community whose *vital interests* are not at stake. . . .[T]oday we find the Liberal Party to consist of a devitalised section of the community—therefore they are *on the whole* a small satisfied (economically) group & people. Therefore, politically, they are *dead*. (Sorry: but I *do* think so) Their day is over in the political field. They no longer represent anybody's vital interests—as they did in the last century."

She points out that "the non-vocal section of the community—labour—began to organise & make itself felt & they represent *real interests*—don't forget that." She wonders: "*Ideals*—ought to generate a feeling for political action? One would feel that this ought to be so—but it isn't. Oddly enough, ideals *follow* the economic system too—they are built up as a justification for what is being done."

The letter ends: "So—Although I love you for trying to have a revival of the Liberals—I don't feel very hopeful. Somehow if you went in for spiritual revival pure & simple it might be more successful. Spirits are languishing sadly to-day. So often I say to myself the words from Isaiah—'Wherefore do ye spend your money for that which is not bread—& your labour for that which satisfieth not?' Ah well, I'm all for the Liberals feeling—& acting—I hope they will—but I do feel you're asking the impossible!" She signs "Clare" with a flourish.

She is quite sure of herself here, not pleading or finding it necessary to be apologetic or diplomatic. She punctures his wish that the Liberals "feel" or respond to an ideal with commentary on man's economic self-interest and the rationalizations that follow from its pursuit. She seems grounded while, by contrast, he does not.

In the letter of April 2, 1943, apparently not given to him for some time after that, she tackles a complex subject closer to his expertise: relationships, society, "the good." She writes: "I'm terribly sorry—but I simply *must* say some things to you—in continuation of part of our discussion." This is reduced in vehemence by: "At least, I must write it—doesn't matter nearly so much that you *read* it." She goes on:

> About the existance [sic] of "good" etc. To make it clear to myself I must sum up a bit first:—
>
> 1. The ultimate "good" thing = the experience in which the inner good world unites with the good in the world of reality through some relationship—as you said for a baby this happens when the inner good mother unites with the real mother.
>
> 2. It is only possible to attain this experience, of the existance [sic] of the inner good world—because only in this way can the *belief* in the goodness be sustained through periods of doubt in the reality

situation—you said that for the baby it means that a relationship with the real mother is *only possible* because of the existance [sic] of the inside good mother.

3. So far so good (?)—Now the *importance* of these experiences is that they are the *only* proof there is that one *is good* oneself. In these moments one is entirely good & entirely *safe*.

4. *Difficulties* arise (a) If there is a lack of good relationship one's good world (& oneself) never *become* good: lack of reality. This is a dangerous situation.

(b): Only in certain moments is the inner good linked up with reality—so that mostly reality does not really satisfy. And you said that this is the great problem of living & perhaps something which must always be reckoned with (i.e. the hate engendered by frustration) [Now *I* think that this is where religion comes in—(religion—in broadest possible terms)]

5. *You* said—that in facing this problem one must be scientific & say that a good experience happened once & *may* happen again (I said that this sounded hopeless) but there is nothing to say that it will.

6. Now *I* want to say it differently (& *please* tell me if you think I am wrong.) If one has a good experience once—it *never ceases* to exist, it is dynamic & creative & enters so deeply into the *fabric* of the personality—that it is independent of *time* & place—& of individuals even—& simply cannot pass like any ordinary event. It is not *only* made up of external reality.

I think that these experiences form part of the background of one's *faith* in life—one's religion, in other words. In this way, they are *stored* up & preserved against the "evil days." And surely this faith *does* help in dealing with reality—(& is not an escape from it). For one thing, there is not the same anxiety about the existance (sic) of good—& of being good—and one is freer to hate—& more independent etc. etc. etc (heaps so say). But this faith comes *only* to those who utterly trust their *feelings* & *experiences* of good. And it is not a blind faith because it has *reality* behind it.

She is not intimidated by his expertise, standing, and scholarship. She has thought about the subject in detail and may well have progressed beyond the limits of his thinking on the subject. She continues:

Well, now just for fun, I want to try your money analogy. I think it will fit rather well! Money = one's experiences of love & goodness which one stored up as an insurance against bankruptcy. It seems to me, that I trust the bank with my money, ultimately I have *faith* in *society*. But you would want to be scientific & say that my money was there yesterday—but it may, or may not, be there to-day! But surely, to be scientific would be irrelevant?—my faith in society which is based on factual experience—is sufficient to make the whole thing *work*—& that is what matters—(Science couldn't make it *work*)

That money must be in circulation I agree—or it is of no use whatever. So must one's "goodness" be in circulation in order to enrich life— otherwise, it becomes a millstone (like so many people's religion) One of *the* problems of reality is how to spend one's goodness—isn't it? It takes so much *courage* & so much real faith *in* one's goodness.

This effort has been entirely for my own benefit & in the hope that you may read it—& tell me where I am wrong—or where you don't agree. [Again, her polite nature, as if to say, "No offense, not an attack on you."] Religion is *so* important to me – that I must get it sorted out a bit.

Good night—shall I tell you 2 lines from a poem by Seigfried [sic] Sassoon (can't remember any more of it): "From you, Beethoven, Bach, Motzart [sic],

the substance of my dreams took fire."
Isn't that *good*?

Did you know that Wordsworth for most of his life was preoccupied with the problem of his great good fortune in that his inner world of imagination linked so much with his real experiences? It was a constant marvel & miracle to him—& he was always seeking the clue to it. Really, that's all.

                                                                                Clare

She is joyful, the substance of her dreams having taken fire from Donald Winnicott. And then the Wordsworth reference, linking reality and the imagination, a quintessentially Winnicottian subject in the years ahead. Marion Milner told me that Clare deepened Donald's interest in the world of poetry, particularly that of Rainer Maria Rilke. And in this letter, with Clare's emphasis on the question of how to "spend one's goodness," she may be responding to Donald's conflicts, since, in the personal area, his spending of goodness is limited, and the unfolding of his bond to Clare begins to encompass a newly expanded capacity to spend his goodness. The joyful expression at the end of the letter suggests that she had found a way to address Winnicott's sexual fear of spending his own goodness. The whole letter is a kind of interpretation of his problem. She offered him this intense focus and degree of interest, and subsequent events demonstrate that he responded to it.

In the letter of May 11, 1943, she once again challenges his views, this time saying that she cannot agree that the delinquent is an optimist: "Then on the same point—the thief who steals penknife thinking it is a good object—Honestly, I may be quibbling—but I do feel that this is too gross a miscalculation for the child to make? It seems to me much more like revenge *because* the good object has not been found." But then, she says, "this must all be *very* childish to you. You see, I never *read* very much about all this—I only *think*. So that I am *very* irreverent."

She probably didn't realize that he did not read very much either on psychoanalytic subjects; he "only" thought, and he too was very irreverent, though his capacity for irreverence had not yet become publicly visible at this early date in his career. Perhaps its emergence was related to Clare's entry into his life.

In the letter of September 21, 1943, Clare refers to the fact that Donald had invited her to work at Paddington Green. Since she loves Oxford, she says, she will need time to decide. She can hardly believe it. "But are you *really* serious? It's terribly nice of you if you are." In the letter of December 8, 1943, three months after his invitation, we find Clare under duress as a result of having been offered a good job as "Principal Officer for Training—Youth Leaders—sponsored by the National Association of Girls Clubs, which she calls parenthetically "a rather pucka job."[12]

There was a threat now to the continuity of their relationship, which had grown ever closer, yet at this time there is still no evidence that it had been consummated. Her suggesting that she could leave him must be seen as an attempt to get him to recognize what she meant in his life and to express in explicit terms that he wanted her to make a choice that would keep her close to him. She often complained about his indecisiveness, and here we see that she refuses to tolerate indecisiveness, on an indefinite basis, particularly since their future was obviously at stake. The issues are laid out in detail:

This is rather out of the blue as I haven't *applied* for the job. I merely said at some stage that I was *interested* in this sort of work. There is no doubt about it that this is a big responsible job—& I am not likely to get such a "good" offer again (much more money for one thing!) Plenty of scope—& a job that I feel *needs* doing badly. Also, between you & me, quite honestly I think I *could* make a useful contribution to the Youth Mvt.:—I could *give*—that's the point & in a small way, I'd be important—& somehow I *need* all that. I could do the job & *believe* in what I was doing—& that what I could give would be of value. And I long—as don't we all!—to be able to *give* (& take) to the limit of my capacity. That has never happened in the job I'm doing now—for various reasons—but it has happened in other jobs—so that I know I am *capable* of giving. So that the one thing that *does* seem clear, is that I must find a better job (i.e. better from *my* point of view) Of course I know that it is important to get married—as you once said to me— but that is so very difficult because of never meeting anybody. (I am *seriously* thinking of joining the Marriage Bureau in Bond St.—do you think it's a good idea?) Oh dear, I'm getting lost—that's because of doing my best writing—

Anxiety about expressing her quest for marriage may make her "get lost." But why because of "doing my best writing"? Expressing herself most deeply perhaps? Addressing directly what really matters to her, such as the question she poses in the very next sentence?

Well, what do I want of you in all this? Perhaps you know better than I—but I know that I'm not asking you to *solve* all my problems for me—I *promise* I will never ask that! But try as I will, I can't make a decision about this job without reference to you—all day I have tried— but then suddenly I felt that you wouldn't mind if I wrote—& it seemed right to do so. And you see, something that *does* affect my decision about the new job—is if you still think I can come to Paddington Green—if you still think it is a good idea—& want it. Is it *really* possible? Because I still think I would like to try it—(although I don't imagine that it will solve all my problems by any means). Its [sic] just come to me that what I am *really* weighing up is—that whereas I *know* that I can be the sort of person who could do the Club Training job—& do it well—& make a name for myself in that field etc.—what

I *don't* know is if I can be the other sort of person who can deal satisfactorily with personal relationships which the other job really means—& *this* is what I want reassurance about—terribly badly. It really *is* a question of deciding what *sort* of a person I am.

Isn't it incredible that anyone could write a *whole* letter about *themselves!* But I'm going to send it—as I mightn't feel like talking when I see you on Tuesday.

I hope you will make a *very good* broadcast—& that it won't be too nerve-racking. I hope it will be successful & that you'll be asked again [it was probably his first]—& will become very famous! Anyway, I've decided to *keep* the plastercine [sic] model I did of you in case one day I can sell it for a large sum (it was *meant* to be Sir William Beveridge but turned into you!)

Clare

She says, in effect, that she is being drawn away from him toward a situation in which she thinks she can make more of her life. And she asks how much he really wants her with him, because if he does, she'll go in that direction, the direction of "personal relationships," by which she refers to the Paddington Green job, but in subtext to *their* relationship, not to be spoken of openly—not quite yet, but almost. Getting married is important, as he has said, but whom could she marry? Perhaps she should reach out via a matchmaking service? She lets her love show its face, in the closing topic, the "plastercine" model. This is reminiscent of her Sassoon quote and Wordsworth comments at the end of the letter of April 2, 1943. It is probably true that the end of a letter often evokes spontaneous disclosures that come from a deeper place than formal and orderly message sending.

The next four letters are undated. They were obviously written after those already discussed, though how long after I cannot determine.

8, Polshead Rd.
Oxford.
Sunday.

My *dear*[13]—I'm afraid you would be terribly tired on Friday night by the time you get home—and hungry too? & I only hope that I haven't made you miserable as well! I hated you to cry & seem unhappy.

You know, it wasn't long enough time—possibly that was why it was difficult. I want you to know that I am better—less depressed—& relaxed somehow. So don't worry about what you've done to me etc. because you've given me so much happiness & to day & I know it & *feel* it & am grateful. Last week had been bad for me—physically—as well as in the job. I was very surprised when I said that you'd *drained* me in the last few months. Well. I suppose in a way, things couldn't happen to you unless they were so—also somehow I'd taken the responsibility of your love for me—as well as mine for you. (Just like me to cope with everything in sight!) Somehow I'd had to—but now you are coping that relieves me of the burden. I loved hearing about you on Friday—and I'm *glad* I called your bluff! I know I shan't regret it—and I only hope that *you* won't—But I don't think you will somehow.

To-day I have eaten an enormous amount of food—had 4 gins—a cider & a lager!! Yesterday I heard Moisezwitch (Sp?) play Chopin preludes—waltzes—*wonderful* Just what I wanted—I let it run all over me like cool water—refreshing & purifying. In the evening I saw "Cherry Orchard" which was also just what I wanted! So—you see— I *am* better! and now I know I'm going to sleep well too—so good night.

Love from Clare

Numerous references to their intimate emotional and physical life leave us as outsiders now. She has been feeling drained. She had taken responsibility for his love for her and hers for him, but now he has relieved her of the burden. He has told her about himself. She had called his bluff. She hated to see him cry, was afraid she had made him miserable, and she offers an explanation (for his impotence?): perhaps there wasn't enough time. She is reassuringly better, no need for him to feel guilty about hurting her. She ate a lot, drank a lot, let music run all over her, is quite functional, so she is definitely better and will sleep well, and he should not feel that he has hurt her. Do we discern in these few remarks the possibility that he was feeling guilty for "inflicting" his excitement on Clare, arousing but not satisfying her? To the expression of sexual excitement, we can add the expression of his dependency. He has been draining her. She would complain of this in later years as well.

This period features the bursting of a dam of constraint. Clare's own needs and their extended period of association have led up to this. He has become masculine and she feminine. She wants a baby. But she is destined never to have one, and would one day tell Marion Milner that she wished she had become pregnant in these years, before she and Donald could marry.

To-day. (Tues) after your letter.
I've actually worked all day— & without feeling sick!

8, Polshead Rd.
Oxford.
Monday—late)

Just back from London—more or less—where I've been all day—& where I exercised my self control by *not* telephoning to you!

Thank you terribly for this letter which is here. You will never know what a relief it is for me—that you've got down to brass tacks. I was afraid you were going to shelve everything—& that would be such dreadful waste somehow—& would have been the hardest thing to bear (for me)—in fact. I would have felt *dreadfully* let down & disappointed in you. You see, I can *stand* being turned down—& frustrated—but I *can't* stand not being faced up to—& well, being just *shelved*—because that makes me feel that I don't exist, that you don't either—& that all my feelings have been wrong & have betrayed me somehow [inserted at bottom of page: "No—I think I should have believed my feelings—& been disappointed that you'd betrayed them—& given over (?)"]. So Thank God, you feel able to go through this—& we *will* come through—I'm terribly tough.

I want you to know that I deeply appreciate & understand your feelings about your home & that it must at all costs be preserved—& I like you for having these feelings & I can realise that all the suffering you must have had has made a very deep bond. But I do wonder if it isn't true that the bit of you that you've given to me—is a bit that has never been given to Alice—therefore you are not taking it away from her?—& perhaps one day you *will* give it to her—but I don't know about this of course. I feel so much that nobody will ever possess all of you—rather in the same way that I know that nobody will ever possess all of me.

I wondered how you would feel about what you told me last Wed.—& if it would be horrid for you. It was wonderful for me that you could tell me—it is so very important to me too. I felt very rich somehow—& very humble too. When I drove away from you I thought—I shall *not* be ill—but I shall go through hell! I had an incredible dream that night too—in which you were just a head—with no body—but I will wait to tell you. [See his own dream at the time of reviewing Jung's autobiography.]

I'm glad that I'm not too heavily leaning on you—& that I'm a bit strengthening too—I would love to be. Best of all I like your dream about giving me the sunflower seeds—because I think sunflower children would be heavenly—they'd have yellow hair & would be *very* gay!

With Love—Clare.

Wednesday

. . . I have seen the New Era with you & me in it—and please. I want to *say* how glad I am to be in it—and *thank you* for letting me be. I only hope I haven't cheated—but you know, it doesn't really *feel* as if I have—it *feels* like having a baby (it was very painful, anyhow!)

It was *so* good to be made to feel & think deeply about the whole job. I am very lucky to have done it with you—(the job I mean) It has been exciting—in spite of all the difficulties—or rather—I should say—*because* of them. So *thank you* my dear—(you know how much)

Clare.

Even with the establishment of this new and probably consummated relationship, Donald continued to live with Alice, reluctant for many years to put an end to their marriage. He suffered heart attacks but nevertheless waited for his father's death before finally, in 1949, moving out of his home in Hampstead. The responsive Clare Britton, deeply interested in his work, able to bring her own intelligence to bear upon it, stands in contrast to the Alice who could never be bothered. Clare, too, was willing to live through an interim period of several years with Donald, with a degree of uncertainty we cannot gauge. He had asserted his wish to preserve his marriage, and without documentary evidence we cannot know when or how he crossed the line from an ongoing affair into a commitment to Clare. It would seem that his 1949 coronaries, which prompted Marion Milner to warn him that if he didn't leave Alice, he would die—played a pivotal role.

There was a new spirit in Donald in his 1945 presentation "Primitive Emotional Development," before the British Society, a strutting display of confidence. Here was a man in full possession of his powers, willing to steal what he felt belonged to him, able to make use of his hate, no longer the "too nice" nine-year-old to whom Clare later refered.[14] By 1947, Donald had presented his arresting paper "Hate in the Countertransference," another landmark in his journey toward harnessing his aggression for constructive purposes.

Clare quotes from a 1946 letter from Donald, three years before he divorced Alice and five years before he married Clare: "In odd moments I have written quite a lot of papers. . . . My work is really quite a lot associated with you. Your effect on me is to make me keen and productive and this is all the more awful—because when I am cut off from you I feel paralysed for all action and originality." The writing in which Winnicott developed his own point of view was largely created with Clare as his companion. But the quoted passage seems to me strangely devoid of matching intensity. Do we see here evidence of an inner division between excitement and deadness? Or does this letter point toward one or more periods in their courtship when he has, in fact, "cut off" from her?

"Why was Clare so important to his work?" asks Daniel Berg in his 1994 manuscript.[15] What was it about her and their relationship that enabled Winnicott to be creative? Clare gives some further clues in her account of a letter she received from him in 1950, in which he described his love for her as being in part the love he had for his "transitional object," a girl doll.[16] One aspect of their relationship therefore was that in her "good-enough mothering" she made herself available to be re-created in the image of his desires and needs in a way that she not only did not challenge but actively encouraged. She also provided him with near-perfect "mirroring" as can be seen in her comments on how she was shown all of his "squiggle" productions, the drawing game in which his unconscious feelings could be manifested. "There were his *endless* squiggle drawings which were part of his daily routine," she later recalled. "He would play the game with himself and produced some very fearful and some very funny drawings, which often had a powerful integrity of their own. If I was away for a night he would send a drawing through the post for me to receive in the morning, because my part in all this was to enjoy and appreciate his productions, which I certainly did, but sometimes I could wish that there were not quite so many of them."[17]

It would seem that it could sometimes be a bit tiresome being Winnicott's lover. But they did play a lot together, in a reciprocal, carefree manner.[18] As Clare said, they could disagree with each other in their play of ideas because they "were strong enough not to be hurt by each other." She went on to say, "In fact the question of hurting each other did not arise because we were operating in the play area where everything is permissible." This playfulness so marked the character of their relationship that a friend of theirs described them as "two crazy people who delighted each other and delighted their friends."[19] Clare told Michael Neve in 1983 that they always reserved Saturdays for themselves, "for play. No work was done by either of us on Saturdays, except enjoying ourselves and thinking what to do. We worked on Sundays sometimes."

By 1979, the time of my acquaintance with Clare Winnicott, she had received the Order of the British Empire (O.B.E.) for work done in the Home Office on behalf of needy children. She was by then a psychoanalyst in her own right, besides being the widow of a famous man. Beginning with the occasion on which she decided to allow me the task of editing Donald's letters, she was, I thought, unusually open with a virtual stranger about her relationship to Donald. I had the impression of a strenuous, joyful sort of relationship in which he clung to her as the tougher of the two.[20] She mentioned his leaping upstairs (after several heart attacks) to play a few loud chords on the piano at the end of the day or during a break in the course of the day. He would awaken in the night and tell her, "I'm potty about you, do you know that?" or express his worries: "What would happen if I never had another original idea?" He actually thought that if he moved out of West London, no one would refer patients to him anymore. She told me over dinner at the Grosvenor Hotel, within walking distance of their home in Lower Belgrave Street, that this was a favorite place of theirs and that they sometimes used to go dancing on a weekend evening.

Clare was now suffering from malignant melanoma, for which she had had several very painful operations on her leg, and she realized that her days were numbered. I felt that in her voluble commentary about herself and Donald, she was handing over a few facts to be remembered and possibly utilized in whatever I might write about the two of them. In fact, she later showed me an angry side because I had procrastinated about putting together the book of their letters. Apart from that, she struck me in the very brief contact I had with her (three weekends, a few letters) as a self-contained, determined, tough-minded, extremely competent woman. Even then, at the end of her life—mourning for her sister, who had died in an automobile accident close to the home they'd shared, and largely occupied with facilitating the publication of the vast Winnicott archive of book manuscripts, still seeing a few psychoanalytic patients—she displayed remarkable clear-mindedness.

— 11 —

Melanie Klein

"It was an important moment in my life," Winnicott recalled in a 1967 talk, "when my analyst broke into his analysis of me and told me about Melanie Klein. He had heard about my careful history-taking and about my trying to apply what I got in my own analysis to the cases of children brought to me for every kind of paediatric disorder. I especially investigated the cases of children brought for nightmares. Strachey said: 'If you are applying psycho-analytic theory to children you should meet Melanie Klein. She has been enticed over to England by Jones to do the analysis of someone special to Jones; she is saying some things that may or may not be true, and you must find out for yourself for you will not get what Melanie Klein teaches in my analysis of you.'"[1]

Donald's father had sent him away to boarding school because he was getting into bad company, and now Strachey was sending him to someone who could enlighten him in ways that he, Strachey, could not. In doing so, both admitted their limitations, sending him on to others who might give him what he needed. In these instances of guidance we see the positive side of the strong father rather than the negative side of the internalized father who prohibited fullness of satisfaction in the nursing baby.

And in Winnicott's relation to Klein, we see again the darling son of a depressed and creative psychoanalytic mother, who eventually found it necessary to insist on expressing his own unique views, which differed from hers. His own mother had died in 1925, just prior to Klein's appearance in his life. She had had a weak heart, and he blamed himself for not having prevented her from walking up a flight of stairs, the proximate cause of her death. (He would defy many such staircases in his own cardiac years.) The lack of physical love in his marriage to Alice Taylor may have added to the intensity with which he responded to Melanie Klein. She was able to nurture the side of him that was professionally preoccupied with babies through her unique speculations and observations, which he could not get from reading Freud or from his analysis with Strachey. Her theory was not, however, a warmly maternal one, even if it focused on the child's earliest development. Instead there was a rigidly "male" tone to her theory. I am hypothesizing that this reflected her own wish to embody maleness, and that her claim to be the true heir of Freud included this personal motive along with whatever scientific arguments she generated in support of that contention. The maleness of the theory attracted Winnicott, for it probably provided him with access to the longed-for father, Freud.

As a pediatrician, Donald was observing a good deal that was not covered by analytic thinking at that time. Freud's devotion to the Oedipal age and its conflicts rested on little study of infancy and early childhood. Later on, Winnicott said that good-enough mothering was simply taken for granted by Freud. But dealing with the emotional illnesses of babies was part of Winnicott's everyday work. He once said: "I gave many tentative and frightened papers to colleagues from the mid-twenties onwards pointing out these facts, and eventually my point of view boiled up into a paper which I called 'Appetite and Emotional Disorder.'"

Melanie Klein (1882–1960),[2] born in Vienna, apparently had six years of analysis with Ferenczi in Budapest, a truly extraordinary length for its time, albeit doubtless interrupted for long periods by Ferenczi's war service. By now she sought relief from depression exacerbated by the death of her mother.[3] Later she had a year and a half more of analysis with Abraham in Berlin, where she went after World War I, when virulent anti-Semitism broke out in Budapest. She had started analyzing her son, and received the transfixed attention of Ferenczi and then the protection of Abraham, who shielded her from the animosity of Franz Alexander and Sándor Radó. She came of a conflict-ridden family. Her early ambition was to be a doctor (her father was a doctor who was forced to become a dentist when the family moved to Vienna), but she set this aside for marriage to the unprepossessing and unfaithful Arthur Klein, a student of chemical engineering. The marriage took place the year after her ambivalently loved sadistic older brother Emanuel died, probably of a combination of tuberculosis and drug abuse. Three children followed. The marriage failed, leaving her to cope with depression, and so she found her way onto a psychoanalytic path. An argument could be made that her deep exploration of the infant mind, with its emphasis on instinct-driven violence, was a penetrating analogue of the doctoring she had given up. Her approach was a phallic, no-nonsense culling out of the ugly disease (the truth consisting primarily of fantasies of destruction). With growing interest in child analysis, she came on the scene around the same time as Hermine von Hug-Hellmuth, who was the first to analyze a child, her own nephew.

Anna Freud, trained originally as an elementary school teacher, had a point of view that could be described as more diffident, or perhaps more sensible. She believed that children could not form transferences and could not free-associate. Play was not, in her view, a substitute for free association, as Klein believed. She emphasized the educational aspects of intervention with children. Her own analysis with her father completes the circle of the three founders of child analysis,[4] all learning from within the family.

A series of lectures Klein gave in Berlin in December 1924 aroused the interest of Ernest Jones and the Stracheys, both of whom had recently been analyzed by Freud. Within psychoanalysis changes were unfolding at a rapid rate. A short experience with Freud led to his imprimatur, which permitted the recipient to analyze others, and to write with authority. Important papers by the master were appearing frequently: "Beyond the Pleasure Principle" in 1920, "The Ego and the Id" in 1923, and "Inhibitions, Symptoms, and Anxiety" in 1926. Revision was in the air within Freudian theory, and new ideas were causing turmoil—Rank's birth trauma for one, and then, out of the depths of her own suffering, a set of stunning ideas boldly advanced by Melanie Klein. These ideas began with the notion that the fantasy life of the infant and small child was rife with destructive ideation. The mother's breast is attacked for its contents, emptied out and appropriated. Sensing the presence of rivals in the form of unborn babies within the mother's womb evokes the impulse in the child to go inside and destroy them. Intercourse between the parents is imagined as the parents bumping up against each other, acted out when the child makes toy figures or objects collide. The child needs words in order to gain relief from this primitive anxiety. Violence, the keynote for Klein, shows itself in play, which the analyst may observe and interpret to good effect. This theory was a continuation of Freud's treatment of adults, Klein believed, with play as the equivalent of the adult's free associations. A disciplined kind of realism thus allowed for the deep analysis of even very young children.

Ernest Jones was looking for an analyst for his children and his wife. He had ideas of his own that Klein spoke to. In the summer of 1913, Jones had been in analysis with Ferenczi, on the advice of Freud. Klein may also have been in analysis with Ferenczi at the same time. Ferenczi, having been Klein's first analyst, was therefore in the picture on both sides. Ferenczi, who had been extremely close to Freud (and who, at the end of his life, was thought to have become psychotic as a result of pernicious anemia with neurological symptoms), was an influence on many, though he was not acknowledged as such at the time. Winnicott once treated a patient of Michael Balint's who had previously been a patient of Ferenczi's. Balint, a Hungarian, was one of the so-called Independents with whom Winnicott was on good terms, but not a social friend. Winnicott learned a good deal about Ferenczi's methods through his treatment of the patient they had in common. He avoided reading Ferenczi, he said, to protect his original thinking, implying thereby that he expected to find, or actually knew, that there were similarities. Ferenczi's experimental methods foreshadow Winnicott's, although they were extreme by comparison (including, for example, mutual analysis of patient and analyst, kissing of patients, and so on). The work of Klein's second analyst, Karl Abraham, was of the more classical variety, and she seems to have been most influenced by him. Although Klein did not acknowledge Ferenczi as a great influence on her, he was her first analyst, and she derived from him considerable benefit in dealing with the depression exacerbated by mother's death.

Jones's interests from 1910 on centered on "the importance of pregenital and innate determinants over and above the influence of external or environmental stress, and their vital role in determining beliefs and perceptions of reality. Of particular importance was the role he ascribed to hate and aggression, and the influence of fear in relation to anxiety.

However, Jones had not put these ideas forward as controversial issues, but as a consolidation of Freud's early formulations."[5] This emphasis on the innate, and the role of hate and aggression, suggest one reason why Jones was ready to welcome Klein and to foster her growth for decades after. Hate and aggression were preoccupations for Winnicott as well, and would have contributed to the favorable impression of him that Jones expresses in his extant letters. Perhaps such a set of ideas also supported an English anti-sentimentalist bias that was congruent with empiricism.[6] Winnicott would eventually make his own antipathy to the sentimental a bulwark of his theory, and it is this that, more than any other quality, differentiates his work from that of Heinz Kohut, who, while attending to the trauma of the early phases of infancy, gave short shrift to the aggressive element intrinsic to mental life.

Here, in the division between Ferenczi, with his emphasis on the behavior of the analyst, which could, in an experimental way, be altered to deal especially with disturbed patients, and Abraham, with his strict adherence to interpretation as the instrument par excellence of psychoanalysis, we see a bifurcation among analysts in their thinking about what is therapeutic in their field. Ferenczi, the environmentalist, gets short shrift because he threatens to dilute the purity of interpretation as the quintessential psychoanalytic method. Melanie Klein jumps away from whatever it was she received from Ferenczi into her own highly exaggerated version of what she received from Abraham. Classical analysts —in the United States, ego psychologists—also followed the work of Abraham much more closely than that of Ferenczi, although in recent years, with the rise of intersubjective or relational methods, Ferenczi has been rediscovered and rehabilitated.

In the 1920s, with the emergence of Melanie Klein, psychoanalysis divided itself not only into those who saw a role for alterations in the behavior of the analyst and those who adhered strictly to interpretation of transference, but also into the sentimental and the anti-sentimental, the crucial matter being the inclusion of an adequate role for aggression in human psychology. One branch led via Anna Freud to the "real relationship," of which Sigmund Freud wrote, and a flourishing of ideas that captured the vision of her close friend Ralph Greenson (and many others who emphasized the therapeutic alliance) and Heinz Kohut. This group, best represented by Leo Stone, was humanely in tune with the needs of patients for "relatedness," in the midst of the deprivation inherent in the analytic procedure. The other branch led via Melanie Klein and similarly disciplined practitioners in parallel with ego psychology to "the classical." Caricatures of each may cause an observer to see one as a form of kitsch, the other as a form of humorless fascism, or one as soft and kindhearted, addressing the human need for empathy, the other as hard and demanding, addressing the need to face up to painful reality. Each, carried to an extreme, engenders a sense of imbalance which evokes a hunger for its opposite. Group dynamics along with an inordinate enthusiasm for "the new" led to coteries, prejudices, and fragmentation of communication. In the United States, ego psychology, presented as the impersonal truth, stretching thin the tie between the ego and the id, between the higher functions of the mind and the wellsprings of instinctual life, set the stage for "self psychology," with its attention to the ever-present subjective and its cure through love. Self psychology provides a background for the renewed assertion of basic psychoanalytic principles by ego psychologists and Kleinians.

The theoreticians behind each school were human beings with personal predilections that derived not only from their "objective" experiences as practitioners but also from their own histories, the sorts of people they were before they became analysts. The study of Winnicott's life amply supports this observation, though in no way were his contributions mere derivatives of personal necessity.

Abraham backed Klein "very positively as the only person who possesses any data on the subject [of child analysis]." Klein, for her part, told Alix Strachey that in her opinion, "Abraham is a sounder person [than Freud] as an actual analyst."[7] She presented her ideas in the form of lectures to the Berlin Society in December 1924.[8] James Strachey responded to Alix's report with a request for an abstract for the British Society, and so word spread, leading through Jones to an open expression of interest among the members. It is interesting, too, to note the impression Klein had given Alix that "she absolutely insists on keeping parental & educative influence apart from analysis & in reducing the former to its minimum, because the most she thinks it can do is to keep the child from actually poisoning itself on mushrooms, to keep it reasonably clean, & to teach it its lessons." I call this interesting because we know that Klein's first patient was her son Erich. The two branches of psychoanalysis to which I have referred each include an ur-event, the analysis of a child by a parent, Freud and Klein. So much seems to have depended on the difference in their views derived from findings that emerged from mixing the two roles.

In Alix's discussion in the British Society, Jones is described as "absolutely heart-and-soul whole-hogging pro-Melanie." Klein arrived in London in July 1925, determined "to drain the dregs & lap the cream of London Life." She bought herself a special hat for her six lectures. Alix described it as "a vasty, voluminous affair in bright yellow, with a huge brim & an enormous cluster, a whole garden, of mixed flowers somewhere up the back, side or front—The total effect is that of an overblown tea-rose with a slightly roug'd core . . . & the [psychoanalysts] will shudder. She looks like a whore run mad—or, no—she really *is* Cleopatra (40 years on), for through it all, there's something very handsome & attractive in her face. She's a dotty woman. But there's no doubt whatever that her mind is stored with things of thrilling interest. And she's a nice character." Her lectures "were received with a warmth well beyond her expectations."

Theoretical battles broke out between with Anna Freud and her followers, still in Vienna, and the ever increasing number of adherents to the camp of Klein. The situation changed dramatically with the advent of the Second World War, when many Jewish analysts from Nazi-occupied countries emigrated to England, with the help of Ernest Jones, Marie Bonaparte, and others. This altered the long-distance contest between Klein and Anna Freud into an intramural struggle in the British Society, for which Klein blamed Ernest Jones. This attitude, which implied that Jones should not have brought the Freuds out of Vienna to England, reveals the dimensions of her obsession at the time. To suggest that Jones should have arranged for them to go instead to the United States would then have left out the preferences of the principles themselves, who wished to come to England. Shortly after Jones's death, however, Klein wrote to Winnicott of Jones's kindness and the fact that he had enabled Freud to die in peace.

Undoubtedly, deep personal dynamics were involved. The threat to Klein's recently acquired Englishness posed by the introduction of the émigrés may well have been a cause of her resentment. She had so taken to being English that she spoke pejoratively of "the Viennese," usually meaning the followers of Anna Freud, as interlopers in the more refined world of English psychoanalysis. For, by then, around 1939 or 1940, there was an "English school," consisting of followers of Klein. Her letters underscore her exaggerated Englishness, paired up with opprobrium for "the Viennese" who did not wish to see deeply, or were incapable of it. Here, I think, is an example of Klein's splitting of herself in two, one part "English" and deep, the other part "Viennese" and shallow, the latter a projection on her part. Her analyses had occurred not in Vienna but with Ferenczi in Budapest and Abraham in Berlin. Thus it was with the pre-analytic Melanie that was associated with the renounced city of her birth and the first eighteen years of her life, and the condition of her mind that she associated with it. A letter to Winnicott from Scotland (quoted in full later in this chapter), where she had gone to escape the bombing of London, includes an intense expression of English pride.

By the time of this letter (1940) she felt confident that in Donald Winnicott she was addressing an adherent to her views. Much had happened by then. She had supervised him (1935–40); he had analyzed her son, now anglicized as Eric, during the same years and would continue beyond; he had finished his first analysis with Strachey and was being analyzed by Joan Riviere, a close follower of Klein, with another year to come. We lack documentation for Winnicott's relation to Klein before 1935, but the likelihood is that there was a good deal of contact, given the fact that she was in London from 1926 onward, where Donald was practicing pediatrics and being trained as an analyst starting in 1927. In 1936 his British Society membership paper, "The Manic Defense," provided evidence that he had taken her theories seriously. Yet, from what we can ascertain, his formal supervision under her began only in 1935.

Winnicott always felt, even during subsequent periods of estrangement, that Klein was the greatest analyst after Freud. He was among her followers until he gradually took up a stance that was entirely his own. Yet as early as 1942, in a letter from Susan Isaacs, Winnicott was said "not [to] give her [i.e., Klein] his contributions early enough for her or the group to vet them, and he made a number of 'blunders.'" He was supposed to be one of the Kleinians, and Klein's frequent letters seem to support this, yet he was already making "blunders," a word that is perfectly suited to Winnicott the clown, the man who enjoyed pratfalls, the gnome, the man who strode unself-consciously into traffic, the playful re-arranger, the non-perfectionist.[9] In spite of his affinity for Klein's ideas and his admiration for her contribution, it is probably fair to say that he was never her disciple, never a Kleinian, was in fact constitutionally unfitted to be anyone's follower. It is more accurate to say that he was once her student, did his best, but was not fitted for the required discipline and—luckily for him, and for us—was a blunderer.

Winnicott says, in his 1962 paper on Klein, "I never had analysis with her, or by any of her analysands, so that I did not qualify to be one of her group of chosen Kleinians." His analysis with Joan Riviere did not, in his view, qualify him to be called a Kleinian (through he was listed by Klein as one of five Kleinian training analysts).[10] Riviere herself, a difficult woman, was eventually alienated from the Kleinian circle. The phrase "chosen Kleinian" implies accurately that he was not one of Klein's "chosen people." Winnicott was not a Jew, as was Klein, and it could be argued that he brought a New Testament gloss to psychoanalysis, mitigating the harsh judgment of the Old Testament God with the forgiving attitude of a non-organizational, pre-Pauline[11] Jesus Christ. The notion of resurrection was inherent in Winnicott's insistence that Klein's ideas be rediscovered and reexpressed in the purely personal language of each individual, or else her language would die or be destroyed. Individual and repeated rebirth was the requirement for continued "aliveness," and personal humility was necessary for the renewal of the living language. It would seem, however, that the complex subject of humility and resurrection, with its religious overtones, was not to be broached publicly. The statement that he was not one of the "chosen Kleinians" perhaps characterizes Winnicott's sense of being an outsider to orthodoxy. This was not a condition imposed on him by Melanie Klein, but one that he embraced as a necessary means of liberation. Only as an outsider to an orthodoxy that he studied so hard, and with which he flirted, could he effectively insist on being himself. This is to say that his pursuit of what was authentic in himself had to be based on conflict, and this conflict had to recruit large areas of his personal being. Paths of obvious divergence from his deeply felt being could be set aside without difficulty. Precisely because Klein's ideas were so immensely appealing, and because she taught him so much, his subsequent struggle to clarify for himself and others where he stood as a separate thinker was difficult and painful.[12]

Even through at least two decades of being a supporter of Klein—first a student, eventually a colleague, and the analyst of her son Eric[13]—through all this, he was never a "chosen Kleinian." Without a Klein, however, there would not have been a Winnicott as we know him. "Being himself" would have taken a different form, and we have no way of knowing whether his name would mean anything at all to us today.

Phyllis Grosskurth believed that Winnicott wanted his second analysis to be with Klein, but he acceded instead to her request that he analyze Eric. Many years later, when his second wife, Clare, was looking for a training analyst who was "tough enough" for her, he is said to have reminded Klein of this sacrifice. We do know that he recommended Klein to Marion Milner and to Enid Balint, as well as to his brother-in-law and friend Jim Taylor. Since he may well have recommended her to many others, her rejection of his contributions in later years must have been especially painful.

In 1939 a cheque for twenty-nine guineas was sent by Klein to "Dr. Winnicott" in payment for his work with Eric. It seems highly probable that this letter of July 25[14] represents the end of the analytic work, at Eric's request. Klein's subsequent letters illustrate the changing nature of her relationship to her supervisee in the sequence of salutations: "Dr. Winnicott" (July 25), "Winnicott" (August 31), and, World War II having begun for England on September 1, "Donald (as I should like to call you, and please call me Melanie"(October 25). On October 31 she wrote of Eric: "He is not taking advantage of the possibility you offered him to continue his analysis. . . . I think he is actually very much in need of it.—He told me Sunday last that he rang you on Friday last but that you were not at home. So I think that it is possible that he will get in touch with you soon. I told you—didn't I?—that his father died at the beginning of Sept. —that and complications about his father's will have affected him apart from all it implies for him." On November 16 she inquired: "I wonder whether Eric has gone back to you and should be grateful if you would drop me a line about this."

A comment on January 19, 1940, indicates that Jim Taylor was coming to Klein for treatment: "I think he is very worth while not only as a person but also as an analysand and hope he will be a good one in time." If there had been any question about Klein's access to information about Donald's marriage, there can be none anymore. Taylor not only knew his sister well but also knew about the marriage from his close friendship with Donald. Alice was at this time in analysis with Clifford Scott, who wrote to me in February 1989: "As you likely know, [Winnicott's] first wife, his brother-in-law, an analyst, Taylor by name, and his second wife were all in long analyses with me with more or less success and more or less failure. He himself once came for analysis but stopped almost at the time he began."

Melanie Klein's first extant letter written from Pitlochry, Scotland,[15] is dated July 2, 1940. On July 30 she writes, "I am sure and feel so with deep gratitude that your work with Eric has been keeping him from going back [i. e., regressing]—a *very great* thing in times as these." On November 18 she writes: "I gather that Eric is not going to see you any-more. Though there is a real point in his wishing to be at home before air raids begin I am sorry that he stopped. I am sure even with twice a week only it has done him a world of good. . . . Does he keep in touch with you?" Several letters have to do with making arrangements for an office and/or playroom in which she could see patients during brief trips to London. Winnicott was very helpful to her.

Klein's letters about Eric are voluminous and often relentless in the pressure they generate on Winnicott to see his condition as she herself does. On March 18, 1941, she pleads with Donald to reach out once more to get Eric back into treatment:

> I should have been very glad to have had an appointment last time I was in London to talk with you about Eric. On the one hand it is quite marvellous and an enormous credit to the work you have done that he should bear up under such strain the way he does, particu-larly keeping on with his work and doing his duty in every way. But there is still much in him which is worrying me. His character seems to have stabilized in a very unpleasant way which is particularly ob-vious in his relation with me, but I am afraid also has a bad effect on his domestic happiness and might even in the longer run be fateful in his relation with Judy [his wife] who (not altogether unconsciously) suffers under it and might even one day refuse to put up with him any longer. She says that she never has any conversation with him,—nothing which could be called so and suffers under this lack of com-mon interests and when he talks he is inclined to nag and be facetious. Clearly the necessity to get away from all feelings led again to a shrinking of his personality and and [sic] he has found a certain stabilization at this cost and also to the detriment of his character.
>
> All this is of course very much on my mind all the more as so much for Michael [his son] and Judy is involved. I don't find it easy to ask you again to help—you have already done so much for him—but if you could possibly find some time and get him back,—now that the days are long, it might make a great difference. He may soon

be called up but if your work could loosen up something in him before he goes it might be a great help. . . .

Yours Melanie

One can understand a mother's worry, especially a mother such as
Melanie Klein. Eric was at the time twenty-seven years old, married and a
father. Her other son, Hans, was dead, possibly a suicide. She was under attack by her daughter Melitta, who charged her with pushing ideas into her.
She was preoccupied with Eric's damaged life, which she herself investigated when he was from three to five years of age, her first source of information about violence in the mind of the child. In her description of what a
parent gives to a child, love is not even mentioned, though the analyst's
cold-blooded objectivity is regarded as indispensable. Naturally, an observer associates such views with the observation that Eric as an adult
tended to be inaccessible. How, without his mother's love, could he be anything but inaccessible? Klein's urgent wish to intervene in his analysis was
an expression of hope that a correct (that is, Kleinian) understanding of his
conflicts would lead to a change for the better.

According to Grosskurth's biography, Klein's own mother seems to
have harbored violent feelings toward her. This experience constituted
part of the setting in which Klein studied the mind of her own child and
found violent ideas. Personal factors must have led to her preoccupation
with the direct study of the mind of the child, as she located the violence
there rather than in the mind of the mother. In fact, one of the oddest aspects of her brilliantly elucidated theories is a "scotoma," or blind spot,
for the mother as an active influence on the child's development. We may
speculate that she allowed herself to see into the child only by blocking
out the mother. The personal implication might be that only in this way
could she concentrate on her own responsibility for her destiny, rather
than seeing herself as the product of her mother's hostility, and, further,
that the fate of her own children would depend more on themselves than
on her influence as their mother. The word "scotoma," which I use here
(and which Winnicott used), largely reminds me of the applicability of
the same word to Winnicott's theories, which largely exclude the father.
This symmetry suggests a factor that may have drawn Klein and Winnicott together, each the completion of the other, at least for a while. Later,
Winnicott would emphasize the mother, and failing, he felt, to convince
Klein of his view, went his own way.

On March 24, Klein opens a long letter with: "Many thanks indeed for the help you intend to give Eric. I hope he will make use of it." In addition to agreeing to further work with Eric (probably at Eric's request), Donald had announced his intention to deliver a paper to the British Society. Her letter is a kind of personal essay that glows with impassioned commitment to her work and reveals her thinking in an undefended way. She seems inspired by Winnicott's capacities and determination. Its 1,500 words are worth quoting at length:

> Dear Donald,
>
> ... I was quite thrilled by your intention to read a paper in our poor decrepit society and it seems that the way you worded this intention struck a chord in me:—I want to hear my voice in the society talking about something that is not—it brought back to my mind happier times, when we left our meetings with a feeling of satisfaction that work and insight were growing and that we had a share in this; that there was hope that a science which might mean so much for mankind was on its way to further achievements.
>
> It seems a long time back,—actually it is nine years now that Glover and Melitta in their Symposium on Ps. An. [psychoanalytic] Education inaugurated *openly* "the New Order" in our Society. Some people have been overrun. I shall never forgive Jones for having been so weak, so undecided and actually treacherous to a cause he himself values so highly and the possibilities of which he never underrated. Others,—afraid of conflict found it more convenient to withdraw— others sit on the fence and feel that to keep the society together at all costs or rather to pretend to the outside world that *this* is *PsAn*. (In contrast to such inferior beings (?) as Tavistockians etc.!—) that to do this work and make it grow—
>
> Does it sound funny. ... This ... work may go under and might be rediscovered again;—that has happened before. But its very nature, the fact that even each of us of those who have got most hold of it have to keep great vigil not to let it slip at *this* point or *that*—because it makes such very great demands and there is a constant temptation to cover it up or to turn away from the points where it strikes terror or causes pain—all this makes one afraid that *if* lost, it might not easily be rediscovered in the entity to which it has progressed in recent years.[16]

In 1927 Jones after his correspondence with Freud about my work told me: It will take a long time to carry your work to people (obviously he meant analysts)—it might take 15 years! When I once mentioned this to Glover (who at this time was still trying to some extent to assimilate it and in any case still *representing* belief in and appreciation of it)—he said: I wonder whether you ever will—it goes too much to the roots—However all this is in some ways beside the point! For in spite of my fear that it all might go under—there is a very strong determination and hope in me that it *won't*. This time in Pitlochry has not been lost. Solitude and greater leisure have done quite a lot for me—I have been *taking in* in various ways (how I enjoy now reading history!) and I have been *thinking* a lot. I am sure that I have progressed and done work with myself and I shall be in a better position to write those books which it is my duty—and perhaps privilege too—to write,—the book on technique and my collected papers with notes and an explanatory preface in which I shall have much to say. . . .

But to go back to your letter which set my thoughts going. It might be as well at present to let things go their course and to allow all these papers to remain uncontradicted—after all people are bound to get bored with always hearing the same and fruitless things and they may be all the more interested if they hear again a paper which has really something to give. On the other hand there is the danger that those people who had already begun to understand are falling back so much into superficial ways of thinking that they might not be able to understand anything which goes beneath the surface. It was long and hard work to get them away from there and much terrain has been lost no doubt in these years in which the deterioration of the scientific standards has gone very far. In addition to this,—there are the Viennese who never even begin to understand our language and don't want to. And yet I feel we must stick to it and try to regain some of the half hearted and at least begin to interest some of those who might wish to learn. We shall all have to be very careful in our presentation and to adjust it more to the understanding of people who either can't take in much of what we have to say or are only too pleased to make capital of one sidedness in our presentation.[17] This warning I am sure applies to all of us who represent this work. For instance I had discussed Susan Isaacs last paper with her and made various suggestions in the direction of not taking too much for granted,—in substantiating material more fully etc.—And yet it should have been of great advantage and improved the effect of this excellent paper had she cut out more of the material and given more proofs reasonable and understandable for the listeners of the remaining material.

To show these people who are obsessed with the fear that penetrating deeper in the ucs. [unconscious] might leave them as it were in mid air—far away from reality—and real people—to show over and over that only interpretations which link up the various layers of the mind and convert every [?] was preconscious and conscious—by means of interpretation of the transference situation which is *the* link to reality; to present and past one—to demonstrate this again and again seems to me one way of impressing and perhaps even winning over those people who might after all wish to learn. Another thing that we should remain or rather make ourselves interested in every one who *might* be taught even if still lacking in understanding as yet. You went toward Miss Evans and it cheered me to think that you keep in contact with her and that she has opportunities to learn from you. But that may be desirable for others who have no opportunity of learning, i.e. MacDonald or [?]. One cannot of course do anything for people who *refuse* to accept as some of the Viennese,—but as I said we should be on the lookout for people who might be induced to learn something. Little as it seems can be done at present in the Society, but perhaps could something by people like you, Heimann & Rosenfeld be done in smaller groups, through getting personal contact and discussions with people who might not be able to ask for enlightenment, and yet wish for it. What is going to happen later on with our Society—one can't foresee yet. I was thinking that we may very much extend for *certain* discussions the circle of our little meetings and thus have kind of meetings in which real work could be done and interest revived and increased,—without formally withdrawing from the Society. Still, in the meantime to hear our voices at meetings and to let others hear them seems very desirable and I am delighted to think of you giving a paper.

Will you be at Queen Anne Street in the week beginning Easter Monday? I shall work there in the week & should be pleased to see you some time or to arrange something with you if this suits you.

All good wishes,

Yours ever,

Melanie. . . [18]

On April 1, just a week later, her letter documents a line of communication that excludes Eric, whose

father and brother are dead, his sister cut herself off from me, he is the only one who owns me so to say. He now has in a deep sense kept me all to himself—robbed the others. If he could do more for me, look a little after me be nice with me he might feel that he replaces the others in a *good* sense. But since the war and a talk with Melitta in which she accused me bitterly, pointing out that I was a God mother to him too—his relation with me has become much worse. He behaved very badly whenever he gave me hospitality in his home sometimes even showing openly reluctance to give me food. Though I always bring with me much more than I need. He used to be affectionate with me and [tried?] to do something for me—of all this there were scarcely any signs in the last 18 months. Recently I found that he was touched by Michael's [his son] affection for me and then became more affectionate with me himself. He is less influenced than I thought he would by Judy's obviously increasing affection for me and trust in me—but in this last year he was more and more shutting himself up. He is aware though that through Michael he is giving me happiness and I feel that unconsciously & also consciously this must mean a great lot in the way of reparation, also bringing the brother back to life sharing me with him and also giving me babies. When Eric was a baby he said repeatedly that he had to produce Michael so that I should have a grand child. I feel all this must be an enormous help against having robbed me and his family—though it was not much apparent in the last year or so.—All this I feel enters into one of the first pieces of material he gave you on his return. Is he not also in the transference situation keeping us apart—having me in his home whenever I come to London when you—the brother—see me but little. He is extremely greedy and dictatorial about my free time when I am in London—resenting when I go out with somebody at a time he could see me but not making good use of the time I keep for him. On the other hand he now has got you, when I have not. And he takes your time and help for nothing—thus also robbing you.[19]—I am so glad he came back to you. Whether you can make much of what I suggested—I don't know. But in any case it shows you something about things which are surely important for him. And I shall be only too glad to make any suggestions whenever you feel like asking me for some.—Could we have an opportunity for a talk while I am in London. I told Eric that on Saturday before Easter I shall do some shopping etc.—if you were available some time in the morning we could meet. If not—perhaps during the week after Easter I shall let you know when I am free.

She makes plain her own formulations here, only a step removed from being her son's analyst even now.

In the same letter Klein supports Donald's misrepresentation to Eric that he has had no contact with his mother: "I am thankful for your giving me an opportunity to be of some help with Eric's analysis. (In these matters it is difficult to make a rule but I personally in your place would do exactly as you are doing,—I should also deny that your communication with me about him and would feel justified because it does not mean to me what he would interpret it for.) " Her rationalizations for these lies are evidence of the breakdown of integrity that took place in this period, and in a subsequent one, as Donald became enmeshed in skeins of compromising relationships.

I was told by Phyllis Grosskurth[20] that Klein tried to persuade Winnicott to write a medical certificate asserting that her son Eric was not fit for military service, but he refused: "According to Clare (my source) 'it was the making of him.'" Presumably she means that Clare thought it was the making of Donald, though there is an ambiguity. This is an instance of his standing up to Kleinian pressure that foreshadows others to come. But it is juxtaposed with his willingness to consult with Klein and hide the fact from his patient. This incident is described by Masud Khan in his Workbook (his personal diary) for 1963, where he reports Winnicott's disclosures to him on this subject, along with Winnicott's feeling that this was the beginning of the rift between himself and Klein.

At this point the trail of letters in which reference is made to Eric's analysis with Donald, and his mother's efforts to have a say in the matter, comes to an end. There are a few more references to Eric in further correspondence, but nothing of the same kind.

A letter of June 6, 1941, addresses Donald's paper "Observation of Infants in a Set Situation"[21]:

Here is at last your paper back. If you don't mind (I am glad that I kept it so long), I kept it until I could set my mind freely to it. I have *thoroughly* enjoyed going through it and making suggestions, not only because I am glad to be able to be of use to you as a friend, but because it is really an excellent paper which should be helpful to our work. There is quite a lot in it and yet *not* too much. As regards my suggestions: You will take them won't you—as what I intended them to be,—suggestions to take or leave and particularly you might find it desirable to alter in some places the wording I suggested—possibly because it is too much my particular way of putting things. I felt very reluctant to cut the paper about as I did, but first I tried to refer to insertions from other pages and finding that I could not get a clear view of the paper in this way I proceeded to put it into the order I suggested by cutting some pages up. You gave me licence—didn't you—to mark it as much as I like and I know you have a copy—so no irreparable harm could have been done—My suggested insertions are I feel things you *meant* to say;—but I am not quite so sure about p. 27a–c. You mentioned something about what you saw in the last five years. I think it refers to insight gained in your analysis and more particularly to depression. As it stands,—one wonders *what* you mean and if what I suggested is *not* what you meant then I think it would be necessary to point out what you meant by the insight gained in the last 5 years.

What you say about the testing of reality—and finding out step by step etc. *particularly p. 24* is of such importance in showing people what we *actually* know and understand about the importance of experiences that it might be—if you think so too—helpful to support this by the reference to my paper on mourning (Journal 1940) the first pages of which are devoted to this particular aspect in development. By the way, I am afraid that the insertion I suggested on p. 22 is very similarly worded as a passage either in this paper or in Love & Hate—so it would be necessary to put this somewhat differently.

I feel it would be very useful if Mrs. Riviere would once more read the paper and judge whether my suggestions or at least some of them—assuming you accept them—are not overloading the paper.

Here, in making a point of asking Donald to be explicit in his paper about knowledge gained about depression in the previous five years from his analysis, she may have been insisting that he provide written credit for her discoveries as transmitted to him through Joan Riviere. One could imagine that she is encouraging the expression of gratitude, a mature emotion which stands in contrast to stealing, which was how he characterized some of his work in his 1945 paper "Primitive Emotional Development." Or she may be applying pressure to turn him into her vassal, with reiterations of his indebtedness to her as the primary source of his knowledge. She also suggests that Riviere read the paper again and judge whether Klein's suggestions might not be "overloading" the paper. (Riviere's letter to Donald of September 2, 1941, indicates that he was still in analysis with her.) Although she is apologetic about cutting up the paper in an effort to provide helpful suggestions, the total effect, combining the request that he be more openly grateful with the suggestion that Riviere review her additions, is overbearing, even crushing. He is being politely nudged toward becoming a manufactured product known as a Kleinian psychoanalyst.

On April 22, 1943, Donald wrote about "a Polish girl treated for one year by David Mathew. Mathew wanted Donald to treat Hallah Poznanska (eventually Hanna Segal) who was seeking training in psychoanalysis. Since Donald was trying to save his time for work with children, he agreed to do the work only if neither Klein nor Paula Heimann would. Seen in the light of what followed, his naïve assent is full of irony. He unself-consciously gave substantial aid to a person who would one day assault him with continual deprecation.

In a letter of July 28, 1944, Klein writes: "I know that your wife has been away for some time and was glad about that. You must have had a very strenuous time, (one does not feel it so much while one is there but afterwards one realises it) and I should be glad to know that you are going to have a real and also not too short holiday." She may be alluding to her own experience of a bad marriage in her parenthetical comment, but it does seem clear that by now his circumstances were openly acknowledged by Klein. This was the period when his affair with Clare was developing.

Klein indicates that Donald was still sensitive to her attempts to influence his work with Eric when, in an undated letter from Upper Quinton, probably soon after the one just referred to, she discusses the urgency of analytic work for Eric's son Michael (he was going to be seen by Marion Milner), who had developed a stammer: "I am not suggesting that you should try to influence Eric—but remembering that in the autumn it did not seem to matter so much if it was postponed, I wanted you to know the facts."

She writes on March 5 that she "very much appreciate[s] your frankness and the spirit in which your letter was written. I know you are my friend and shall never doubt this.—I have no intention to participate in the discussion about Glover, but this does not mean that I agree with you on a number of points you raise in your letter." And on May 3: "I shall have a seminar on Tuesday next and am reminding you of that. But please do not take it otherwise but as a reminder, as if you do have anything else urgent to do, do not come."

This is further evidence of the delicate emotions now in play. Winnicott appears to have begun his long, slow withdrawal from the intense tie to Klein. If he truly had sacrificed analysis with her to treat Eric, his withdrawal probably started in 1936, for we know with certainty that he was seeing Riviere by then. He resumed analysis, having finished ten years with Mr. Strachey three years earlier, his marriage still unconsummated. He undoubtedly needed what support he could find. But there was probably more than that at stake, given the knowledge we have of his ongoing self-analysis, which seems never to have ceased. Was it Kleinian thinking, not available from Strachey, or from Klein herself in a context of his own analysis, that promised him some form of personal liberation? Was it Klein's suggestion that he consult Riviere to foster the work with children that she was supervising? He had refused to be supervised by Klein in the treatment of her son, but she managed to communicate some of her fears and formulations to Donald anyway, as the extant letters indicate. She was, of course, supervising his other work during this period, so a conflict between Klein as supervisor and Klein as the mother of a non-supervised patient is certain to have existed. Where exactly did he, could he, stand in relation to her? And, given the fact that Riviere was so close to Klein, a supervisor of Klein's writing (as a quintessentially literary and artistic person), could Donald have been assured of the confidentiality of his analysis? Could he feel certain that this work was kept segregated from Riviere's relationship with Klein? Events in the 1950s would bring Klein and Riviere together in his mind, and he found it necessary to stand up to them as a pair.

The letter of April 1, 1941, in which Klein confirms their secret arrangement with respect to Eric suggests a weakened Donald, not a chosen Kleinian (at least in his own mind, as expressed in 1962), but chosen by Klein for the analysis of her precious son, trying to keep her in abeyance and failing. He could not reconcile the demands of analysis free of external influence with Klein's constant pressure to have her say. It was Klein who furnished the rationalization and the words I quote in this account. Therefore she was given a kind of triumph over Donald's struggle, one that implicated both of them in a dishonest pact. Or is it more fair to say that under extremely difficult circumstances such an abrogation was minor, and that Winnicott maintained his independence to a remarkable degree, given the unrelenting will of Melanie Klein? In Winnicott's life there are examples of other, much more destructive acts.

We know that Klein and Riviere were very closely associated, but there is no documentation to support the conjecture that they talked about Donald's analysis. Riviere did intervene in at least one unseemly and unanalytic way. In Winnicott's words: "I was at that time having analysis with Mrs. Riviere who was a great friend of Mrs. Klein's, and I said that I was writing a paper on the classification of the environment, and she just wouldn't have it. This was a pity because I'd got a tremendous amount from my five years with Mrs. Riviere, but I had to wait a long time before I could recover from her reaction."[22]

I return to Klein's letter of June 1941, in which she writes, "I feel it would be very useful if Mrs. Riviere would once more read the paper and judge whether my suggestions or at least some of them—assuming you accept them—are not overloading the paper." Since Donald was still in analysis with Riviere, her role was being compromised under the influence of Klein's judgment. If Donald accepted the recommendations, this would have brought him within their combined purview in a published work. What comes to mind is a statement from a famous letter James Strachey wrote to Edward Glover[23] urging compromise in the British Society, in which he said, "The aim of a training analysis [is] to put the trainee into a position to arrive at his own decisions upon moot points—not to stuff him with your own private dogmas." Certainly Donald's 1956 letter to Riviere represents his ultimate statement to the two of them:

> After Mrs. Klein's paper ["A Study of Envy and Gratitude"] you and
> she spoke to me and within the framework of friendliness you gave

me to understand that both of you are absolutely certain that there is
no positive contribution to be made from me to the interesting attempt Melanie is making all the time to state the psychology of the
earliest stages. You will agree that you implied that the trouble is that
I am unable to recognize that Melanie does say the very things that I
am asking her to say. In other words, there is a block in me. . . . My
trouble when I start to speak to Melanie about her statement of early
infancy is that I feel as if I were talking about colour to the colour-
blind. She simply says that she has not forgotten the mother and the
part the mother plays, but in fact I find that she has shown no evidence of understanding the part the mother plays at the very beginning. I must say this quite boldly in spite of the fact that I have never
been a mother and she, of course, has. . . . I shall understand if you
have too much on hand to be willing to take up this matter with me. I
feel, however, that I want you to know that I do not accept what you
and Melanie implied, namely that my concern about Melanie's statement of the psychology of earliest infancy is based on subjective
rather than objective factors.

By the time fifteen years had passed, he had taken up a strong position against the privileged criticism of his analyst and her close colleague, his admired former mentor. He does not, in the end, fall within
their purview. While he lent himself to their sometimes destructive influence when he might have chosen not to, unlike so many others Winnicott
proved to have the personal wherewithal to extract himself from external
influence in time to fashion a statement of his own.

Looking now at the larger context of the direction of development of psychoanalytic thinking after Freud, we may take note of the impressions of
Klein's biographer, Phyllis Grosskurth: "It is a chilling conclusion that
Libussa [Klein's mother] did not want her daughter to be happy, that she
did not want [Melanie] to find fulfillment, that she begrudged her the en-
joyments of which she herself was deprived when she was young."[24]
With her mother as the enemy of her happiness, Klein developed a theory that excluded the influence of the mother on the development of the
child. This was a defense against a too-active, too-influential, destructive
mother. Her defiance of her mother, possibly even a requirement for
maintaining her own sanity, was codified in her theory. No wonder that

her formulation of what the mother gives the child does not include love. That was her own experience.

This denial of the mother gave Klein the power to observe the child in a clear field, as if what she saw in the consulting room could be taken in itself to be evidence of what the child generated *ex nihilo.* She was the icy observer of the objective child. Her commentary gained, and continues to gain, convincing authority from this attitude. I will call a theory that takes account of the influence of another person "the real" and the opposite, the theory that excludes the influence of the other, "the unreal."[25] Klein's theory was an instance of "the unreal," with the emphasis on the dark interior of the mind, as opposed to the mind as illuminated and transformed by the influence of one or more others, the mother or the analyst, for example, which are instances of "the real."

Klein's fearless pursuit of the earliest, destructively ugly emotions may have represented the deflection of her early, doctorly (male) ambition into the exploration of the primitive mind. The initial hostility in England toward Anna Freud's approach to the child represented, in part, the negative side of the attitude of many toward Freud himself, a protest of sorts against having to continue to toe the Freudian line just because Anna was his daughter and carried his name. Ernest Jones, who backed Klein, was a leader in fostering pro-Klein and anti–Anna Freud sentiment. Because [Klein] often formulated her ideas in descriptive rather than conceptual terms her theories were easy to apply to a quick understanding of a patient's material and could easily be shared with colleagues without the hard work that would have been involved in conceptualizing them in terms of the metapsychology of classical theory.[26] Robert Waelder, a member of the Vienna Society who came to England to present a paper in the exchange between the two societies in the 1930s, would write one day of "experience-near" and "experience-distant" theories. Theories like Klein's that are continuously rooted in direct observation of patients are consistent with the tradition of British empiricism.[27]

Freud's sense of balance guaranteed an awareness of the real relationship of analyst and patient, as well as the relationship based on transference. With Anna Freud as a fulcrum, the "real" aspect received support from many like-minded colleagues, including her Los Angeles friend and benefactor Ralph Greenson.[28] The emphasis on the "real" came through as a commonsense corrective for theories that exaggerated the role of transference in treatment. The Klein theory was the major example, but the work of American ego psychologists was also seen to be similar. Strachey, not a Kleinian, advanced the notion that the mutative interpretation was a transference interpretation. In my view, the attention to the "real" was intended, consciously or otherwise, to suppress awareness of the depth of the "unreal," which Klein approached in her own way, and may have represented a general yearning for a corrective of this sort, part of the ongoing, cyclic exaggeration-and-correction flow of psychoanalytic thinking. Kohut's much later emphasis on failures of early parenting as an ultimate cause of psychopathology derived from the same theoretical tradition as Greenson's, with a consequent appeal to all those who preferred to focus on the "real" as opposed to the "unreal." This left behind those who continued to be preoccupied with the "unreal," some of whom did not wish to dispense entirely with the "real" either.

Winnicott welcomed Klein's emphasis on the primitive, savage elements of aggression in the small child. In these ideas he had found an avenue of approach to his own hatefulness, on which he would focus for a long time to come. The "too good" little boy could now see an underlying dynamic of destructiveness. This would have been a relief to him. He had considered himself much too adaptive to his mother's depression, much too devoted to being the good child. Now he had support for his own "badness." In time, his natural inclinations in other directions would reassert themselves and make his initial loyalty to Klein problematic.

Prepared by his early loyalty to Freud and then to Klein, Winnicott was able to go on and add to that groundwork what was unique to him, and unique to his own experience as the observer of mothers and infants. He would pay close attention to the environment in the development of infants and in the treatment of patients with "early damage," that is, disturbances of development that originated in the early mother-child relationship. This was the "real" element in Winnicott, derided by Klein, Riviere, and more recently by Hanna Segal. To them it was a dilution of the sturdy, the indispensable "unreal" Freudian theory, as transformed by the extremism of Melanie Klein.

The motto of the early part of his career, "There is no such thing as a baby" (because wherever you see a baby you also see a mother), is the apotheosis of the "real" point of view. This became the location of maximum disagreement with Klein. Having established to his own satisfaction, however, that his formulation of the role of the environment was valid and lasting, he became more and more preoccupied with what might be called the darker side, another term for the "unreal." This line of thinking reached its zenith in the 1960s, with his assertion that he believed there was a permanent incommunicado aspect of the True Self, sealed off from any external influence, and after that, his belief that the continuous unconscious destruction of the real, external object (who survives) is a precondition for "the use of an object." The creation of reality from within the individual absolutely reversed the prior commonsense notion that reality is always "out there," to be perceived and understood by the individual, or not.

Freud's single theory thus gave rise to two branches, one with an emphasis on the dark and demonic "unreal" elements, the other taking into account the influence of other people, beginning with the mother and progressing to the analyst.[29] The second branch led to today's widespread and widely welcomed development of an interpersonal emphasis in analysis. Winnicott, known generally as a member who is part of the second group, in fact combines the two. That may be one of the sources of his tremendous and growing appeal. He represents the reinstatement of balance between real and unreal, much as Freud himself had maintained throughout his career. According to this point of view, it was Anna Freud who, with all her clearly articulated formulations and voluminous writings based on the direct observation of children, nonetheless fostered a distortion in the development of psychoanalytic thinking, leaning so far in the direction of the "real" that the dark and demonic underpinnings of human psychology were given short shrift. Klein's ideas were held dear by the group around her and have been advanced by them, possibly to an exaggerated degree, in order to safeguard the insights, which she regarded, as stated in her letter to Winnicott from Scotland in 1941, as easily lost.

The advent of World War II occurred in the same month as Freud's death (September 1939): this is the approximate dividing line between two phases. A period for Donald of involvement with Klein, marked by the combination of supervision by her, his work with Eric, and his second analysis, would come to an end within two years. In the war era, the "controversial discussions" occurred, and the Klein/Anna Freud battles broke out in the open. Donald's life began to show an ever more independent strain of thought and action, manifested in and probably supported by his new relationship with Clare Britton, starting in 1944. But even by then, the complicated structure of Winnicott/Klein/Eric/Riviere was beginning to give way to a new and even more complicated agglomeration of Winnicott/Alice/Clare/Marion Milner/the patient Susan. We will ask whether the early condition of his life—with mother, sisters, nanny, and extended family,—ruptured by his expulsion to boarding school at age fourteen—was repeated at various phases of his later life, as complicated relationships required extrication and clarification in order for a new sense of freedom to become possible.

— 12 —

Marion Milner

The year 1943, when Donald was forty-seven, included several events that both evidenced his confusion and added to it. In Oxfordshire, where he spent most Fridays, his relationship to Clare Britton was progressing to an affair. And in London, his relationship to Marion Milner was becoming quite complicated. (Later on the mischievous Masud Khan would say that Marion was jealous that Donald had married Clare instead of her.)

Marion Milner was born Marion Blackett in 1900. Her brother Patrick, a physicist, won the Nobel Prize in 1948. His twenty-first birthday gift to her of Freud's *Introductory Lectures* introduced her to psychoanalysis.[1] Marion and Donald had been colleagues ever since she had attended the 1938 lecture that had prompted her to begin her own analysis. (She was four years younger than he.) He was the only person willing to undertake the analysis of her husband, Derm, a lawyer who suffered from severe asthma. Winnicott was then being analyzed by Joan Riviere and, according to Milner, "he still thought clever interpretations were important"; yet, in contrast to Riviere, he was interested in the potential value of physical contact with patients and would hold Derm Milner during an attack. He visited him one weekend thirteen separate times, which shows his dedication and perhaps a belief in his power to restore his patient's health by giving him faith in a reliable helper. The physical gesture would be around ten years later in the analysis of Margaret Little, whose hands he would hold. Little was psychotic at the time, and Derm Milner he considered to have been "mad" as well, whatever that was supposed to mean. Winnicott was taking into account the patient's dependency needs, which he tried to meet directly.[2] Eventually the Milners were divorced. Derm Milner subsequently died of asthma.

Donald and Marion were close colleagues from the beginning. He sometimes drove her home after meetings, and entrusted her with personal confidences. Marion Milner's *The Hands of the Living God* (1969)[3] tells the story of her treatment of "Susan," who lives with the Winnicotts, designated in the book as "Mr. and Mrs. X."

> It was in the autumn of 1943 that I was rung up by a Mr. X, a man of independent means, who was interested in problems to do with mental health. He asked if I would undertake a research analysis with a girl, Susan, aged twenty-three, who was just about to come out of a hospital for functional and nervous diseases. (I will call the hospital N.I.) He told me how his wife had been visiting there and had become interested in this girl and had invited her to come and live with them. Much later, Mr. X was to tell me that his wife had become interested in Susan because she was so beautiful—"She looked like the Botticelli Venus rising from the waves."
>
> Mr. X went on to explain that although they had invited Susan and she could have left the hospital, her woman psychotherapist, Dr. F., had been telling her that she should have ECT, and that Susan had been in acute conflict as to whether to have it or not. She had visited him and his wife in their home, but had been unable to decide to come, since to leave the hospital would have meant opposing Dr. F. Susan had therefore ECT twice, but when Mrs. X saw the "terrible state" she was in after it she had finally persuaded her to leave the hospital and come and stay with them. Mr. X added that he thought I might not want to take on such a difficult problem but that the main treatment would be the fact that he and his wife were providing her with a home. He also said he would pay for the analysis; he added that before going into hospital Susan had been living and working on a farm for four years but had been unable to accept any payment.

In her discussion of this case, Judith Hughes[4] has written:

Alice Winnicott had found Susan "in great distress" at "N.I.," a hospital for functional and nervous diseases. Susan had been admitted in the summer of 1943 following a breakdown: the presenting symptoms were hypochondriacal heart pains, torturing obsessional doubts, guilt, and depression. When after a couple of months she showed no improvement, the hospital psychiatrist recommended electroconvulsive therapy (E.C.T.), otherwise known as shock. Susan resisted but finally gave way: "She was asked," Milner wrote, "to give her permission about 19 times and she refused, but after the 20th time when she said yes, the shock therapy was started." She "had two doses and following these she had a great disturbance of the right side apart from a very severe degree of the usual amnesia and confusion."[5] (The longer term effect of the E.C.T. remained unclear. The treatment itself and Susan's experience of it, however, figured prominently in the analysis.)

Winnicott recognized, whereas his wife did not, the full extent of what she was taking on. Susan herself recalled much later how "she would 'just sit'—her head down, knees up, for hours and hours, 'how awful for them'—and how Mr. X would come in and put a hand out and maybe she would take no notice." By 1949 Milner had begun to observe an "inner movement that seemed to be bringing her alive as a person."At the same time she began to see "that there was another acute anxiety, a very realistic one, dominating her feelings. . . . there were increasing signs that the X's marriage was not going to last very long." When Winnicott's home broke up near the turn of the year, he found her a new one: "She was taken in by a seventy-year old friend . . . Mrs. Brown, who took total charge of her and expected nothing from her in the way of help in running the house." Indeed by the time Susan moved in with Mrs. Brown, she had become unable to help. Her daily routine—so she reported to a psychiatric consultant in July 1950—consisted of going to bed at 10:30 P.M., sleeping with sedation, and sometimes remaining in bed until one o'clock the following afternoon, in sum, just sitting about and having her psychoanalytic sessions, and she usually went to them in a taxi. Obviously the breakup of the marriage had produced a serious regression.

Of Susan's move, Marion said,[6] "Donald himself told me he felt he owed it to Alice because she had recently to cope with the difficult boy that he had asked her to accept in the house.[7] . . . The tragedy was that, when Alice brought Susan to see them both and the house being offered her, Donald said nothing, did not say 'Don't have the ECT.' At least this is what Susan told me, as I remember it." Perhaps Donald harbored some degree of guilt about this, not to mention his possible guilt over being unfaithful to Alice, and this prompted him to pay for Susan's treatment. At this point he was trying to hold together a domestic situation which, he told Clare, should and must be preserved. Beginning in July 1943, not long *before* Susan's appearance in his life, Donald had launched an attack on the use of electroconvulsive therapy in the pages of the *British Medical Journal* and before the British Psycho-Analytical Society.[8] He had very strong feelings on the subject, which makes his behavior all the more strange. His discussion includes due attention to the potentially suicidal or self-destructive impulse which might lay behind a willingness to undergo ECT. He expressed elsewhere the belief that a person does have the right to take his or her own life,[9] and it is possible that he was holding his influence in abeyance for that reason, or that he was at least in a state of conflict about what he should or should not advise. The result was that it was Alice who came to Susan's rescue and Donald who exposed her to the terrors of ECT. He then arranged for her to undergo analysis with his most esteemed colleague. His failure to defend her against ECT provides an interesting counterpoint to his extraordinary effort to meet the dependency needs of regressed patients.

After beginning the work with Susan, her marriage now dissolved, Milner asked Donald to recommend an analyst for her "mad part," left untouched, she felt, by her earlier work with Sylvia Payne.[10] She did not think that Donald believed there was such a part, though when she asked, he made a facial expression as if to confirm that he did believe there was. He considered her request for a day and then offered himself as analyst. She accepted. "I'm not sure when I began P. A. with Donald," she told me, "certainly after I began with Susan, which was 1943."[11] To Marion, Donald was now a colleague, friend, supervisor (of her work with Susan), provider of a home for her patient, fee payer (for Susan), and personal analyst, whom she paid. That the analysis itself took place in Mrs. Milner's consulting room added an extra bizarre effect. This location was chosen ostensibly because it was between Winnicott's home in Hampstead and his consulting room in Queen Anne Place. But of course the choice illustrated and added to the confusion of roles between the two.

It would seem that after a lifetime of propriety, of adhering to the boundaries of acceptable behavior, a life that did not even allow for sexual intercourse, Donald began, in 1943, to cross boundaries in a reckless fashion, finding his freedom in the process, but making mistakes as well.

"As for offering himself as my analyst," Milner told me, "it could be partly making amends. He always said that when I came and asked him to be my husband's analyst in 1937 or 1938, it was the worst consultation he ever did and that I was really asking him to be *my* analyst. Also I think because he felt he was the only person who could really do my analysis! He told M[argaret] Little that she was the only person, having been analysed by him, who could do [J. D.'s] analysis." Little did not want to do this. The results for J. D., said Milner, were disastrous. Donald, she added, "simply failed to think of the effects on my analysis with him of having 'Susan' living in the house. . . . About the effect of his treatment on my husband . . . certainly the war stopped it. What with gas masks and all that we decided on a cottage in the country. And he did come down once or twice for a session, but obviously it could not go on." One might add here that Milner seems simply to have done what she was told, though she might have resisted, but perhaps the sway of transference was too great for her, as it often is around charismatic analysts. At the end of her life, she told one of her close friends, Nina Farhi,[12] that she was obsessed about her own unanalyzed aggression and expressed tremendous regret that she had not been able to defend herself when required, as in the instance when Donald suggested he be her analyst. To the analyst Judith Issroff she complained that Donald had failed to analyze the effect on her of having had a depressed mother.[13] Mrs. Milner's training as an analyst had been prompted by Winnicott's lecture in the first place, so perhaps it was not so strange that she was now in an advanced state of "training" under his aegis, which combined roles as analyst and supervisor.

The work went on for several years until Milner consulted Clifford Scott, who thought the arrangement a travesty of analysis and advised her to quit, which she did. (Scott had analyzed Alice Winnicott until his services were required in the war, and he would also become Clare Winnicott's analyst.) She felt that there had been in her case a powerful transference to Donald, but that she got little out of her analysis. Scott suggested that since what she sought was "the genital thing, why not find it?" So she did.[14] She found a Polish mathematician and artist, who became her lover of many years.

One theme that arose in the countertransference, as it were, was that of Donald as marital sufferer, manifested most graphically one day during his treatment of Milner in the form of a figure that he fashioned during the hour and then left behind. Milner described it as a "little crucifix" made of three matches and an elastic band. "The [match] that was Christ had its top end broken and bent forward, so like a dying man; that's why I said it was beautiful." In the poem Donald wrote in 1963, "The Tree," he also likens himself to Christ. It seemed to Milner in retrospect that he wished to communicate something of his personal agony. His loyalties were deeply confused, as he sought to find a way out of his unhappiness. She could understand this only after she learned about his marital situation and his health, which was in 1949,[15] at an art school in Suffolk (undoubtedly the place described by Hannah Henry), where he told her about Clare. She advised him to leave Alice, because otherwise he would die. It was not until the very end of 1949 that he did leave his wife, though he communicated with Mrs. Milner repeatedly on the subject of his personal suffering.

Within the British Society, Marion Milner was closest in temperament and talent to Winnicott. Her far-ranging visual imagination was always put in the service of those intellectual attributes that made her thinking so original and articulate. When I was in the early stages of gathering material for the book of letters to come, Clare Winnicott asked me whether there was anyone I would like to meet. I thought immediately of Marion Milner, whose *On Not Being Able to Paint*[16] was just the sort of quirky psychoanalytic book that continued to give pleasure and knowledge with repeated rereadings. Then, during my research, I came across an undated letter from Milner to Winnicott which hinted at a prior period of analysis: "There's another thing. I've been doing Mental Accounts about my 3 analyses—Somehow I feel there's something more to be said about my analysis with you; I don't know what it is, but do you think it a good idea, or a bad one, if I came to see you, professionally, for just one session, to see if we can perhaps get it said? And if good, then perhaps fairly soon, before things get too cluttered up?" I do not know what she meant by the last clause.

I asked her about this in a letter but received no response for quite a while. She finally acknowledged that she did have analysis with Winnicott, but she did not wish it known generally. The reason is, I think, that she wanted to provide her own account of their relationship rather than to have someone else do it. Perhaps such an account would be central to a discussion of a good many related topics. I do think that the subject of that analysis is central to Winnicott's life, since it demonstrates his failure of judgment (not the only instance), as well as his self-indulgence, overestimation of his capacities, and use of his privileged position as a means of getting help for himself. He had been coping for decades with personal deprivation. His two analyses had not led to any immediate liberating action, although one may speculate, in a way that gratuitously credits his analysts, that he could not have left Alice for Clare without the work that was done.

His messages to Milner, within and outside their psychoanalytic relationship, may have been a way to find relief by communicating, and getting advice from one who had a sense of his pain. He did put Milner in a position to tell him to leave his wife, after all. We see no such evidence of such a decision in the letters of 1943 and 1944 from Clare. In fact, at that early stage he was determined not to break up his home, and Clare was in agreement. So Marion's advice, in that special Suffolk location described by Hannah Henry, that flower-filled and artistic place of inspiration, advice that he would die if he did not leave Alice, created a major moment of choice.

This would have been all the more startling if Milner had still been his patient, as she may well have been. Susan was still being treated. She had several more months in the Winnicott home before the Winnicotts' separation induced in her another breakdown and the move to the home of "Mrs. Brown." Milner was thus in possession of information not only from Donald directly but also from Susan, her patient, about the marriage of Donald and Alice.

One way of understanding this complex interplay of roles is that Donald was participating in an arrangement in which he gave help to Milner, which might be thought to foster her ability to help her patient, Susan, whose improvement would ultimately be helpful to Alice, who had brought her into their home in the first place: thus a filtering down of help originating in Donald, with Susan as a sort of daughter to Alice. Yet, he was also at this time deeply involved with Clare Britton, on the brink of the first sexual relationship of his life. It makes a certain sense that he would have extended himself to help Alice at a time when he was being unfaithful. However one may wish to view the skein of roles he had spun at this time in his life, they must have expressed his personal struggle to emerge from the sterility of his caretaker marriage to Alice into a fruitful relationship with Clare. He was moving out of an enclosing, protective cocoon, from pupa to adult.

According to Joyce Coles, Susan was at Donald's seventieth birthday party at the institute, in 1966, frying sausages in the kitchen.

Marion Milner provided me with a great deal of information about herself and Donald Winnicott in the few short years during which I knew her. Each time I came to London we had a discussion, and there was an ongoing exchange of letters. She was a beautiful woman, even in her nineties, graceful, alert, and responsive, if in obvious decline. I knew that each occasion could well be the last.

It was a surprise to me, rereading *Eternity's Sunrise*, Marion's study of diary-keeping, when I came across this paragraph: "On the first day, looking seawards from the port [Thallos, a Greek island she was visiting], away on the right in a small cove, I saw two sailing ships drawn up on the beach. Delighting in them, I walked over to the cove and made a fairly accurate drawing of them in ink and oil chalks. But, deeply discontented with the result, after a day or two I had cut up the drawing, dismembered it and reassembled the bits in a tiny collage, its shapes only determined by the formal qualities of the rhythms of colour and line."[17] I was reminded then that in the years when I was acquainted with her, she had taken to cutting up old paintings and drawings and reassembling them into collages. And I had failed to note the parallel to Winnicott's own habit of rearranging the parts of his papers, as he had done with the furniture in the rooms of his childhood home, and as he had done in the house he shared with Alice and the one he later shared with Clare. This common trait probably has meaning in the context of the complicated friendship between Donald and Marion.

If I say that Milner was Winnicott's only intellectual and imaginative peer in the British Society, it is not to depreciate others. It is their preoccupation with play that leads me to that opinion—that and a relentless clinical-introspective devotion without off-putting posturing or demands on others. The capacity to encompass infinite complexity in a simple vocabulary perfectly mimics the child's undertakings, with "the child" always identical to the mind that is pondering those complexities.

The last time I saw Marion was in November 1996. I came to her London home in Provost Road of a morning. She told me she was working hard on a book, beginning with her son's notebook and his analysis of her when he was seven, in stories and pictures. She showed it to me proudly. Then we talked about Winnicott. I asked her if he had been in love with her. She responded that she had seen a light in his blue eyes when he was helping her with her luggage at Liverpool Station as she evacuated to the country at the outset of World War II to be with her husband, whom he had treated. I suppose that her answer to my question was a conditional yes.

She had been puzzling about why he had volunteered to treat the "mad part" of her which Sylvia Payne had missed. She hadn't been "hooked" on Sylvia, she said; that is, there had been no transference. She then had four years of analysis with Donald, who finally said that the analysis was wrong and that he would take the guilt over his treatment of her to his grave. I told her it seemed as if *he* had wanted treatment from *her*, needed it, and communicated this via the crucifix and the arrangement of seeing her at her house. He was trapped, I thought, in his Christ situation.

I asked about the exact beginning of the analysis, but she did not remember with precision. She thought it had begun perhaps in 1944. This was around the time things started up with Clare, I noted. Clare was tough and competitive, she said. She didn't like Donald's beautiful drawings in the colored pencils that Marion had introduced him to. I wondered whether this had been an expression of Clare's jealousy of Marion, more evidence that there was a feeling between Donald and Marion that merited jealousy.

Marion showed me a squiggle by Donald of a mother and child, similar to one I described earlier—another of the same subject but with a much more marked "spine" in a dark herringbone pattern down the middle. This was when she told me that Donald had said he was weaned early because his mother got too excited, and it had had something to do with her own father. Marion wondered whether the spine might represent the internalized anti-sexual father, coming between mother and child. I found this an interesting idea, with many levels of potential inference. The idea of the grandfather's interference in his daughter's pleasure with her baby was a speculative addition to Winnicott's belief that he was weaned early because of his mother's excitement. I believed then and continue to believe that this disclosure to Marion was a crucial piece of information that explains a great deal about him.[18]

Marion Milner died in June 1998.[19]

— 13 —

"Human Contact with External Reality": 1945–52

D onald Winnicott suffered a coronary thrombosis[1] in February 1949[2] shortly after the death of his ninety-four-year old father. Recuperating, Donald took Alice for a holiday together at Hannah Henry's guest house in Suffolk. At the end of that year he finally separated from Alice and soon thereafter had another coronary, described by Margaret Little,[3] who was in analysis with him at the time: "One day his secretary told me that he was not well and would be a little late for my session. He came, looking *grey* and very ill, saying he had laryngitis. I said, 'You haven't got laryngitis, you've got a coronary. *Go home.*' He insisted that it was laryngitis, but he couldn't carry on; he rang me that evening and said, 'You were right, it *is* a coronary.'" She tells of its significance for their work, which was arduous: "This meant quite a long break which was very painful, but at last I was *allowed* to know the truth: I could be right, and I could trust my own perceptions."

According to Joyce Coles, Donald's secretary, he had a coronary at Queen Anne Street around October 1949, soon after she started to work for him.[4] They had met in August, when Donald and Alice were going to their cottage in New Quay, Gloucestershire. It was evening before he ad-

142

mitted he was ill. He went home to bed in Pilgrim's Lane and stayed there for five weeks. It was not long after this that he left Alice. "He knew he couldn't stand the strain of Alice anymore," Coles told me.

Between July and September 1950 he suffered a third coronary. As a result, he could not give his paper "Transitional Objects" before the British Psycho-Analytic Society when first scheduled. He finally did deliver this work, for which he became famous and by which he is still best known, on May 30, 1951.

Until the end of 1949 he was living with Alice, continuing to see Clare, and practicing in Queen Anne Street. The end of 1949 brought his separation, followed by an interim period of two full years, until the end of 1951, when he no longer lived in Hampstead and often slept in his office or at Clare's flat in Chelsea. When they finally married and moved into 87 Chester Square in Belgravia, his private life and his work were spatially united.

Within the context of separation and marriage, of compromised physical capacity and the threat of sudden death, the various stresses in his life undoubtedly forced out of Winnicott certain kinds of behavior that made manifest his ongoing personal struggles. These included seeking approval from important women in his life with highly aggressive behavior accompanying or alternating with his overtures. It seems as if his absolute need for a good reception gave rise to a frustration which drove him to make his own views clear in an insistent way, with the result that he often received back, understandably, not approval but disagreement or resentment.

A propos the question of the potentially psychosomatic background of coronary thrombosis, he wrote a short paper, "Excitement in the Aetiology of Coronary Thrombosis," given to the Society for Psycho-Somatic Research, University College, London, on December 5, 1957,[5] which is not accompanied by any case material. Sexual frustration is given as the primary cause. "[We]. . . need to know," he wrote, "what happens in the body when excitement 'goes cold,' that is to say, does not reach a climax."[6] He differentiates between those conditions in which excitement leads to climax and relaxation, and those in which there is no climax, but a recovery anyway and relaxation. His third category is one in which there is delay, displaced excitements, congestions, and "disaster," meaning hysteria, depression, depersonalization, disintegration, a sense of unreality, (or a mixture) and/or general tension (chaotic defenses). About this last he says: "Only the passage of time cures this phase in which there is impotence or frigidity, and probably there is an incapacity to masturbate, or masturbation is only possible by the dragging in of pervert and regression mechanisms." He continues: "Excitement is the pre-condition for instinctual experience. There are many zones at which excitement occurs locally, but for the integrated personality local excitements are part of the build-up for a general state of excitement, and purely local satisfaction of a major instinctual locality is a frustration to the whole person who expected more result—in fact, a whole experience on the basis of the experience of the past." The paper concludes: "The common state of affairs in men and women who like to link their instinctual experiences with the enrichment of relationships is that many excitements must remain unrequited, and must find a way of dying down. Here we come near to the physiology of such a psycho-somatic disorder as coronary thrombosis."

Since impotence was a major factor in his life, as were repeated instances of coronary thrombosis, we are led to see in his words a statement about his own despair, translated into clinical terms. That "many excitements must remain unrequited" undoubtedly speaks of his own frustrations and his effort to accept them, even though they produced in him at least some of the symptoms described in the third category.

The comments in this paper may be connected to other statements he makes in various of his surviving works, including letters, with the principal point of interest being the effect on an infant of a depressed mother. He wrote, for example, to a younger colleague about one of her patients: "I think that this mother, because she was depressed, took great care that her infant did not get excited and of course in thinking this I am using the clinical notes that you gave."[7] He assures her that he is not disclosing anything from anywhere else, least of all his own life. That he may have been taught by his mother not to feel excitement would help to explain his conflict about excitement leading to impotence, and his preference for theorizing about what might be called the freedom of the ego, rather than the id. This kind of antiorgiastic attitude accords well with the fact that he married a woman who found ways not to bring her work to fruition. That the consequent syndrome of noncoordination would lead to a kind of disastrous excitement and coronary thrombosis is a reasonable conclusion. Discussing the patient cited, he says further that "breathing excitement is the thing that the patient is trying to get to. This, as you know, is a very important part of sexual intercourse."

The Winnicott Family at Rockville, Plymouth, 1900. Donald's father and mother stand at the far left. Frederick's brother Richard is seated left with his wife standing behind him. Donald's sister Violet is fifth from left and his other sister, Kathleen, is in the front row to the left. Donald himself is the baby in the center of the photo. *Courtesy of Peter Woolland*

The parents of Frederick
Winnicott: Richard and
Caroline Winnicott. Car-
oline may be on the far
right in the family pho-
tograph.

Sir Frederick Winnicott

Frederick and Elizabeth Winnicott at the Royal Regatta, Plymouth Hoe, 1922. *From the Mayoral Yearbook.*

Donald, 1935

Manor House, Theberton, Suffolk, 1920s. Donald kneeling, Alice in front of him, Lilian Bentley at back, Hannah Henry next to dog. *Courtesy of Hannah Henry.*

Four friends at Dartmoor, 1931. Violet the older sister is marked with an X and Kathleen the younger sister is second from the left. Hannah Henry is second from the right. *Courtesy of Hannah Henry*

Kathleen is on the far left and Violet the far right.

Melanie Klein

Marion Milner. *Courtesy of Brenda Prince/Format*

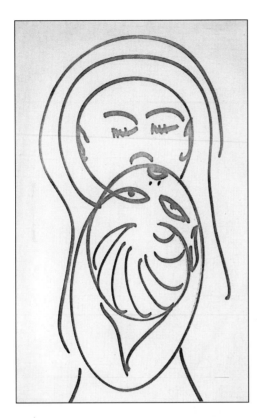

Drawings

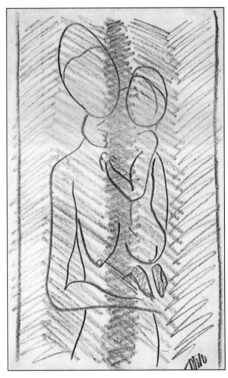

Three coronaries were closely associated with loss: his father, his first marriage, and, later, the suicide of a patient. Was he, then, forcibly reminded, somatically reminded, of an early time when "the object"—that is, his mother—had withdrawn from his excited self?

Winnicott needed to allow himself freedom of expression, very often of an excited type. We have seen the development of this freedom over many years of his life, and we see it still in the 1950s, in his aggressive reaction to what he takes to be Kleinian political maneuvers. In a letter to Hanna Segal of February 21, 1952, he writes: "You will see that I have let myself go writing to you. My intention is to let myself go in the Society meetings whenever the trend is taken away from scientific statement towards the statement of a political position." As he fights for his life through these years, both physically and emotionally, we see how he pleads (excitedly, or at least with excitement attending his discoveries) for verification from important figures that he does have a contribution to make, that what he offers is valuable and should not be rejected. These figures are principally Joan Riviere, Melanie Klein, and Anna Freud, the last of whom grew ever more appreciative and ever more important to him for that reason, especially in the 1960s, after the death of Klein. Anna Freud, however, was a completely different kind of figure, much less related to his deeply internal life, yet also valuable for that very reason. On James Strachey and Ernest Jones he could always rely for admiration and support.[8]

The papers Winnicott wrote during this period after the war were "Primitive Emotional Development" (November 1945), "Hate in the Countertransference" (February 5, 1947), "Reparation in Respect of Mother's Organized Defence against Depression" (January 7, 1948), "Paediatrics and Psychiatry" (January, 28 1948), "Birth Memories, Birth Trauma and Anxiety" (May 18, 1949), "Mind and its Relation to Psyche-Soma" (December 14, 1949), and "Aggression in Relation to Emotional Development" (1950). His "Transitional Objects and Transitional Phenomena" of 1951 represented a dividing line in his own development. In the ensuing period, during which he pondered whether to contribute it to a book honoring Melanie Klein, he laid claim to a voice and a point of view that were uniquely his own, which would be enunciated powerfully, even tragically, in a 1952 letter to Klein.

These eight papers, beginning with "Primitive Emotional Development," show him advancing fruitfully at a pace not previously seen. These were years of crisis for him, as he was leading a double life.

Among the many themes and ideas contributing to his advancing theory of infant development correlated with adult psychology, as especially revealed in his work with patients who "regressed to dependency," is the concept of the True Self. This idea would not become the central theme of a paper of its own until 1960, but the phrase appears in his papers of 1949, first in "Birth Memories," then in "Mind and Its Relation to Psyche-Soma," and in his 1950 paper on aggression. The True Self is a way of describing the surviving unscathed inmost aspect of the individual through the vicissitudes of infant existence. It is easy to say that his urgent concern with or his ongoing focus on understanding the conditions under which the True Self may exist stemmed from his personal odyssey. His own path of development was henceforth often discernible in his published and unpublished writings.

Early in this period, an exchange with Ella Freeman Sharpe (1875–1947), a leading figure in the British Society, reveals his evolving views about psychoanalytic work. She was moved by his presentation of a case, to be described eventually as a therapeutic consultation, to write about his "art." She incidentally mentions a new candidate, Masud Khan, with a prescient comment, given the significant role he would play in Winnicott's life, and vice versa, in years to come. She was also one of those who preceded Winnicott in the attempt to analyze Margaret Little. She wrote, on November 7, 1946:

> I want you to know how much I appreciated what you said last night. As "consultations" have never been my business I could freely enjoy the whole import and spirit of your communication. You give so freely of your experience, I do hope your generosity will make it possible for others to follow your lead—in your simple direct sincerity.
>
> As an original worker, dealing first hand with your experiences, with such disinterested zeal you will surely add not only to the general body of scientific knowledge, *but* (for me more important still) to the technique of dealing with human beings—i.e. the *art* of p. a treatment. . . .
>
> I am just starting the analysis of an Indian (a *candidate*). I can think no one more than yourself would enjoy the constant need I have to shift out of ruts and see the world through other eyes than Western ones.

He replied on November 13:

> As a matter of fact, I am not certain that I agree with you about psycho-analysis as an art. Out of your very wide experience there is something that you want to say, and which you express in this way. But from my point of view I enjoy my true psycho-analytic work more than the other kinds, and the reason is to some extent bound up with the fact that in psycho-analysis the art is less and the technique based on scientific considerations more. Therefore, when I hear you speak about psycho-analysis as an art I find myself in difficulties: not wishing to completely disagree with you, but fearing lest this comment which you make should be given too much importance. There is obviously plenty of room for discussion here, but I thought I would let you know what I feel, because I usually find [when] I talk on non-analytic aspects of psychiatric work, that I am making an indirect comment on true analysis which I am not making.

In the same spirit, he wrote on November 11, 1946, to Dr. Kate Friedlander and staff at the Hampstead Clinic, urging continued reservation of the word "psychoanalysis" for psychoanalysis itself. Articles in the *New Era* had called their work in child guidance "psychoanalysis," and it was quite important to him that, just as psychoanalysis is mainly science, so the word itself should be reserved for "the interpretation of the unconscious as it gradually becomes demonstrated and ready for interpretation in the transference." In the Sharpe and Friedlander replies he shows how important to him is precise delineation of his field.

"Hate in the Countertransference" (1947) is a rather short paper, which continues the freewheeling style of the 1945 "Primitive Emotional Development." One might say that he is putting his True Self on display here, in contradistinction to the False Self tones of what usually passes for scientific writing.[9] He makes reference to his own dreams and to his analysis, and describes the problems he and his wife had in dealing with a nine-year-old foster child, all in the service of illustrating and developing his concept of objective hate, and associated countertransference ideas. The reader is taken into Winnicott's personal life.

He writes, "However much [the analyst] loves his patients he cannot avoid hating them and fearing them." About dealing with psychotics, he says "If the analyst is going to have crude feelings imputed to him he is best forewarned and so forearmed, for he must tolerate being placed in that position." He tells us about "healing dreams," from his own experience as a patient, and then describes at length one dream precipitated by a mistake he made in the treatment of a psychotic patient. It began with images of castration anxiety, and then featured psychotic anxiety traceable to the patient. He goes on to discuss the foster child: "My wife very generously took him in and kept him for three months, three months of hell." He hated the boy at times of provocation and, voicing the hate, made him stand outside the door. From this he proceeds to the notion that "the mother . . . hates her infant from the word go," and gives a long list of the reasons why, with elaborations. One conclusion he draws is that "it seems to me doubtful whether a human child as he develops is capable of tolerating the full extent of his own hate in a sentimental environment. He needs hate to hate."[10] As part of his deepening appreciation of the role of mothers, he writes: "The most remarkable thing about a mother is her ability to be hurt so much by her baby and to hate so much without paying the child out, and her ability to wait for rewards that may or may not come at a later date." The presentation of these deeply human but never acknowledged aspects of the psychology of the analyst electrified me fifteen years after the paper was first given and constituted the beginning of my absorption with Winnicott's work.

His January 1948 paper "Reparation in Respect of Mother's Organized Defence against Depression" addresses a subject that was of more than purely professional interest to him because of his own situation as the child of a depressed mother. The primary theme is that a child's reparative behavior may represent the mother's reparative needs rather than those of the child itself. "The depression of the child can be the mother's depression in reflection," he writes, and "in the typical case of the delightful girl . . . the mother's need for help in respect of the deadness and blackness in her inner world finds a response in the child's liveliness and colour." In this he raises complicated questions, quotes Edward Glover's criticism of Klein as putting forth fantasies attributed to patients that in fact belong to Klein herself, goes on to acknowledge that patients often produce material that they think Winnicott himself would like to hear, and states that Jungian patients produce Jungian dreams, while Freudians seldom hear of such dreams. He asks whether "due recognition has been given to the need for everything to be discovered afresh by every individual analyst?" and adds immediately, "At any rate there must be kept clear the distinction between the value of ideas and the feeling about them roused by the way they have been presented."

He is walking a line here between Glover's complaint about Klein and Klein's insistence on her objectivity. The comment about every analyst rediscovering everything afresh is directed to Klein (and would figure in his climactic 1952 letter to her). To Anna Freud, he evidently wrote expressing intense criticism of Glover, prompting her to explain, on April 11, 1947, why the invitation Glover received from the Amsterdam Society to join its ranks did not represent an attack on the British, from whose society he had resigned. Here we see Winnicott's position between the two women.

In his study of the depressed mother, we naturally ask what he may be revealing about his own condition as the child of such a mother, and the struggle he had probably undergone, and perhaps continued to undergo, to differentiate his own depression, with his own reparation, from that of his mother. Such a question may be particularly applicable at this time with respect to Melanie Klein, from whom he was trying to disengage without depreciating her contributions to psychoanalysis. This was the subtext of his short paper.

Only three weeks after giving his "Reparation" paper to the British Society, he delivered another, much longer work to the medical section of the British Psychological Society titled "Paediatrics and Psychiatry."[11] It is a rambling essay containing the usual bright insights. His remark that "in the first interview it is often possible, and not harmful, to do a sort of analytic treatment in miniature" foreshadows *Therapeutic Consultations in Child Psychiatry*, not to appear until just after his death in 1971. The material in the book was collected over many years. He agrees with Anna Freud about the absence of object relations at birth and the need for a certain measure of psychic organization before this is possible, a point of view that he reiterated to Michael Balint in a 1960 letter. This differentiates him sharply from other so-called object relations theoreticians and allies him, as he says explicitly, with the viewpoint of Anna Freud and her father before her, and the ego psychologists generally. It would seem to arise directly from his experience as a close observer of infants and children in his role as a pediatrician. This kind of experience gave him something in common with Anna Freud, who, though not a medical practitioner, was a longtime overseer and organizer of children's nurseries in Vienna and in London. Such views were not likely to endear him to Melanie Klein.

The belief that babies go through an early stage before they can recognize another person's existence stands in sharp contrast with the belief that the baby can recognize at birth that there is a "mother." Klein's theory emphasizes the savage aggression of fantasies about the mother from the very beginning. Winnicott would one day differentiate between "early" and "deep" states, making the point he stated here that they are not the same. It takes some amount of development before there can be a state that will be called, later in life, deep. In these distinctions Winnicott is laying the foundation for a theory of infant development.

In this long paper Winnicott outlines the ways in which the mother's behavior helps the baby sustain the illusion of having created the satisfying external world, with all the consequences. It was the outcome of his combined experience as pediatrician and analyst, his identity as pediatrician obviously now given a more fully realized standing in the work that he was developing. He observes, "Unreality feelings show as a craving for the new," such as "love of. . . . gangster films, crashing Spitfires and bombers" (this was written just after the war—today we might add horror films, science fiction, and psychedelic experiences). "But the new can also hurt. It would be wise to keep in mind that for the infant the new, whether its taste, texture, sight, or sound, can . . . physically hurt." The urge to dispel feelings of unreality can lead to a craving for sensory input, which may be accompanied by pain. His observation could apply as well to the conceptual world, in which the new idea, the new observation may also inflict pain. Thus the urge to put up a defense against the unanticipated as well as the possibility that one's judgment about the value of the new may be compromised by the craving for it. Major personal errors may occur as a result of the craving for the new.

An exchange of letters with Anna Freud (July 6 and August 7) prior to a mental health conference tells us something of their relationship at the time. His letter, expressing a bit of irritation, emphasizes the Kleinian contribution to the study of aggression, while her reply acknowledges a lack of agreement on the subject, and makes reference to environmental factors, which must have appealed to him, given the direction of his thinking and writing. The role of the environment differentiates the two sharply with respect to Klein. Her emphasis is on the emergence of aggression from the libidinal drives, a continuity with

Freud, as well as the connection to the life and death instincts. His is on the British contribution (i.e., Klein) with guilt, reparation, and depression in the forefront.

Although we do not know the nature of Winnicott's own reaction to Anna Freud's letter, her calm response to his somewhat slightly irritable note is a reminder that he characteristically modifies his hostility in response to such replies. The ability of others to absorb his sharp words without retaliating calls to mind his principle, in the treatment of patients who are regressed to dependency, that the analyst must never retaliate for attacks by the patient. Her calm responses to his excited attacks must have had therapeutic value for him.

On February 11, 1949, Winnicott wrote to her again, this time about her associate Kate Friedlander's illness, expressing his concern that Anna would now have extra responsibility for the training of child therapists. He does not fail to mention his difference with Dr. Friedlander, but goes on: "These things, however, now become utterly unimportant, because of Dr. Friedlander's illness—It would be wonderful if she could be completely restored to health so that we could all start telling each other what we think of each other again and enjoy our disagreements as well as the very considerable overlap in our scientific theory. A lot of psycho-analysts are getting ill at the moment, and I am quite sure that the Society as a whole is overloading itself. I sincerely hope that you will not allow the increased pressure of work due to Dr. Friedlander's illness to get you down."

He is referring here to his own heart attack, without saying so, as his letter to Ernest Jones four days later (February 15) attests: "I have another thing in common with yourself now in that I have recently had a coronary thrombosis, which is fortunately slight in degree." There is later evidence that he attempted to conceal this event, calling the next one, late that same year, his first.

After Dr. Friedlander's death, Anna Freud wrote to him in a letter dated February 16, 1949:

> It was very nice indeed that you wrote to me about Dr. Friedlander and I appreciate it very much. I am very glad that you do such things, like your last letter before the Congress which was a great help to me [she notes nothing objectionable in his underscoring of Klein's contributions], and like your coming to the door here in 1939

to ask whether we were all right [when "we" included her father]. I do not know whether you remember that but I do; no one else had thought of doing it.

Actually, Dr. Friedlander's fate is the very worst. . . . It is rather horrible to see somebody overtaken by death who was so eager to live. Apart from these feelings, it is really a great blow to me and the plans for work. I am trying to substitute for some of the things she had taken over. But every person has a special function and special ways of doing things. In analysis we somehow seem to lose our workers before they have had time to make their full contribution. It is very sad.

Thank you very much for your paper; I have heard a great deal about that address after you gave it; I am very glad to have it [perhaps she is referring to "Mind and Its Relation to the Psyche-Soma"].

Do keep well!

To Michael Fordham on April 26 (two and a half months after his coronary), he wrote: "You may have wondered why we have not written to you and your wife following your very generous offer of the cottage at Jordans. The fact is that we went away very satisfactorily to a Guest House run by a friend of ours in Suffolk, and there we forgot everything including the letters we ought to have written. I am able to do a great deal now without noticing anything wrong. For instance, on Sunday, taking the car from Oxford to the White Horse at Uffington, I was able to enjoy the walk on the downs and all round the old Roman remains at the top and with no signs of heart limitation. From May 1st I shall be gradually coming back into circulation."

On May 18, Winnicott presented his paper "Birth Memories, Birth Trauma, and Anxiety" to the British Society, the fruit of an interest already evident in the early days of his first analysis with James Strachey. He had not yet read Phyllis Greenacre's work on the subject, but would revise the paper in 1954 in the light of it. The two of them established this subject as entirely worthy of patient scientific study rather than speculation. Again, one sees the pediatrician at work here as he describes a dramatic case, and his understanding that the infant, under good conditions, will have rehearsed the birth experience in utero, so that "in the natural process *the birth experience is an exaggerated sample of something already known to the infant.*" He goes on, "In health the infant is prepared before birth for some

environmental impingement, and already has had the experience of a natural return from reacting to a state of not having to react, which is the only
state in which the self can begin to be."

Winnicott's capacity for extrapolation makes for an abrupt shift of
reference that illuminates an intellectual landscape not previously
glimpsed. "Among features typical of the true birth memory is the feeling of being in the grips of something external, so that one is helpless,"
he writes. "Belonging to this feeling of helplessness is the intolerable nature of experiencing something without any knowledge whatever of
when it will end." Thus, "it is for this reason fundamentally that *form in
music* [my italics] is so important. Through form, the end is in sight from
the beginning. One could say that many babies could be helped if one
could only convey to them during prolonged birth that the birth process
would last only a certain limited length of time." Winnicott's own musical abilities and interests must have been the personal background for
this observation. He allows himself the association to music, not, it
would seem, part of his subject. But without the freedom to include it, the
paper would be diminished. Readers are now positioned to wonder,
from their own experiences, about the role of form in music in their lives,
or the role of form generally, and about the experience of the endless, the
unlimited.

Toward the end of the paper he considers "congenital paranoia" as
possibly stemming from a traumatic birth experience: "No paranoid case
can be analysed by enabling the patient simply to relive the birth trauma,
[but]. . . in a percentage of paranoid cases there is this additional fact that
birth was traumatic, and placed a pattern on the infant of expected interference with basic 'being.'" Here he is in another way differentiating himself from Klein's understanding and her technical approach via the
analysis of the paranoid-schizoid position.[12] He emphasizes the etiological role of the environment here, as opposed to the intrapsychic origins in
certain cases of paranoia.

The following day, May 19, he sent a copy of the paper to Riviere,
with various comments, including reference to his heart condition, now
more than three months after his "slight" coronary:

> I am sending you a rather long paper at your request. I was unable to
> get this paper down to proper proportions for reading at the Society,
> and although I chose from it as I went along, I had to leave the last

few pages out, and I should think a fairly chaotic impression was
given. At any rate it was decided to give me another chance in a few
weeks' time, when I shall be able to pull together the threads of what
I did manage to say and finish reading the paper. This should leave
time for a long discussion, and I think that a lot of people are wanting
to make comments.

The paper I am sending you contains a great deal that I did not
read, nor did I intend to read; for instance, the episode of the dream
of my own which I had when I was ill, in which the heart took over
every other function. . . .

At present I am very fit and I am keeping my life down to what I
can do without rush and with nice intervals for sleep and wandering
in the park. This I enjoy. It is something new for me to stay calm and
be not rushed around. Unfortunately this last fortnight has been disturbed a little by the fact that we were suddenly told at Paddington
Green that the hospital was to be closed and reopened as an adult
skin and throat hospital. I had to decide whether to fight for the existence of this hospital, which I consider to be a very valuable one to
the local community, or to let it slip. I found that a great deal depended on me, and in fact I have had to attend about ten committee
meetings dealing with the matter.

The reason why I am mentioning this is because my reading
round the subject of this lecture was seriously interfered with by
these committees, and I was especially sorry not to be able to make a
fuller study of the work of Greenacre, whose three articles on this
subject really contain everything that I want to say.[13] The worst part
of it was that the vital committee meeting at St. Mary's Hospital was
timed for 5 o'clock yesterday, and it was my business to represent the
hospital, the only other possible person, the present chairman, being
away on holiday. The meeting was very tense, and I am glad to say
that we managed to get the matter referred back, which was all that
we could get the committee to do at 7 o'clock. I had come very near
to the end of the somewhat limited capacity of my heart, which is a
maddening thing to have to take into consideration when I feel absolutely well. I was able to rest a little, but at the meeting I was all the
time conscious of being near to the limit of my present capacity. This
spoilt my enjoyment of the evening, and probably made me rather
bad at choosing what to leave out.

However, I believe the Society somehow or other managed to get something out of what I said. I certainly got something out of it myself, and now feel that in a year's time, when I try to write this out as a paper with the co-operation of two patients who are too ill to co-operate at the moment, I shall start from a firmer foundation through having made this first attempt.

We see in this letter an ongoing affection for Mrs. Riviere, against the background of conflict that so often characterizes their correspondence. To some extent he seeks to be "held" by her.

On May 23, 1949, Winnicott wrote to Melanie Klein: "I enclose a copy of what I might send round before the renewed discussion on birth. I also enclose for your amusement a note on a dream of mine. I think you may recognise in it something of your own contribution to the understanding of the human being. This was so important to me at the time that I can almost say that *I could not have lived through the episode without the understanding about depression which you have given us* [my italics]. I have marked the relevant detail with an X. On reading them more carefully, I find the articles by Greenacre more and more interesting, and I am remembering that I said I would hand on to you a volume that I have borrowed from the library." The dream material is not included with the saved letter. His gratitude to Klein is explicitly for his own survival through the depression that probably accompanied or caused, in his view, his thrombosis.

Only one month after his friendly letter to Riviere, he launched an attack. In this precarious era of his life he was battling ambivalence, trying to tame his rage, but succeeding only temporarily. Writing on June 24, he takes her to task for many offenses having to do with a candidate in analysis with him who consulted Riviere for supervision:

[M]'s relation to you was undoubtedly very disturbed and one could say that [M] is only just coming round into being able to be a human being in your presence. You might of course have got round this by taking what [M] had to say and seeing what there was that was good or bad in it and pointing out [M's] deficiencies. Probably the method that you adopted was the better one, by which I think you told [M] what to do and rather expected [M] to put it into practice. This method, however, had to generate difficulties because of the particular quality of [M's] mother's attitude towards [M] in which [M] was dominated and had no other method but to be dominated from early infancy, the mother being a teacher and not being able to stop teaching or to do anything much else.

He goes on to the next complaint: "There was no question of your being asked to do this supervision in order that I should avoid the negative mother transference.[14] You have suggested this in conversation with me, and I want to make it quite clear that this suggestion is not founded on fact. It is important for me that you should understand that this is so because I do not like to be misunderstood, especially by yourself. Dr. Heimann has also expressed a view that I try to avoid the negative transference, especially the transference in which I am the bad mother."

This accusation is important to him because of his work on regression to dependence:

I think the misunderstanding . . . comes from my pointing out that in the treatment of a severely regressed patient the analyst needs to adapt to the regression of the patient. It is easy to feel that I am saying that the analyst has to be a good mother if the patient is a small infant. What I really do say, however, is not that, but it is that in the transference situation when the patient is in the very early stages of infancy the analyst is in the role of the devoted mother. This is quite different from good mother. In fact it antedates a splitting of the good and bad mother. It pays tribute to the fact that at the beginning the infant is absolutely dependent on the devotion of a mother figure, without which the very early stages of emotional development cannot be made.

He goes on with other complaints: first, that the attitude of supervisors must be that the teaching of the candidate is the most important thing, more important than the progress of the case. Second, his opinion of the candidate's ability, in this case, is very high, in comparison to Riviere's. Third, he asserts his authority in judging that the candidate undertook the case in question at the right moment and not too early. And he closes with the usual pleasantries: "With good wishes."

The excellent study of Joan Riviere published by Athol Hughes[15] includes a discussion of her mother's diary of her earliest life: "It would seem that Joan Riviere could have felt that she, like her mother, assumed a mask of maternity. One may surmise that since, as recorded in her mother's diary, her infantile distress was denied or ignored, she found infantile distress hard to bear in her own child. This could be particularly the case since Diana [her daughter] was only a year or two old at a time of Joan's breakdown after her father's death." The exchange with Winnicott concerned dependency and early neediness in a patient, and may well have evoked old themes in Riviere's life.

Riviere's reply of June 26, 1949, begins: "I am very sorry that you have so much feeling about the matter of [M] in relation to me. I can only tell you that I accept the situation quite readily as it is, and that all along I have not had any noticeable emotions about [M], or you, or anything that has happened.[16] On receiving your letter *now*, I am a little disturbed: as if *the child* [my italics] might be succeeding in making a breach between her father and mother, and for her sake I do suggest you might be careful not to play into that phantasy." Of the "serious misunderstandings" she says, first, that the idea that he tries to avoid the negative mother transference never crossed her mind: "My method anyhow in supervision is not to concern myself with the candidate's emotional reactions, leaving them to the analyst, unless they become very manifest and one has to take notice in some way." Then, "as for having brilliant intellectual capacity, the fact remains that [M] has not used it over [the] work with [the] patient." She goes on: "Another point which impressed me badly (though I expressly did *not* mention it in my report) was [M's] serious slackness about keeping notes. No supervisor can do anything if the candidate does not keep sufficient notes, and the Training Committee recognises this necessity fully. The first few weeks [M] really had nothing; a casual excuse about having no time was almost all [M] brought. I had to point out that that system made supervision useless. Even now [M] obviously misses out some days in [the] notes, but I do not comment on it. M was also hardly ever on time, and is the only student in supervision I have had who has constantly been late."

She continues: "Your letter practically begins with a criticism of my methods of supervision and with the suggestion that I am so inhuman that '[M] can't be a human being in my presence.' This is then justified by the statement that I never listen to what [M] has to say and see what is good or bad in it, and then point out . . . deficiencies. Don't you think you might reflect here that this description of what I do can only come from one source, namely, from the child [it]self (a severely regressed patient, you say), who apparently admits having a negative mother-transference, and yet seems to have succeeded in putting many of [the patient's] own ideas about the mother into the father and stirred him up against the mother on [the patient's] behalf?"

Then, at the end: "And I shall be still more sorry, after all I have said here, if you still have to go on being so angry with me because I don't think the child is as wonderful as you want me to."[17]

He seems to be overidentified with his patient, who, unlike most candidates in psychoanalysis, requires an experience of regression to dependence, which in turn demands protracted devoted adaptation on the part of the analyst. This generates in Winnicott the sense of a contrast between his own views and methods and those of his former analyst, who is seen as cold and critical and quite unadapted to the candidate's supervisory needs. The repeated use of "the child" hints at the patronizing idea that summarizes the adult candidate in terms of surviving childish wishes and manipulations. Winnicott was up against this sort of an attitude in the Kleinian group and, fighting as he was for a point of view that was new and unaccepted, he was also fighting for recognition of his own needs by his former analyst. It is not incidental that at the same time he was fighting for his life. And, side by side with immense productivity, fighting off despair.

Interposed among Winnicotts's letters to and from Riviere is another that bears on the topic of dependency. On June 30 he wrote to a colleague to discuss the need for a general practitioner on the National Health Service for a patient addicted to "Secconal."[18] The cost of this medication in the amounts being taken could not be borne by the patient: "It will be difficult to explain every detail to a visiting doctor, and I am hoping that he and yourself will let me take full responsibility for the drug situation. The matter of drug addiction is not the important thing at the present time in this case. It is more important that with the aid of a certain amount of Secconal the patient is able to make use of me, whereas without it there are very great inherent difficulties."

He goes on: "While [the patient] is working with me in the way she is working at present, I am able to let her be the judge as to how much she takes, that is to say, I am able to take whatever risk there is in regard to this. The stakes are rather high in any case because the illness includes the impulse to suicide, and if we succeed in getting behind this illness we shall also get behind the need for drugs." The subject of dependency preoccupied Winnicott—its various manifestations in his patients, his own, made acute by his present physical limitations, and in his role as the person on whom others needed to depend.

He also continued his correspondence with Riviere in the matter of "M," writing on July 4, 1949: "It was good of you to write at length in reply to my letter. . . . I am trying very hard to take in and make use of the help which you give in your letter. The fact that I do not agree with some of the assumptions does not really seem to matter."

Only a month before he was describing to her how limited he was by his heart condition, and, to Melanie Klein, how he could not have survived without the understanding of depression which he learned from her. Riviere took his letter at face value and responded without reference to his state of mind. She comes across as cool to cold, forbiddingly objective, and only slightly empathic, until she reveals, toward the end, how upset she is that he is angry with her. It may be that this little bit made visible in the inadvertent way that the ending of the letter allowed got through to him and led to the much softer tone in his reply. In the letter that initiated the exchange, he was defending his analysand full-throttle, stepping out from behind the anonymity of the consulting room and demonstrating what he would call "management"[19] of a regressed person who could not advance under orthodox psychoanalytic conditions. He was defending her in his role as a senior person defending a junior one.

This cold-blooded attitude as experienced in his own analysis (he uses the phrase "cold-blooded" in a favorable way when speaking of Strachey's work with him in a letter of July 17, 1952, to Ernest Jones) may be what underlay both his revised idea of what a regressed patient required and how his claim that Riviere's attitude was disturbing to his own regressed patient. This exchange may also help us understand his procrastination over contributing to a book in honor of Melanie Klein, which was being edited by Riviere. His use of the word "help" in his reply to Riviere may be sarcastic, but is more likely an attempt to acknowledge that this woman to whom he had looked for support was actually trying to help. In the light of her effort to disabuse him of some of the notions behind his accusations against her, this may be an appropriate word.

The letter on behalf of his addicted patient reveals another aspect of his thinking and his state of mind at this time, as he strained to find conditions under which she might go on getting treatment and survive. He was fighting for two patients in this period, defending them with strenuous action while, simultaneously, his own survival was in question. All of this was taking place in late 1949, the aftermath of his father's death and with the imminent prospect of a definitive separation from his wife of twenty-six years and the emergence into view of his hidden six-year relationship to Clare Britton.

The paper "Mind and Its Relation to the Psyche-Soma," given before the medical section of the British Psycho-Analytic Society, must have followed both his heart attack and his separation from Alice. It is a study that takes off from Ernest Jones's comment that the mind does not exist as an entity. Winnicott's discussion is a reexamination of beginnings. "The mental activity of the infant turns a *good-enough* environment into a perfect environment, that is to say, turns relative failure of adaptation into adaptive success. What releases the mother from her need to be near-perfect is the infant's understanding." And "in the development of every individual, the mind has a root, perhaps its most important root, in the need of the individual, at the core of the self, for a perfect environment." Elaborating toward pathology, he writes: "One might ask what happens if the strain that is put on mental functioning organized in defence against a tantalizing early environment is greater and greater? One would expect confusional states, and (in the extreme) mental defect of the kind that is not dependent on brain-tissue deficiency. As a more common result of the lesser degrees of tantalizing infant care in the earliest stages we find *mental functioning becoming a thing in itself*, practically replacing the good mother and making her unnecessary. Clinically," he asserts, "this can go along with dependence on the actual mother and a false personal growth on a compliance basis. This is a most uncomfortable state of affairs, especially because the psyche of the individual gets 'seduced' away into this mind from the intimate relationship which the psyche originally had with the soma. The result is a mind-psyche, which is pathological."

Environmental interferences during the birth process, he tells us, are memorized pending future disposition "until the individual is able to make them his own after having experienced libidinous and especially aggressive drives, which can be projected. In this way, and it is essentially a false way, the individual gets to feel responsible for the bad environment for which in fact he was not responsible and which he could (if he knew) justly blame on the world because it disturbed the continuity of his innate developmental processes before the psyche-soma had become sufficiently well organized to hate or to love. Instead of hating these environmental failures the individual becomes disorganized by them because the process existed prior to hating."

Such a conceptualization sheds light on the dilemmas of patients who center responsibility on themselves for circumstances that clearly derive from parents and others. Such a willingness to shoulder responsibility may be greatly appealing because of the contribution of psychoanalysis toward demonstrating that we have so much more control over our destiny than we had thought. It would seem obvious by now, however, that there is no escape from differentiating between those elements over which we had no control and those over which we did. Frequent reference to these two categories, and the complementary series (Freud's term) that lies between, is an indispensable part of any analysis that hopes to generate respect for real human circumstances.

This was the beginning of a line of thinking that would result, in 1963, in Winnicott's posthumously published paper, "Fear of Breakdown" (1974). In the case of a woman with a severe birth trauma who regressed in analysis toward recovering an experience of annihilation, there was a gap in the continuity of her being which she needed to reach. He speaks of having held this patient during a "temporary phase in which there was no mind and no mental functioning." He would eventually write that where there is early trauma for which there is an inadequate psychic organization with which to experience it, the patient will fear the breakdown for which he or she yearns, in order to encompass the trauma and have the opportunity of integrating its results into the total being.

Again, still recovering from a heart attack and in the midst of a radical rearrangement of his private life, he gave a paper in January 1950, "Aggression in Relation to Emotional Development," in a symposium with Anna Freud at the Royal Society of Medicine's psychiatry section. This paper was substantially enlarged for publication by the addition of two talks given to private groups in 1954 and 1955. It is a difficult, dense, theoretical paper without clinical illustrations. At origin, according to Winnicott, aggressiveness is almost synonymous with activity; it is a matter of part-function. That is to say that there is no separate instinct of aggression. He dwells on the "stage of concern," his revision of Klein's "depressive position,"[20] as a central consideration in the evolution of aggression, the infant's capacity to recognize that his aggressive urges are directed at the same person (the "object mother") who provides a "holding environment" (the "environment mother"), which leads to guilt, a great achievement, and the urge for reparation. "Frustration," he writes, "acts as a seduction away from guilt and fosters a defence mechanism, namely, the direction of love and hate along separate lines. If this splitting of objects into good and bad takes place, there is an easing of guilt feeling; but in payment the love loses some of its valuable aggressive component, and the hate becomes the more disruptive."

Speaking of children who withdraw into introversion and then return to the world, as it were, he notes that they regularly become aggressive and require special sensitivity to avoid a return to the introverted state. As a corollary he points out, "An individual is in a sensitive state on coming round after a period of concentration on a personal task." This comment resonates with his later remark to Klein about the sensitive state of people who read papers to the society, and their special requirements at that time. He represents them in his plea for a sign of appreciation from Klein, especially since he did not receive such a sign in either of his two analyses. Obviously he raised the subject of approbation in that 1952 letter because he was in need of it.

In July 1950 the hospitalized patient who was addicted to Seconal committed suicide. She had become one of those "special patients" discussed some years later in Thomas Main's famous paper "The Ailment." About that patient, Margaret Little writes: "He told me of one patient who for many months had threatened suicide seriously enough for him to arrange hospitalization. The suicide happened, unnecessarily and for the wrong reason as he felt, because his instructions had been ignored. He had gone through a long period of anxiety before it, and guilt because he hated the patient for making him suffer. He wanted to scream, 'For God's sake, get on and *do* it.'[21] When it did happen, there were fresh guilt and helplessness (he should have been able to prevent it), fury with those who had failed to carry out his instructions, and finally a deep sense of loss of someone about whom he cared intensely and in whom he had invested so much feeling." This is of interest when juxtaposed with Milner's account of Winnicott's failure to prevent her patient "Susan" from having ECT, and raises the subject of his hate for the dependent patient, in glaring contrast to his consummate adaptation to patients' need. He refers, in "Hate in the Countertransference" to the analyst's "hate and fear" of his patients. Although I cannot cite a reference, I have been told that Winnicott once spoke of his hatred of women.

On July 18 one of the nurses who had cared for his patient wrote him an emotional letter about her own sense of loss, and gave him her support: "I shall always be very pleased to work with you at any time should you feel I might be able to help any of your patients. It seems so tragic to me that everything has ended this way, after all you have done. What a lot there is to know, and so much to learn."

He replied: "I think we shall use [the patient's] influence to gather together something that will be of value to psychiatric nursing, but it will take time and first of all we all have to recover from the loss."

On July 20, Michael Balint[22] wrote to Winnicott about contributing a paper, with incidental remarks about the suicide: "Using our files I telephoned up a number of people, got a lot of vague promises but not one certain paper. Thus, I am afraid you will have to be the first victim of the season. Could you let me have the title of your paper, and will October 4 be a possible date for you? I have heard the news about the suicide of your patient. I am very sorry for it as I know how much honest and painstaking work you put into this analysis. Such events raise the great problem of the limits of analysability, of which we have so many phantasies and so little knowledge." The next day, Winnicott responded: "Thank you for your letter. October 4th is all right for me and the title of my paper is 'Transition Phenomena; a study of neutral territory between the subjective and the objective in terms of the toys of infants.'"

Some measure of the toll his patient's suicide took on him may be gauged from the fact that a little over a month later (around August 30) he suffered yet another coronary, his third at least.[23] Melanie Klein wrote on September 14: "My dear Donald, I was very grieved to hear about your illness. It is a comfort to know that the attack was a mild one and that you are being well cared for. I do hope that you will not make any efforts to return to work earlier than you should. Needless to say—this would not only possibly harm you but not even pay. So please be careful and *patient!* It is a great shame that your plans are upset and that we shall not have you functioning as training secretary at present,—but that will only be temporary! There seems an abundance of applicants—I am seeing the second one this week." She closes "Love and very best wishes." Winnicott's letter to Hannah Henry (see chapter 7) put into his own words his situation at the time: the end of his first marriage and the recent heart attack.

Klein remained friendly and sent an invitation in April 1951 to a little gathering of people, including Marion Milner and Klein's children. He could not accept because he was going to be out of London.

To Strachey he wrote on May 1:

> You may have seen from the notices sent round that I am due to give a paper on 30th May on what I am calling "Transition Objects." Actually I am trying to get some of this written before Whitsun so that it can be circulated. The full paper would be rather a long one.
>
> I am writing to you because I am wondering whether you would agree to read through what I have roughly made of this paper already and let me come and discuss it with you. I am particularly keen to pick up the ordinary psychoanalytic theory in the theoretical section of the paper enough to make what I think is my contribution acceptable.
>
> You will be relieved to hear that I have done quite a bit of psychoanalytic reading,[24] thanks to having been ill twice; however, it is still true to say that if I were to take a year off and do nothing but read, I would be in a better position for writing papers.
>
> I will be ringing you up about this. . . . I know that you will tell me if you would rather not burden yourself with this.

The concept of the transitional object (and the transitional phenomenon, not an object) is a way of understanding the overlap between the needs of the infant and the devotion of the mother through the mother's provision of an object (such as a soft piece of blanket or a stuffed animal) or a bit of behavior (such as a little bedtime tune or ritual). The baby, according to Winnicott, is positioned to feel that he or she has created the thing provided, and he makes a point of emphasizing that the paradox must not be resolved. The baby must never be asked, "Did you find that or did you invent it?" From this experiential overlap, which fosters the omnipotence in the child that once characterized its in utero life, develops the whole of cultural experience. Much more derives from this extraordinary idea, the concept of potential space, and Winnicott gave much of his subsequent career to exploring its implications.

The action of his mind had led from one bright, original, or frankly stunning observation to the next and the next, with this paper emerging to dazzle and then continue to dazzle people of all persuasions almost fifty years later. I heard Robert Stoller in the 1970s tell an audience at the Los Angeles Psychoanalytic Society and Institute that it was time to declare a moratorium on the use of the concept of the transitional object as applied to phenomena other than those to which Winnicott originally applied it.[25] I do not believe that I have ever heard a comparable statement about anyone else's theory. Such, however, is the candlepower of the beam that emanates from that paper that someone like Stoller, and others as well, have felt compelled to put filters in front of it. The concept seems to be too applicable to too many phenomena.

It does not seem to have been Winnicott's habit to consult Strachey regularly about his papers, so he probably felt that this one needed special attention, or perhaps special support from the man who had taught him psychoanalysis in the first place. Strachey having had an analysis with Freud, and having been Freud's translator, could direct him to the relevant literature by Freud. Or perhaps he knew that this was destined to be a particularly important contribution. Winnicott's inhibition about reading Freud was his own way of putting a filter in front of a too intense beam. It is interesting that even with this inhibition, or perhaps as a natural accompaniment to it, Winnicott never wavered from his acknowledgement that Freud was the founder and the undeniable progenitor of Winnicott himself and all other analysts. He never succumbed to either petty or grand criticisms of Freud, though he did discuss Freud's limitations in the psychology of infancy and babyhood. He said on more than one occasion that Freud provided psychoanalysts with a method and that it was up to them to use that method to extend his findings. One could develop a case for this Freudian ambivalence (inhibition versus respect) as a version of ambivalence toward his natural father, for which there is much evidence, most spectacularly in the nearly total scotoma for fathers in his vast body of work about child development.

The paper "Transitional Objects and Transitional Phenomena," which had been postponed twice because of Winnicott's health, was finally delivered on May 30, 1951. Thereafter he developed it further, as he considered whether it would be finished "in time" for the Klein book which Joan Riviere was editing. The period of gestation of this paper appears to have been one of decisive change leading to his 1952 letter to Klein and his decision to withhold his paper from the book.

In a letter of July 25, 1951, to Willi Hoffer, Winnicott complains that Freud's study in the house in Maresfield Gardens which he occupied with his daughter during his last months in England was not a good location for seminars because it inhibited the candidates from criticizing Freud's work. This objection grew out of his abiding and extremely personal concern with freedom of expression.

To Ernest Jones, at the end of November, he wrote about various matters and concludes: "My private affairs develop steadily and I am rather expecting to be re-married before the end of the year." This is the first letter with his new address on it. He and Clare were married on December 28, 1951.[26] This marriage brought a seven-year romance to fruition.

When the war ended, Clare had continued to work with children in Oxfordshire. After that she helped returning British prisoners of war. The death of a foster child generated a good deal of public awareness of the plight of children in the form of the Curtis Report, and resulted in a law, the Children's Act of 1948, which led to an emphasis on training social workers in the care of children. Clare was appointed to head up the child care course at the LSE, to which she devoted her energies until 1958. In 1948 she started an analysis with Clifford Scott, Melanie Klein's first candidate. She found him not very Kleinian. At the time of their 1951 marriage, therefore, Clare was in analysis and was very much at the forefront of social worker training at the LSE.

Klein wrote in January: "My dear Donald, I am sending you my heartfelt good wishes on the occasion of your marriage. I wish you much happiness in your married life and in your new home and good health. May I add that I also wish you should become very interested in keeping well and therefore avoid doing too much? Please give my best wishes to your wife. With love, Yours, Melanie."

Winnicott had found his way through a jungle of personal difficulties to this moment of renewal and was generating a series of highly original psychoanalytic ideas. One might expect a period of calm, of recuperation perhaps, as he settled into his new marriage and new home and office. But this turned out not to be the case. Perhaps he felt *empowered* by his newly consolidated domestic situation as well as the reception beginning to be accorded to his paper on transitional objects. In the process of reading his correspondence, we get a sense of the storms raging within his breast, and of the seriousness with which he took the progress of psychoanalysis, but critical letters, as we have seen, were nothing new for him. He wrote first to Hanna Segal, a follower of Melanie Klein, and then to Ilse Hellman, an associate of Anna Freud. In the first instance, his scathing attack on Segal's know-it-all attitude was met with a calm response, leading to a peaceful outcome. His attack was undoubtedly part of his response to seeing his ideas ignored by the Kleinians. In the second, a less critical statement about Hellman's failure to reveal how she worked in the presentation of a membership paper, became a complicated matter involving Anna Freud, whom Winnicott had to visit hat in hand before matters could be set to rest.

The overall impression is of a man defending his views but with a special vehemence that comes close to outright provocation, or even of a man who is actively looking for trouble. To Segal he wrote on February 21, 1952:

What I am afraid of is that, unless somebody tells you, you will never know that the way you started off talking last night gives the impression that you are unbearably conceited. I know perfectly well that you are capable of being as humble as anyone else at the right moment, but I think you cannot have any idea how much antagonism you rouse against yourself when you get up at a meeting and say you are amazed to find that your colleagues (junior of course) have shown that they are capable of doing a good piece of analysis and reporting their findings in English which can be understood etc. etc. I do think that just at times for a few minutes you are tremendously cocksure of yourself, and if you happen to be speaking just then it shows. Perhaps what I am afraid of is that there is a terrible disillusionment inherent in all this and I would much rather you knew about it before you come to it. The fact is that you are capable of failing just as other analysts are, because there is so much that we do not yet know. When you talk at these moments of cocksureness you give no indication whatever that you believe that there could be anything that you do not understand.

There are several reasons why I take the trouble to write a letter of this kind. One is because I have a genuine concern for you, having been of some use to you at an early stage when you were trying to get to London from Edinburgh. I saw you trying to be a house surgeon at Paddington Green and there I think you will agree that you were not a great success, but that does not matter because you never claimed to be any good at surgery and we knew perfectly well that you were using the job as a stepping-stone to London and to Melanie Klein.

With the very greatest pleasure I have watched you develop in analysis and I know of no analysis which has been more successful in producing a mature from an immature personality.

With all this in mind naturally I am concerned that you shall not spoil it all by getting into some sort of ugly state in which you are sitting perched up on top of a Mount Everest of an internalised good breast.

There is another reason why I am writing this letter and that is that I am very genuinely concerned with Melanie Klein's contribution to psycho-analysis. This contribution of hers is steadily being made unacceptable because of the propaganda indulged in at every meeting, by Dr. Heimann and yourself in particular. There is a saying that good wine needs no bush. In a similar way the good in Melanie's contribution need not be pushed forward at Scientific Meetings. It can be expressed and discussed. At present it is seldom discussed because it is put forward aggressively and then defended in a way which can only be called paranoid. In other words, Dr. Glover's efforts are at last bearing fruit and the Kleinian psychology is organising itself into something which the Klein disciples will preach until it is hated. . . .

What is so strange about all this is that Melanie herself is not, as far as I can tell, a bit like this herself. I often feel that she must be very severely hurt by the actions of her friends just as she is hurt by those who refuse to see the value of her contributions. It is notorious that it is more galling to be hurt by one's friends. . . .

I sincerely believe that you yourself will want to go into this matter in order to try to see whether what I say is true, which is that Melanie's contributions are being made unacceptable to the Society by the way that about six or eight persons are presenting them in a propagandist way.

Dr. Segal replied: "Thank you very much for your letter. I must say I felt pretty hurt by some [of] it, but I can appreciate the spirit in which it was written and the trouble you took in writing it. It seems to me however that the points you make are so grave that they cannot be properly done justice to by letters especially that I am a very bad correspondent. Would it be terrible for you to spend some time [for]. . . a short discussion? I should certainly very much appreciate that. P. S. If you do have some time to talk about your letter, would you think it a good idea to have Heimann as well, as many of the points seem to refer to her?"

He wrote back to Segal on the twenty-seventh: "After a letter like the one I wrote to you and which you have taken in the spirit in which it was intended, for which I am grateful, I would naturally do all I could to make it possible for us to have a talk. I would very much like it if Dr. Heimann could be there at the same time."

He continued to write papers such as "Psychoses and Child Care," which was given to the psychiatry section of the Royal Society of Medicine in March 1952. It is essentially a review of previously articulated material, this time with the emphasis on hidden instances of childhood psychosis effectively cured within the family. A curious aspect of this paper is a comment Winnicott makes about "how a tendency for a basic split in the environment-individual set-up can start through failure of active adaptation on the part of the environment at the beginning," and that "in the extreme case of splitting the secret inner life has very little in it derived from external reality. It is truly incommunicable." This is of interest in view of his 1963 comment about the True Self as always existing incommunicado. His remarks in 1952 would indicate that the secret inner life is incommunicable as the result of pathogenic circumstances and not a normal condition. The two views may be partially reconciled by noting that the True Self, while always incommunicado, does express itself through the spontaneous gesture ("the True Self in action") while the split-off secret inner life cannot do so. The difference here is that under circumstances of environmental impingement, the True Self is driven deeper within, out of touch with the external world, whereas where there is good-enough environmental care, it is willing to express itself on occasion.

Elaborating, he goes on to write that "where there is a high degree of the tendency to split at this early stage, the individual is in danger of being seduced into a false life, and the instincts then come in on the side of the seducing environment. . . . A successful seduction of this kind may produce a False Self that seems satisfactory." One would tend to think of the instincts, native to physical being, as unlikely to ally themselves with the seducing environment that enforces splits in the self. It seems reasonable to think that his mother's intolerance of his states of excitement might have tended to alienate him from his own instinctual life.

In the critical spirit that characterizes his letter to Hanna Segal, he next (on March 20) turned toward one of Anna Freud's close associates, Ilse Hellman. He criticized the paper she gave as part of her application for membership in the British Society for failing to reveal her working methods. It seemed to him that much of the patient's difficulties were not brought into the transference, where they could be analyzed. It was a long letter ending with a declaration of "full support" for her membership. She replied that she was surprised at his support, writing, "I am sorry to have caused you this disappointment; it must be due to the fact that you expected me to work on lines which I have in fact never followed."

Out of this came a meeting with Anna Freud as he sought to mend the damage done. Writing to a colleague, W. H. Gillespie, on March 28, he says that "the unwisdom of my method is clear by the fact that it made Miss Freud feel that the letter was part of a general attack, whereas really it was something that arises out of the friendship which I feel in my relationship to Miss Hellman. I had no idea that she would show it round, and I think she herself is sorry about it, but I must take the blame for this because undoubtedly the letter had undesirable qualities mixed in with the attempt to be honest. In my opinion the latter is so important that the rest can be dealt with quite easily."

To Willi Hoffer on April 4 he said, "I want to write you about two things":

> The first is I want to thank you myself, although I know others have done so, for the very great trouble you took over the Melanie Klein number of the Journal. My regret at not having an article in it is very great, but I have been rather busy re-arranging my private life, which I thought was more important. If the number comes out in book form I hope to have my little bit in it. In any case I feel that the number as it stands is an extremely good birthday present for Melanie, and as I am fond of her as well as deeply appreciating her work I am glad.
>
> I would like also to write a word about what you said at the meeting, partly to agree and partly not. I do agree that Associate

Members who are reading membership papers are in a state in which they cannot easily stand criticism. I say this in spite of the fact that I recently wrote a letter which caused a good deal of trouble. If you have heard of this letter I hope you have also heard that I have expressed very deep grief that it was written as it was a thoroughly bad letter. It hurt the reader of the paper but it also hurt me because it obscured the point that I was trying to make which was that I thought the paper was too tidy, not giving away enough of the analyst's way of carrying on. . . .

What I really want to say is this, that there is a great deal to be said for giving the reader of a membership paper every encouragement that can be given. I would not feel, however, that we should sterilise our discussions by feeling unable to use such papers for argument especially as a high proportion of the scientific papers must be membership papers. I well remember my own, which was not a very good one ["The Manic Defence," given in 1936]; I remember the discussion became a sort of wrangle between factions which I had no notion of and I just sat back bewildered, quite unable to take part. I cannot remember it having been very traumatic, however. I think I took it as an interesting way into the Society which was evidently not as much in agreement with itself as I had thought.

You may remember some membership papers have been brutally treated. For instance, Rickman's attack on Mrs. Warburg was quite open; he just said he hated her and the paper and that it was an insult to the Society that the paper was read. I think that there was not much protection of Mrs. Warburg going on that evening. I remember trying to protect her myself without any success, because I could not think of anything to say.

I would like to suggest that the ability of a reader of a membership paper to stand getting involved in the disagreements in the Society should be one of the many tests of maturity which we require of an Associate Member when electing to membership. I would personally say that the absence of a direct attack on Anderson when he read a really irritating paper was just as harmful to the internal politics of the Society as the open criticism which you felt was made on [Augusta] Bonnard by Melanie Klein when she said that there were things that are already well known which could have been used to do with persecutory anxiety etc. etc.

Before I finish this rather long letter I want to make quite sure that you understand that I am trying to write something within the framework of friendship. I have to be on my guard just at the moment because apparently in writing letters I can so easily seem to be quite different from what I feel.

On May 9, 1952, Winnicott wrote to Klein about reviewing Adrian Stokes's book *Smooth and Rough*,[27] as she had wished him to do. But he said, "a review which satisfies the editor has already been received by Hoffer; probably you know about this, and it is by Masud Khan." Nevertheless, "if I find that I think I can write a review of some interest I will write one and offer it to Hoffer who I think will accept it as a second comment to be published alongside that of Masud Khan."

He did not actually like the book, and eventually attacked it privately. Nevertheless, he wanted to please Klein, yet at the same time did not want to hurt Khan's feelings by displacing him. So he offered a compromise: two reviews, by Khan and himself. Here we see him in a reflective state of mind about his loyalties.

In 1953, with Masud Khan in analysis with him, Winnicott and Khan would write a joint book review,[28] the only instance of collaborative writing in his career except for papers with Clare Britton. Khan wrote most of it. By the time the review appeared, Khan had been rejected for membership in the society on his first try, though Winnicott had spoken in his favor. His letter in support of his candidate "M" in the correspondence with Joan Riviere was another attempt to defend one of his analysands. His behavior on these occasions may well reflect his views on what certain patients required for therapeutic purposes. Or it may simply reflect Winnicott's identification with his rejected candidates and thus a particular difficulty in adhering to the usual properties of a psychoanalyst's behavior.

Ernest Jones wrote him a note on July 17, prompting a response on the twenty-second:

I was very grateful to you for reading and commenting on my lecture "What is Psycho-Analysis?" It is strange how a stupid thing like "not very voluminous" creeps in. It might interest you to know the explanation for this. In 10 years' analysis Strachey made practically no mistakes and he adhered to a classical technique in a cold-blooded way for which I have always been grateful. He did, however, say two or three things that were not interpretations at a time when interpretation was needed. Each one of these has bothered me and at some time or other have come out in an unexpected way. One day, instead of making the interpretation which I can now easily see for myself, about my inhibitions in regard to the reading of Freud, he took up the attitude of trying to persuade me to make the effort and he used the words: "after all the part that you need to read is not very voluminous." I am very angry indeed that I have allowed this to come in and I am getting these words crossed out in all the copies that I am sending round.

I am not so ashamed about saying that Shakespeare knew as much as a psycho-analyst although I agree that the word "knew" is wrong, at any rate it is a point of interest for discussion and not a mistake like the other.[29]

From Joan Riviere on September 14:

I meant to write to you while I was away about the article you sent me,[30] but found I had inadvertently omitted to take it with me! Which I am sure you will forgive!

I thought it was a good article to the boys of St. Pauls in its way—in *your* way, I really mean. And I thought it better and more clearly put together than yours have sometimes been. It has one invariable feature, however, which to my mind is always a pity: your emphasis is either apologetic, or truculent, sometimes both at once— on having your *own* angle spoils the perspective, & is irrelevant + unnecessary. (Everybody has their own angle + one can see quick enough what it is as a rule.)

A less personal point is the question: Did the paper tell the boys enough of what *they* want to know about PsaA? I am inclined to feel that not to mention sex to that audience amounts to shirking it + would be felt as such by them. (I suppose they were the top form.) It is like a big piece of fluff—possibly it would come off—I can't tell.

The main idea, that PsA is a science does impress me as a very good one + I think you have worked it out well. It might be a bit easier for people to grasp your meaning if you were to connect the "unconscious" rather more clearly + specifically with emotions + feelings (i.e. which have to be suppressed). As you refer to the unconscious (part of the personality, etc.) it sounds something static, + perhaps

dead, a "cause of what is unhealthy in us" + so on. You don't mention love + hate at all, but speak of instinctual drives, which must be
nearly Greek to them.

　　I don't know Zilboorg's books. Should I know them?

In the month prior to his long letter to Klein, foretastes of his decision appear. First, on October 17, 1952:

> Dear Melanie, This letter is only about one small detail; you may
> have wondered why I have done nothing about Adrian Stokes' book
> 'Smooth and Rough.' This is not because I neglected it after you
> asked me to read it and possibly to write a note on it. The fact is that I
> do not consider it to be a good book. . . .
>
> 　　You may be interested to know that I am slowly and in my own
> way working at a simplification of the Transitional Objects paper just
> in case it should be ready in time for inclusion in your Birthday Book.
> I think Marion Milner will be asking you whether this would prove a
> suitable discussion for one of your seminars. I should very much like
> to hear the ideas I have put forward discussed by that group.

On the same date he wrote to Roger Money-Kyrle, an adherent of
Klein's views: "In regard to the Klein Birthday Book, I think you know
that I would very much like to have something in it; this depends entirely
on myself and I am working at a version of the Transitional Object paper
although I know that by the time it is ready it may be too late for you to
include it. I would like you and Dr. Heimann to know, however, that this
is going on in a slow sort of way, as fast as real growth can allow it to go
and no faster." Here he is taking a stand in favor of a rate of personal
growth over and above any external demand, in the form of a deadline for
contributing to the Klein birthday book. On this occasion, he was not
going to pay homage to this mother figure or to subsume his own uniqueness in a celebration of hers. Matters came to a head one month later.

　　The presentation that gave rise to his 1952 letter to Klein was "Anxiety Associated with Insecurity," a very short paper on a subject prompted
by a paper by Charles Rycroft on a case of vertigo. In a succinct way Winnicott addresses the results of the failure of child care in very early stages:
"Three main types of anxiety resulting from failure in technique of child
care are: unintegration, becoming a feeling of disintegration; lack of rela-

tionship of psyche to soma, becoming a sense of depersonalization; also the feeling that the centre of gravity of consciousness transfers from the kernel to the shell, from the individual to the care, the technique." He refers to his comment ten years before, for which he became famous that, that "there is no such thing as a baby," and, bringing it up to date, writes that "before object relationships the state of affairs is this: that the unit is not the individual, the unit is an environment-individual set-up. The centre of gravity of the being does not start off in the individual." The technique of child care—"technique" in this context being a word he attributes to Anna Freud—sets the stage for the emergence of the individual as a unit. The paper ends with an emphasis on a kind of automatic, unnoticed failure of development, a catastrophe: "It is normal for the infant to feel anxiety if there is a failure of infant-care technique. An infant at the very beginning, however, would go into an unintegrated state, or lose contact with the body, or shift over to being the socket instead of the content, *without pain*. . . . There is a state of affairs in which the fear is of a madness, that is to say a fear of a *lack of anxiety at regression* to an unintegrated state, to absence of a sense of living in the body, etc. The fear is that there will be no anxiety, that is to say, that there will be a regression, from which there may be no return." He goes on: "The analysis of the hysteric (popular term) is the analysis of the madness that is feared but is not reached without the provision of a new example of infant care, better infant care in the analysis than was provided at the time of the patient's infancy. But, please note, the analysis does and must get to the madness, although the diagnosis remains neurosis, not psychosis."

With this statement about the role of the environment, and the incidental mention of Anna Freud, he has enunciated a position much at odds with Klein's strenuous emphasis on the intrapsychic from the inception of life, and it is not difficult to think that she would have taken exception, to the extent that she had previously held out some hope that Winnicott was still, in some way, a Kleinian. One may also guess that, knowing the extent of their differences, Winnicott would have been especially sensitive to signs of rejection from this teacher and mother figure from whom he was continuing to diverge so widely. "Dear Melanie," he wrote, on November 17, 1952:

> I want to write to you about last Friday evening's meeting in order to
> try to turn it into something constructive.

The first thing I want to say is that I can see how annoying it is that when something develops in me out of my own growth and out of my analytic experience I want to put it in my own language. This is annoying because I suppose everyone wants to do the same thing, and in a scientific society one of our aims is to find a common language. This language must, however, be kept alive as there is nothing worse than a dead language.

I said that what I am doing is annoying, but I do also think that it has its good side. Firstly, there are not very many creative people in the Society having ideas that are personal and original. I think that anyone who has ideas is really welcome and I always do feel in the Society that I am tolerated because I have ideas even although my method is an annoying one.

Secondly, I feel that corresponding to my wish to say things my way there is something from your end, namely a need to have everything that is new restated in your own terms.

What I was wanting on Friday undoubtedly was that there should be some move from your direction towards the gesture that I make in this paper. It is a creative gesture and I cannot make any relationship through this gesture except if someone come to meet it. I think that I was wanting something which I have no right to expect from your group, and it is really of the nature of a therapeutic act, something which I could not get in either of my two long analyses, although I got so much else. There is no doubt that my criticism of Mrs. Riviere was not only a straightforward criticism based on objective observation but also it was coloured by the fact that it was just exactly here that her analysis failed with me.

I personally think that it is very important that your work should be restated by people discovering in their own way and presenting what they discover in their own language. It is only in this way that the language will be kept alive. If you make the stipulation that in the future only your language shall be used for the statement of other people's discoveries then the language becomes a dead language, as it has already become in the Society. You would be surprised at the sighs and groans that accompany every restatement of the internal object cliches by what I am going to call Kleinians. Your own statements are of course in quite a different category as the work is your own personal work and everyone is pleased that you have your own way of stating it. The worst example, perhaps, was Anderson's paper in which he simply bandied about a lot of that which has now come to be known as Kleinian stuff without giving any impression of having an appreciation of the process personal to the patient. One felt that if he were growing a daffodil he would think that he was making the daffodil out of a bulb instead of enabling the bulb to develop into a daffodil by good enough nurture.

You will see that I am concerned with something which I consider to be much more important than this paper of mine. I am concerned with this set-up which might be called Kleinian which I believe to be the real danger to the diffusion of your work. Your ideas will only live in so far as they are rediscovered and reformulated by original people in the psycho-analytic movement and outside it.[31] It is of course necessary for you to have a group in which you can feel at home. Every original worker requires a coterie in which there can be a resting place from controversy and in which one can feel cosy. The danger is, however, that the coterie develops a system based on the defence of the position gained by the original worker, in this case yourself. Freud, I believe, saw the danger of this. You are the only one who can destroy this language called the Kleinian doctrine and Kleinism and all that with a constructive aim.[32] If you do not destroy it then this artificially integrated phenomenon must be attacked destructively. It invites attack, and as I tried to point out, Mrs. Riviere's unfortunate sentence[33] in her otherwise excellent introduction puts the matter exactly into words which can be quoted by people who are not necessarily the enemies of your ideas but who are the enemies of systems. Mrs. Riviere's sentence, which I believe you yourself dislike, gives the impression that there is a jigsaw of which all the pieces exist; further work will only consist in the fitting together of the pieces.

The fact is that further understanding such as you have been able to bring through your work does not bring us towards a narrowing of the field of investigation; as you know, any advance in scientific work achieves an arrival at a new platform from which a wider range of the unknown can be sensed. Your work has made us see that the insanities will one day be understood mainly in psychological terms. It is no disgrace that psycho-analysis even represented by its chief exponent, which is yourself, cannot give a clear statement as to why a child is a bed-wetter or why we smoke; that the psychology of delinquency has not yet been tackled in the Society because the main clues are missing; and that you carefully choose patients for teaching purposes and also for therapeutic work.

Those who know your work extremely well nevertheless have their failures, including suicides.

Further I would say that a book like that of Adrian Stokes (Smooth and Rough) shows that it is not yet safe to do the analysis of a poet. The psychology of artistic creation and therefore of the creativity that infuses life in general is not covered even if one studies all the work of yourself and those who help to explain your work. All this is a great stimulus and anyone who has an original idea is welcome and I believe we will always be able to tolerate an initial statement in personal terms. The initial statement is usually made at great cost and for sometime afterwards the man or woman who has done this work is in a sensitive place as he is personally involved.

In recent weeks a paper of Rowley, with his use of the word collusion, contains original work which can be withered by the sort of treatment Dr. Heimann gave it. Fortunately there are others who can see that he is a sincere and creative person who is at present speaking his own language, nevertheless using words that we can come to understand.

There is one more point, and that is that I feel that you are so well surrounded by those who are fond of you and who value your work and who try to put it into practice that you are liable to get out of touch with others who are doing good work but who do not happen to have come under your influence. I would have mentioned this on the evening that we were there in your house with the Stracheys if it had not been for the fact that Eric and Judy [Klein's son and daughter-in-law] were present. When you took it for granted that it is impossible that Miss Hellman could do a good analysis of Tyson I felt that you were making a great mistake. Mr. Strachey is too polite and in any case too lazy to take up the matter with you but of course he knows that Miss Hellman is capable of doing a good analysis and so do I. It is true that wrong things will be done and that a great deal will be left out that could be done; nevertheless an opportunity will be given to this man to be creative in a regular setting and he will be able to grow in a way that he was not able to grow without analysis. I think that some of the patients that go to "Kleinian enthusiasts" for analysis are not really allowed to grow or to create in the analysis and I am not basing this on loose fantasy but I am seriously bringing it forward as a matter for thought. I believe that the idea expressed in my paper, however badly it is done, is in the direction of giving a new emphasis so that those who use your concepts and your ideas and your technique may not forget something which it is disastrous to leave out.

I do know that in your analyses nothing of this that I am criticising occurs. I have no difficulty whatever in telling anyone who asks me, from the bottom of my heart, that you are the best analyst as well as the most creative in the analytic movement. What you do not meet, however, is the opposition to Kleinism which I used to think was simply an invention of [Edward] Glover's but which I now have to admit exists as something which is as much a barrier to the growth of scientific thought in the Society as Darwinism was to the growth in biology so greatly stimulated by the work of Darwin himself. I suppose this is a phenomenon which recurs and may be expected to recur whenever there is a really big original thinker; there arises an "ism" which becomes a nuisance.

I am writing all this down to show why it is that I have a real difficulty in writing a chapter for your book although I want to do so so very badly. This matter which I am discussing touches the very root of my own personal difficulty so that what you see can always be dismissed as Winnicott's illness, but if you dismiss it in this way you may miss something which is in the end a positive contribution. My illness is something which I can deal with in my own way and it is not far away from being the inherent difficulty in regard to human contact with external reality.[34]

This was perhaps his defining moment with Klein. Note that he had courted trouble not long before this, with Segal and Hellman and Riviere, all in the period of his remarriage, new home, heart attacks, transitional object paper, and his patient's suicide. Here he is particularly articulate, and in the very length of the letter, he gives himself an opportunity to reach deep down for a commentary that is fully grounded in his life experience and the thinking that has flowed from it. He makes the powerful case against fixity, even in scientific theory, and especially in psychoanalytic theory, taking account of the fact that human beings are continuously rediscovering principles that come to life only when personal language is employed. The idea of narcissism of theory, a phrase not used here, is nonetheless implied, wherein some thinkers of great liveliness and originality, himself as their representative, are to be excluded from the closed coterie within which final judgment is rendered. One may conjure the infant whose excitement is not allowed an outlet in the arms of the rigid mother as an image from Winnicott's early life that may well be part of his brilliant complaint.

This is the means by which his own artistic temperament, standing for that of others doing the same work, is given room to express itself. It will not be hampered by the inherited authority of a theory. Science, he says, is not thereby discarded; the accumulation of knowledge proceeds over time, leading to a progression of understanding, but personal rediscovery is given its legitimate place. This view is the product of the agony of one who must express himself without reservation or perish. It is a view that is closely related to the idea of external reality as the creation of individuals. There is therefore no room for an authoritarian imposition of a particular arrangement of that reality. Winnicott is driven to questions of epistemology as a philosopher of science out of the exigencies of personal experience.

He has located the source of his strength within himself rather than from Klein, whether as herself or as his psychoanalytic mother. With Clare at his side and the evidence of his power constantly made manifest, still able to remain grateful to Klein, he chooses a path now entirely his own.

PART TWO

Imagination is the true fire, stolen from heaven.
—Mary Wollstonecraft

I'm the orphan of a dream, stranded by the outgoing sea.
—Fernando Pessoa

14

Regression: 1953–54

Having traversed the immediate postwar period, with its confusing intellectual topography, and its coronary dangers, Winnicott regained his health and became an ever more visible presence among psychoanalysts. He embraced his status as an outsider. His hard-earned conviction that certain patients require a psychoanalytic situation that makes possible a regression to dependence in the search for a new healing link set him apart from most analysts of his time. This was where his history, temperament, and accumulated experience directed him. He spoke as an authority into the living ferment of contemporary thought.

In the 1950s, largely through the appearance in print of his papers for lay and professional audiences, readers in Great Britain, and, gradually, others in the world at large, began to encounter Winnicott's brilliant, probing, idiosyncratic intelligence. Although his attentiveness to both unconscious and conscious human dilemmas was finely focused, he did not present his ideas as definitive statements. Instead there is in his work a sense that what is being communicated is in an unfinished condition. Very often a seemingly casual reflectiveness gives way to a sudden bearing down on a given subject, or a jolt of insight, a profound dive into the unknown. His psychoanalytic undertaking is very much "in process."

In this period his writings show a growing ability to capture the wonder of human experience in all its innocence and complexity. This ability was derived from his research into the earliest stages of life, which in turn was based on his work with patients, children and adults, as well as with himself as a patient in a self-analysis that seems never to have ceased. His efforts for the benefit of others resonated with his efforts on his own behalf.

He published three collections of essays in the mid-fifties: *The Child and the Family; The Child and the Outside World*, combined later into *The Child, the Family, and the Outside World*; and *Collected Papers: Through Paediatrics to Psycho-Analysis*. The wide circulation of these books, together with his BBC broadcast talks, now published as *The Child and the Outside World*, brought his insights to ever larger circles of readers at many levels of sophistication.

The great arc of his development in the fifties and sixties comprised a series of closely related concepts. These include the increasingly familiar regression to dependence, management, the spontaneous gesture, the concepts of the "True and False Self," object usage, and, near the end, a new and brilliant grasp of the role of the father as the first whole object.

Much of his writing is arrayed in relation to a central preoccupation with regression. Regression emerges as the patient's quest to recapture early experiences in which development had been interrupted, resulting in a catastrophic loss of access to aggressive energy. For Winnicott, the search to tap this energy with which to assert himself had a long history in his own life. Now this personal preoccupation found application in profound work with a broad category of patients who had thus far exceeded the clinical grasp of psychoanalysis.

Starting in the late 1940s, when he was struggling with his personal life and suffered the first of a series of heart attacks, there was a sense of urgency to his formulations, as if at any time his work might be cut short and his gifts left unconsummated. Out of this urgency came a stark emphasis on the life-enhancing uses of destructiveness. This was an extension of the personal trajectory that had started at the age of nine, when he considered himself "too nice," and continued for many years thereafter, during which he cultivated an awareness of what he seemed to enjoy calling "hate."

The preoccupation with aggression took shape in his idea that "in its earliest form aggression is part of movement, beginning with motility of the fetus in utero. With adequate holding by the mother the stage is set for the maximum of infusion of motility into id experiences. When that motility encounters resistance, the external world is brought into consciousness. It feels 'real.'" Erotic experience, he would maintain, derives its highly valued sense of reality from the aggression that has been fused with it. At the other end of the spectrum of his ideas around aggression came his formulations on "the use of an object." Within the context of one's relationships, the other person, seen as external and beyond one's personal omnipotence, is, he maintains, subjected to continuous unconscious destruction. To the extent that that other person survives this destruction, he or she becomes of "use," by which he meant capable of contributing something new to one's life. He contrasted this with the taking in of what is projected, or thought to be projected, a kind of self-feeding that yields no reward. It was the genuinely new that concerned him, the novel emotional and psychological experience that feeds personal growth. Reality for him gained intensity from surviving continuous destruction.

Between the two poles of simple fetal motility and continuous destruction of the object lay many shades and stages in the development of his comprehensive theory of aggression. Without invoking a death instinct (as, following Freud, did Melanie Klein and a few others), Winnicott supplements Freud's ideas about libido, just as his attention to the very earliest stages of development within the context of the mother-infant relation supplemented Freud's attention to later development.

Although Winnicott always deferred to Freud with great and genuine humility, there were instances when he was aware of a conflict, of his own views as different from Freud's. In addition, as I will show, he seemed to see himself as the son figure to Freud that Carl Jung had originally been before falling out of favor. Winnicott, however, was not the childhood schizophrenic that he thought Jung had been, but a person capable of overcoming dissociations to make both himself and psychoanalysis whole again. In Keats's words (which he used as the epigraph to one of his papers), he put himself and psychoanalysis at "the centre of an intellectual world." Many consider Winnicott to have been the most influential psychoanalyst since Freud. There is a strong implication in his writings about Jung that he, Winnicott, was Freud's true successor, although such an explicit claim is nowhere to be found and would never have been put forth in so many words by Winnicott.

He probably suffered his fourth coronary in January 1954,[1] and possibly another in September of the year.[2] After that, there were apparently no others until 1968, although, because he was sometimes secretive on the subject, this is not absolutely certain.[3]

In a portrait of Donald in his late sixties or, more likely, seventies, which appeared in the *International Journal of Psychoanalysis* with his obituary, we see him holding a cigarette. Given his cardiac history, we can ask whether smoking represented a suicidal aspect of himself. In the portrait (his face is heavily creased—as criss-crossed, in fact, as that of W. H. Auden) the cigarette is held upward, perhaps a defiant gesture, like his running up staircases after a coronary. This was an aspect of his bearing, this defiant pose—rushing into traffic, say, or doing a pratfall on entering a room, or standing up in the driver's seat of a car while steering with a stick. His writing style exhibits analogous features. It frequently gives the impression of a man dueling with and defying death. His comments to Paul Roazen in 1965[4] on Freud's smoking are undoubtedly applicable to himself: it was, he says, an attempt to "recapture and make up for the loss of the experience of omnipotence." He made an analogous comment about driving to Marion Milner while taking her home after a lecture. He said that when he drove, "that means I'm less deprived."[5] He was referring to his problematic marriage to Alice Taylor.

This defiance manifested itself in his original point of view, the fount of so many new psychoanalytic ideas. He provided himself with a term, "research analysis," by which he meant all those analyses that fell outside the range of the usually accepted criteria. In this way he could allow for experiment, and learn what worked and what didn't as he sorted through his ideas. He could also rationalize behavior that some others would have found objectionable. His "management" methods certainly drew a large measure of criticism, especially from Kleinians, from which he defended himself vigorously. And his fifteen-year analysis of Masud Khan, if "analysis" is the apposite word, was research with a vengeance, as we shall see.

Not being "too nice" was an avenue that gave Winnicott the freedom to realize more of what he could be, including the freedom to adopt certain behavior, outside of ordinarily accepted ethical standards, which would anger him if exhibited in others. He kept this defiant attitude—or, better, his insistence on both being himself and not being ignored—for the rest of his life. In letters to followers of Melanie Klein, he focuses on contentious issues, maintaining that Klein's work was being diluted, distorted, or defiled by those who claimed to be advancing it. He knew better, he was sure, and, far from being a compliant or passive member of her coterie, he would make use of her theory as he saw fit. He would preserve what he felt was the core of it, striking that note of aggressiveness for which he strove.

These concerns become evident two months after the 1952 letter to her that defined the end of an era. To Herbert Rosenfeld, one of Klein's adherents, on January 22, 1953, he wrote at length on the subject of the psychoanalytic treatment of psychotics. As is so often the case, he was concerned with the subject of regression in psychoanalysis and, most pointedly, with the behavior of the analyst. He wished to emphasize that more than interpretations are required for such patients, that "management" is indispensable, management that reflects what the mother provides to her infant in normal development. "I fully support the idea that psycho-analysis of psychotics can be done," he told Rosenfeld. "This still needs working out, especially in view of the fact that you slur over management problems. . . . If you would acknowledge [that]. . . the bit of work which you did by analysis made no appreciable difference to the patient . . . , I would support your idea that the work you did is valid as research and interesting enough to report." He goes on: "I find myself in quite violent disagreement with the general tendency of your paper. I really am extremely concerned with the way in which [Mrs. Klein's] position as a pioneer is being undermined by her followers at the present time. You who know her work so well should be helping her to see that the work has its natural limitations. . . . The dullness [i.e., deadness] of yesterday's meeting is the result of the years of propaganda by which these supporters have battered down the gestures of those who feel, indeed know, that there are other things in human nature than those tremendously important mechanisms which Melanie Klein has shown us how to see and use."[6]

The letter picks up steam and becomes now propelled by outrage:

> I tried very hard to get you to allow yourself to bring in the importance of the mother's behaviour at the very beginning but you got away from this as quickly as possible. If it is possible for an analyst or for a mental hospital to cure a schizophrenic patient it must certainly

be possible for a mother to do so while the infant is right at the very beginning, and the logical conclusion is that the mother often prevents schizophrenia by ordinary good management. You spoke about the distress of the mother whose baby is already paranoid, and I well know this to be true. What you left out is the fact that a high proportion of infants of the world are seen through infancy by their mothers in such a way that they do not have to have subsequently the therapeutic care of the mental hospital or the psycho-analyst. I was hoping that you would find it possible just to mention the role of the mother in her adaptation to the needs of the infant who is not disturbed; otherwise you are implying that there is nothing but a technique which the infant requires, and this would be an adoption of the worst bit of Anna Freud's way of talking[7] without allowing for all the things that she says about infant care which show that she really knows that there is more in it than a series of techniques.

The idea of a technique, implying manipulation from an objective distance rather than a subjective gesture, is to Winnicott out of keeping with the therapeutic requirements of a regressed patient with early damage. He continues:

I am also worried when people like yourself take back the origin of the sense of guilt too early, thereby failing to give the impression that they understand the fact that it is a very great achievement in the development of the human infant when guilt is experienced.[8] Melanie Klein's most important contribution from my point of view is her theory of the gradual build-up of the capacity to feel guilt, and if somebody says that this is almost a quality of the newborn infant, as you seemed to do last night, then in my opinion what is being shown is that Mrs. Klein's work on the depressive position is not fundamentally understood. You would no doubt be able to show me where I have misunderstood you if we had opportunity for conversation.

I am not able to forget, and I am sure you would not wish me to forget, that those who follow Mrs. Klein have their failures just the same as other people do. Melanie Klein herself has turned down one or two students as unanalysable, a very brave thing to do. You yourself have recently had a failure with Mr. Q., who had several years with Susan Isaacs, four I believe with Fieldman, and then a certain

period with yourself. You felt that you understood him although I
myself felt that you were wrong in what you interpreted to me. This
would not have mattered, however, had you been able to manage the
external situation in which you failed and the man committed suicide. He was a man known to a lot of my friends and had value; nevertheless he was very ill and you have nothing to be ashamed of in
the fact that you failed. Nevertheless failure has to be acknowledged.
I believe that you could contribute in a very important way if you
could give a paper on Q. to the Society, so that the discussion could
range around the reasons for failure.

The patient had been a lover of Clare Britton's (she told me this in 1981).
He committed suicide while she kept a date with Donald. This could indicate that Donald and Clare were not faithful to each other in the long
period before they finally married. I do not know the details. There was,
however, a two-year period between Donald's separation from Alice and
his marriage to Clare in which they did not share a home. A curtain has
been drawn over this period and over other details of their marriage, except for what Clare chose to reveal in her interviews. Of course, it is none
of our business anyway, though she did volunteer the information about
"Q" without any prompting. She wanted someone to know. This casts
further light on the episode with Rosenfeld.

In the letter Winnicott is fighting against Kleinian perfectionism, the
idea that a perfect approach to patients is attainable, as well as the idea
that a perfect theory is possible. He is emphasizing, in an English way,
the empirical nature of psychoanalytic work, with its bits and pieces and
slow accretion and systematization, rather than its unitary perfection
under the umbrella of a big single principle, in the spirit of Middle Europe. Already as an adolescent he felt similarly, as in the paper he wrote
comparing two forms of town planning: English and German.

This all seems heartfelt and straightforward. But what about the patient "Q"? What about the personal connection? Doesn't this fact taint the
veracity of Winnicott's earnestness? "In regard to the patient that you reported," he continues, "I believe that the treatment ceased, did it not, because the parents came home? This is the sort of thing that requires
management. You did not have time to tell us what you did in regard to
the man's mother so that we could not discuss whether someone else
would have been able to have dealt with that factor, which is a part of the

man's illness, a bit of the early mismanagement followed through to the present day." Having written all this, he had the gall to add: "I will not burden you with further comments but I am writing and sending them to you because I believe that you would like me to do so. I do value your work."

Rosenfeld replied in a cool and ironic tone on February 14:

> Dear Dr. Winnicott,
>   Thank you for your letter, which arrived in the middle of my "flu." I found the discussion of my papers stimulating, but of course the time was short and only certain aspects were discussed. I quite agree that in all psychotics the dealing with relatives and nurses and hospitals is important. I certainly have not found the answer for many of the problems of hospital, nursing, time and expense I have come up against. I am certainly very interested if you have found some solution to these problems. As to Q.: I saw him for 4 weeks and I was unable to avert the severe psychotic breakdown against which he was struggling at the time he saw me. I don't understand what you mean about management there. He got in touch with you and obviously needed you after he left me. Perhaps you had no time to see him in hospital. I certainly don't blame you. Everybody has to decide how far he is willing to go and where one's responsibilities lie.
>   . . .
>   I hope you are keeping well.

He signed himself "Yours sincerely." Here we discover another interesting fact: the patient consulted Winnicott, too—yet a further complication, a further crossing of lines, with still more doubt about the purity of Winnicott's protests. The student of this interchange must wonder about a possible motive in Winnicott's sense of guilt driving him toward his criticisms. Even with such a personal background, however, those criticisms must be judged valid or not on their merits.

Winnicott wrote again on February 17:

> Dear Dr. Rosenfeld,
>   I am sorry that you had 'flu and I am glad that you are now recovering. Thank you very much for answering my letter, which did not really need an answer.

In regard to Q., you are quite right to point out that I was involved myself, and if I was critical of you in my letter I am also critical of myself[9] although I only went to see him in order to get him into hospital without certification. I feel that Q. gives us all a good deal of reason for humility since he had several years with Susan Isaacs and, I believe, five with Fieldman and then made use of several of us but in the end could not get the help he so very much wanted to find. I am not of course forgetting that he was very ill.

My good wishes to your wife and to yourself.

On January 22, 1953, Winnicott started in on Hanna Segal, once again on management, directly tied to regression: "I am writing assuming that you would welcome a further discussion of the point you made at the meeting last night. You seemed to say that of course every analyst knows that the patient has management needs. You mentioned the fact that no-one would analyse somebody who had not had food for five days. Presumably you would give food. You went on to imply that there is no essential difference between the management needs of a psychotic and a neurotic patient. If you really mean this, heaven help your psychotic patients, and until you recover from this point of view I am afraid you will not make a very interesting contribution to the theory of psychosis."

Winnicott was always concerned with diagnosis, that is, with differentiating among patients, whose treatment requirements differ accordingly.

If you really believe, as many of us do, that the psychotic patient is in an infantile state in the transference situation, then what you are really saying is that there is no essential difference between the management needs of an infant and those of a grownup. Yet in conversation I am sure you would admit that whereas a mature person can take part in his own management a child can only take part to some extent and an infant at the beginning is absolutely dependent on an environment which can either choose to adapt to the infant's needs or fail to adapt and to ignore those needs.

I would say that the management problems are essentially different according to the level of development. If this is so, then management problems must be different in the analysis of psychotics and neurotics. As you know, I am one of those who go a little bit further and who say that in the analysis of psychotics we must actually study what we do when we take part, as we always must do, in management. It is not necessary for you to agree with this but your extreme view which you expressed last night seems to me to be one that you might easily wish to correct on another occasion.

One day when we meet we will be able to discuss this. Meanwhile, every good wish.

A third chastising letter was sent to Esther Bick on June 11, 1953, the day after she gave her paper at the British Psycho-Analytical Society.[10] He wrote:

I do hope that you will give a lot of thought to this idea of splitting and not take for granted that you are right. In your answer you talked about this woman's splitting mechanisms and used the word "she." She, by various means, cut and split objects. If the personality of this woman were split, you would not be able to use the word she in this simple way. It would almost seem as if you have not yet met someone fundamentally split. The gentleman who invented the word schizophrenia really did believe in the splitting of a personality, whereas it seems to me that you have got as far as seeing that a person who is whole can be concerned with dissociated elements in the inner and external world. I think this is rather an important point in view of the fact that in your use of the word splitting you are joining in with the current tendency.

You will understand that this is mostly a use of terms and therefore is not very fundamental. Nevertheless it can be fundamental if those who use the word split in your way then proceed to feel that they have dealt with the true splitting of schizophrenia, which they have not done.[11]

I am writing this to you because it arises out of your paper, which I found an interesting one, and you understand that I would not criticise or appraise your paper on a detail like this.

[Reference here to the patient described in the paper] I . . . think you will find that breathing excitement is the thing that the patient is trying to get to. This, as you know, is a very important part of sexual intercourse.

I am reminded of a case of compulsive over-breathing which came my way when I was a House Physician in 1922; this went on for many hours and was leading to serious physical effects, but it disappeared when in the history-taking I and the patient discovered that it started during intercourse and as part of a phobia of intercourse. I know that all this suffocation difficulty will be mixed up with body memories of the birth process but in my experience it is eventually the breathing at the climax of instinctual experience that is the thing that has to be found. I think that this mother, because she was depressed, took great care that her infant did not get excited, and of course in thinking this I am using the clinical notes that you gave.[12]

Whenever he writes, for any purpose, he almost always includes something new or different, something to think about: "There was a point which struck some of us, " he tells Bick, "which was to do with a psychotic element in the patient's material. It had to do with her annihilation of you when she, according to your description, noticed everything in one corner of the room. I am thinking of what would happen if you were to give a long period without making interpretations, and perhaps you have done this; but it can easily be that by interpreting you reassure the patient against her anxiety of having annihilated you and that conversely, a period of leaving her alone would produce a severe anxiety attack which might have value in itself."

In all three letters Winnicott is a scold, demanding self-discipline, which, in the Rosenfeld episode, he himself has not shown. Yet, he *was* dealing with an entrenched and determined orthodoxy that continued to be impervious to what he regarded as his empirical findings.

In the three-year period 1953 to 1956, Winnicott produced several brilliant papers, most pointedly on the subject of regression, on the theory of aggression, and on transference. The heart attack he suffered in January 1954 did not put a stop to his activity. He gave a paper on the depressive position, and then the regression paper during the immediate aftermath of this event. He did withdraw from his duties as training secretary of the British Society during that period, and Charles Rycroft took over for him, but he did not stop presenting his ideas.[13] The coexistence of health difficulties with personal productivity gained additional drama from his ongoing efforts to deal with the two women who dominated the psychoanalytic scene in Britain: Melanie Klein and Anna Freud. He found himself defending Klein, as he often did, in a letter to a colleague,[14] and he argued with Klein about the topic of Masud Khan's rejection, on his first attempt, for membership in the British Society. He wrote a letter to the two of them proposing the dissolution of the training scheme (it was rejected by both), and at the end of 1955, probably under great duress as a result of Klein's turning away from him (though this is not documented in materials available to me), he communicated with Anna Freud obsequiously, needing a place in which to give his point of view—a particular kind of a place, since he had plenty of listeners throughout Britain. These women, who carried Freud inside them,[15] were important to him for personal reasons. He wanted to be worthy of Freud the father, and approached him through the women who were available to him, since Freud, like his own father, was not. And further, the idea of the powerful father was well served through Freud's women, since his actual father, superficially successful and popular, had been weak. Probably his own maximum output could not have been delivered without a correspondingly maximum stimulus and evaluator.

The theme of regression is evident in "Symptom Tolerance in Paediatrics: A Case History," Winnicott's presidential address to the paediatrics section of the Royal Society of Medicine, February 27, 1953. The case was one that called for a therapeutic consultation (one or a few sessions of intense psychoanalytic interaction, usually with a clinical result), although the term had not yet been coined. The message to pediatricians is that in order to understand and approach symptoms of psychogenic origin, the usual attempts to eradicate them must be set aside in favor of an attitude of tolerance. This may involve conditions that favor the appearance of regression, sometimes extreme. Winnicott reassures them, via his case, that a bottom will be reached, and from it a change that makes possible much more adaptive behavior. The last sentence reads: "It would have been futile to have tried to cure Philip's enuresis without dealing with the regressive need that lay behind it." As the very embodiment of both professions, he is mainly trying to educate pediatricians about the methods and thinking of child analysts and, as part of that effort, to foster a condition of awareness of and tolerance for states of regression, which tend to evoke in observers an urge to do everything possible to reverse the process immediately. It had not been very long since he was unable to restrain himself from intervening in order to place a limit on the full extent of a regression to dependence.

Anna Freud's impressions expressed in a letter dated February 17, 1953, were favorable:

> I was fascinated by your paper and I greatly enjoyed the simplicity of the presentation, your comparisons with the work of the paediatrician and the whole aspect of symptom-intolerance with which I agree heartily. . . .
>
> The idea of the beneficent regression is a very intriguing one and it would be equally intriguing to know how to distinguish between these and the malignant regressions which we see so often.
>
> I had a curious therapeutic experience once of which your case reminds me. On that occasion I never saw the child, the mother only twice and the rest was correspondence. But it cured the child of the "beneficent regression" into soiling which stood for his longing for the mother at a certain early time of separation.

This marked one step toward an ever more friendly relationship with Anna Freud, which paralleled his distancing himself from Klein.[16] They had in common an exposure to large numbers of children, in contrast to the experience of Klein and most of her followers of limited numbers studied in psychoanalysis. Miss Freud's experience stretches back to her work as an elementary school teacher, her Vienna nursery schools, the Hampstead War Nurseries, and her ongoing observation of children in the normal nursery in Hampstead. Winnicott's came from dealing with 60,000 mother-child pairs in his pediatric and psychoanalytic career.

In the immediate aftermath of another cardiac illness, on March 17, 1954, he gave an extraordinary presentation to the British Society titled "Metapsychological and Clinical Aspects of Regression within the Psycho-Analytical Set-Up," a lengthy, strenuously argued presentation in which he unpacks his great experience and thought on the subject. His idea differs sharply from Freud's notion of libidinal regression from Oedipal conflict toward fixation points in the pregenital stages.[17] The emphasis is on regression to dependency. Winnicott wished to rescue this side of analytic experience, with its special demands on the analyst, from the rubric of "art" or "intuition." (This calls to mind his response to Ella Sharpe's enthusiastic response to one of his presentations as art.) Here he continues to lodge protests against this presumably complimentary viewpoint, as if to be an artist is a higher calling than to be a scientist. Always aware that "diagnosis matters" (as he put it in a letter to me in January 1969), he divides patients into three categories: those suited to classical technique, those at the depressive position who need some management, and those whose problems are centered in the earliest stages, where the accent has to be on management. He expresses himself in this paper in quite a confident tone, as when he writes: "An analytical diagnosis needed to be made that took into account a very early development of a False Self. For treatment to be effectual, there had to be a regression in search of the True Self." By subdividing patients diagnostically, he allows for the notion that his theory is something in addition, applicable to those patients who require management, leaving "well-chosen neurotic cases" to be approached according to Freud's teachings.

Among the many themes and ideas contributing to his advancing theory of infant development correlated with adult psychology is the concept of the True Self. This idea would become the central topic of a paper of its own only in 1960, but it had its roots in this post-war period. The idea of a False Self developing in utero appears ("Birth Memories," 1949), then as a False Self on a compliance basis ("Mind and Its Relation to the Psyche-Soma," 1949), and was then more fully developed in his 1950 paper on aggression. The True Self is a focal point of his theory, a way of describing the survival of a most essential and unharmed aspect of the individual, soul-like in its undiluted and undenatured truthful being. As the regression paper progresses, he gives more and more weight to the True and False Self, a sign of the direction of thinking that would lead him toward his 1960 and 1962–63 papers directly addressing the subject. By 1963, "The Tree" would illustrate his state of despair, as expressed poetically, or, through his having transcended it, as a healing dream, to use his own phrase, or, through the writing itself, as a vehicle of self-cure. Clearly, it is his own pursuit of conditions for the expression of his True Self that underlies the sequence of papers that were now pouring out of him. Who is to say where communication of his meditations to others can be separated from communication to himself, with accompanying inner revisions?[18]

He restates the notion that a defense against specific environmental failure is a *"freezing of the failure situation,"* which allows for future unfreezing when conditions may be better. Here he elaborates his observa-

tion of a patient whose traumatic birth was relived step by step in perfect detail under regressed conditions in analysis. He sees the possibility
that this freezing phenomenon is related to the concept of fixation
points. Yet, diverging from Freud, or adding on to Freud, he writes: "We
can build theories of *instinct* development and agree to leave out the environment, but there is no possibility of doing this in regard to formulation of *early ego* development. We must always remember, I suggest, that
the end result of our thinking about ego development is primary narcissism. In primary narcissism the environment is holding the individual,
and *at the same time* the individual knows of no environment and is at
one with it."

"It takes a great deal of courage to have a breakdown," he writes, " but
it may be that the alternative is a *flight to sanity* , a condition comparable to
the manic defence against depression."[19] Here he is emphasizing his feeling
that "apparent health with a False Self is of no value to the patient." Later he
writes: "The development of a False Self is one of *the most successful defence
organizations* designed for the protection of the True Self's core, and its existence results in a sense of futility." And "from this one can formulate a fundamental principle of existence: that which proceeds from the True Self
feels real (later good) whatever its nature, however aggressive; that which
happens in the individual as a reaction to environmental impingement feels
unreal, futile (later bad), however sensually satisfactory."

Out of this thorough look at regression as he understands it "comes
a fresh understanding of the 'True Self' and the 'False Self,' and of the observing ego, and also of the ego organization which enables regression to
be a healing mechanism, one that remains potential unless there be provided a new and reliable environmental adaptation which can be used by
the patient in correction of the original adaptive failure."

A long letter to Clifford Scott on March 19,[20] the day after he gave this
paper ranges over a wide swath of topics. He starts with a discussion of
the difference between the criminal and the lunatic. Then he continues on
"the difference between the first and subsequent interviews." He comments on the shift from his position in the mind of the patient as a "subjective object" at the beginning toward being seen as an ordinary person.
No one before Winnicott had grasped the notion of the subjective object,
or the object objectively perceived, which is a precondition for understanding the shifts he describes to Scott:

I did just mention that the regression was not a simple return to infancy but contained the element of withdrawal and rather paranoid state needing a specialised protective environment. I do believe, however, that this can be said to be normal in a theoretical way if one refers to a very early stage of emotional development, something which is passed over and hardly noticed at the very beginning if all goes well. This is a matter for discussion, and it is exactly here that I am particularly interested in the subject.

In regard to the duration of the regression, I could not of course predict its length. I had indications, however, which perhaps are rather subtle, and I might have been absolutely wrong. I took as my main platform the relatively normal first two years, and following this the way in which the child dealt with the considerable environmental disturbances which started at the age of two by using the mother and by his technique of living in a slightly withdrawn state. In regard to this particular point I am now very much strengthened by my experience of having allowed a psycho-analytic patient to regress as far as was necessary. It did really happen that there was a bottom to the regression and no indication whatever of a need to return following the experience of having reached the bottom.[21]

P. S. I have just thought of the other point which was important. I agree with you that in ordinary analyses one tries to make it unnecessary for regression to have to take place, and one succeeds in the ordinary neurotic case. I do believe, however, that the experience of a few regressing cases enables one to see more clearly what to interpret. As an example I would say that since experiencing regressions I more often interpret to the patient in terms of need and less often in terms of wish. In many cases it seems to me sufficient that one says, for instance, "At this point you need me to see you this weekend," the implication being that from my point of view I can benefit from the weekend, which indirectly helps the patient, but from the patient's point of view at that particular moment there is nothing but harm from the existence of a gap in continuity of the treatment. If at such a moment one says "You would like me to give up my weekend" one is on the wrong track and one is in fact wrong. I expect you more or less agree with this too.

This idea came to Winnicott in 1944, suggesting a change in his own life when he and Clare Britton became lovers. The shift of wording reflects a deep shift in meaning, from an objectivization, expressed as "wish," with its attendant responsibility, toward the perception of an existential state of incompleteness, more characteristic of the infant as experienced by empathic adults than the infant as a little adult with a heavy responsibility for "wishes."

It is also possible that Winnicott's changing emphasis from "wish" to "need" was in response to Ronald Fairbairn's 1944 paper that emphasized the absence of instincts in human beings.[22] Fairbairn conceptualized an inborn search for relatedness, congruent with need over wish. In this period of Winnicott's life, it is possible that he gained support from reading Fairbairn for a softening of attitude toward his own needs, thus facilitating his progressing relationship with Clare.

Fairbairn was one of the very few colleagues who was capable of grasping Winnicott's idiosyncratic ideas. He worked in a sort of isolation in Edinburgh, far from London, but Winnicott too, in the very midst of London, was an isolated figure, not part of a coterie, and insistently so. Fairbairn wrote to him about this paper (March 18):

> I gather that the Regression which you have most in mind is psychotic regression; but I have come to be very interested in the Regression which is liable to occur in certain hysterics, and which is not obviously psychotic. These cases require a great deal of what you describe as "management"; but, from the object-relations point of view which I adopt, I feel it is rather artificial to draw a hard and fast line between management and analysis, as I take the view that some degree of management enters into analysis in all cases. But, of course, in regressed cases management assumes greater proportions than in non-regressed cases.
>
> In general, I am rather against what might be described as "purism" in analysis, viz. making the standard analytical technique an end in itself. The main thing is to get the patient better; and it seems to me a mistake to subordinate the psychotherapeutic aim to the aim of psycho-analysis pure and undefiled. Such subordination [has]. . . too much of the attitude involved in "C'est magnifique, mais ce n'est pas la guerre."

I don't know if you have heard of Guntrip who does analytical work in Leeds, and of whom I have a high opinion. He is an analysand of mine as a matter of fact; and he is interested in the same problems as I am. He has one or two cases of regressed hysterics, and, like me, has been trying to work out a technique for dealing with such cases. It occurs to me that he would be very interested to have a copy of your paper, if this is in order and you have a spare copy. Should you feel in a position to let him have one, would you be kind enough to send him a copy.

This was Winnicott's first knowledge of Harry Guntrip.[23] It turned out that Guntrip was seeking a regressive experience by which to capture his condition of mind at the time of the death of his younger brother, an experience that he would eventually have in the aftermath of his work with Winnicott. Guntrip would one day write a fascinating paper on his analytic experiences with Fairbairn and Winnicott.[24] The excellent biography by Jeremy Hazell[25] gives an extensive firsthand account (based on Guntrip's notes) of Winnicott in action. As such, it exceeds in value the note-based account of Winnicott's own work, published in *Holding and Interpretation*. That work was constructed sometimes long after the experiences described,[26] and of all his writings is the least accessible and human.[27] Hazell's account shows us a Winnicott that rings true.[28]

To Anna Freud on March 18, Winnicott wrote "We all missed you at the meeting. . . . My paper produced a really interesting discussion I believe. My aim will be now to try to correlate my ideas with those of Kris and Hartmann as I feel when I read what they have recently written that we are all trying to express the same things, only I have an irritating way of saying things in my own language instead of learning how to use the terms of psycho-analytic metapsychology. I am trying to find out why it is that I am so deeply suspicious of these terms. Is it because they can give the appearance of a common understanding when such understanding does not exist? Or is it because of something in myself? It can, of course, be both." A nearly apologetic letter, as if to admit to his shortcomings, as he imagines she might see them, and to demonstrate that he is concerned with doing something about them (like a good boy). Here he is expressing doubts about the ego psychologists which are similar to those he had about Klein, but more mildly put: an overstatement which leaves out the fact that the "common understanding" was far from complete. Of course, his idea of regression to dependence was new, and might not merely supplement but replace Freud's notion of regression through psychosexual stages to a fixation point with its emphasis on the ego rather than the id.

Ernest Jones wrote from his home, The Plat, on March 15 to say that Winnicott's "paper on regression impresses me enormously. I think it is the best thing you have done, which is saying a very great deal. It has made a good deal clearer to me in my own work. I had patients who worked through that intense regression two or three times at different periods with only partial benefit from doing so. I would remark about your picture of the 'false self' that it sometimes may contain valuable elements, particularly moral and aesthetic ones, which of course have to be salvaged."

Michael Fordham, Winnicott's Jungian friend, wrote on April 20: "I am at present involved in trying to develop a theory of development starting from Jung's ideas. I am repeatedly startled by the way in which the conclusions are simply the same as yours. . . . [T]he notion that a patient needs the analyst to undertake self analysis as part of *the process*—I think that is the substance of it—is much too much neglected. It is often important that a patient should do and realise that he or she has done the analyst some good in the same sense that it has been done to him or her."

The third paper on the subject of regression during this period, "Withdrawal and Regression," is a compact work presented in Paris in November 1954. In it he focuses on patient behavior during individual hours, specifically illuminating the concept of converting withdrawal into regression, a useful transformation, by "holding," which is illustrated by a series of apt interpretations which show the patient that the analyst understands the need to be held:

> If we know about regression in the analytic hour, we can meet it immediately and in this way enable certain patients who are not too ill to make necessary regressions in short phases, perhaps even almost momentarily. I would say that *in the withdrawn state a patient is holding the self* and that if immediately the withdrawn state appears *the analyst can hold the patient*, then what would otherwise have been a withdrawal state becomes a regression. The advantage of a *regression* is that it carries with it the opportunity for correction of inadequate

adaptation-to-need in the past history of the patient, that is to say, in the patient's infancy management. By contrast the *withdrawn* state is not profitable and when the patient recovers from a withdrawn state he or she is not changed.

He is showing how his concept can be applied in here-and-now instances, and is thus not limited to the lengthy process through which certain patients regress to dependency. Dependency and its need for action is in front of the analyst in any given hour, and can be met with a therapeutic act, given the necessary understanding.

Winnicott's close analysis of the nature of regression, expressed in several papers in this period, prepared him to recognize the phenomenon and the need, as well as the means by which regression can be met by the analyst. This is true for long analyses so often required for patients with early damage, but it is also true in the short run, even within a given hour. His view generates hope for change—sometimes immediate change. By finding it possible to alter one's viewpoint, even slightly, a process of great internal revision may be set in motion. Winnicott's ideas on regression are central to a long career in which he attempted to rescue individuals who were otherwise beyond reach.

— 15 —

Masud Khan

M asud Khan, a tall, handsome Pakistani émigré,[1] was born the youngest son of a wealthy landowner in his seventies, and his fourth wife, nineteen years old, a beautiful former courtesan of Persian origin who already had a child. Khan had come to London after World War II, still in his twenties, before the partition of India. Hannah Henry recalled that Donald had once asked her to look after "'a lovely ballet dancer, having a dreadful time with a difficult husband. She's Jane Shaw of Bernard Shaw.' Well imagine my reaction. 'Donald how can that be. B. S. hasn't any children.' 'Ah, but this isn't that B. S. This is Bernard *Shore*, the famous viola player.'" He also said that she might arrive in the company of "a very handsome Pakistani. Well she didn't. I met her at the station, a charming lovely girl. She stayed a couple of weeks, but this handsome husband turned up and off she went. We kept in touch for a long time, but the marriage ended eventually. He was Masud Khan, brother of the then president of Pakistan,[2] a social climber. After divorce from Jane [he] married a famous ballerina—Beri[o]sova, but she ditched him too. I think he was training to follow Donald's career." In his request to Hannah Henry, Winnicott was seeking help for Khan's first fiancée, whom he would eventually analyze for ten years, much of the analysis simultaneous with that of Masud Khan himself.[3]

Khan's effort to get into analysis in 1946 for help with his anxiety was mistakenly understood by John Bowlby to be an application for training. Khan thus became an analyst by accident. His analysis began with Ella Freeman Sharpe, who mentions him in a letter to Winnicott dated November 7, 1946. Sharpe died not long after. Khan then went to John Rickman, a disciple of Melanie Klein, who also died during his treatment.

Linda Hopkins, biographer of Khan, told me in March 2001: "Masud was analyzed [by Winnicott] from 1951 to 1966. He quit treatment in 1966 and continued (intensified) his editorial relationship with Winnicott from that point on. Winnicott also saw Khan's first wife, Jane Shore, in analysis starting in 1952. For awhile, she even took Khan's spot because Winnicott didn't have enough time for both.[4] Jane had a breakdown but stayed in treatment with Winnicott for almost a decade, throughout her estrangement and then divorce from Khan."

Khan's second wife, the ballerina Svetlana Beriosova, was thought by many to have had analysis with Winnicott, but this was not the case. "Winnicott and Khan tried to get her to see Balint," according to Hopkins, "but she did not believe in psychoanalysis, would not come four times a week. She was an alcoholic. She had treatment with drugs and also the electric coma treatment, but nothing worked.[5] She had been expecting to become the prima ballerina of the Royal Ballet, but when Rudolph Nureyev escaped from the Soviet Union, Margot Fonteyn came out of retirement and this destroyed her chances. She had even sacrificed having children for the professional opportunity, and she fell into drinking when it was clear that she would never make it. Masud lived vicariously through her fame—he became alcoholic after her, partly in response to the deterioration in their marriage, which had sustained him for a long time."

Khan's application for membership in the British Society was turned down on his first try. Winnicott rose to Khan's defense during the meeting, believing as he did that it was the Kleinians who, voting as a bloc, had made sure that Khan would not be accepted, just as they usually did when opposing Winnicott in other ways. In fact, Khan's case presentation "gave away" the patient, that is, the members could tell who it was, and they found this distasteful or unethical. John Bowlby in particular objected. Winnicott thought that Khan had provided excellent case material for a good discussion, whereas, by contrast, another candidate, the

Kleinian Betty Joseph did not provide good material for discussion.[6] On his next attempt, Khan was elected, and he became a training analyst only on Winnicott's fourth attempt on his behalf, in November 1959. As it turned out, he would become a disruptive, troublesome member with a long history of ethical violations and exploitations of candidates and patients—not to mention a book that featured anti-Semitic commentary. He was eventually regarded as the most disgraceful individual ever associated with the British Society, notwithstanding his good mind and services as editor of the International Psychoanalytic Library, as well as his books and his editing tasks on behalf of Donald Winnicott.

Hopkins cited a variety of evidence (discounting the boastful element in Khan's remarks on this subject) which leads to the conclusion that Khan edited *much* of Winnicott's output in the last 20 years of his life, although Joyce Coles, Winnicott's secretary, expressed doubt about this claim.[7] Winnicott collaborated with Khan in co-authoring a review of Ronald Fairbairn's book on object relations theory[8] soon after Khan began his analysis, in 1952, and there were many referrals to Khan during this period as well.

The surviving correspondence with Khan in Winnicott's file is all very businesslike and a reflection of Khan's devotion to Winnicott's published oeuvre and his wish to enhance it. There are little social notes here and there and some snide commentary about colleagues as well. A perusal of this archive would lead one to the conclusion that Khan was, as advertised, an editor of superb skills, which were brought to bear in the cause of psychoanalysis generally and Winnicott in particular. But the public record shows us another side of Khan, reprehensible to such a degree as to prompt searching questions about Winnicott's own ethical standing. In a letter to the brilliant theoretician David Rappaport (October 9, 1953), Winnicott indicates that if he and Khan got together, Winnicott would benefit. Khan would be the emissary who would bring the wide world back to Winnicott. In a letter to Riviere, he passes along Khan's idea that Gregory Zilboorg was worth reading. [9]

Khan, the analysand and suitor of Winnicott, was, according to Madeleine Davis, never his real friend, never in his inner circle, always held at a distance. He would arrive on Sunday mornings after he had been out horseback riding. There is a description of such visits in *When Spring Comes*,[10] Khan's memoir. Of this book Enid Balint has said: "I couldn't recognize Winnicott at all. . . . [H]e gave examples of what Winnicott said to him, and he claims that Winnicott [called him] 'Mr. Khan.' Winnicott would never have said Mr. Khan. He called him 'Masud.' The whole thing was phony and unpleasant."[11] Charles Rycroft, who shared a flat with Khan in the 1950s, said: "He was mad. . . . He was a psychopath, a creative psychopath. He wrote a paper on collage, and as I look back on it, that is what Masud himself was. He was a picker-up of other people's ideas, which he didn't properly integrate. The whole of his mind was a kind of muddle of all sorts of people, including me, except that he hardly ever quoted me. Like many Moslems, he would get on to alcohol and start drinking too much. I knew both his wives. He married dancers. The second was Svetlana Berizova [sic], who was a prima donna of Russian origin. That was all a disaster."[12]

According to Marion Milner, Khan became a kind of servant to Winnicott, who was ruthless with him. "Maybe he [Winnicott] felt he [Khan] was unanalyzable."[13] This comment, the truth of which appears now to be self-evident, would help to explain Winnicott's participation in a relationship that probably included sessions on the couch of a psychoanalytic appearance but otherwise dispensing with all psychoanalytic rules, except perhaps for drawing the line on Sundays, when, the Winnicotts's lunchtime would bring the editorial sessions to an abrupt end. This iron rule was probably enforced more by Clare than by Donald. Yet if, throughout the fifteen years of "analysis," there were regular psychoanalytic sessions between Winnicott and Khan, along with a full range of nonanalytic incidents and behaviors of which we have some idea now, can we say on that basis that this did not deserve to be called psychoanalysis, with the appended word "research" as qualification? To what extent does one's indignant response to the disturbed, self-aggrandizing, and self-destructive Khan color one's attitude toward the person who had undertaken his treatment?

I recently heard of a definition of "borderline" patients: those who, in consultation with another therapist, will describe their therapy in a way that would make the original therapist ashamed of the work he or she had done.[14] In the present climate (2002), prompted by an article in the British press, of which more shortly, Winnicott is being subjected to posthumous shame through the actions of his longtime analysand.

And those actions were indeed egregious. Khan told a new candidate who had just started analysis with him, and was naturally in a sensitive condition as he started to reveal himself, that he was behaving like a hysterical woman.[15] The candidate could not bear the humiliation and quit. Khan acted the part of a privileged royal, a prince, as he would eventually call himself (as the author of an introduction to a book, he would style himself Prince Masud Khan), although there was no evidence that, despite his wealth, he was in fact a prince.[16] He had a long relationship with Anna Freud, who favored him. Charles Rycroft voiced the rumor that he had been in analysis with her, while doubting the truth of it himself. Hopkins's research indicates that Khan did have an analysis with Anna Freud twice a week after Winnicott died.[17]

In an article in the *London Review of Books*,[18] Wynne Godley, a former analysand of Khan's, describes behavior that can only be called dangerous, self-indulgent, and destructive. In a description of his analysis, undertaken for what he called an "artificial self," Godley asserts that Khan "knew how to exploit and defy the conventions which govern social intercourse in England, taking full advantage of the fact that the English saw him instinctively as inferior—as 'a native'—and tried to patronise him." (Khan had very dark skin, with Aryan features.) From the start of his work with this patient of aristocratic background, Khan subverted the analysis. Ultimately his behavior became bizarre. He treated the patient sadistically. He told him that he, Khan, had exhausted "every manoeuvre that I know. You are a tiresome and disappointing man." He told tales of his own life, with the repetitive theme of his "getting the better of someone," usually someone famous. Khan boasted of his contacts with such well-known people and revealed confidences about other patients. He secretly asked the patient's wife to come to him for an interview. Eventually, there were social occasions involving Khan himself, the patient, and another woman, also a patient, as Khan tried to foster a liaison between his two patients. Khan gave Godley expensive gifts. He and Beriosova hosted Godley and his wife on one occasion in their flat, where Khan, discovered lying on the floor moaning, told the patient, "My wife has kicked me in the balls." There were episodes of mockery and, near the end of the relationship, with the two couples at dinner, a verbal attack on Mrs. Godley, who was pregnant with a much-wished-for child. (The couple had not been able to have a baby.) His wife felt a sharp pain, which Godley interpreted as evidence of a direct attack on the pregnancy.

After they went home, Godley "rang up Winnicott and said, 'Khan is mad,'" to which Winnicott replied emphatically, "'Yes,' adding: 'All this social stuff'. . . . He didn't finish the sentence but he came round to our house immediately, saying that he had told Khan not to communicate with me again. As he said this, the telephone rang and it was, indeed, Khan wanting not only to speak to me but to see me, which I refused to do. And that was the end of my 'analysis.'"

Godley, who now lives in the United States and has been writing an autobiography, was told by Linda Hopkins that throughout his analysis, Khan was himself in analysis with Winnicott. Winnicott had referred Godley to Khan, and was naturally aware of the aberrations and ethical violations of which Khan was capable, as far back at least as the seduction of his patient Barbara Corke.[19]

Because Godley was married to the former wife of Lucian Freud (the famous painter, son of Anna Freud's brother Ernst), the Winnicott referral may have been preceded by an original referral from Anna Freud to Winnicott.[20] Miss Freud was a supporter of Khan, whom she supervised without taking a fee,[21] and would presumably have had veto rights over Winnicott's choice. Thus the approval of Khan as analyst may have been agreed to by both Anna Freud and Winnicott. Godley's autobiography may shed further light on his experience. In the meantime, judgment about the behavior of Winnicott in this instance has to be tempered by knowledge of the context from which Godley's complaints arose.

Winnicott had shown a willingness to cross boundaries on several previous occasions. As we have seen, in the treatment of Melanie Klein's son, who was in his twenties, he colluded with her to prevent the young man from realizing that his analyst and his mother were discussing his treatment and his life. Winnicott undertook a bewildering array of roles with Marion Milner during the period described in her book about the patient known as Susan. And, irrespective of problems in his marriage that might excuse his infidelity, he did lead a secret, parallel life with a professional colleague, unknown to Alice, for at least five years. Of course, he was also willing to cross boundaries in his clinical and theoretical work, as part of the extraordinary advances he was making. In addition, in his dealings with Khan, it is possible that Winnicott, as an outsider, overidentified with another outsider. His relationship with Khan began at about the time of his marriage to Clare Britton. He thus had a strengthened, consolidated personal life as a base from which to proceed. Linda Hopkins thinks that Khan was the closest thing to a son that Donald ever had.

The end of Khan's analysis is indicated by his notation, "DWW ... faltered in 1965. ... Not his fault, my lapse! This I respected in DWW. We loved each other from an uneasy—no, a *traumatic* alliance."[22] According to Linda Hopkins, "it seems likely that Khan had protected Winnicott by leaving analysis. He knew that Winnicott couldn't handle his intensity." This is consistent with Hopkins's belief that Winnicott failed to provide conditions under which he could have been of "use."[23]

Further, Hopkins notes, "the ending of analysis was not peaceful at first. Although the facts are not known re. what happened exactly, a letter from [Wladimir] Granoff (on a business topic) to Khan reveals that there had been bitterness: 'To quote your own words re. Dr. Winnicott, you said you did not speak to each other anymore, all was finished between you, and you had no other communication except what was strictly formal. And in the company of two people besides myself, you said that Dr. Winnicott had failed you completely when you were in trouble.' Masud didn't mention to Wladimir that his marriage was in shambles as Svetlana continued her alcoholism and Masud started an affair with a patient (after transferring her to Marion Milner)."[24] It is easy to wonder what effect on their relationship the disastrous work with Wynne Godley might have had. Yet "even after the analysis ended," Hopkins adds, "Masud still talked to Winnicott whenever he had a problem."[25]

"In some 15 years of analytic relationship with DWW," Khan writes in his diary, known as his "Workbooks" (May 3, 1971), "I did succeed at three points or occasions to sink into my Self, be silent, present in my person and related to him. All these three occasions were physical or rather psychosomatic. He was in the chair seated and I had got off the couch and buried my head into the side of his coat. I can still hear his heart and watch beating. All else was still and sentiently neutral and I was at peace. And DWW never interpreted those three occasions. He had enabled me to reach to that point, allowed it to actualise, and let it pass—without comment. And these three occasions were my only experience of the Self in me in analysis. Of course, I always talked a lot and often quite insightfully. But my language, spoken, was always other to me."

Arlene Kramer Richards has recently suggested a sexual component in Winnicott's holding of Margaret Little.[26] She might very well see something similar in the analysis of Masud Khan. Such behavior would, of course, be considered destructive of the analytic process, an indulgence in the satisfaction of instinctual urges in the transference (and countertransference) quite at odds with the growth of insight. Yet patients like Dr. Little were not, as Winnicott sometimes put it, "well-chosen neurotic cases." They required something else of their analysts if a clinical result were to supervene. Of course, it is always possible to claim that persistence under orthodox conditions will eventually succeed, in good enough hands. But in the living moment with a patient, will the analyst think about a referral, or will he reach down within himself for whatever seems to be useful and constructive, knowing as he always does that it is up to him, and no one else, to do what he judges to be right? And knowing as well that a colleague would, naturally, have chosen something else.

Winnicott's ship proceeded into uncharted waters, where no device could provide him with coordinates. Dodi Goldman writes:[27] "In 1968, three years before his death, Winnicott spoke before a closed meeting on 'The Transmission of Technique.'[28] According to the notes of one of the participants, Winnicott remarked: 'It is not a very great thing to fail in analysis. The awful thing is to go on with an analysis after it has failed.'" Goldman adds: "I think Winnicott went on with his analysis of Khan long after he felt it not only had failed, but that it could never succeed. I think he did this because of his dedication to the 'three per cent that was creative and vital'[29] and because he never imagined curing *himself* from taking responsibility for Masud Khan's uncure." There did come an end to the analysis, assumed to be Winnicott's decision, but there is no supporting evidence, and in general any attempt to understand the dynamics of the fifteen-year analysis is hobbled, or perhaps invalidated, by the fact that we are, one and all, rank outsiders. One is tempted by Khan's Workbook and all the collateral evidence of Winnicott's convictions and behavior, but the subject is material for projections and speculations. Analysts are always trying to gather "the material" into coherent and communicable form, and, of course, we will never stop trying. But as analysts and patients, we know how ineffable experiences in a given hour or a whole analysis inevitably are.

Khan believed himself to be above the ordinary rules of human civility. He seduced many of his patients, and descended into a condition in which he felt privileged to behave however he wished. For that he lost his editorship of the International Psychoanalytic Library and his status as a training analyst, and was eventually expelled from membership in the British Society. He died persona non grata. By this point he had been living under the stress of a fatal illness for some time. Cancer of the lung had led to a pneumonectomy, and he had lost his larynx and his trachea as well. This was how his life came to an end. Nevertheless, he had no such illness during the long period when he indulged himself in a kind of abuse which borders on the criminal.

When Winnicott died in 1971, Khan expected to be named his literary executor. He insisted in his arrogant way to Clare Winnicott that he must have complete charge of all papers and documents or nothing. She chose to give him nothing. She told me this with a look of distinct satisfaction in her face—the look of a woman capable of making a solid judgment. Vengeance, too, may have played a role. I wondered about the extent to which she had stood in opposition to Khan's role during her husband's lifetime. Certainly her calling a halt to Khan's weekend editorial meetings at an exact time and her failure ever to invite him to lunch indicate her attitude. As far back as the early 1940s, Clare had complained of Donald's vacillation. In this instance we may be seeing her role as the enforcer of a limit.

In the history of psychoanalysis there have been examples of similarly charismatic figures who brought life to the field but also incited disruption and discord. This is true today as well. No one else in the history of the British Society, however, so abused his position for so long, until public awareness of his exploitation of others rose to an intolerable pitch and he fell into ignominy. By then Winnicott had died, not knowing the eventual outcome of Khan's career.

Given the fact that the work with Khan came into being at precisely the same time as Winnicott's second marriage and lasted until the end of his life, even if the "analysis" was terminated in 1966, the question occurs whether what one supposes to have been Donald's fully realized heterosexual relation to Clare was paralleled by a sort of homosexual counterpart with Khan. This analytical relationship brought an ongoing excitement and mutual self-indulgence that hint at a sexual component. Khan told one patient that he knew of a discreditable incident in Winnicott's life that Donald would not wish to have disclosed.[30] How could Khan have come into possession of such information except from a Winnicott in a confessional mode, a Winnicott who was out of control? Like Khan, in the 1950s and 1960s, Winnicott was at least sometimes out of control, while struggling to understand himself and writing papers of the deepest and most lasting value. Yet, we also have to ask what is true in Khan's assertions and what is fabrication.

Christopher Bollas has written:

> Winnicott never courted students and declined the many invitations to form a group or school that would study, teach and elaborate his ideas. He did, however, accept his own need for at least one person to occupy the place of *the other*, and so, throughout his marriage to Clare, and his complex relation to an analysand, Masud Khan, and more subtly, yet as influentially, with Marion Milner, he tested his thinking and used criticism. Winnicott's style cannot be understood, in my view, unless the place of the impishly critical *other* is understood, a psychic location that certainly reflected a part of his personality, but one which a few close friends occupied throughout his life. He could only write about the essentials of aloneness, indeed celebrate the unreachable areas of the self, because he was always at play with a puckish *other* who foiled him to his heart's delight.[31]

This is an interesting angle of view on the foiling "other," given Winnicott's late description of an encounter with an "other" who knows too much and is so terrifying that his thought process ceases.[32] Was that lethal "other" the extreme version of the "impishly critical other" to which Bollas refers? If so, then the serious pursuit of a thought process might lead him into dangerous territory, where his mind could go dead. Hypothesizing beyond reason now, one could ask whether he could attempt to analyze Khan only as "impishly critical" other, not with the full seriousness that ran the risk of bringing the process to a halt. As Khan's behavior grew more reprehensible, Winnicott's more serious side ("all that social stuff") may have supervened, leaving no more room for fun.

Adam Phillips, one of Khan's analysands, told a conference in 1987 that Winnicott's father had specialized in selling women's corsets.[33] I was amazed to hear this assertion and learned in time that it was completely false. Phillips's statement carried overtones suggesting certain vague preoccupations of a possibly perverse nature. The claim is reminiscent of Khan's erroneous comments about Winnicott, made with equal assurance, such as that he was a member of the Plymouth Brethren. In Phillips's case this is especially unnerving, because his *Winnicott* is a most powerful statement, an incisive port of entry into Winnicott's life and, especially, his work.

A letter from Madeleine Davis on June 11, 1989, the week after Khan's death, quotes from a paper of mine: "'We get further [reading Winnicott] than we get with most analytic writers because the subjective element, Winnicott's internal life, while continuously present, is kept in the background, and not permitted to burst onto the page.' To me," she continues, "this is what is meant by Masud Khan's phrase 'the privacy of the self'—something which M. K. sought after all his life, and therefore, and especially, *knew* about, though he himself couldn't find it. It has to do with depth, has it not?—with the understanding of oneself as being a 3 or 4 dimensional being. The . . . central self 'in a state of immanence' is the same thing as being found and yet inviolate. If someone violates themselves (or another) by attempting to reduce the central self to explication or analysis (that is, to a *list*), it disappears. Ergo, its only real definition is D. W.'s—the place that gives rise to the spontaneous gesture." The insights of Madeleine Davis are a small indication of what was lost to the world when she died of breast cancer in 1992.

In the same letter, Davis makes a comment that is, I believe, applicable to the plight of Masud Khan, though not specifically intended as such: "One has to love one's patients very much, doesn't one, when they find out how bitterly they can hate, etc. and are humiliated by it? How to convey in a manner befitting the analytic situation that one loves them especially for the grand courage of these moments? And respects them more than before? Difficult. But perhaps that is something that is needed from psychotherapists (and parents) if humiliation is to turn into humility—into the realisation of ordinariness. And that can bring *such* relief, if only one can find it." Khan never seemed capable of such a realization of ordinariness, with its attendant relief, although he probably did receive more than a full measure of Winnicott's capacity to love during times of Khan's intense and humiliating hatred. In fact, as Khan said, at Winnicott's memorial meeting,[34] "Some of us, and I am one of those, think he let the side down by his special stance of humility, which is larger than arrogance and authority."

— 16 —

"We Analysts Want to Be Eaten"

Winnicott suffered considerably throughout his professional career from not being allowed to teach in the British Institute, except in a token way. He did eventually achieve worldwide recognition, of course, but in 1953, before his major books appeared, before his lecture tours in the United States, and in the immediate aftermath of his brilliant paper on transitional objects, he was aggrieved at being largely ignored. His letter to Sylvia Payne (October 7, 1953) shows how disregarded he felt as a teacher, an indication of his total sense of rejection at this time.

I personally am one of those who feels that I have been fairly seriously neglected as a teacher. The only teaching that I have ever done to students has been confined to the three lectures which I give to the third year students, and I certainly would not have been asked to give these. It was entirely my own suggestion. I used to give another small group of lectures but I saw that these had to be crowded out to make the training scheme less patchy and I gave them up voluntarily. The fact is that my own very considerable experience in the psychoanalysis of children has been absolutely wasted although as a matter of fact I have had more experience of long child analysis than almost anyone else. I realised a long time ago that I would not be asked to teach in the Society and therefore I concentrated on teaching teachers and I have had to develop my views through the 10 yearly lectures which I give at the Institute of Education as a result of Susan Isaacs' original recommendation. I also give a large number of sporadic lectures all round the place which are based on personal reputation.

He felt estranged from official circles, in spite of having served a three-year term as president of the British Psycho-Analytical Society, and the fact that soon he would serve again. There were those who thought of him as pursuing ideas that were outside the realm of accepted, sober psychoanalytic thought (many were put off by the degree of innovation in his writings), and some believed that he did not understand analysis at all. He was not recommended by Anna Freud as a supervisor of her Jewish candidates,[1] and it was clear from the early 1940s that he was not accepted as a member of Melanie Klein's circle and did not wish to be. This contributed to his estrangement and must have added to the rage that erupts in his vituperative letters.

Yet it is evidence of the other side of Winnicott that he could respond with concern when Klein was ill. She replied on April 21, 1953: "Thank you very much for your kind wishes. I am much better—in fact I feel better than I was before the attacks started. I shall go slowly for the next months and not come to meetings, but I feel confident that by taking precautions I may still last a long time. I much appreciate your friendly feelings."

This was five months after his significant criticism of her. He stayed friendly, and she absorbed what he had to say and stayed friendly too. In some continuous way, there was acknowledgment of an underlying mutuality, a notable achievement for two such headstrong persons so frequently and deeply at odds. They were both aging, both susceptible to illness, and soon it was Winnicott's turn once more. In the context of an interesting letter (January 27, 1954) to Clifford Scott, he makes reference to his latest brush with cardiac illness:

A patient of mine . . . is dangerous just after expressing genuine love. In fact it was necessary for me over a long period of time to hold this patient's hands throughout the analysis,[2] this being the equivalent of certifying her and putting her in a padded cell for the analytic hour. In this way she was able to proceed and to express love and hate. If I

failed in this physical way then in actual practice I got hit and hurt
and this did no good either to me or to the patient. In this case the os-
cillations between love and hate seemed to me to have been almost
measurable but what is more important they were painful to the patient. . . .

It was very good indeed of you to come and see me the other
day. I am now, I suppose, well, but I am staying in bed a few days
longer than necessary.

In spite of his illness, the very next month he addressed the medical
section of the British Psychological Society, delivering "The Depressive
Position in Normal Emotional Development." Anna Freud was
present[3]—more evidence of her esteem, especially because this paper
was an attempt to deal in detail with Melanie Klein's concept of the depressive position. As such it is bursting with intricacy and logic that cannot be summarized. Among many interesting remarks is that "for me the
weaning age is that at which the infant becomes able to play at dropping
things," which is from five months to perhaps eighteen months. (This reminds us of Winnicott's 1941 paper "The Observation of Infants in a Set
Situation," in which he makes cogent inferences from seeing what the infants in his clinic do with tongue depressors.)

In his talk before the society he notes, "To reach the depressive position a baby must have become established as a whole person, and to be
related to whole persons as a whole person." Before this the infant is
ruthless: "It should be noted that the infant does not feel ruthless, but
looking back (and this does occur in regressions) the individual can say: I
was ruthless then! The stage is one that is pre-ruth." He goes on: "It
seems to me to be a postulate of Klein's theory that the human individual
cannot accept the crude fact of the excited or instinctual relationship or
assault on the 'quiet' mother. Integration in the child's mind of the split
between the child-care environment and the exciting environment (the
two aspects of mother) cannot be made except by good-enough mothering and the mother's survival over a period of time."

Thus, "the result of a day-after-day reinforcement of the benign circle is that the infant became able to tolerate the hole [in the mother as a
result of the infant's drawing out nourishment]. Here then is the beginning of *guilt* feeling. This is the only true guilt, since implanted guilt is
false to the self." That is, *"The healthy child has a personal source of sense of*

guilt, and need not be taught to feel guilty or concerned." So we find that "in the operation of the benign circle, concern becomes tolerable to the infant through a dawning recognition that, given time, something can be done about the hole, and the various effects of id impulse on the mother's body. Thus instinct becomes more free, and more risk can be taken. Greater guilt is generated, but there follows also an intensification of instinctual experience with its imaginative elaboration, so that a richer inner world results, followed in turn by a bigger gift potential." He concludes, "Love of the internal representation of an external object lost can lessen the hate of the introjected loved object which loss entails."[4]

In the end Winnicott answers the question not asked then but asked nowadays: What do analysts want? (a postmodern echo of Freud's "What do women want?"). The answer: "We want to be eaten, not magically introjected. There is no masochism in this. To be eaten is the wish and indeed the need of a mother at a very early stage in the care of an infant. This means that whoever is not cannibalistically attacked tends to feel outside the range of people's reparative and restitutive activities, and so outside society. If and only if we have been eaten, worn down, stolen from, can we stand in a minor degree being also magically introjected, and being placed in the preserve department in someone's inner world." In gender terms, this is the view of the analyst as female, the mother, and in its summarizing implications, it takes transference as far back as it can go, underscoring Winnicott's fundamental preoccupation.

In a letter dated October 31, 1990, Madeleine Davis reports on a presentation to the 1952 Club by Adam Phillips in which, according to her, he spoke of the horror of the ideas in "The Use of an Object "(1968) which nullify the whole idea of reparation: the object (see below) must be totally destroyed before it can be "of use." She thinks that Winnicott did not intend this meaning and quotes me, in a paper, as saying, "Ruthlessness must go on co-existing with concern, if we can claim to be adults, so long as we live."[5] "How complex it all is if one is trying to be intellectual!" she adds. Here she is addressing the simultaneity of stages of development, and underscoring the importance of the survival of earlier stages as development goes forward and generates successive stages. In addition, I can infer from this awareness that it is not always a matter of regression from one stage to another as an explanation for the ongoing simultaneity of stages, but more of a normal aspect of daily life. The destruction of the object, the result of the ruthlessness that began in infancy, which allows for the noticing of its survival, and therefore its new status as "useful," is there every day, along with our appreciation of the object as whole, ambivalently loved and hated, and worthy of our reparative efforts, part of a total relationship.

On June 3, 1954 Winnicott's ongoing struggle with the tripartite arrangement within the British Society, and most probably the corresponding dissociations within his own mind, including his position as one who stands alone outside all other groupings, prompted him to propose to Melanie Klein and Anna Freud that the organization that underlay the training program be dissolved.[6] He believed that with the death of either of the leaders, the division would continue indefinitely, based on political considerations. As usual, he presented his ideas with great earnestness.

The responses were negative, first from Klein and later from Anna Freud, who wrote on June 24 to say that she agreed with Klein. She stressed the confusion that a candidate would have to deal with if analyst and supervisors were of different theoretical persuasions. Harmony, she said, was important.[7]

We are reminded of the precariousness of Winnicott's health by a letter dated June 6, 1954, from Sylvia Payne. After Clifford Scott moved to Canada (interrupting the analysis of Clare Winnicott, just as war service had interrupted his work with Alice), Payne wrote: "It is obvious that you would be thought of first to fill Dr. Scott's place. I do not think that you ought to be asked as it would be a threat to your health to take on another administrative task of this calibre. It's hard to refuse if you are asked. I feel that your contributions to Psycho-Analysis + the scientific world are in the nature of creative ideas + that executive duties tend to destroy you."

Winnicott's concern for the direction child analysis was taking is heard in his unpublished "Meeting of Analysts Who Are Doing the Child Training Course" of July 14, 1954. In a powerful, authoritative voice, he gives freely of his wisdom, with reference to cases that fail. He notes that the training program of the institute began because he was able to supply cases from his Paddington Green clinic, that his assistant Norma Williams is likely to be the person to whom he would refer private cases, because she can do the work, in spite of not having received official training, and that there were talented therapists without training who could work with psychotic children in a way that hardly anyone with training could. The overall message is one of support for psychoanalysis and psychoanalytic training juxtaposed with a willingness to recognize ability that lies outside official circles. The intellectual air is brilliantly clear in this piece of writing.

The stark idea that analysts want to be eaten is paralleled by his preoccupation with the vexed subject of aggression, its origin, development, and relationship to libido. Winnicott's capacity to reflect upon aggression originating in mere mobility to wished-for (by the analyst) cannibalistic attacks *on* the analyst illustrates his intellectual range and audacity. The portion of his three-part paper on "Aggression in Relation to Emotional Development (1950)" which is entitled "The External Nature of Objects" was presented to a private group in the same month as his paper on withdrawal and regression. "Patients let us know that the aggressive experiences (more or less de-fused) feel real, much more real than do erotic experiences (also de-fused). Both are real, but the former carry a feeling of real, which is greatly valued. The fusion of the aggression along with the erotic component of an experience enhances the feeling of the reality of the experience. . . . confusion exists through our using the term aggression sometimes when we mean spontaneity. The impulsive gesture reaches out and becomes aggressive when opposition is reached. There is reality in this experience, and it very easily fuses into the erotic experiences that await the new-born infant. I am suggesting: *it is this impulsiveness, and the aggression that develops out of it, that makes the infant need an external object,* and not merely a satisfying object."

The second portion of his paper "Very Early Roots of Aggression" was given to a private group in January 1955. In it he asks: "[D]oes aggression come ultimately from anger aroused by frustration, or has it a root of its own?" He continues, "It is convenient . . . to say that the primitive love impulse (id) has a destructive quality, though it is not the infant's aim to destroy since the impulse is experienced in the pre-ruth era," by which he means in the era before the development of concern, which signifies the point when the mother is seen as a whole person. The paper contains his most explicit statement about the origins and nature of aggression. In its earliest form, he writes, aggression is allied with movement, beginning with motility of the fetus in utero. With adequate holding by the mother, the stage is set for the maximum of infusion of motility into id experiences. There is a fusion of the x per cent of the motility potential with erotic potential (with x quantitatively high). Nevertheless even here there is (100 − x) per cent of motility potential left out of the pattern of fusion, and available for pure motility use. It must be remembered that fusion allows of experience *apart from the action of opposition* (reaction to frustration). That which is fused with the erotic potential is satisfied in instinctual gratification. By contrast, the (100 − x) per cent unfused motility potential *needs to find opposition*. Crudely, it needs something to push against, unless it is to remain inexperienced and a threat to well-being. In health, however, by definition, the individual can enjoy going around looking for appropriate opposition.

Thus, the aggression built into movement itself is expressed both in its fusion with the erotic (potential) and in its opposition to resistance, or response to frustration.

Furthermore, "the sense of the real comes especially from the motility (and corresponding sensory) roots, and erotic experiences with a weak infusion of the motility element do not strengthen the sense of reality or of existing." Here he links the sense of reality, or, more likely, the intensity of the feeling of reality, with the expression of aggression, or motility. This foreshadows his climactic "Use of an Object" (1968), in which it is not motility as such but the continuous unconscious fantasy of destroying the object which is the backdrop for the survival of the object and thus of its availability for "use." Reality, he says there, is created by destruction of the object, a conception that was still some distance away in 1955.[8]

Anna Freud responded excitedly to the draft of his paper for the transference symposium to be held in Geneva that summer. The draft is a coherent description of Winnicott's "research" analysis for patients with borderline psychotic conditions, or neurotic patients with a pocket of psychosis. It is a plainly written document that reaffirms his belief in and use of psychoanalysis, as inherited from Freud, for suitable cases, and expands into the area of management and regression to dependence for patients who require this sort of experience. His question for Anna Freud was uncomplicated: he wanted to know whether what he had written was suitable for the symposium. He signs his letter of January 25, 1955, "Donald W. Winnicott." After 1963 he signed himself "Donald W. W." when writing to her, sometimes addressing her as "Anna Freud." These signatures are obvious attempts to induce a greater measure of closeness to Anna Freud, who continued to address him as "Dr. Winnicott."

In another letter soon after (February 19) Miss Freud wrote: "I do not think that I ever used the word 'technique of child care' myself. What I have in mind is the ministering to the child's body needs,—in distinction from his emotional needs and his instinctive urges, or rather, as a fore-runner to both of these. But I believe that it comes very near to what you have in mind yourself."

In the summer of 1955, at the Geneva Congress, he presented "Clinical Varieties of Transference." This short paper begins with reference to the True and False Self, with attendant theorizing about the early mother-child relationship. In light of the commentary in his paper on aggression on the sense of reality, it is worthy of note that he says that the hidden True Self, not involved in reacting to external impingements, "suffers an impoverishment that derives from lack of experience." It would appear that to the extent that the True Self is protected from collision with the external world, it does not develop the sense of reality that is so closely linked to the expression of oppositional motility and/or aggression. Essentially, it lacks experience of the external world. Yet the False Self, brought into being in order to shield the True Self and to face the external world, "cannot . . . experience life or feel real," so the total person is impoverished where the False Self grows beyond a certain stage: "The behaviour of the analyst, represented by what I have called the setting, by being good enough in the matter of adaptation to need, is gradually perceived by the patient as something that raises a hope that the True Self may at last be able to take the risks involved in its starting to experience living." He goes on in this vein, with the early failures of development reproduced in the transference, in which case "the patient is able to take an example of original failure and to be angry about it. Only when the patient reaches this point (which is preceded by a long period of near-perfect adaptation to need by the analyst) . . . can there be a beginning of reality-testing."

Continuing his effort to draw closer to Anna Freud, he wrote on November 18:

> I am trying to put together a small contribution which seems to me to follow your paper Psycho-Analysis and Education and the discus-

sion as reported in Volume 9 of the Psycho-Analytic Study of the Child.

I feel that so many important things were said by you in the course of that discussion that they lead naturally on to a more definite statement than was made of the emotional state of the mother at the very beginning of the infant's existence. This has been referred to but rather in terms of a biological state, and the word symbiosis has been used.

All this ties up very much with the difficulties that the Society is having at the moment in tracing the early roots of unfused aggression, this being reflected in my opinion in Mrs. Klein's temporary (I hope) insistence on what she calls innate envy, something which involves the idea of a variable genetic factor.

I am writing to you because I am wondering whether you have a group that I could write this short paper for so that it could be discussed. I would be quite contented, of course, if you were to say that it would be best if I were to write it and send it to you and have a talk with you about it personally. I somehow feel that, being human, I need an audience of at least one so that I may orientate to the presentation of my idea.

I know how busy you are but I know also that you can defend yourself and I need not mind asking you this favour.

I would like to say how very much I have enjoyed this contribution of yours in Volume 7 [a slip?] and I want to thank you again for mentioning my name.

Yours very sincerely,
D. W. Winnicott

This is a very needy letter, a plea, really, for recognition, an expression of gratitude for her mentioning his name, and a peculiar comment about her defending herself, indicating his urge to be nurtured by her in an unfettered way. She is an object of his desire. He is being obsequious, courting and whining. There is something desperate going on, which is probably illuminated by his letter to Riviere and Klein on February 3, 1956. He must have felt himself being forcibly expelled by them, and possibly all the more in need of Anna Freud's support.

The following is another landmark letter (February 3, 1956) in his attempt to defend himself against what appears to have been the expression, by Klein and Riviere, of a humiliating insult.

Dear Mrs. Riviere:

After Mrs. Klein's paper ["A Study of Envy and Gratitude"] you and she spoke to me and within the framework of friendliness you gave me to understand that both of you are absolutely certain that there is no positive contribution to be made from me to the interesting attempt Melanie is making all the time to state the psychology of the earliest stages. You will agree that you implied that the trouble is that I am unable to recognize that Melanie does say the very things that I am asking her to say. In other words, there is a block in me. This naturally concerns me very deeply and I very much hope you will give me a little bit of your time. I would willingly call on you if you do not feel like writing a letter. Enclosed are the notes from which I chose certain passages when speaking after Melanie's paper.

There is no need for me to try to tell Melanie how to do analysis. If I am any good at analysis myself it is largely due to her work and also to yourself. Also the work Melanie has done recently, drawing our attention to projective identification and now to envy, is undoubtedly valuable, although I would like to say that her contributions in these respects can be overvalued since analysts have surely been using these ideas for a long time. It was useful to be reminded of projective identification. In regard to envy, I think it valuable that Melanie has drawn our attention to the fact that the concept of penis envy, which has come into analysis for years and years, can have roots in breast envy. In other words, when envy turns up in the transference, it is not necessary for us to assume that the analyst is in the father role. The question arises, however, when envy turns up and the analyst is in the maternal role, whether it is not better to stick to the idea of potency even though a modified idea of potency must be ascribed when it is of the mother figure that we speak.

Surely Melanie's paper had three themes which were mixed up in a way which made discussion almost impossible. I am surprised to find Melanie writing such a muddled paper. The first theme is the theme of envy as it appears in analysis, and here her contribution is positive and acceptable and valuable, although not new. The second theme is that of the infant's envy of the good breast. Here Melanie is looking at the infant as brought to the analysis by the child or adult patient. The third is her attempt to state the psychology of earliest infancy. In the second I feel that she has raised problems which are by no means solved and in the third I feel that she has let herself down badly by making a statement which it is very easy to pull to pieces, and which can easily hold up the study of the development of Ego stability and the researches which are going on in various parts of the world into the treatment of psychosis. I think it is necessary that Melanie does not deal with psychotic patients although of course she has a vast experience of psychotic material as it appears in patients who are not actually mental hospital material.[9]

It is little wonder that a paper which muddles up these three distinct themes produced a poor discussion. The only thing that can happen is that those who like to support Melanie produce, as we could all do, clinical material or quotations from the Bible which support her theme. Anyone dealing with the other two subjects must be in an odd position because the themes are in odd positions relative to each other.

My trouble when I start to speak to Melanie about her statement of early infancy is that I feel as if I were talking about colour to the colour-blind. She simply says that she has not forgotten the mother and the part the mother plays, but in fact I find that she has shown no evidence of understanding the part the mother plays at the very beginning. I must say this quite boldly in spite of the fact that I have never been a mother and she, of course, has. You, too, have been a mother, and you are entitled to your own opinion about my capacity to deal with these matters. You have expressed to me often that you value my statements of the mother-infant relationship, and I want to ask you whether you could carry the matter a little further and consider perhaps whether there is not something in the theory at this point that I can contribute. If I contribute to psychoanalytic theory it is not of course necessary for me to be accepted by either yourself or Melanie Klein, but I do in fact mind tremendously if I really have a positive contribution to make, however small, and if this cannot find acceptance either with you or with Melanie.

An example of the way in which communication with Melanie is difficult on this point—I would take the matter of her statement to the effect that there is the "good breast" and there is the infant, and the result is an attack on the breast. I know very well indeed that this is true and I know that it is the good breast and not the bad breast that the infant bites. Nevertheless in talking in this way we are leaving out the Ego development of the infant and we are therefore not making a statement of earliest infancy. The "good breast" is not a thing, it is a name given to a technique.[10] It is the name given to the presentation of breast (or bottle) to the infant, a most delicate affair and one which can only be done well enough at the beginning, if the mother is in a most curious state of sensitivity which I for the time-being call the State of Primary Maternal Preoccupation. Unless she can identify very closely with her infant at the beginning, she cannot "have a good breast," because just having the thing means nothing whatever to the infant. This theme can be developed, and I have frequently attempted to develop it because I know of its great importance not only to mothers with infants but also to analysts who are dealing with patients who have for the moment or over longer phases been deeply regressed.

It is a matter of great grief to me that I cannot get Melanie to take up this point or to see that there is a point here to be discussed.

You may wonder why I am writing you and not to Melanie. It would seem likely that Melanie will not want to be bothered with me and my ideas especially in view of the fact that she will not meet any analysts except those who are glad to welcome her contribution in respect of its first theme. I know, however, that you have always been in close touch with Melanie and in any case I have an interest in your opinion of me for obvious reasons. The one thing that would make me doubt about writing to you is the sentence in the preface to the Klein book [see his letter to Klein, November 17, 1952] which you wrote and which you know shocked me, in which you implied that the Klein system of thought had covered everything so that there was nothing left to be done but to widen the application of the theories.

I shall understand if you have too much on hand to be willing to take up this matter with me. I feel, however, that I want you to know that I do not accept what you and Melanie implied, namely that my concern about Melanie's statement of the psychology of earliest infancy is based on subjective rather than objective factors.

Riviere replied with a postcard (February 10) about having had "2–3 weeks bronchitis" (her recurrent pulmonary condition), as well as "the most formidable arrears and obligations all round to be urgently off! When I feel freer and stronger I shall be glad to see you + talk."

Donald responded on February 14: "I am very glad that you have put my letter aside. Some time when you are feeling quite well you may be able to look at it in spite of its length. Meanwhile I hope that you will get well quickly. Some letters have to be written but they do not have to be read." And again, on February 24: "I would be grateful if you would destroy the letter I sent you. If you have time to consider the matters raised in that letter I would rather that you were to read the enclosed." The enclosure remains unidentified. Given the change in climate between Riviere and Klein in the 1950s,[11] I speculate that their joint expulsion of Winnicott had some sort of meaning for the two of them. Perhaps Riviere's alliance with Klein against Winnicott represented an effort to ingratiate herself with Klein during a time of alienation. Hanna Segal quotes a letter to Klein in which Riviere begged: "What have I done? Why have you turned against me? What's gone wrong?"[12] Did Klein turn against Riviere? Or did Riviere withdraw as the group grew larger? A four-year period full of new ideas and underlying personal struggle was reaching a point of punctuation.[13]

— 17 —

Patients Who May Kill Psychoanalysts

Loyal member that he was, Winnicott went on contributing according to his developing understanding, and serving the British Society. He was president of the society between 1956 (when he turned sixty) and 1959. The correspondence that he collected in his personal files attests to the many demands placed on him by colleagues who wished him to speak or to write or to see patients, and from nonprofessionals who wished to communicate with him about one thing or another. He seems to have responded actively to all requests. His productivity continued to expand in the number of presentations he gave, not to mention the books that began to appear. These extended his work deeper into the professional world and stimulated the invitations he would receive over the next decade from analytic groups in various parts of the world.

A conference in celebration of the centenary of Freud's birth gave him an opportunity to dwell again on a subject of perennial interest, perhaps especially because it brought Anna Freud, Melanie Klein, and himself together. His conference paper, "Psycho-Analysis and the Sense of Guilt," given in April 1956, is an encyclopedic work in which he attempts "to study guilt-feeling, not as a thing to be inculcated, but as an aspect of the development of the human individual." He writes, "Those who hold the view that morality needs to be inculcated teach small children accordingly, and they forgo the pleasure of watching morality develop naturally in their children, who are thriving in a good setting that is provided in a personal and individual way." In his review of Freud's work, he reminds us that early statements on the subject did not include the aggressive impulse, and adds that "in the concept of the superego can be seen the proposition that the genesis of guilt is a matter of inner reality, or that guilt resides in the intention." In obsessional neurosis, "in some specific setting of which the patient is unaware, hate is more powerful than love," and in melancholia, where the patient has the same fear (hate stronger than love), "the illness is an attempt to do the impossible. The patient absurdly claims responsibility for general disaster, but in so doing avoids reaching his or her personal destructiveness. . . . [I]t is only Freud's instrument of psycho-analysis and its derivatives that have made it possible for us to help the individual who is burdened by guilt-feeling to find the true origin of the sense of guilt in his or her own nature. The sense of guilt, seen this way, is a special form of anxiety associated with ambivalence, or co-existing love and hate."

In the middle section of the paper, headed "Guilt at Its Point of Origin," he outlines Klein's theory of the depressive position in his own language, with emphasis on reparation or "the restitutive gesture." It is crucial to "the benign circle" of development that the mother be present to receive the child's gesture, which helps him cope with the sense of guilt that is part of this stage of growth. The infant can begin to accept full responsibility "for the total fantasy of the full instinctual impulse that was previously ruthless." He concludes this section by saying: "From my personal point of view, the work of Klein has enabled psycho-analytic theory to begin to include the idea of an individual's *value*, whereas in early psycho-analysis the statement was in terms of *health* and neurotic *ill-health*. Value is intimately bound up with the capacity for guilt-feeling."

In the last section, "Sense of Guilt Conspicuous by Its Absence," he concentrates on the antisocial tendency, the subject of a separate paper. What I would call his characteristic leap—a sudden inspiration that leads to a comment discontinuous from what went just before, as if he has left out some of his own associations—comes in a paragraph headed "The Creative Artist": "It is interesting to note that the creative artist is able to reach to a kind of socialization which obviates the need for guilt-feeling and the associated reparative and restitutive activity that forms the basis for ordinary constructive work. The creative artist or thinker may, in fact, fail to understand, or even may despise, the feelings of concern that motivate a less creative person; and of artists it may be said that some have no capacity for guilt and yet achieve a socialization through their exceptional talent. Ordinary guilt-ridden people find this bewildering; yet they have a sneaking regard for ruthlessness that does in fact, in such circumstances, achieve more than guilt-driven labour." There are no clinical illustrations; his statements, made in an authoritative tone, can only suggest the possibility that he has observed a phenomenon that deserves our attention. This is a leap of thought analogous to the moment at which the artists he describes make a gestural leap in the elaboration of a work of art. Perhaps the use of the word "ruthlessness" is the clue to what he meant, since it was reserved quite specifically for the infant at the breast before awareness of an object. Elsewhere[1] he speaks of the necessity of prepared reparative gestures before the full expression of destructiveness is possible. Does he mean that the creative artist may indulge ruthlessly at the very moment he or she is being most reparative? Given what we now know of the behavior of Masud Khan, Winnicott's analysand, and even though Khan was not an artist, perhaps Winnicott awarded him this title (which, for Winnicott, has pejorative overtones if applied to a psychoanalyst) on the basis of an absent sense of guilt combined with flashes of deep understanding. If Khan were this peculiar subtype, he would not have to be called a sociopath.

In "Primary Maternal Preoccupation" (1956), Winnicott writes of the special condition of mind that women attain in the final weeks of pregnancy and the first few weeks after giving birth. It would be called pathological were it not that pregnancy and early motherhood are normal features of life. The mother is preoccupied with her infant almost to the exclusion of all else, and this condition makes it possible for her to adapt to its needs in a near-perfect way, to be the good-enough mother that a baby requires to start its life. This paper includes a comment that differentiates his point of view from those of the other "object relations" analysts. He writes: "Miss Freud shows that we have gone far beyond that awkward stage in psycho-analytic theory in which we spoke as if life started for the infant with oral instinctual experience. We are now engaged in the study of early development and of the early self which, if development has gone far enough, can be strengthened instead of disrupted by id experiences. Miss Freud says, developing the theme of

Freud's term 'anaclitic': 'The relationship to the mother, although the first to another human being, is not the infant's first relationship to the environment. What precedes it is an earlier phase in which not the object world but the body needs and their satisfaction or frustration play the decisive part.'" He means that it takes a period of development before the infant is capable of relating to "the object world." This capacity is not there at birth.

A woman who is tending her infant in the state of primary maternal preoccupation allows the silent "building up of the ego" In the child: "The first ego organisation comes from the experience of threats of annihilation which do not lead to annihilation and from which, repeatedly, there is *recovery*. Out of such experiences confidence in recovery begins to be something which leads to an ego and to an ego capacity for coping with frustration." He goes on: "A good enough environmental provision in the earliest phase enables the infant to begin to exist, to have experience, to build a personal ego, to ride instincts, and to meet with all the difficulties inherent in life. All this feels real to the infant who becomes able to have a self that can eventually even afford to sacrifice spontaneity, even to die. On the other hand, without the initial good-enough environmental provision, the self that can afford to die never develops." This last is the typical startling Winnicottian extension of thinking into uncharted territory. In a letter to me during the Vietnam War, he spoke of young soldiers with False Self personalities who were afraid to die because they had not lived. He was not speaking about life as chronological age.

"The Antisocial Tendency"[2] makes use of Winnicott's experiences during World War II in Oxfordshire and much more, to propound the notion that deprivation is not a primary condition but, by definition, comes after a period of satisfaction. It is not the same as privation. The antisocial act is an expression of hope, a sign, for anyone who can read it, that the perpetrator feels that what he once had by right has been taken away unfairly. He is expressing his need. "The antisocial tendency is characterized by an *element in it which compels the environment to be important*. The patient through unconscious drives compels someone to attend to management," he writes. "The child who steals an object is not looking for *the object stolen but seeks the mother over whom he or she has rights*. These rights derive from the fact that (from the child's point of view) the mother was created by the child." And, extending further into the realm of the normal: "Any exaggeration of the nuisance value of an infant may indicate the existence of a degree of deprivation and antisocial tendency." He adds, "In a more complete study of stealing I would need to refer to the compulsion to go out and buy something, which is a common manifestation of the antisocial tendency that we meet in our psycho-analytic patients." He connects here to the phenomenon now familiar to all, indicated by such current *bons mots* as "Shop Till You Drop" and "Born to Shop," or even "Shut Up and Shop," a true pathology of material acquisition, though not often treated as such.

Another 1956 paper, "Paediatrics and Childhood Neurosis,"[3] consists of two parts. In the first section Winnicott reviews the nature of neurosis, with its origin in unconscious conflict and the central role of anxiety, which pediatricians are in a position to observe *in statu nascendi*, if they but knew it. In the second part he emphasizes the indispensable value of psychoanalytic training for those who wish to treat effectively. He seeks recognition of the value of psychoanalysis for pediatrics, as one who practices both.

At about the same time, in response to a letter from a Cuban analyst who had received training in London on the subject of his son's discovery of his penis, Winnicott had some interesting observations to make. They may be considered in relation to two ideas. The first, which came late in Winnicott's life, was that the father is the first whole object, later endowed by the child with a part object. The second is my theory that Winnicott related to his "father" Freud through the two women (Melanie Klein and Anna Freud) who carried within them his (phallic) legacy. In his letter of July 4, 1956, he writes:

> It seems to me that the idea of what in psychoanalytic terms is called a penis originally turns up in respect of certain qualities in the mother such as rules and regulations, timing, hardness, indestructibility. At a variable date these ideas gather together and may be handed over to the father if he happens to be around. Here is building up the idea of an indestructible element that easily forms a root for eventual appreciation of a paternal phallus. Before this happens there are several side-tracks, one of which is the idea of a maternal phallus. . . .
>
> What a task the infant has, bringing together these ideas of his own genitality and the concept of the paternal phallus which is formed from another root in the way I have tried to describe! It seems

to me that observations of the paternal phallus sometimes join up
with the one and sometimes with the other root.

Winnicott's insights were now being recognized as sympathetic to
other groups. This is demonstrated in a letter of December 9, 1956, to his
friend Michael Fordham in which he writes: "From my point of view, I
wish you people [the Jungians] did not exist separately from us, and I
have no doubt that you wish we did not exist separately from you. In the
course of time it will certainly be necessary for the two trainings to discuss the points they have in common."

In this period there were also several cordial letters from Jacques
Lacan. Winnicott had chaired a committee of the International Psychoanalytic Association that investigated a split in the French societies
prompted by Lacan and his followers.[4] Other members were Phyllis
Greenacre, Willi Hoffer, and Jeanne Lampl de Groot. Lacan was being
criticized for his short sessions (they might be as little as ten minutes long
if he felt like it). "He exercised too much attraction on his pupils, he was
no good at analyzing transference, and it was thought his influence inside the SFP might be excessive and unhealthy."[5] Further investigations
without Winnicott led ultimately to the expulsion of Lacan from the IPA
at the Stockholm Congress of 1963.

On January 10, 1957, Klein wrote that she would be pleased to attend
the dinner before the Margaret Mead lecture—a sign of their ongoing relationship despite Winnicott's powerful criticism. But there was little
time left for them to communicate with each other. Very shortly Clare's
analysis with Klein would bring a virtual end to the relationship.

That same month Winnicott wrote to Dr. Anna Kulka of Los Angeles,[6] offering a fulsome response to a paper she had written:

> I have read "Kinesthetic Needs and Motility in Earliest Infancy." Per-
> sonally I am most interested in the study of the movements in prema-
> ture infants which give an indication of what happens in the foetal
> state which indicates life and liveliness. For instance, it has often
> come my way in an analysis to interpret a snake not as a phallic sym-
> bol but as a symbol of the infant's whole self as represented in the
> body and body movements that are characteristic round the birth
> date. You seem to me to be dealing with this difficult problem of the
> infant's task, and therefore the task of those who are caring for the in-

fant, which is to gather up as much as possible of whatever there is of the early vitality into the general service of love and hate. No doubt there is always a certain residue of the earliest activities and muscular urges which is never assimilated to the whole means of expression, and one of the most difficult things I find in analyses is the technique for dealing with unassimilated destructive or aggressive or simply vital urges which turn up clinically in the form of maniacal attacks or more commonly in the form of an inability on the part of the patient to relax. Vigilance has to be maintained against the maniacal episode.

I think that an awfully important part of hypermotility is its relationship to inhibition of oral erotism or, shall I say, the hopelessness about object relationships in oral terms. . . . It appears in the common statement of parents that the restless child is restless "even at meals." If the mother knew more psychology she would say "especially at meals" because it appears as a substitute for the greedy impulse that can be satisfied.

Certainly we have gone a long way beyond thinking that the infant starts with the oral erotic relationship to the breast and there is a great deal of Ego development prior to the establishment of feeding if this be looked at in terms of an experience of the infant and not simply as a mechanical taking in of food that is offered.

During this time, among the now classic papers there arose some unpublished speculations about patients who were capable of "killing" psychoanalysis and psychoanalysts. Extrapolating from the notion that analysts want to be eaten, Winnicott may have meant that analysts offer themselves to patients for consumption, the extreme expression of which is "being eaten." Short of that, especially in what he called "the well-chosen neurotic case," the analyst offers insight for consumption, at first at a distance from crude instinctual eating. But as patients with earlier damage are treated, the analyst offers himself or herself in a way that may be experienced as being closer and closer to actual nutrition, to the breast, the flesh itself. Patients who regress to dependency require analysts with protracted adaptation and a readiness to provide what is needed at the right time—close, it seems, to feeding, and sometimes even food itself. Freud gave food to his famous patient the Rat Man, and Winnicott offered tea and biscuits to his patients.

Although the analyst may protect himself or herself during the delicate process by which he makes himself available to his patient, the process may lead to exposure to danger if the patient's destructive urges are not counterbalanced adequately by gratitude or love. In the nether reaches of instinctual life, where the patient, stimulated by hope, attacks the "bad mother," as a transference figure or as a psychotically perceived, here-and-now, actual bad mother, the analyst, especially the adventurous analyst who believes deeply in his capacities under all circumstances, may be in dire straits. By that I mean that he may be subjected to physical attack (Winnicott was physically attacked by Margaret Little) on any basis, including that of delusion, or may sense that he is in physical danger, for example, from a coronary constriction. I once had a patient with whom I came to the edge of understanding but also to imminent danger of some sort of physical event, which I sensed was going to occur in my chest. In this period, it felt frightening to be in the presence of this patient. A paranoid countertransference had supervened, but not necessarily without actual physical danger.

Such concerns were the focus of Winnicott's correspondence with Thomas Main about his patient who committed suicide. Winnicott's letter of January 24, 1957, is a response to Main's paper, "The Ailment." Winnicott, referring to "the second [part], the long part dealing with the Nurses' problems and the research method, and this is what I found fascinating," suggested that it be discussed at the British Society.

"The Ailment"[7] is a densely written, unrelenting tour de force of observation and inference about twelve "special patients." It quickly became a classic in the era of "milieu therapy," about the time that the phenothiazine tranquilizers (Thorazine, Stelazine, Mellaril) were introduced, but prior to the availability of the vast array of psychotropic medications that would follow, and the emphasis on medical cost accounting that would reduce all hospital stays to an absolute minimum. These patients required new experiences to help overcome deficits in their development, wrote Main. They elicited unusually privileged handling by the staff, with extraordinary devotion as the perceived precondition for therapeutic progress. Many staff members, ever more sensitive to failure, suffered breakdowns, and the outcome for almost all these patients was unfavorable. Staff resentment of one another was characteristic, with florid suspicion that others were incapable of the necessary intelligence, sensitivity, and devotion. These patients were studied through a long series of staff discussions under Main's direction.

The one patient who committed suicide was Winnicott's. She was the person for whom he had sought access to Seconal. "The Ailment" shows us the dark side of analytic devotedness, which, on the surface, appears to be an exceptional and admirable pattern of behavior on behalf of those who require it. The paper leads one to wonder about the less apparent side of Winnicott's devotion to patients who are seen individually but who may also require occasional institutionalization or other special arrangements. Main calls attention to ambivalence and the potential risk of failing to acknowledge and integrate the negative side.

During this period Winnicott was developing his theory of "management" and defending it vigorously to Riviere, Klein, Rosenfeld, and others. Management considerations allowed for an expansion of psychoanalysis to include more disturbed patients. In his hands, it would seem to have accomplished the otherwise unaccomplishable. There were casualties, such as his special patient at the Cassel, and later on a woman who committed suicide when Winnicott was detained by illness in New York. We know as well of a psychoanalyst who had two-month periods of twice-daily analysis with Winnicott and who, in 1980, killed himself. This man had made a suicide attempt with drugs, had been unconscious for at least two weeks, then recovered and resumed the analysis of a woman who later wrote about her experience. Margaret Little compares his case to that of Masud Khan in the sense that he required "a greater degree of reliability in dealing with his psychotic anxieties than DWW could, in fact, provide—hence failures—breakdown into madness and suicide."[8]

"The Ailment" looks down into the abyss at the dangers of regression for both patient and caretaking person. At the time of this episode, the perils of Seconal addiction were known in medical circles, and yet Winnicott overrode the usual cautions to get access to supplies that the patient could use. We do not know whether it was Seconal that was used in the suicide, but this is probable. Winnicott's judgment, as he reached for a cure, seems, in retrospect, clouded. His own hope and his overestimation of his abilities lured him into the dangerous situation that resulted in his patient's death.

Winnicott retained a handwritten note in his file: "Mrs. Coles: I have lost my only daughter. C. died yesterday. She was a nuisance. In the end it was my own limitations that killed her, quite unnecessarily. I would like to have Saturday over again. Mrs. R. [probably his patient's mother] will come 1:16 PM King's Cross. Will you go and meet her with me? Perhaps you would take her to Ham Common [the location of Cassel]. Thank you for all the help you have given me over this maddening person who was so nearly through but not quite. She was coping with reality. Most people don't have to, or they skim it over and around its problem. DWW."

The insistence on special status for these patients is reminiscent of Marion Milner's comments about Winnicott's conviction that "only he," or someone of his choice, could analyze a particular person. The patient "J." was sent to Margaret Little, and the outcome was, according to Marion Milner, "disastrous." The solitary conditions of psychoanalytic practice make it easy for an analyst to become convinced of his special status and expertise. Main writes of the doctors he studied that "it was plainly difficult for them to relinquish to others full responsibility for the patient," and that "concern for the patient was emphasized, impatience or hatred never." But Little reports Winnicott's extreme frustration with the woman who committed suicide. He wanted her to "get it over with!!!" This underlying attitude—revealed, it seems, to a patient in a regressed analysis—makes sense, even if it is misguided, in the light of the frustrations intrinsic to such exacting work. Of course the analyst would want to be rid of a patient who required so much of him. But the urge to get it over with undoubtedly coexisted with the urge to see it through successfully.

The discussion with Main generated unprecedented insights into potentially life-endangering features of certain psychoanalytic patients, the realization that the strain of devotion may lead to the death of the analyst. Winnicott was able to recognize himself in this discussion and in his letter to Main. Main's absolutely unflinching research into a most difficult subject is a tribute to what appears to be an especially British ability to make room for failure and ugliness in the larger context of personal effort.

On January 29, 1957, Main told Winnicott that "the whole business [the suicide] was too near and painful for me at least to be able to discuss it without wanting to blame somebody. [It took both of them seven years before they could deal with it.] Now that I am easy about it, I am wondering if the time has come when discussion would be fruitful. I would very much like to spend an evening with you (not on this occasion social) to discuss not only [your patient] but the phenomena surrounding other patients also."

On February 25, Winnicott reflected on their meeting:

Dear Dr. Main,

It was natural that at the half-way stage we should have arrived in our discussions at a point where [my patient] is under discussion as my special patient. I had to take the opportunity to obtain personal relief after waiting many years before speaking about this case which I believe had in it the possibilities of a clinical result. . . .

Your collecting together of all the fragments of nursing reactions adds up to a real contribution to psycho-analysis.

Roughly speaking I would say that there are two obvious extremes of people in the world; those who are having psycho-analysis or could make use of psycho-analysis as we know it, and by contrast those who have no reason to hope and who therefore do not worry us. The second category includes a large amount of the mental hospital population and also a great number of people living in ordinary society but who have no knowledge that life could be more satisfactory than it is. I am concerned at the moment about the intermediate area between these two extremes. We can divide this again into three groups. The first would be those who have needs derived from early infancy and who just manage to get through in the course of analysis, partly because they happen to have gone to analysis with an analyst who is willing to adapt the classical technique where necessary. The third category in this intermediate area of those who have some hope is largely made up of those who commit suicide. At the centre is the second in this category and here we have the kind of patient that you are describing. The characteristic of this kind of patient is that hope forces them to bang on the door of all therapies which might give the answer. They cannot rest from this and, as you know so well, their technique for mobilizing activity is terrific in its efficiency. In this particular grouping I think there is a dynamic force which might destroy psycho-analysis. In practice these patients could wear down all the available nursing and actual psycho-analytic personnel. Psycho-analysis cannot ignore this group any longer but must know that it provides a threat. The psycho-analyst's life is likely to be threatened by one or two of these patients who always happen to be in his practice. . . . Constructive work at the Cassel, you have pointed out, can be disrupted by a few of these patients.

What I am trying to put down in black and white is that these patients make us try hard because they have hope and because it is the hope which makes them so clever; yet at the same time the fact that we cannot provide what is needed produces disaster. In other words, it is only contributing a little if one can show that what these patients need is a very complex situation in which they can regress and in which the psycho-analyst can help them to make use of a regression. Whatever can be done and is done here must be only a small bit of what would have to be done to neutralise the destructive potential of this group of people. Indeed I would say that the more psycho-analysts become able to do this kind of work with a few patients the more patients there are who will begin to have hope and therefore will begin to bash around in a ruthless search for a life that feels real. I do consider, therefore, that if psycho-analysts ignore the problem that you have raised in your paper, they are ignoring a group of forces that could destroy psycho-analysis, and in practice could account for the deaths of analysts and psychiatric nursing staff and the breakup of the better type of mental institution.

Members of Main's staff did suffer breakdowns, but no one died, as far as I know. Still, Winnicott perceived death itself as a possible risk of arousing hope without the resources to neutralize destructiveness. With disturbed patients who present themselves as possibly amenable to the kind of work Winnicott did and others do, it may be said that they have hope, and their analysts may have hope as well—hope that is misguided. But the analysts do not know at the outset that there is no hope. They do not know the extent of disturbance in combination with their own limitations. They may be subjected to a process of consumption from which they do not survive. Those who wish to be eaten may be physically destroyed—not able, as they assume, to survive in the face of being eaten, thereby establishing themselves as "of use." There may therefore be moments in work with such patients when the analysts decide that they must cease to expose themselves to these forces. Younger analysts may show the necessary persistence and energy to work with such patients, while older ones may not. I have written a book-length account of such work with a patient in the beginning of my career.[9]

The word "ruthless" in the penultimate paragraph of Winnicott's letter expresses the idea that the analyst of such patients is subjected to forces that do not take account of him as a person. Thus, he is not compensated in a human, non-monetary way for what the patient takes. And with such a group of patients he will not be able to deliver what they are after and will never be compensated for all it has cost him to try. In the effort to gain a result, he may exceed his psychoanalytic capacity to understand and temporize, and may find that, in a regressed way, his physical health is now at stake. This seems to have happened with members of Main's staff, and Winnicott himself had a heart attack not long after his patient killed herself. While not having suffered a coronary, I sensed the imminence of something similar in the case to which I referred.

Several years later (July 26, 1965), Charles Rycroft tried to refer a patient to Winnicott. He felt pessimistic about being able to help her. She idealized him, treated him as if he were a transitional object. Winnicott replied (August 2): "I feel really frightened about seeing her myself as I know that if I am any use to her at all she will try to go on using me in a way that I am not willing to fit in with; in other words, I feel very much like you do in spite of the fact that I have allowed certain patients of mine to make claims on me so that I might know what these claims are."

While speculating about patients who can kill psychoanalysts, Winnicott continued to write classic papers, beautifully reasoned. He continued to see patients, to serve the British Psycho-Analytical Society, to deal with correspondence, mundane and otherwise, all while leading his fuller married life.

The question of failure continued as a concern. "I would like to write a note," he wrote to Michael Balint on March 27, 1957, "to thank you for the trouble you took preparing and giving the lecture last Wednesday. I think the best part of it is that you start from a position of humility with the acknowledgement that we all have failures to our account. This is a great relief as compared with the tone of many speakers who seem to suggest that they can tackle everything." Winnicott was one of those who overestimated his own abilities repeatedly, either his analytic powers themselves, or his ability to judge who could analyze particular patients effectively and who could not. He continued: "I cannot say that I agree with your idea that the only worth while contribution was in my opening remarks, but I think you wrote this the next morning in the negative phase that occurs after the reading of a paper. It is certainly important for the Society to be reminded over and over again that man cannot live by bread alone—bread here meaning verbal interpretations."

On April 11, 1957, there is a grateful letter from Ilse Hellman for his sending two books during a hospital siege with her daughter Margaret. She would miss his seminar, she said. "As a mother and an analyst I want to say a doublefold 'thank you' for all the help you have given me through your work in all these years." This is further evidence of his capacity (or was it true of everyone in the society?) to transcend difficult moments over the long haul. After her bitter response to his criticism of her membership paper, how grateful she was now.

Amidst all that was so serious, we find a note of humor[10] also typical of Winnicott in a letter to the editor of *The Times* (April 11, 1957):

I *QANT* STAND IT

It is reported that Qantas pilots are to strike for higher pay. Could they not strike at the same time for the restoration of the U to their Q? This Q without U has been planted on the English-speaking world and causes irritation. Surely this mutilation tends to put people against trusting their lives to Q. E. A.!

Winnicott stayed in touch with his relatives in Plymouth, as a few letters from his cousin Harold attest, though there were none either to or from his sisters in his files. Harold writes about taxes coming due on the estate (of Donald's father, no doubt) and the problem presented for Violet and Kathleen, who, in the end, are left to go on living at Rockville without financial worry, although the estate fell into disrepair, the sisters took to sleeping on the ground floor instead of in the bedrooms upstairs, and at one point a homeless man took up residence in one of the outbuildings on the property. "I have been thinking over your letter," Harold wrote on October 26, 1957, "and really feel it would come very hard on V & K if they had to sell up an investment to meet this Estate duty demand as so far as I can make out they only just make ends meet, the upkeep of Rockville what with wages, repairs, rates, etc. are pretty heavy. If their income was reduced very much they would certainly have to try and sell Rockville. It has been their home for so many years that anywhere else would not be the same. You have asked my views and I have been frank in saying what I feel." Harold then offered to take over the house Donald owned on Evelyn Terrace for £500, just to help out. Donald declined the offer. The house came up for sale after rent controls were lifted, but Winnicott, though wishing to sell, decided to keep it when the renters indicated that they could not afford to buy it.

A note from Marion Milner on May 19 includes, at the end, "I'm sending a cheque because I expect I'll want to ask for another talk one of these days. Love to you both." An analytic strand continued, seven or eight years after the end of analysis proper, as part of their relationship.

In June 1957, John Bowlby gave a paper[11] at the British Society which occasioned some interesting correspondence. Winnicott wrote to Joan Riviere on June 21, 1957, thanking her for taking part in the discussion of the paper: "It was certainly a very difficult paper to appreciate without at the same time giving away almost everything that has been fought for by Freud." (Riviere had analyzed Bowlby in the thirties.)

The next day he got a letter from Anna Freud thanking him for his letter and then commenting that Bowlby was too valuable to lose. "But in the present paper," she says, " he sacrifices most of the gains of the analytic theory, such as the libido theory, the principles of mental functioning (the pleasure principle), ego-psychology etc. with very little return. I suppose he is put off by the ante-dating of complex mental events in the Kleinian psychology, but that is no real excuse for going too far in the other direction." Analysts in general paid little attention to Bowlby with his attachment theory, and would not have anticipated that his work would become central to a major development of psychoanalytic thought in the early part of the twenty-first century.

Winnicott wrote on July 17, 1957, to Augusta Bonnard, an analyst who was in charge of a clinic for children in East London. They were in quite frequent touch. On this occasion the subject was secret tongue-sucking. Bonnard had an adopted patient who did this.[12] Winnicott writes that "in my anorexia nervosa case that I have talked about sometimes, secret tongue-sucking was very important, and I took a long time to discover it." Such secret forms of satisfaction would make it more difficult for an analyst to become a vital force in the lives of such children. Discovering them could thus mobilize a new therapeutic direction.

In "On the Contribution of Direct Child Observation to Psycho-Analysis,"[13] Winnicott makes the point that "deep," as in the "deep" stage, is not synonymous with "early." This distinction is based on the notion that an infant needs a certain amount of maturation before it can have experiences associated with the word "deep," and that in the beginning there is an environment-baby combination out of which, if the environment is good enough, develops a capacity for object relations with growing complexity. He quotes Strachey and concludes that Strachey accepts "the words as synonymous," in which case he is correcting his revered analyst. "What is found repeatedly in analysis," he says, "is not annulled by being proved to be wrong through direct observation. Direct observation only proves that the patients have been antedating certain phenomena and therefore giving the analyst the impression that things were happening at an age when they could not have happened." Toward the beginning of the paper he presents his credentials as a direct observer by citing his paper "Observation of Infants in a Set Situation" (1941), but the emphasis is primarily on the importance of conclusions drawn from psychoanalysis as opposed to any notion by direct observers that they may be displacing such conclusions by looking.

In the same month as his direct child observation paper, he gave another, "The Capacity to Be Alone."[14] It is one of the many by which he is known, with the distinct Winnicottian stamp of paradox. In this case, the capacity of the title arises out of the infant's first being alone in the presence of the mother, that is to say, the infant's "relaxing," not having to be integrated, and eventually feeling an impulse that may be directed to the mother, who has been there all along. The capacity to be alone, based on good-enough mothering, is "one of the most important signs of maturity in emotional development." In the clinical setting, "the patient who falls into silence may be showing a capacity to be alone for the first time."

He approaches the subject under various headings, and as usual, the abundance of ideas is never presented as if it were truly exhaustive. He does not aim to cover all the ground, it would seem, even with abundance. "I consider that if one compares the meaning of the word 'like' with that of the word 'love,'" he writes, "one can see that liking is a matter of ego-relatedness, whereas loving is more a matter of id-relationships, either crude or in sublimated form." After intercourse, "being alone along with another person who is also alone is in itself an experience of health." He adds, "It could be said that an individual's capacity to be alone depends on his ability to deal with the feelings aroused by the primal scene," and "the capacity to be alone depends on the existence of a good object in the psychic reality of the individual."[15]

"Ego-relatedness" refers to the state of mind of the infant who is alone in the presence of his mother. "It may turn out to be the *matrix of transference*," writes Winnicott. "The individual who has developed the capacity to be alone is constantly able to rediscover the personal impulse, and the personal impulse is not wasted because the state of being alone is something which (though paradoxically) always implies that someone else is there. . . .[I]f there is such a thing as an ego orgasm, those who are inhibited in instinctual experience will tend to specialize in such orgasms, so that there would be a pathology of the tendency to ego orgasm." Here we have to consider that he is being ironic about himself, unbeknownst to his readers. He goes on: "There can be value in thinking of *ecstasy* as an ego orgasm . . . the climax that may occur in satisfactory ego-relatedness." He states that "the so-called normal child is able to play, to get excited while playing, and to feel *satisfied with the game*, without feeling threatened by a physical orgasm of local excitement."

The Child and the Family was published in 1957. In October, Arthur Rosenthal, his publisher at Basic Books, sent along a copy of the American edition. It was then that Winnicott wrote back to him about not using "M.D." after his name, but he eventually agreed to its use for an American audience, since it indicates the same qualification that his fellowship in the Royal College of Physicians signifies in Britain.

The Ordinary Devoted Mother and Her Baby (a BBC publication) had been included in *The Child and the Family*. By the end of that year, publishing plans were far advanced for *Collected Papers: Through Paediatrics to Psycho-Analysis*. In addition, a small book titled *Mother and Child: A Primer of First Relationships* came out. All at once, it seemed, the large backlog of Winnicott writings was becoming available. Many new readers were going to be exposed to his thinking. Both the lay public and fellow professionals would have easy access now to his original and immensely appealing contributions to psychoanalysis.

In April 1958, R.D. Laing, an analysand of Charles Rycroft (he said), wrote to Winnicott: "You may or may not remember me. I've written a study (c. 80,000 words)[16] on schizoid and schizophrenic states, in particular trying to describe the transition from a sane to a mad way of being in the world. It draws its inspiration very largely from your writings. May I send it to you?" Yes, Winnicott replied the day after. On July 28, he wrote back appreciatively to Laing, "Something you said about being watched in paranoid states made me see that one of my patients is being watched by a projection of her true self." He had read through the manuscript in two hours, a measure of his enthusiasm. He felt quite adequately cited in the text.

On February 16, 1959, in a memorandum about Gisburne House, a facility for insane and borderline girls whom he felt needed a lower standard of expectations, he suggested that since they were just staying only a year, continuity would be an achievement worthy of note, rather than cure, which was out of reach. This approach is typical of Winnicott—a recasting of a clinical situation in terms that might yield a sense of success, which for these girls was so rare as to be almost unattainable. He had an extraordinary capacity for reaching for ways to restore hope, as where he asserts in "Thinking and Symbol-Formation" that some patients require the delusion of a failed analysis and ought to be allowed this.[17] The analyst, armed with such an idea, may retain the sense of success without having to have his patient agree. Here we see his ability to address the loneliness of the analyst, as in the Gisburne memorandum, where he addressed the loneliness and sense of failure in the staff as well as the patients.

The tremendous importance of hope to Winnicott is evident in these writings. He cherishes hope as the fuel by which life may advance, the opposite of depression and discouragement, the antidote to loneliness. He understands what it means to others as well and finds ways to arrange reality so as to include hope. Somehow he realizes that to this end reality may be arranged and rearranged according to the perspective adopted toward parts of it. In his demanding work as the psychoanalyst of men and women with early damage, he tries to exploit his capacities to their fullest, to keep hope alive, and, in reaching the end point of possibility, he comes to understand that there are limits to the fulfillment of hope, limits that may expose the analyst to danger, even to death itself. This, in a way, is the fullest expression of living: to come to the end of one's powers.

— 18 —

Melanie, Donald, and Clare

In the period preceding Melanie Klein's death from colon cancer in 1960, Clare was her training analysand, a situation that was naturally complicated by the long prior history of Donald and Melanie.

On June 12, 1958, Klein wrote to Winnicott at great length offering suggestions for the Ernest Jones obituary Winnicott had prepared. Jones had died very shortly after the completion of his three-volume biography of Freud. He had been supremely important in supporting Klein's emigration to and acceptance in England. A calculating and manipulative person, devoted to psychoanalysis as he saw it, and devoted to Freud up to a point, Jones had been partly responsible for stoking the fires of controversy that burned between Klein and Anna Freud. He questioned Anna's theories of child analysis with the accusation that she had not been well enough analyzed. This was, of course, an insult to Freud himself, even if Jones did not realize that Freud had been his daughter's analyst. Even if scientifically justified, it was presumptuous of him to discuss her with her father as if she were just another theorist. His accusation led to repercussions from the side of Freud, thus allowing Jones to depict Anna as excessive and unreasonable. Such a transaction has a Kleinian stamp—the know-it-all interpretation from "on high," giving rise to protest, followed by new interpretations of the demonstrated "pathology."

Jones's remarks were made in a letter to Freud[1] written on May 16, 1927: "It is a pain to me that I cannot agree with *some* of the tendencies in Anna's book [on child analysis, just published] and cannot help thinking that they must be due to some imperfectly analysed resistances; in fact I think it is possible to prove this in detail." He goes on in the same patronizing vein. In 1935, he implied that Freud had copied some of Klein's work. "I was glad you liked my Instinct paper, but was very astonished at your thinking I had made such a mistake as to suppose you had used any of Melanie Klein's work as a starting point for any thoughts of yours."[2] Freud had written to Max Eitingon on May 30, 1927: "I don't find Jones's behavior very puzzling. For a long time he has been looking for 'conflicts' or fights that hold the temptation to become independent from Europe and to establish his own Anglo-American realm, something he cannot very well do before my demise, and he believes he has found a good opportunity in the partial contradiction between Anna and Mrs. Klein. Perhaps one should add to it a partial anger with Anna dating since 1914 when she refused him."

In 1908, Jones had emigrated to Canada after a scandal involving womanizing and did not return until 1913. Riccardo Steiner indicates that Jones may have had an affair with Joan Riviere while she was his patient. Yes, Jones was a contributor. He saved the Freuds from the Nazis. He ran the British Society with an iron hand, for better or worse. Yet he was sometimes unscrupulous.

Klein's wish that Jones's memory be treated with special care is evident in her detailed suggestions in the June 1958 letter, in a tone still reflecting the attitude of teacher to student:

> You will see that, in some places, I am suggesting both bringing in something more positive about Jones' personality and also paying more tribute to his enthusiasm for analysis, his devotion to Freud and his work. As it is now, I do not think it is quite balanced enough. I hope that my very short remarks in the margin will convey to you what I mean. By stressing more certain points, for instance; the great importance of his principle that every psycho-analyst be analysed, (whatever his personal qualities) and his achievement that Ps. analysis should only be applied to Freudian teaching, and, furthermore, by stressing what you perhaps have not so strongly experienced,[3] that is, a great deal of kindness and helpfulness, as against his at times

forbidding approach, the picture of his personality would appear in a different light.

. . . I do not believe that Jones was in principle against giving up his position as president, but that he was rather sensitive on the point that it should not be an expression of dissatisfaction with him personally. I think that this personal sensitivity would be sufficiently indicated by the "nevertheless" which would follow a better formulation of my suggestion in the margin.

. . . [I] would prefer you to refer to me as Melanie Klein, not Mrs. Klein. I am more concerned with the picture you give of his personality, and you will see that . . . I have braketted [sic] half a sentence, which I really feel will, in wider circles, give rise to misinterpretation. I think the counterpart of Jones's at times sharp and caustic attitude needs much more stressing, that is, the great deal of kindness, which expressed itself in helping so many people, and which had its root in a dislike of falsity and mediocrity, and in a real enthusiasm for the value of psycho-analysis. He hated to see it badly or not genuinely represented. It is true that, with his intellectual brilliance, it was not easy for him to put up with stupidity and excessive mediocrity, but this rather sharp attitude was apt to pass over quickly and give way to a real appreciation as soon as he found something interesting, new or true. You were right in mentioning that, in some degree, his defensive attitude was due to a fight with very hostile and stupid opponents in his medical profession, but, as you say, his bitterness did not go deep and there was a good deal of optimism and hope for the future in his personality. If this side is more stressed than you have done, and also the enormous amount of work and devotion which he put into supporting Freud and his work, his personality appears in a different light. I think it is most understandable that a very brilliant man, with his enormously quick perception of what is true or false, would at times be awe-inspiring, would appear very much sharper to someone feeling very much more inferior. There is something in people that makes them feel more at ease with somebody less outstanding and more equal to themselves. For instance, Freud was very awe-inspiring. I had full opportunity of seeing the other and deeper side of Jones' capacity to admire and support what he thought valuable. He was always on the look-out, as Mrs. Riviere very well puts it, for new ideas to help to establish psycho-analysis and to develop it. You are quite right that later on this sharpness very much diminished, but by then I think he had done what everybody in a similar position has to do—he had arrived at a state of resignation.

I prefer to make these suggestions to you instead of adding a passage to your obituary, because I think the whole of it should be altered in the sense I am suggesting, and I do not really think that can be done by adding anything. I believe that the nearer we came to the war, and during the war, resignation and therefore greater mildness had already set in. However, he showed great courage and devotion in the way in which he saved Freud from Vienna and enabled him to die peacefully. As you have noticed in my remarks, Jones had a second attack of coronary thrombosis and actually was not a healthy man after that, which may account for his retiring, not only to the country, but also to a change of attitude.

I hope that you won't mind my criticism, since you invited it and since I have very much at heart that the obituary should do justice to Jones and to the writer of it.

I received your letter referring to the election and thank you for it.

Yours ["sincerely" is crossed out],
Melanie

P. S. You refer, of course, to Jones' biography of Freud, but I believe that, as this was his magnum opus, at least of the last part of his life, the value and importance of it should be more stressed. Jones has, to some extent, been able to bring to life Freud's personality, and he has done invaluable work in doing so. He also had to put aside his own autobiography in order to write this, not because he was indifferent to his own autobiography, which he was longing to write; but it is typical of his attitude towards Freud and his conviction of Freud's greatness that he set aside a piece of work which would have given him great satisfaction and have been of considerable interest. . . .

A Congress on Child Psychiatry in Portugal was the setting, in June 1958, for Winnicott's paper "Child Analysis in the Latency Period." This entails a discussion of latency, with its characteristic decline of instinct, and the difference between Melanie Klein and Anna Freud in analytic technique. Winnicott expresses his belief in addressing the unconscious as quickly as possible to show what the treatment is all about and to render aid, but he gives plenty of room to Anna Freud's method of consciously evoking cooperation in the child for the process. He cites the work of Berta Bornstein, quoting her comment that "*free association by the child [is] a particular threat to his ego organization*" (Winnicott's italics). His liberating final comment addresses the need for practitioners to pool their work, there being so few cases in the experience of any one, and the need for "not being afraid to make suggestions which turn out to be stupid when examined by a group." This is his mark—not being afraid to sound stupid or foolish—out of which comes so much that is unheralded, startling, and fruitful, though this paper on latency is not one of his most brilliant.

On July 29, 1958, Winnicott agreed to Lacan's request for a French translation of his paper on transitional objects. Victor Smirnoff would do the translation. There followed a correspondence about this project.

There is also an undated note from Masud Khan, who says, "We are looking forward to seeing you and Mrs. Winnicott on Wednesday + shall collect you at 7 PM."[4] If Winnicott was willing to socialize with an analysand in this way, he would very likely not have objected to Khan's doing the same with Wynne and Kitty Godley. Or, to put it another way, Khan could have acquired such willingness from the example of his analyst. Such socializing is incompatible with psychoanalytic practice as we know it.

The title of Winnicott's 1959 paper "Classification: Is There a Psycho-Analytic Contribution to Psychiatric Classification?" given to the British Society on March 18, 1959, has much to do, I think, with his relationship to Joan Riviere, who objected to his plan for a classification of the environment,[5] which, he said, set him back considerably. This paper does contain such a classification, although there is, he says, much more work to be done. The use of the word "contribution" in the title in this context also calls to mind his 1956 letter to Riviere in which he objected to the comment she and Klein had made to the effect that he had no contribution to make to the psychology of earliest infancy. In this case it is psychoanalysis that is the contributor, psychiatry the recipient. Winnicott, a child psychiatrist by extensive experience, had not been trained as an adult psychiatrist. This form of the title, expressed as a question, points to something more personal than a simple declarative phrase would. The spirit of this rather long paper is a bit unusual for Winnicott and calls to mind his 1945 paper "Primitive Emotional Development," in which there is a measure of swagger. Here we see a self-possessed writer and contributor (his books were out by now) most uncharacteristically reviewing the literature. He cites Freud, Anna Freud, and Melanie Klein as usual, but he also includes Ferenczi.[6] He also brings in Rickman and Glover, Menninger, Abraham, Hartmann, James, Kris, and Aichhorn. The overall impression is of someone coming to grips with his subject.[7]

He writes, "In a classification based on those areas of interest which Freud covered in the early years of his work the patients were either psychotic or hysterical." This is his first flat statement that some of Freud's patients were psychotic, and it indicates a level of confidence reflected also in his citing Ferenczi as someone who discussed a failed case in terms of a deficiency in psychoanalytic technique. He goes on: "In the study of the *actual* infant it is no longer possible to avoid taking into account the environment. . . . The term regression . . . has now a clinical application *regression to dependence.*" His work is established; there is no apology and nothing tentative about it. He then indicates that the dichotomy between "those who almost confine their researches to a study of the internal processes [like Melanie Klein] and those who are interested in infant-care [like Anna Freud and Dorothy Burlingham]" is "temporary, one which will eventually disappear by natural processes." How optimistic he is![8]

This paper is a summary of psychoanalytic thinking which lays emphasis on what is "probably the most important contribution from psycho-analysis to psychiatry and to psychiatric classification . . . the destruction of the old idea of disease entities." In coming to "Positive Suggestions," he gives special consideration to "(i) The idea of the true and the false self. (ii) The idea of delinquency and psychopathy as derivations of perceived, actual emotional deprivation. (iii) The idea of psychosis as related to emotional privation at a stage before the individual could perceive a deprivation." A reference to Riviere is concealed in the remark that "some may feel that in putting forward a method of classifying which includes a classification of environment I am leaving aside all that psychoanalysis has gained in the study of the individual."[9]

Nevertheless, he says, "For the time being I find it valuable to use the concepts which I have put forward in other papers, of independence arising out of dependence, which in turn arises out of double dependence. By double dependence I mean dependence which could not at the time be appreciated even unconsciously by the individual, and which therefore cannot be communicated to an analyst in a patient's analysis. As I have said elsewhere, the analyst has to reclothe the patient's material, using his or her imagination in so doing." This is a brilliant sentence which, in the word "reclothe," incorporates the necessary sequential action of the imagination.

The 1964 postscript to this paper is essentially a summary of "Fear of Breakdown," which did not appear until four years after his death. He must have written it out in 1963 or 1964.

In spite of Klein's reduced contact because of Clare's analysis, she writes on May 21, 1959: "Since you have shown so kind an interest in my Manchester lecture, I send you a copy of part of the letter which Dr. Peters, the acting head of the Department of Anthropology and Sociology, has written to me. I assume it will interest you." Peters had written, unremarkably: "Thank you very much indeed for coming up to Manchester to give your talk. We were delighted to have you and thoroughly enjoyed the private discussion we had with you. Since your departure I have spoken to many people who attended your lecture and they were all highly delighted with it. Many of us have had a number of new ideas as a result of your visit."

Winnicott replied on May 22: "It was very good of you to let me have a copy of the letter from Dr. Peters. You must feel that it was very well worth while going to Manchester and I am sure that it is good for the Society as a whole." Just a kind, polite exchange between old friends, a small occasion that serves as a vehicle for acknowledging each other, this in spite of her caution that they minimize contact because Clare was in analysis with her.

During this period Klein must have been preparing her paper on loneliness,[10] which was to be given that summer at the Copenhagen Congress. There is, in this paper, a greater acknowledgment of the actual mother in the development of the child than she has previously been willing to make. "[T]he close contact between the unconscious of the mother and of the child . . . is the foundation of the most complete experience of being understood. . . . However gratifying it is in later life to express thoughts and feelings to a congenial person, there remains an unsatisfied longing for an understanding without words—ultimately for the earliest relation with the mother. This longing contributes to a sense of loneliness and derives from the depressive feeling of an irretrievable loss." One can never face reality without idealization, she wrote, because life is otherwise colorless. At this point in her life, she showed a depth of longing. After a lifetime devoted to facing reality as she understood it in the most unadorned terms, she resigned herself to the idea that reality alone is not enough to make life satisfying; Winnicott's paper ("On the Capacity to Be Alone"), by contrast, stresses the stages in the achievement of solitude, and its pleasures.

On May 21, 1959, he commented to Donald Meltzer about a paper of his, "It is unfortunate that the sort of presentation which you gave last night makes people think that the followers of Mrs. Klein talk more than their patients do."

Addressing the issue of what we would now call day care, he wrote,[11] "My view on the matter in hand is not a blind recommendation that all babies and children should be with their mothers. I am in fact tremendously in support of the good nursery school which mothers can use to enlarge the world of their more normal children while they themselves get on with their own jobs. This is an extension of the old-fashioned system of the nanny in the home. You will understand that the good nursery school is very different from the day nursery in which mothers are encouraged to dump their children while going to work, and often these schools are used for the rather difficult small children who are most in need of their mothers. Such mothers in my view should be encouraged to look after their own infants and not encouraged to go to work."

A questionnaire from Thomas Szasz[12] elicited a refusal to cooperate (November, 19, 1959) because answers can be manipulated to produce an impression that is not accurate. Although he did fill in a few answers, he did not send the form back to Szasz. According to his responses, he testified in court fewer than three times per year, did belong to or hold membership in an organized religious group, had attended services fewer than three times in the past year, and he did believe that training analysts should communicate with officers of institutes and societies concerning their patient-candidates.

His prepared examination for students at the London School of Economics is, as always, provocative and searching. He provides numerous essay questions, such as:

> Compare aspects of "guilt": legal guilt, moral guilt, sense of guilt, aetiology of guilt.

Discuss the concept of absolute dependence—relative dependence—towards independence, in the theory of human emotional development.

Use cases you have had to do with to illustrate: the boy in the girl, and the girl in the boy (keep to the latency period of development).

What importance may the real father have in the life of:

1. a baby girl under one year;
2. a boy of 4 years;
3. a girl of 14 years;
4. a boy of 21 years?

Choose an aspect of adolescence that interests you and write on it. (Adolescence here means a phase of development, becoming adult.)

A boy or girl of 10 is kept in bed for a year on a mistaken diagnosis of rheumatic heart disease. What effect might this have in respect of the development of personality and character?

We are familiar with the various phases of his thought behind these essay questions. We know how fluent he could be on any of these subjects and can easily infer with what receptivity he could contemplate the responses of any of his students. We can say with certainty, based on these questions alone, that he was an effective, fully engaged teacher. Dr. Judith Issroff described his lecturing style as follows:

Winnicott [was] almost never [spruce], but, rather, crumpled and rumpled, glasses perched atop his head, hands and furrowed brow working as an integral part of his mobile embodiedness. . . . He was astonishingly adept at capturing his audience, would roam about, or be very still, somehow building things in such a way that one's appetite was whetted, one's excitement grew, and he drew one with him to his climax, the main thrust of wherever he was inviting one to follow along his thinking with him if one could. He didn't express himself in ordinary linear language, and definitely not in an unwritten lecture about communication and interpretation. . . . He was a theatrical lecturer-performer. Sometimes he would entice his audience into a state of high expectancy, taking everyone with him to the delayed climax. But sometimes, usually because of his idiosyncratic language and novelty of exposition that broke new ground for psychoanalysis . . . his audience did not "get it."[13]

A symposium on countertransference was held by the medical section of the British Psychological Society on November 25, 1959. Michael Fordham, representing a Jungian viewpoint, participated, as did Winnicott, whose contribution was published as "Counter-Transference." He expressed the view that the term had been stretched too far and that it should be defined in the original way, as an interference in the analyst's functioning because of aroused transferences to the patient. He discusses the professional attitude of the analyst, which produces a strain. His own analysis is undertaken not to free him from neurosis but to

> increase the stability of character and the maturity of the personality of the worker, this being the basis of his or her professional work and of our ability to maintain a professional relationship. . . .[A]ny structuring of his ego-defences lessens his ability to meet the new situation. The psychotherapist . . . must remain vulnerable, and yet retain his professional role in his actual working hours. . . . What the patient meets is surely the professional attitude of the analyst, not the unreliable men and women we happen to be in private life."[14] . . . [I]n between the patient and the analyst is the analyst's professional attitude, his technique, *the work he does with his mind*. . . . The analyst is objective and consistent, for the hour, and he is not a rescuer, a teacher, an ally, or a moralist. The important effect of the analyst's own analysis in this connexion is that it has strengthened his own ego so that he can remain *professionally* involved, and this without too much strain. In so far as all this is true the meaning of the word counter-transference can only be the neurotic features *which spoil the professional attitude* and disturb the course of the analytic process as determined by the patient.

He discusses the borderline patient who "gradually breaks through the barriers . . . and forces a direct relationship of a primitive kind, even to the extent of merging." But this fact does not alter his fundamental opinion about both the concept and the word "countertransference."

On February 5, 1960, he wrote to Michael Balint about his paper on primary love, offering many meaty comments, for example, that it did not matter how Freud had changed; people who cared about the evolution of Freud's concepts as a basis for their own would soon be dead. Claiming that he couldn't take part in metapsychological discussions, Winnicott acknowledged, "We are alike in our concern but you were probably here first." He confessed:

> I personally wonder very much whether an infant is aware when the environment is satisfactory, and I have actually stated in positive terms that I think the infant is not aware of this early environmental provision but is affected when it fails. For this reason I am unable to use the word primary love here because I cannot see that there is a relationship. The infant has not yet established the capacity to make relationships and in fact is not there to be related except in an unintegrated way. I become more definitely in disagreement with you when you use the word harmonious in description of the relationship which you call primary love. As soon as the word harmonious is used I feel I do know that a highly complex and sophisticated defence organization is at work in the child who is no longer a newly born baby or a pre-natal infant.

This statement takes him definitively away from Klein and Fairbairn and toward Freud and Anna Freud. As we have seen, he distanced himself from those who think that an object relation is possible for a newborn infant, believing instead that it takes time for the infant to become sufficiently mature to have such a relation.

On February 11, 1960, he wrote Lacan thanking him for the translation of his paper on transitional objects. He regretted the split in French psychoanalysis, which lay behind the sequence of invitations rendered by the British to French analysts to give papers, first to a member of the Paris group, and after that to Lacan. Things in France seemed beyond repair, he observed, and thought that was too bad. His files contain a very friendly eight-page letter from Lacan in French.[15]

He writes appreciatively to Dr. G.T. de Racker of Argentina (April 26, 1960) for a paper[16] that had helped him "join up my own ideas with the Kanner descriptive article on autism.[17] No doubt you are familiar with the other descriptive work on autism in which the patient's use of machines is emphasized." Winnicott's reference to machines as associated with autism suggests the work of Frances Tustin, yet to come.

Melanie Klein died of colon cancer on September 22, 1960. Her decline was relatively swift. Their polite exchange about her Manchester visit takes on an empty, haunting quality in view of all the intensity that marked their long acquaintance. The subject of loneliness addressed in her last paper, with its tragic longing for an unrealizable past, evokes something of Klein's internal life that paralleled her attitude of certainty about her findings and theories. She had been chastened by age, as most of us are.

Clare had undergone analysis with Clifford Scott starting in 1948, before her marriage to Donald, and probably at the same time as Marion Milner's analysis with Scott. A few years after he left for Canada in 1954, she worked with Melanie Klein, a training analysis that ended shortly before Klein's death. Her supervisors were Michael Balint (later removed from her list because he was not acceptable in a Kleinian line of training), Hanna Segal, and Herbert Rosenfeld. Prior to her analytic practice in the 1960s and after, Clare had been carrying on her distinguished social work career, much of it in the Home Office, for which she was eventually awarded the Order of the British Empire. She was in charge of the child care course at the London School of Economics from 1947 through 1958, a program originating in a collaboration between the LSE and the Home Office. She was regarded as an inspiring and dedicated teacher, with the child's inner life her central preoccupation. Donald accompanied her as lecturer in many courses. This served as his teaching outlet, largely because he was not welcome to lecture in the British Institute more than three times a year. He taught a ten-lecture series, "The Inter-relation of Physical and Psychological Aspects of Development," eventually adding on five more lectures on the subject of adult personality patterns.

Only a small group of students (about twelve) took this course, and there was therefore a personal quality to the teaching. An annual Christmas party was held at Chester Square with singing around the piano, Donald playing. In the same celebratory spirit, the Winnicotts sent out a much-anticipated Christmas card every year to their friends, illustrated by Donald—a different motif each year derived from their Chester

Square home—each one hand-colored. They became reliable signs of Christmas until the end.

The child care course was not given after 1958 as the result of a major reorganization of social work teaching in Great Britain, the emphasis having turned to an attempt to unify all instruction, rather than continue specialized attention in separate fields. This created a complicated situation to which Clare tried to adapt, but with great ambivalence, and she finally withdrew. During their time teaching together, however, Donald and Clare continued the collaboration that had begun in Oxfordshire, with many travels all over Britain, so that the termination of the course was a great loss to them as a couple. Donald continued giving lectures in the mental health course and the applied social studies course. Clare taught as well, here and there, at the LSE. After the child care course came to an end, she identified herself as Mrs. Clare Winnicott, having called herself by her maiden name before this time. This watershed moment occurred during her work with Melanie Klein and undoubtedly had considerable personal significance.

According to Grosskurth,[18] Clare "had been greatly impressed by Klein's paper on mourning[19] and wanted a Kleinian analysis—'but I wouldn't get there in a hundred years with Scott.' She recalled that when she related a dream to him, she would sometimes plead, 'You're supposed to be a Kleinian—give me a Kleinian interpretation of it'—but he never could." After Scott's departure, Clare "told her husband that she wanted to have an analysis with Klein herself—'I think she's tough enough for me'—and in retrospect she was bemused and impressed that he raised no objections, in view of the fact that, as he had told her two years before, 'I find that she no longer considers me a Kleinian.'. . . [Donald] approached [Klein], reminding her that she owed him a favor: he had sacrificed his analysis with her by going to Riviere instead, freeing him to analyze Eric [Klein's son] as she had wanted him to do. Surely now she would agree to take Clare?" There is no supporting citation for this.

Winnicott's relation to Klein in the last years was conditioned by the fact that his wife was in a training analysis with her. Klein wrote him on January 14, 1958:

> I am glad that you feel that our talk was useful but I don't think that
> to see you from time to time is advisable for it would disturb your
> wife's analysis.

I am very concerned to keep her analysis as free from external disturbances as possible—and as we know, this is not at all easy in the circumstances.

I am sure you will agree with me on this point and understand that it is only for that reason that I would rather not meet you frequently nor correspond frequently.

Of course as far as work is concerned we need not agree about everything and as you say no one has a monopoly of the truth.

With kind regards . . .

This letter probably did not mark the very outset of the analytic work, which apparently began in 1957. Inevitably it calls back the late 1930s when Donald was analyzing Eric, with tremendous input from Melanie.

Grosskurth believes that

this analysis was an extraordinary battle of wills; at one point Winnicott told his wife that he could see no forseeable end to it: "You'll kill Melanie or she'll kill you." Clare Winnicott recalled its positive aspects: Klein's "fantastic memory for detail" and "She gave you a feeling of strength behind you." But there were aspects of the analysis that troubled her greatly—for instance, the impersonality of the situation which was exemplified by the fact that Klein never greeted her or said good-bye. She found her a brilliant theoretician but not a clinician: "She implanted her own theory on what you gave her. You took it or left it." Clare Winnicott was also troubled by her total disregard for the environmental factor. "It's no good our talking about your mother," she was told one day. "We can't do anything about it now." There was not much room for tears on the couch. One crisis occurred after Mrs. Winnicott had been hospitalized for meningitis. On her return, speaking of the helpful nurses, she said: "You have enabled me to trust other people, Mrs. Klein." "No," Klein said, "this is simply a cover-up for your fear of death." Her illness and dependency were discounted. Clare believed that in the analytic situation it was very hard for Klein to accept love and reparation, and she always emphasized the destructive side, so that positive acts were interpreted as a disguise for hate. Clare felt that hostility emanated from Klein except for one epiphany, when she knew that she had touched a deep chord in the older woman. One day, on entering the room, she was startled by a vase of beautiful red and white tulips. She remarked that it must be Mrs. Klein's birthday, and went on to say that they symbolized the fusion of love and hate. "I shall send red and white flowers like that when you die." Klein did not reply— a period of uncharacteristic silence—and Mrs. Winnicott felt that she was very deeply moved. "I shall never forget those tulips—*never*!!" Mrs. Winnicott's comment on her analyst's death and its aftermath, no matter how stated with respect to beautiful love/hate tulips— seems cruel, and therefore uncharacteristic of Clare Winnicott. Perhaps she did have a cruel streak, or at least, given her complaints about Klein's approach to her, she may well have wanted to inflict pain in return.

Klein's birthday was a matter of interest to Winnicott, as this note to her on April 2, 1957, attests: "I had it firmly fixed in my mind that your birthday was on Wednesday. Last night when I told Clare that I would be sending flowers from both of us she let me know that I was already two days late. This makes me very sad. I look forward to Wednesday's meeting with much more than usual pleasure." Given Klein's 1958 warning about communication, in view of Clare's analysis, it is unlikely that she had begun at the time of "Wednesday's meeting."

Grosskurth reports that "a year before Mrs. Klein's death, Clare Winnicott brought her 'a thoroughly Kleinian dream.' 'Mrs. Klein will be very pleased with this dream,' she remembered thinking at the time. Klein then proceeded to analyze it, and her irritated patient timed the interpretation by her watch: twenty-five minutes. Furiously Mrs. Winnicott exclaimed, 'How dare you take my dream and serve it up to me?' and slammed out of the room. Winnicott tried to mediate. He went to see Klein, who told him, 'She's too aggressive to analyze.' On his return he advised his wife, 'If you give it up, she'll never let you qualify.' After a week Clare Winnicott returned, still truculent: 'I have come back on your terms, Mrs. Klein, not on mine.' "

We do not know the extent to which Clare's anger at Klein was rooted in feelings about her husband's relationship to Klein. Furthermore, a patient's aggressiveness is not necessarily unrelated to the sort of attitudes and commentary made by the analyst. She may have been "too aggressive" for Klein to analyze, but not necessarily too aggressive for someone else. Descriptions of Klein's attitudes and methods in the treatment of Clare suggest a high level of provocation, with preexisting theory stamped on associations, just the sort of attitude that would elicit stubborn, even furious protest from the self-possessed Clare Winnicott.

Grosskurth's research leads her to conclude that "Clare Winnicott believed in retrospect that she made a great mistake in going to Klein for analysis, especially as it put her husband in a highly embarrassing position, even though he did nothing to discourage her." This assertion is not supported by documentation. After Klein's death, Clare had a further analysis (her third) with Lois Munro, about whom she spoke enthusiastically,[20] and consulted Peter Lomas as well, after Donald died.[21] She was aware, of course, that Klein was in failing health. "She ventured: 'I do use her ideas all the time—*my* way.'" One may add: precisely as was the case in Donald's use of those ideas.

Grosskurth writes that

> the whole situation seems bizarre. What were the conscious and unconscious motives of the people involved? Mrs. Winnicott went to Klein because she was deeply impressed by her paper on mourning; but why did she not apply to her in the first place, rather than to Clifford Scott, who had analyzed Winnicott's first wife? It is hard not to entertain the conjecture that both Winnicott and Klein, for conscious and unconscious motives, were using her as a stalking horse. And what were Clare Winnicott's own unconscious motives? No wonder the woman was confused, caught as she was in a difficult situation. Occasionally Winnicott would inquire about the analysis. "Does she ever mention sex?" "No." "Did she ever mention the Oedipus complex?" "No." His wife recalled him then asserting, "*That* is because she knows nothing about it!"

It is most unlikely that there were any more ulterior motives in Clare Winnicott's choice of Klein as an analyst than is the case whenever an individual seeks out a particular analyst. The primary motive, subsuming all others, must have had to do with her personal need for the best and deepest possible experience. Donald always considered Klein the very best analyst. Speculation to the effect that Winnicott might have "sent" Clare to Klein in order to advance his own ideas is not supported by evidence. Other people are said to have been captivated by Klein, and this makes her behavior as an analyst highly suspect, inasmuch as the state of being captivated is out of keeping with that degree of sobriety and reason necessary for the work to proceed. Any attempt to inculcate Kleinian principles through the vehicle of analysis would be met, properly, with resistance in a patient who was not captivated, not brought under an emotional current leading to a sort of conversion. Clare was of an independent mind, as her letters to Donald in the early 1940s already attest.

The outcome of the work has not been documented. Even under circumstances of conflict, it is quite possible for good results to emerge. Certainly we do not know that the analysis failed. What we do know is that after all these years in which Donald related to Melanie Klein in his various non-patient roles, the person closest to him had an experience out of which she could accumulate impressions and draw conclusions that were based on firsthand observation. This must have been of tremendous interest to Donald. Of course, the history of conflict between Winnicott and Klein would enter into the analysis, and we can only speculate about the transferences that were evoked. We do know that Clare belonged to no religious organization as an adult in spite of the fact that her father had been a notable Baptist minister.

Just before she died, writes Grosskurth, Klein "told her colleagues that they were to convey to the Society that Clare Winnicott was now qualified as an analyst."

Winnicott wrote "An Appreciation of Mrs. Melanie Klein" for the *British Medical Journal* (September 20, 1960). He begins by noting that she "was not medically qualified; yet because of her work on the psychology of childhood and infancy she will be honoured among doctors. . . . It is certainly possible that in the course of time Mrs. Klein will rank as the most important of those who have built on the work of Freud." She had a "fine intellect and a spacious personality, and she enjoyed being a pioneer and a teacher. Above all she was a very fine practising analyst. She was able to go over in her mind at the end of a week's work every detail of every hour of each of her patients, each seen for an hour daily." Mrs. Klein "had a sense of humour which made her a good friend. She knew humility, but she did not like to compromise, and this cost her some friendships."

Almost forty years after her death, Klein's successor as leader of the group, Hanna Segal, gave her venomous account of the Klein-Winnicott relationship. In a 1999 interview conducted by Joseph Aguayo she says:

Yes, I can tell you a lot about Winnicott. He was another person, like Melitta [Schmideberg], whom Klein never attacked. This is actually strange because on a technical level, he did all these things that Klein abhorred, like feeding patients milk and wrapping them in blankets—in short, enacting and mobilizing primitive transferences rather than analyzing them. But no matter, Klein never attacked him for this. Who came in for sharp criticism was Margaret Little, one of Winnicott's followers. The story about Winnicott that Klein told me was that after being in London for a while, Winnicott came to her and asked to become her analysand. Klein told Winnicott that of all people in London, he was the only one who could analyze her son Eric. She asked him to take Eric and she then sent him to Joan Riviere. It was a mistake. Somehow she felt so bad about Winnicott, so she didn't say that much when he started with his active techniques.* He always complained that he was not recognized as a Kleinian, but how could he be? Kleinians don't feed their patients or cover them with blankets. When it comes right down to it, there are fewer differences between Freudians and Kleinians when it comes to the setting and the analytical posture than there are with the Winnicott group. Yet Mrs. Klein always respected her debt to him. Then, of course, Winnicott later asked Klein to take his wife into analysis, which she felt obligated to do.

Aguayo then notes: "It's curious that in reading the correspondence between Winnicott and the London Klein group in the 1950s, there seems to be an assessment on his part that the Klein group was a rigid, almost paranoid organization. He wondered why he had been marginalized by the Klein group." Segal responds:

Well, he was! Besides his techniques, there was the question of his theories—he wanted to make Klein's theories into his own, such as taking Klein's depressive position and calling it the "position of concern." Neither of them at that time recognized their different views on narcissism. Winnicott went along with the view of primary narcissism—what you have to do is notice and sustain the narcissism for a period of time before it would go away; whereas Klein saw object

---

*The phrase "active techniques" is associated in psychoanalytic writing with the work of Sándor Ferenczi.

relations existing from birth—yes, there is narcissistic desire, but she later connected it to projective identification. She always saw narcissism as part of a relationship. A lot of basic differences between Klein and Winnicott come from that. Also, from Winnicott's point of view, everything comes to the mother, and when it came right down to it, there was only one good mother, and that was Winnicott himself. He did not analyze negative transference, but sought to become the good mother. He actually did not have a good relation to his own mother.

When Aguayo remarks, "Winnicott's active techniques sound so much like those of Sandor Ferenczi," she replies, "Oh, worse than Ferenczi." It is this final hyperbolic comment that underscores Segal's intensely felt wish to depreciate Winnicott, to deprive him of any credit as a contributor. In this she maintains the attitude of Melanie Klein and Joan Riviere. In another interview reported to me by the same interviewer, Joseph Aguayo,[22] Betty Joseph responded to his question as to why the Kleinians never answered Winnicott's criticisms by saying that there was really nothing to respond to. The criticisms were meaningless and trivial. This illustrates in contemporary times what Winnicott had to face during his career.

19

The True and False Self and "The Right Not to Communicate"

Winnicott's continuing attempt to understand himself in the context of advancing age reached a number of climactic expressions in the early 1960s. He jolted readers into a new perspective on the totality of human relations with his concept of the True and False Self. He altered the psychoanalytic agenda with such encyclopedic statements as "The Theory of the Parent-Infant Relationship" and the startling "Communicating and Not Communicating Leading to a Study of Certain Opposites." He wrote with newfound confidence, having found it possible to bring together his personal strivings and his professional observations and speculations. Not having experienced any coronary attacks since 1954, he was confident enough to undertake three arduous tours of the United States (in the autumn of 1962, again in 1963, and in 1967) prior to the one in 1968 during which he was felled by cardiopulmonary illness.

He had first mentioned his concept of the True and False Self in his 1949 paper "Mind and Its Relation to the Psyche-Soma," and made frequent reference to the subject after that. In a 1959 note[1] he describes an actress patient whose "nothingness at the centre" is a representation of her True Self, empty, hungry, and waiting—"the emptiness before impregna-

264

tion as well as sexual and oral desire." "Ego Distortion in Terms of True and False Self" (1960) brings together his thinking on the subject up till then, with numerous additions: "One recent development in psychoanalysis has been the increasing use of the concept of the False Self. . . . This concept is not in itself new. . . . Evidently a real clinical state exists." One could ask: Who else besides Winnicott uses the concept? He refers to the phrase "as-if personality," coined earlier by Helene Deutsch,[2] and elsewhere to Jung's use of these terms. He places his contribution at a distance from its inventor, within the larger "not-me" universe called psychoanalysis. He associates this idea with Freud's division of the self into "a part that is central and powered by the instincts . . . and a part that is turned outward and is related to the world." He states that there is more to be learned by analytic work with deeply regressed patients than by direct observation or contact with infants. He believes that, in contrast, experience in adult psychiatry can have the deleterious effect on psychoanalysts of opening a gap between their assessment of clinical state and their understanding of etiology, a problem he did not have to experience since he never trained in adult psychiatry (and refused to "take beds").[3] In his "Classification" paper, he sees psychoanalysis educating psychiatry.

"Ego Distortion in Terms of the True and False Self" is a crystallization of his ideas on the subject. The mother implements the baby's omnipotence in her state of identification with the infant. Out of this comes the spontaneous gesture, which is the True Self in action. The not-good-enough mother fails to meet the gesture and substitutes her own, with which the infant complies with the beginning of a False Self. "It is an essential part of my theory," writes Winnicott, "that the True Self does not become a living reality except as a result of the mother's repeated success in meeting the infant's spontaneous gesture or sensory hallucination."

"The protest against being forced into a false existence," he finds, "can be detected from the earliest stages," since "at the earliest stage the True Self is the theoretical position from which come the spontaneous gesture and the personal idea." (His addition here of the phrase "the personal idea" is an example of the way in which the process of writing and rewriting gives rise to new thoughts that spin off from the momentum of previously established statements. I am reminded of the sparks flying off a Catherine wheel, Marion Milner's metaphor for her first encounter with Winnicott.) He continues, "Only the True Self can be creative and only the True Self can feel real."

One idea previously unstated—and, in this case, also unexplained—is that "there is a compliant aspect to the True Self in healthy living, an ability of the infant to comply and not to be exposed. The ability to compromise is an achievement." Winnicott customarily states characteristics of the True Self in absolutes, but here he relativizes it. This comment (and another similar comment in "The Theory of the Parent-Infant Relationship") attributes to the True Self a measure of compromise, a quality that has been associated up to now only with the False Self. The idea may well precede and provide the springboard for the notion in his 1963 paper "Communicating," which I will discuss later, of "the right not to communicate." What I mean is that the spirit of compromise may have given rise to a restatement of its opposite. Perhaps this shift reflects a larger phenomenon in Winnicott's life, in which he moves his focus from what I called, in the chapter on Melanie Klein, "the real" toward the world of the "unreal." I am speaking of attentiveness to external reality giving rise to a *shutting out* of the external, and a corresponding focus on the hermetically internal. His own version of this extreme position is unique among psychoanalysts and is the strange twin to Melanie Klein's exclusion of the mother. The great papers of the 1960s emerged from this extremity.

The penultimate paragraph of "Ego Distortion" states: "One could say that the False Self . . . deceives the analyst if the latter fails to notice that, regarded as a whole functioning person, the False Self, however well set up, lacks something, and that something is the essential central element of creative originality."

Masud Khan, prompted by a request by Dr. Liselotte Frankl of the Hampstead Clinic for information about Winnicott's use of the concept of integration, wrote out for Winnicott his own concept of the meaning of dissociation,[4] and in so doing redefined the origins of the True and False Self as "states of primitive dissociation [that] become organised into separate areas of personality functioning. . . . [These] can also lend themselves to pathological integration into split off dissociated parts, which I think form the basis of what you term 'True and the False Self.'" Khan begins his incisive discussion by speaking of dissociation as a normal phase in which the infant's changing states of mind are not yet felt as aspects of a single entity, and are held together by the mother's care until such time as they are. Here I am reminded of Michael Fordham's theory of "deintegrates."[5]

"The Theory of the Parent-Infant Relationship" (1960) is a nineteen-page tour de force entirely worthy of its rather grand title. It shows the maturing of thoughts that were first broached in "Primitive Emotional Development" (1945). At the forefront in the paper are the terms "holding" and "the holding environment," which, at the very end of the paper, in a footnote, Winnicott attributes to his wife, Clare, with reference to a 1954 paper of hers on casework.[6] "Holding" applies to the good-enough mother expressing love for her infant and also to the psychoanalyst treating a regressed, dependent patient. It refers to the physical act when describing the mother, but also includes all those aspects of attitude that result in the feeling in the infant of being held, and it is these that apply to the psychoanalyst who is focused on his or her patient in a dependent state. In this paper Winnicott does not deal with the physical holding of the patient by the analyst.

In deepening his description of infantile omnipotence, he fills in for us the details of a stage for which the term "projection" is useful: "The paradox is that what is good and bad in the infant's environment is not in fact a projection, but in spite of this it is necessary, if the individual infant is to develop healthily, that everything shall seem to him to be a projection. Here we find omnipotence and the pleasure principle in operation, as they certainly are in earliest infancy; and to this observation we can add that the recognition of a true 'not-me' is a matter of the intellect; it belongs to extreme sophistication and to the maturity of the individual."

He cites a sentence from Freud that supports his fundamental idea that an infant must always be seen as part of a combination of itself and its mother. And later on, quoting Freud again, he takes issue with Freud and judges that Freud's statement actually applies to a phase later than the one Freud intended. Here he subtly interconnects the inherited writing on his subject with his own additions and elaborations. Perhaps he is demonstrating through this review the way in which he has taken possession of inherited knowledge through his own projections.

The same is true of the way he now interprets Klein's ideas: "Melanie Klein made it clear that she recognized that the environment was important at this period, and in various ways at all stages. I suggest, however, that her work and that of her co-workers leaves open for further consideration the development of the theme of full dependence, that which appears in Freud's phrase: '. . . the infant, provided one includes with it the care it receives from its mother'. . . . There is nothing in Klein's work that contradicts the idea of absolute dependence, but there seems to me to be no specific reference to a stage at which the infant exists only because of the maternal care, together with which it forms a unit." He seems to have succumbed to Riviere's and Klein's argument, to which he objected in his 1956 letter, that Klein says the very things he says she doesn't. Yet, while he modifies his contention that she neglects absolute dependence by now indicating that there is nothing in her writings that contradicts that idea, he then restates his observation that she fails to be explicit about a stage of absolute dependence. Here he forges a bond with Freud that precedes the one with Klein. Further on, however, he presents a revisionist and clearly Winnicottian view of her work when he writes: "The work of Klein on the splitting defence mechanisms and on the projections and introjections and so on, is an attempt to state the effects of failure of environmental provision in terms of the individual."

In his discussion of the True and False Self, he again, as in the 1960 paper, makes a comment inconsistent with prior absolutes: "In health, object relationships can be developed on the basis of a compromise, one which involves the individual in what later would be called cheating and dishonesty, whereas a direct relationship is possible only on the basis of regression to a state of being merged with the mother." He is speaking of object relationships here, not the expression of the True Self, so the idea of compromise is a fitting one. One can only wonder what he means when he speaks of "cheating and dishonesty," unless he is including under object relationships those aspects of the False Self that are indispensable to daily living, such as courtesy, and not wearing one's heart on one's sleeve, or implying that because of the ambivalence intrinsic to all object relationships, a True Self relationship is, in its pure form, impossible.

Perhaps related to and consistent with his view is a letter from Harry Guntrip dated October 21, 1954, in which he refers to a book "by de Forest on Ferenczi."[7] De Forest quotes a note written by Ferenczi as late as 1931: "Only in earliest childhood or before the original splitting, was anyone 'one with himself.' Deep analysis must go back under the level of reality into pretraumatic times and traumatic moments, but one cannot expect a proper resolution unless this time the resolution is different from the original one. Here intervention is necessary (regression and a new beginning)."

On the subject of the mother who is too well adapted to her baby's needs, to the extent that she anticipates them and deprives him of the opportunity to signal his needs, Winnicott writes that "by being a seemingly good mother, [she] does something worse than castrate the infant. The latter is left with two alternatives: either being in a permanent state of regression and of being merged with the mother, or else staging a total rejection of the mother, even of the seemingly good mother." This is a valuable insight for the clinician who works with patients of any age.

In this paper we find the phrase "projective identification" for, I believe, the first time in his work. Masud Khan used it in his attempt to clarify and enlarge upon Winnicott's concept of dissociation, but this was after the initial paper had been published. His June 28, 1961, memorandum includes projective identification among those defense mechanisms with which "primitive dissociation states" can get involved. This is Kleinian language, which Winnicott had attacked with single-mindedness.

Discussion of the paper continued at the Edinburgh Congress in the summer of 1961. In any case, the phrase was used in the period around Klein's death and could be considered either a tribute to her or a sign that he felt he no longer needed to differentiate himself from her quite so assiduously. Perhaps his revisionist ideas about her reflect the same thing. I am reminded that Joseph Sandler organized a conference on projective identification right after Anna Freud died.[8] Did this represent secret admiration for a term and a concept that is officially *verboten*? Is the phenomenon similar to the liberation of the son by the death of the father? Does it expose, retroactively, hypocrisy during the life of the now deceased individual? Or merely respect? Although Sandler was a close adherent of Anna Freud while she was alive, he eventually advanced a theory that featured a subdivision of the unconscious into present and past, thought by Pearl King for one[9] to have entailed the discarding of numerous basic Freudian ideas in favor of "turning psychoanalysis into relationship therapy."

A 1962 lecture to the London Institute of Education titled "Morals and Education" contains a statement of the notion that "man continues to create and re-create God as a place to put that which is good in himself, and which he might spoil if he kept it in himself along with all the hate and destructiveness which is also found to be there. Religion (or is it theology?) has stolen the good from the developing individual child, and has then set up an artificial scheme for injecting this that has been stolen back into the child, and has called it 'moral education.'"

In 1962 he wrote "Ego Integration in Child Development," a "bare bones statement," as he put it, of his conception of the beginnings of the ego:

> There is no id before ego. Only from this premise can a study of the ego be justified. It will be seen that the ego offers itself for study long before the word self has relevance. The word self arrives after the child has begun to use the intellect to look at what others see or feel or hear and what they conceive of when they meet this infant body. . . . At the stage which is being discussed it is necessary not to think of the baby as a person who gets hungry, and whose instinctual drives may be met or frustrated, but to think of the baby as an immature being who is all the time *on the brink of unthinkable anxiety.*
>
> Unthinkable anxiety has only a few varieties, each being the clue to one aspect of normal growth.
>
> 1. Going to pieces.
> 2. Falling for ever.
> 3. Having no relationship to the body.
> 4. Having no orientation.
>
> It will be recognized that these are specifically the stuff of the psychotic anxieties.
>
> With good-enough mothering at the beginning the baby is not subjected to instinctual gratifications except in so far as there is ego-participation.

He differentiated between *unintegration*, which refers to the infant's not feeling the need to integrate as mother's supportive function is taken for granted, and *disintegration*, which "is an active production of chaos in defence against unintegration in the absence of maternal ego-support, that is, against the unthinkable or archaic anxiety that results from failure of holding in the stage of absolute dependence."

Terms found here but not previously included in his writings are "handling" (as the maternal action that leads to "personalization"), "object-presenting" (the maternal action that leads to "object-relating"), and "ego-coverage" (by the mother, which enables the baby to have the indispensable experience of "going-on-being").

On January 14, 1962, Anna Freud wrote enthusiastically: "I am delighted with your present for me and the Clinic which arrived yesterday. Thank you very much indeed. As you perhaps know, I admire your 'Devoted Mother' talks very much, and I feel no student of our subject should miss either reading or hearing them. I can promise that the records will be kept busy."

On March 7, 1962, Winnicott made a short presentation, "The Aims of Psycho-Analytical Treatment," to the British Society. He stated that he was satisfied with one interpretation per session, and discussed phases of analysis and various types of analysts, since "analysts are not alike." He remarked: "If our aim continues to be to verbalize the nascent conscious in terms of the transference, then we are practising analysis; if not, then we are analysts practising something else that we deem to be appropriate to the occasion. And why not?"

To Benjamin Spock (April 9, 1962), he sent a nine-page discussion of "Striving for Autonomy and Regressive Object Relationships." The letter is a brilliant summary and analysis, always emphasizing the role of the mother, with comments on regressive objects that are reminiscent of autistic objects. Here is a link to the work of Frances Tustin (to come later), perhaps, in his mention of hard objects and contraptions, or, specifically, the mother as a washing machine.[10] Winnicott once wrote about autism as a product of deficient mothering but was challenged by a correspondent (and probably others), and he recanted that position. Prior to the advent of neurological studies of autism, the notion of a psychogenic origin was widespread, and even with the new knowledge of the condition as one with physical roots, a separate school of thinking, led by Tustin, generated ideas about the treatment of psychogenic autism through psychological means and demonstrated degrees of autistic defenses in otherwise non-autistic individuals.

Joan Riviere died of emphysema on May 20, 1962. James Strachey, Paula Heimann, and Lois Munro, who spoke at the memorial meeting at the Institute of Psycho-Analysis, and Riviere's daughter Diana all emphasized her deep interest in fine workmanship of all kinds, not only in writing and verbal expression, but also in painting, design, music, and ballet. (According to Athol Hughes, "she was an active supporter of the Camargo Society, a society that was concerned with ballet.")[11] Paula Heimann remarked in her eulogy, "the dominant force in her design for living, the key to her personality, was the striving after beauty, beauty in nature and in man-made things. . . . To Joan Riviere the beautiful was the expression of the life instinct, and it demanded the exertion, the caring, the workmanship, the blood and sweat, the toil and tears that go to the act of creating or discovering beauty."

This preoccupation with beauty adds to our understanding of Riviere's frequently critical remarks about Donald Winnicott, who was in no way tidy. It may also help to explain the appeal to her of Klein's theory.[12] It is easy to understand that in Riviere's mind Klein's theory was an intellectual artifact of great beauty, possibly the achievement of maternal perfection with which to replace the cold mother of her childhood, or by which to express the coldness.

Riviere suffered from a disorder characterized by violent unconscious self-criticism,[13] which was frequently projected onto others, a not uncommon condition in those who are obsessed with the beautiful, which is to suggest that difficulty in achieving an internal harmony is seen in the unceasing struggle to achieve such a harmony in the external world, through the production of a work of art, or through the achievement of an understanding of art, or through recognition of the beautiful object or pattern. Paula Heimann's use of words such as "blood and sweat, toil and tears [taken from Churchill's inspiring speech when Britain stood alone against Nazi Germany] that go to the act of creating or discovering beauty" suggests the pain that necessarily accompanied Riviere's search for the beautiful, and contrasts with Winnicott's discovery of spontaneous, accidental beauty in the ordinary. The interplay between external and internal would have been outside Riviere's concern, since, as Bowlby said of her attitude toward his own work, "she held strong views that psychoanalysis was in no way concerned with external events."[14]

Winnicott's concept of the "good-enough mother," which could be extended to apply to the "good-enough analyst," would stand in striking contrast to Riviere's perfectionism in the pursuit of the beautiful and the well made. The tragic element in Riviere may be glimpsed in her paper on the negative therapeutic reaction and Anton Kris's study of her analysis as reported by Freud: The tragedy is that she knew how vital positive feelings toward the analyst were to the advancement of the analysis of patients such as herself, but, on the evidence of surviving written materials, was unable to behave, or had great difficulty behaving, in a way that would foster the expression of such feelings, or, better, not interfere with the growth and awareness of such emotions in her analysand Winnicott. Perfectionism is the natural enemy of imperfect emotion.

There is in her correspondence with him recurrent mention of her respiratory illnesses. She suffered from tuberculosis and died of emphysema. And there is, too, a sort of harshness typical of the judgmental know-it-all, which seems to have included a rejection of Winnicott as a contributor to early development theory. It is easy to imagine that Donald represented the living core of herself which existed as an object of constant rejection.

Another death in the ranks of psychoanalysis occurred at about this time as well, that of Princess Marie Bonaparte (suddenly, of leukemia), one of the founders of psychoanalysis in France, who had been instrumental in saving the Freuds at the start of World War II and who had also bought the early Freud letters, thereby saving them from oblivion. On September 29, 1962, Anna Freud wrote to thank Winnicott for writing about Bonaparte's death.

Max Schur wrote as well, a letter that exists now only as a fragment: "My dear Dr. Winnicott, I too was quite shocked by the death of this really unusual person. She played a great role in my life: it was through her that I became Freud's physician. We decided to publish the book as a memorial volume. This was also the immediate wish of her son, Prince Peter, who will also contribute a paper. . . . I assume . . . you will [be pleased?] with this decision. She knew . . . you will be one of the contributors and was genuinely pleased about it."

In the fall of 1962, Winnicott made a tour of the United States and presented papers in several cities. The number of lectures scheduled was evidence of the vast interest that had been generated by his work, now available in book form and in journals, especially the *International Journal of Psycho-Analysis.* "A Personal View of the Kleinian Contribution" was presented on October 3 to the candidates of the Los Angeles Psychoanalytic Society. In it he makes the startling statement that "Melanie Klein and Anna Freud had a relationship in the Vienna days"—startling because Klein was fourteen years years older than Anna Freud, and when she left Vienna in 1900 at the age of eighteen, Anna was four. This statement represents a fantasy of earlier friendliness for which we have no documentation, unless he was tangentially referring to Anna Freud's "Vienna days" prior to Klein's presentations in Berlin and London, or perhaps unconsciously thinking of his own sisters, or hoping for a rapprochement. It is a rich paper from the standpoint of his own personal history, and I have incorporated much of what he says in it into this book. At the end he provides a list of Klein's contributions but leaves out "projective identification."

He read "The Development of the Capacity for Concern" to the Topeka Psychoanalytic Society On October 12. In it he makes the useful point that "most of the processes that start up in early infancy are never fully established, and continue to be strengthened by the growth that continues in later childhood, and indeed in adult life, even in old age." This calm was part of his effort to discourage a preoccupation with being too precise about the dating of the depressive position, or, as he called it, "the phase of concern." He gives a concise account of drive fusion: "This is the achievement of emotional development in which the baby experiences erotic and aggressive drives toward the same object at the same time. On the erotic side there is both satisfaction-seeking and object-seeking, and on the aggressive side, there is a complex of anger employing muscle erotism and of hate, which involves the retention of a good object-imago for comparison. Also in the whole aggressive-destructive impulse is contained a primitive type of object relationship in which love involves destruction. . . . Ambivalence has been reached." This is a precarious condition of mind, which might be called "'the humpty dumpty stage,' the wall on which Humpty Dumpty is precariously perched being the mother who has ceased to offer her lap."

He then elaborates on the two mothers, the object mother and the environment mother, with the environment mother continuing to arrange for comfort and being ready to receive reparative gestures after the object mother has been the recipient of instinctual feelings and acts: "I would say that human beings cannot accept the destructive aim in their very early loving attempts. The idea of destruction of the object-mother in loving can be tolerated, however, if the individual who is getting towards it has evidence of a constructive aim already at hand, and an environment-mother ready to accept." He uses case material to illustrate the point that "his [the patient's] capacity to have an idea of ultimately contributing . . . was making it possible for him to get into more intimate contact with his destructiveness. But constructive effort is false and meaningless unless . . . one has first reached to the destruction." With regard to another patient, he underscores what might be regarded as a counterintuitive idea: "The constructive and creative experiences were making it possible for the child to get to the experience of her destructiveness."

Also in October, the Boston Psychoanalytic Society heard him deliver his paper "Dependence in Infant-Care, in Child-Care, and in the Psycho-Analytic Setting." He told them: "You will see that I am involved in an attempt to evaluate the external factor. May I be allowed to do this without being thought to be going back on what psycho-analysis has stood for over the past forty years in child psychiatry? Psycho-analysis has stood for the personal factor, the mechanisms involved in individual human growth, the internal strains and stresses that lead to the individual's defence organization, and the view of psycho-neurotic illness as evidence of intrapsychic tension that is based on id-drives that threaten the individual ego. But here we return to ego vulnerability and therefore to dependence." As an incidental comment, he suggested that fathers may go through a special state like mothers do in primary maternal preoccupation. Fathers, however, have less opportunity to show it.

Much of the paper is occupied by a case presentation that illustrates the clinical factors in the dependency environment of analysis with a patient whose pathology began during early life. He speaks of the requirement that the analyst be reliable and not leave at inopportune moments, thereby provoking discouragement that is not part and parcel of the transference. In other words, failure—if the analyst can stand to fail his patient—should occur out of the re-living of original failure. In that case the failure becomes useful as a means of recovering what could not otherwise be recovered.

"Providing for the Child in Health and in Crisis," presented to the Extension Division of the San Francisco Institute in October, is notable for his pointing out a tendency in personality growth. He speaks of "the development of a capacity to make relationships with objects in spite of the fact that in one sense, and an important sense, the individual is an isolated phenomenon and defends this isolation at all costs." Here he is dealing with a contradiction, struggling, I believe, with the simultaneity of isolation and relatedness, of absolute inviolability and compromise. Also, he says, "Always, I include the father," but in fact he does not, and this requires an assertion to the contrary.

In this paper he remarks that "theology, by denying to the developing individual the creating of whatever is bound up in the concept of

God and of goodness and of moral values, depletes the individual of an important aspect of creativeness." His point of view is, as ever, that morality develops naturally in the child without having to be inculcated. But "there is a special reason why a moral code should be available, namely, that the infant's and the small child's innate moral code has a quality so fierce, so crude, and so crippling. Your adult moral code is necessary because it humanizes what for the child is subhuman. The infant suffers talion fears."[15] And further: "This principle affecting the handing on of moral values applies likewise to the handing on of the whole torch of culture and civilization."

In October 1962 the San Francisco Psychoanalytic Society was privileged to hear his great work "Communicating and Not Communicating Leading to a Study of Certain Opposites." The paper was given to the British Society the following May.[16] It is a climactic expression of an insight that arises from his own private condition of mind and the train of thought that he pursued as a psychoanalyst. "The Tree," the poem about his own enslavement by a depressed mother, would be written a year later, in November 1963, and would demonstrate his preoccupation with the same subject.

The paper starts with a comment about the process of writing it, when he was surprised to find himself staking a claim "to the right not to communicate. This was a protest from the core of me to the frightening fantasy of being infinitely exploited." Infinite exploitation is an idea that recurs in "The Tree," in which, Christlike, he cannot have a life of his own. From this surprising awareness he extrapolates to the principle that is, in Keats's words (quoted in the epigraph to the paper) "the centre of an intellectual world," that "although healthy persons communicate and enjoy communicating, the other fact is equally true, that *each individual is an isolate, permanently non-communicating, permanently unknown, in fact unfound.*" He goes on: "I suggest that in health there is a core to the personality that corresponds to the True Self of the split personality; I suggest that this core never communicates with the world of perceived objects, and that the individual person knows that it must never be communicated with or be influenced by external reality."[17]

To get to this point he reviews in detail his ideas about the attainment of ambivalence, which allows for a differentiation to be made between the me and the repudiated not-me. After this, there is either communication or noncommunication, with environmental failures tending to promote splits between the inward-turning True Self, which silently communicates with subjective objects and alone feels real, and the outward-turning, compliant False Self, which does not feel real. He sees a third area in the transitional world that represents a compromise. He does not demonstrate but suggests or declares that there is something like this split in everyone, from which he draws certain conclusions that are difficult to understand or accept. The idea of the True Self silently communicating with subjective objects and never to be communicated with, let alone influenced by the external world, the feeling of real being limited to its experience—this notion nullifies any feeling of reality that might be part of what he says is the indirect method of communicating through the use of words. People enjoy using words, and they enjoy the cultural elements of the transitional world, but somehow he is unwilling to say that a feeling of the real may go with them: "It may be necessary [this is grudgingly put] . . . to speak in terms of man's cultural life, which is the adult equivalent of the transitional phenomena of infancy and early childhood, and in which area communication is made without reference to the object's state of being either subjectively or objectively perceived."

Included in this paper are these words: "In the artist of all kinds I think one can detect an inherent dilemma, which belongs to the co-existence of two trends, the urgent need to communicate and the still more urgent need not to be found. This might account for the fact that we cannot conceive of an artist's coming to the end of the task that occupies his whole nature."

He also refers to "the special clarity of certain first hours," which he writes about, and about which he would write much more, the situation in which the child (perhaps the adult as well) treats the analyst as a subjective object, before he is seen objectively, as is bound to happen after awhile.[18] The subjective object dwells within, has not yet been perceived as the not-me.

About mystics, he remarks: "Perhaps not enough attention has been paid to the mystic's retreat to a position in which he can communicate secretly with subjective objects and phenomena, the loss of contact with the world of shared reality being counterbalanced by a gain in terms of feeling real." Winnicott's ideas about Jung, and the value of a dialogue with Jung, may have to do with such notions about the mystic's heightened sense of the real.

He further observes: "By the time mothers become objectively perceived their infants have become masters of various techniques for indirect communication, the most obvious of which is the use of language." He notes that "there is a link here with the idea of being alone in the presence of someone," and continues: "I have always felt that an important function of the interpretation is the establishment of the *limits* of the analyst's understanding. . . . This being alive is the early communication of a healthy infant with the mother-figure, and it is as unselfconscious as can be. Liveliness that negates maternal depression is a communication designed to meet what is to be expected. The aliveness of the child whose mother is depressed is a communication of a reassuring nature, and it is unnatural and an intolerable handicap to the immature ego in its function of integrating and generally maturing according to inherited process."

His summary, which I quote in full, reads:

> I have tried to state the need that we have to recognize this aspect of health: the non-communicating central self, for ever immune from the reality principle, and for ever silent. Here communication is not non-verbal; it is, like the music of the spheres, absolutely personal. It belongs to being alive. And in health, it is out of this that communication naturally arises.
>
> Explicit communication is pleasurable and it involves extremely interesting techniques, including that of language. The two extremes, explicit communication that is indirect, and silent or personal communication that feels real, each of these has its place, and in the intermediate cultural area there exists for many, but not for all, a mode of communication which is a most valuable compromise.

He does not explain further what he means when he refers to the cultural area that does not exist for all. Nor does he elaborate on the "extremely interesting techniques, including that of language," which allow for explicit communication. The phrase "extremely interesting techniques" is a strange one for Winnicott, "technique" having a somewhat pejorative connotation in his usage, and the overall phrase failing to define anything at all. He is not forthcoming about what he has in mind, or he is at the edges of his own speculations and does not know what he has in mind.

Personal matters are probably so immanent in this field of thought that they sow confusion. It may be that in this urgent statement protesting being infinitely exploited, he has drawn the line against his ongoing personal condition of mind, which would soon be expressed in "The Tree." By reclassifying all behavior apart from the only kind that feels real—silent communication with subjective objects—he has negated the significance of a lifetime of restituting liveliness to his depressed mother. The later material relating to a review of Jung's autobiography, including a dream in which he conceives of a kind of cure for his lifelong emotional malady, is closely related to this struggle. These elements are part of a crucial late period of resolution in Winnicott's life.

Trying to understand his discourse requires a reexamination of the meaning of "real," the meaning of "words," and the meaning of "gestures." Previously he saw aggression as indispensable to experiences of the real. He described the expression of an aggressive urge that finds resistance in the external world as having the quality of the real about it, in contrast to the expression of an erotic urge, which gains in its sense of reality through fusion with aggressive urges.

Thus, there now appear to be two distinct explanations for the experience of the real. While continuing to provide commentary that connects with various previous contributions, such as the capacity to be alone, he nonetheless seems willing to allow contradictions to exist, driven as he now appears to be to express what he feels to be deeply true, no matter its relationship to other theories of his own. This is an exaggeration of a long-present transgressive streak in Winnicott. He is propelled by the urgent need to unburden himself of thoughts that derive from his deepest personal struggles in a way that evokes the word "demonic," by which I mean to suggest that he is striving to rid himself of a demon or to put a feeling of personal dissociation into words.

In "Psychotherapy of Character Disorders,"[19] he defines character disorder as "[a] personality distortion that comes about *when the child needs to accomodate* [sic] *some degree of antisocial tendency.*" He thus joins all of his writing on the antisocial tendency to character disorder, and the logic of psychotherapy follows. He gives us the range of possible courses in a child with an anti-social tendency:

> The child in accomodating [sic] the antisocial tendency that is his or
> hers may hide it, may develop a reaction formation to it, such as

becoming a prig, may develop a grievance and acquire a complaining character, may specialize in day-dreaming, lying, mild chronic
masturbating activity, bed-wetting, compulsive thumb-sucking,
thigh-rubbing, etc. or may periodically manifest the antisocial tendency (that is his or hers) in a *behavioral disorder.* . . . . Character disorders in some way and to some degree actively involve society. [They]
may be divided according to: Success or failure—to hide the illness
element. Success here means that the personality, though impoverished, has become able to socialize the character distortion, to find
secondary gains, or to fit in with a social custom. Failure here means
that the impoverishment of the personality carries along with a failure in establishment of a relation to society as a whole, on account of
the hidden illness element.

This paper is a very finely developed analysis of the antisocial tendency and its associated phenomena and as such is the companion piece
to the original "Antisocial Tendency" paper itself. Winnicott notes here
that acting-out is evoked in psychotherapy and must be expected: "[it] is
the alternative to despair. Most of the time the patient is hopeless about
correcting the original trauma and so lives in a state of relative depression or of dissociations that mask the chaotic state that is always threatening. When, however, the patient starts to make an object relationship,
or to cathect a person, then there starts up an anti-social tendency, a compulsion either to lay claims (steal) or by destructive behaviour to activate
harsh or even vindictive management." He outlines the various ways
character disorders may be treated: by psychoanalysis with various out-
comes, in the home itself, and by society's reaction if legal transgressions
are a feature. In regard to society's responsibility, he makes the striking
statement that "it is best to give up all attempts to cure prostitution, and
instead to concentrate on giving these girls food and shelter and opportunity for keeping healthy and clean."

In speaking toward the end of the paper about parents who had
been curing their child, he says, "I helped them in this long task by giving them some understanding of what they were doing." This has relevance to the work of the psychoanalyst, who may strengthen his patients
or increase their desire to delve deeper into their lives and those of others
who are close to them, by providing understanding of what they are
doing and have done. This leads toward a framework of thought in

which to place previously bewildering facts and experiences, and it is a means of giving credit to their strivings.

Another paper from these years, "The Mentally Ill in Your Caseload," given before a group of social workers in 1963, is a summary of varieties of mental illness. Reflecting his preoccupation of the time, Winnicott makes a startling statement: "It has to be acknowledged that the normal person cannot achieve a feeling of reality in the world comparable with the schizophrenic's feeling of reality in the absolutely private world of the schizophrenic's relation to subjective objects. For normal persons the only approach that can be made to this quality of feeling is in the cultural field." This is a corollary of his theory that "the feeling of real" attaches to the relationship between the true self and subjective objects. But his statement is so strenuously put ("it has to be acknowledged") that one wonders how he knows. What are the data that support this inference?

Also on the subject of a feeling of reality he writes: "A mental breakdown is often a 'healthy' sign in that it implies a capacity of the individual to use an environment that has become available in order to re-establish an existence on a basis that feels real. Naturally such a device does not by any means always succeed, and it is very puzzling to society to see a compliant and perhaps valuable False Self destroy good prospects by a renunciation of every obvious advantage simply for the hidden advantage of gaining a feeling of reality." In this same paper he reminds his audience that "we need to acknowledge that there are cases that are outside remedy."

On July 18, 1963, he received a letter from Mrs. Bernard Brandchaft, who writes of her disappointment that Masud Khan did not call when he was in Los Angeles.[20] Khan was an extremely close friend of Robert Stoller. He stayed at his home whenever visiting Los Angeles, and, as we saw, left a copy of his Workbooks in the care of the Stollers. Leo Rangell, then president of the International Psychoanalytic Association, received Stoller and Khan at his nearby home. Stoller told Rangell, when he was alone with him, that Khan was all right to sit and drink wine with, but "I wouldn't trust him as far as I can see him.[21]"

On September 14, 1963, a letter came from Nelly Wolffheim, who said she had written a biography of Klein in the Berlin days. Winnicott consulted Khan about Wolffheim's proposal that the book be published.[22] (Khan was in his eleventh year of analysis with Winnicott at the time.) Further exchanges led him to the conclusion that the biography was not a book but only an essay. A few weeks later, on October 9, Khan sent good wishes on Winnicott's trip to America and added, with respect to a Winnicott paper, a new definition of self: "Always personal, isolated and unaffected by experience."

In "Psychiatric Disorder in Terms of Infantile Maturational Processes," given in October 1963 to the Philadelphia Psychiatric Society, Winnicott takes up the subject of patients who are dependent on the ego support of the analyst: "If the interpretation is incomprehensible then, whatever the reason, the patient feels hopeless, and may feel attacked, destroyed and even annihilated." In a case presentation he describes, "I took part naturally in the conversation, not knowing what was going on." The participants were discussing horse jumping. Here is Winnicott being himself, without straining to practice according to a technique, able to be a participant, yet not compromised as an observer in readiness to understand "what was going on" and develop whatever insight seemed well founded and useful.

Discussing dependence and its risks in treatment, he writes: "The risk is not that the analyst will die so much as that the analyst will suddenly be unable to believe in the reality and the intensity of the patient's primitive anxiety, a fear of disintegration, or of annihilation, or of falling for ever and ever." He goes on: "Occasionally holding must take a physical form, but I think this is only because there is a delay in the analyst's understanding which he can use for verbalizing what is afoot."

In "Hospital Care Supplementing Intensive Psychotherapy in Adolescence," delivered that same month at McLean Hospital in Belmont, Massachusetts, he adds an important observation to his developing theories about the nature of reality: "Will not society clamp down on dangerous sport and make even this unrespectable or even anti-social? We do not know the answer to this broad question yet, but we do know that a localized war, with all its immense tragedy, used to do something positive for the relief of individual tensions, enabling paranoia to remain potential and giving a sense of REAL to persons who do not always feel real when peace reigns supreme. Especially in boys, violence feels real, while a life of ease brings a threat of depersonalization." Further on he notes that "the adolescent has a fierce intolerance of the false solution" and that "adolescents in the doldrums phase seem to me to use the ill individuals on the fringe of the group to give reality to their own potential symptomatology."

He observes that "the false-self personality that threatens to break down at the period of examinations" gives the analyst a way of approaching those extremely common conflicts that arise out of the stresses of examinations, and suggest as well a point of view about examination dreams, prototypically in the form of a sudden awareness of an examination for which one is in no way prepared.

In this same talk Winnicott warns of deceptive recoveries: "The unsuccessful case can be used to illustrate the fact that a successful rehabilitation department can alter the clinical picture and make it seem that a patient has got well so that the original diagnosis is lost sight of. . . . You will not be deceived. . . by excellent artistic productions which can indeed denote potential health in the patient but which do not stand for health itself."

Overall, Winnicott's discussion of problems relating to adolescence underscores issues relating to the True and False Self. This rings true for the period in which a major revision of the self takes place, often painfully, often—to observing adults—quite confusingly.

In the early 1960s, Winnicott's writings entered into wide circulation, and new papers appeared in rapid succession. These were not simply the workmanlike harvest of an intent observer and thinker but the audacious output of a new kind of analyst. Following the directions indicated by his imagination, he put into words a tremendous succession of previously unarticulated ideas. He dealt with the notion of truth and falsity in life as lived, the double urge to be known and to be unknown, the complicated study of the quality of the real. This last area remained unclear, but Winnicott never purchased clarity at the cost of the complexity of human existence. One has the sense of ongoing struggle, eminently worth all the effort it took, and greatly fertile for those who could and would listen and read carefully.

— 20 —

The Ever-Deepening Journey

Between the end of 1962 and 1965, a number of topics emerge into view, showing Winnicott's formidable capacity to engage and grapple with new and surprising issues. This period began with a fuller acceptance from Anna Freud. It proceeded into Jungian territory, where Winnicott produced a complex narrative that interconnected himself, Jung, and Sigmund Freud. He wrote his poem "The Tree," the most profound autobiographical statement of his life. He defended himself against attacks based on the virulent and stupid accusation that he was nothing but a poet. He also wrote a paper on psychosomatic disease which underscored its essential dissociation between mind and body. That vast continent of illness, so neglected even now, is an area of bewilderment for physicians and others unable to find a set of words and concepts that can do justice to it.

This was the middle of the final decade of Winnicott's life. He made other, not insignificant contributions in this period. Winnicott showed more and more daring in his raids on the unknown, and would continue to do so in his last years. By now he had exceeded the total clinical and literary output of everyone else in his field with the exception of Freud.

Martin James, a psychoanalyst on good terms with Winnicott, reviewed *The Collected Papers*, which had appeared in 1958. James's remarks in a December 6, 1961, letter to Winnicott exemplify a climate of change toward Winnicott's writings that was then coming about. He spoke of the "mixture of fright and misunderstanding that has surrounded your work in some circles. Those with literal or obsessional minded approaches cannot comprehend your allusive and illustrative skills, which I find so attractive. I do think that your approach is typically British and totally beyond the comprehension of the Teutonic Hartmann style of theorist."[1] This, like Rycroft's "Dr. Livingston, I presume" anecdote, gives evidence of a lingering sense of being an embattled minority among the non-Jewish English members.

James also writes: "It seems from Miss Freud's ongoing comments in the Clinic since the holidays, and from her reaction to the Review, that she has really changed and, if so, then 'when Mother says turn—we all turn' and this whole climate will fall away. Winnicott will now no longer have to be thought of as, at best, incomprehensible and, at worst, quite absurd, malignantly Kleinian and wrongheaded." James fails to see the irony in the notion that it is the "Teutonic" Anna Freud (is Jewishness Teutonic?) who has changed. I think he means that Winnicott tended to be beyond the comprehension of most people anywhere. Or perhaps he was segregating the Freuds from Hartmann and certain unnamed others.

On November 27, 1961, Anna Freud had written to James: "I read your review of Dr. Winnicott's collected papers yesterday and I am full of admiration for the thorough and insightful work which you have done. I must confess that this is the first time that I fully understood Dr. Winnicott's theoretical position as well as all of his therapeutic intentions." She comments, too, about Winnicott's divergence from Freud in the meaning of the concept of regression.

This was a watershed moment, a year after Klein's passing.[2]

Outside of the evidence of extant materials, we have no way to date precisely when any particular turn of growth occurred in Winnicott's life, or what events contributed to it. We try to reconstruct, knowing that what we generate is bound to be a particular version of a particular moment in a particular life. This, of course, is the problem with any attempt at biography, but it is good to acknowledge this as an antidote to any sense of certainty that may bleed into a narrative. In the period under focus, the early 1960s and, for that matter, the remainder of Winnicott's life, we are studying a juncture, or series of junctures, when, stepwise, he seems to have moved into new and ever more profound territory.

In 1963, Winnicott's mastery of his clinical work is evident in two brief pieces, "A Note on a Case Involving Envy" and "Two Notes on the Use of Silence," not published until 1989.[3] We get access to the idiosyncratic person when we read: "To some extent I always listen with my throat, and my larynx follows the sounds that I hear in the world and particularly a voice of someone talking to me. This has always been characteristic of me and at one time was a serious symptom." We want to know more, but there is no more told. With this sort of interjection, as with so many others not generally seen in the psychoanalytic literature, more or less gratuitous identifications of his own peculiarities, we feel sure that we are in the presence of a human being, and not at all a psychoanalytic machine that has ironed out its distinctness and its irrelevant fullness of being.

That person was now working at the top of his form. He had given a number of talks in the United States the previous fall and was planning to do the same later in the year. This was also the year in which he wrote "The Tree" (in November). The theme expressed there of living with a depressed mother also appears in a dream related to reviewing Jung's autobiography, in the review itself, and in "Fear of Breakdown," probably also written in 1963, published in 1974. The subject continues into writings related to "The Use of an Object." In a 1963 letter to Michael Fordham, Winnicott describes his significant dream which "cleared up the mystery of an element of my psychology that analysis could not reach, namely, the feeling that I would be all right if someone would split my head open (front to back) and take out something (tumour, abscess, sinus, suppuration) that exists and makes itself felt right in the centre behind the root of the nose." The dream came in three parts, first one of absolute destruction, of which he was a part and was therefore being destroyed, the second one of absolute destruction of which he was the agent. In the third part he awakened, in the dream, and knew he had dreamed the first two parts. With this there was no longer a dissociation: the three I's were in touch with one another. He felt this resolution to be "immensely satisfactory, although the work done had made tremendous demands on [him]."

He felt that he had dreamed this dream for Jung and for some of his own patients, in addition to himself.[4] This idea grew out of his preoccupation with Jung's autobiography, which shows Jung to have been a childhood schizophrenic in dire need of integration, and it suggests the possibility that Winnicott felt himself to be Jung's twin, a gentile (my own designation) representative in psychoanalysis.[5] Instead of the dissociation between the work of Freud and Jung, however, which he describes in his review there is in his case an integration, in which his own discoveries and theories about early development and psychosis are themselves a development of, and can be integrated with, Freud's findings. His own ongoing struggle to mend the splits in himself is congruent with such a viewpoint and suggests the material of "Fear of Breakdown," which deals with patients who are preoccupied with the possibility of such an event. The analyst, he writes, should understand that what is needed is the recovery of a breakdown that happened too early to be experienced and therefore was never gathered into the omnipotence of the child, not integrated into the total personality. In other words, there was a failure of support by the mother at a stage when support was indispensable for going-on-being and progression to what he calls "unit status." There was a failure before this wholeness could be achieved. The patient fears what he or she wishes for, which is to experience the breakdown as if for the first time, with the equipment necessary to deal with it. Such a breakdown occurs in the transference, in re-living or, more correctly, living for the first time.

The dream described to Fordham, a Jungian analyst and friend of Winnicott's, suggests the climactic overcoming of a condition so extreme that he needed to have his "head split open" (i.e., he needed treatment that would bring back the original split) so that he could experience it in the present and overcome it. Winnicott's inference that Jung's mother was depressed matches up with his own situation and enhances the implication of a twinship. The plea that he makes for psychoanalysts to come to terms with Jung, however, is never supported by evidence of the value of Jung's contributions to analysis and is all the more suggestive of a personal stake in the outcome, that is, in the healing of an original (professional) dissociation that has personal meaning in Winnicott's own life. Jung's lack of contact "with his own primitive destructive impulses" is corrected by Winnicott's enlargement of the role of destructive impulses in early development and ongoing emotional life, the sense of the real and the creation of reality. And his recent interest in the hyperreality of the experience of mystics who commune with subjective objects may suggest another link to Jung, with his spiritual and mystical preoccupations. These topics have been totally outside the interest of psychoanalysts.

The review is sometimes difficult to follow. Winnicott draws conclusions and arranges a sequence of landmarks in Jung's early life that are commanding evidence of his own capacity for inference on the basis of what is presented. He takes hold of Jung's facts and forges a developmental line from which he draws powerful conclusions, making himself a kind of undissociated successor to Jung. Along the way he pays tribute to Jung: "If I want to say that Jung was mad, and that he recovered, I am doing nothing worse than I would do in saying of myself that I was sane and that through analysis and self-analysis I achieved some measure of insanity. Freud's flight to sanity could be something we psycho-analysts are trying to recover from, just as Jungians are trying to recover from Jung's 'divided self,' and from the way he himself dealt with it." Describing Jung's plight, he says: "It is not possible for a split personality to have an unconscious, because there is no place for it to be." Jung's concept of the collective unconscious "was part of his attempt to deal with his lack of contact with what could now be called the unconscious-according-to-Freud." Winnicott claims that Jung's development precluded a genuine Oedipal struggle and that as a result he was "unprepared as a man to clash with Freud." He goes on: "An imaginative clash with Freud would alone have formed a basis for a friendship (sublimated homosexuality), and there is evidence that Freud would have welcomed such an imaginative clash." Emphasizing Jung's failure to see in himself the origin for his fantasies of destruction and repeated acts of destructiveness in childhood, he adds, "It is precisely this primitive destructiveness that is difficult to get at when an infant is cared for by a mother who is clinically depressed. (Fordham has referred to Jung's fear of his own destructiveness.)"

This fear of destructiveness emanating from very early contact with a depressed mother was Winnicott's burden as portrayed in "The Tree." He was preoccupied throughout his life with recovering the means by which to overcome this deficit. His long history of using the word "hate" and of expressing his hatred,[6] and his protracted struggle to differentiate himself from the power of Melanie Klein and Joan Riviere, culminating in his dream and the further development of his ideas in "The Use of an Object," is the proof. The deeply disturbed Alice Taylor, whose unwillingness to have intercourse met with his own impotence, was succeeded by the tougher Clare Britton, who could meet him on his own ground and with whom he could transform aggression into potency.

Winnicott's side reference to "True Self" as "Jung's Language" suggests Jung as the source of the term he used as his own. Jung's "persona" was thought by Michael Fordham[7] to correspond to Winnicott's "False Self": Jung's idea was that "so long as the individual core of the personality is not lost behind the mask it is useful to have a mask to put on." Winnicott's description of gradations of False Self in his 1960 paper shows him to have been in agreement.

The upward trajectory of Winnicott's fame was accompanied by an intensifying preoccupation with understanding his inner life and resulted in a new level of personal integration. This came about through the combination of self-expression (the dream, the poem) and the continuous scrutiny of what was emerging. Much as he had given the world up to this time, there was going to be still more, none of it of a trivial nature, if only we could comprehend it. On November 4, 1963, he composed "The Tree":

Someone touched the hem of my garment
Someone, someone and someone

I had much virtue to give
I was the source of virtue
*   the grape of the vine of the wine*

I could have loved a woman
*   Mary, Mary, Mary*
There was not time for loving
I must be about my father's business
There were publicans and sinners
The poor we had always with us
There were those sick of the palsy
*   and the blind and the maimed*
*   and widows bereft and grieving*
*   women wailing for their children*
*   fathers with prodigal sons*
*   prostitutes drawing their own water*
*   from deep wells in the hot sun*

Mother below is weeping
                    weeping
                    weeping

Thus I knew her

Once, stretched out on her lap
            as now on a dead tree
I learned to make her smile
                to stem her tears
                to undo her guilt
                to cure her inward death

To enliven her was my living

So she became wife, mother, home
The carpenter enjoyed his craft
Children came and loved and were loved
Suffer little children to come unto me

Now mother is weeping
She must weep

The sins of the whole world weigh less than this
            woman's heaviness

O Glastonbury

Must I bring even these thorns to flower?
            even this dead tree to leaf?

How, in agony
Held by dead wood that has no need of me
        by the cruelty of the nail's hatred
                    of gravity's inexorable and heartless
pull
I thirst

No garment now

No hem to be touched
It is I who need virtue
Eloi, Eloi, lama sabachthani?

It is I who die
    I who die
    I die
    I[8]

This poem was sent to his good friend Jim Taylor, brother of his first wife, and a doctor himself.[9] Winnicott's agonizing task, to bring his dead mother back to life, and to tend to all those others as well, continues as a dynamic preoccupation, coloring everything else. It does not follow from this late articulation of a theme that dates from the inception of his life that Winnicott was, on the whole, miserably laboring at the same task. One aspect of his wisdom, expressed in various places, is that many pursuits and preoccupations exist at once in any given life, not canceling one another out but part of the multidirectional nature of human development. This is not to understate the ongoing work that he was doing in the attempt to get free of that which was stamped on him from the beginning. This privately stated commentary on his plight as a Jesus figure startles by contrast with his well-crafted and voluminous professional output. It also reminds me of his paper on communicating and not communicating. It is as if this poem comes from the land of non-communication, a contradiction in terms since that place is never to be known or else it would be destroyed. It has that feel because it emerges in the context of his deep psychological burrowing, as in the papers bearing on revelation and non-revelation. It comes during a particular period in his effort. Yet, more simply, it could be called a spontaneous gesture, the true self in action, to return to an earlier conception— a spontaneous gesture entrusted to a good friend. The other good friend that we know about who received a similar gesture was Marion Milner, for whom he left an assemblage of matches, bent in such a way as to represent Christ on the cross. This was his message as her analyst, still married to Alice Taylor. From at least the mid-1940s to the mid-1960s, Jesus Christ was clearly a figure with whom he identified.

The examination Winnicott prepared for students at the LSE for March 25, 1964, reveals, alongside the probing, personally driven, far-ranging and struggling seeker, the perennially practical Winnicott. Questions include:

"'Health is, in one sense, a pattern of defences.' Do you agree with this, and if you do can you say what the defences would be against?"; "Take any case that has come your way to illustrate some form of depressive illness. A brief clinical description should include an indication as to the type of depression, and the degree of illness of the individual being described"; "What ideas have you concerning the Beatles' appeal to the teenager?"

Upon reading an article in *The Times* ("Freud or St. Peter") which implied that Freud urged uninhibited behavior on the general population, Winnicott was exercised enough to write a letter in defense of Freud (who, he indicates, "suffered depressions"). He sent it to Anna Freud, who replied from Yale Law School, where she was collaborating with some analytically trained lawyers on practical matters having to do with child custody: "Thank you for sending me the letter. I was very interested and I am glad that you can get so indignant. (But did my father have depressions? I never saw him in one.)"[10] He must have been primarily making reference to his own depressions, as "The Tree" would indicate.

For a seminar for psychoanalytic students on July 9, 1964, Winnicott wrote "The Importance of the Setting in Meeting Regression in Psycho-Analysis," essentially a review of material that had already appeared. Responding to what he regarded as an error in technique with a regressed patient (the placement of a pile of papers in other than their usual spot), he "was able to say that as far as I could see this disastrous mistake that I had made had unconscious motivation. I could guess at some of my reasons for making the mistake but in my own opinion, I said, the mistake lies within me and is not a reaction to something in the patient." Thus, "In the end I was able to say: 'The thing is, this is what I am like, and if you continue with me you will find I shall do similar things with unconscious motivation again because that is what I am like.'" He also told the student, "The work is not only difficult but it absorbs a great deal of one's capacity for cathexis."

In his review of aspects of the indispensable facilitating environment, he lists holding and handling but adds now, instead of object-presenting, the term"realising." He says that erotic satisfaction comes from "successful realising," but does not go further into definition. He continues:

> An important aspect of growth is the change from relating to subjective objects to a recognition of objects that are outside the area of omnipotence, that is to say are objectively perceived but not explained

on the basis of projection. In this area of change there is the maximum opportunity for the individual to make sense of the aggressive components. Making sense of the aggressive components leads to the baby's experience of anger (related to the Klein concept of envy of the good breast) and leads on in the favourable case to fusion of aggressive and erotic components eventuating in eating. In health by the time eating has become established as part of the relationship to objects there has become organised a fantasy[11] existence which is parallel to actual living and which carries its own sense of real.

Is this fantasy existence the equivalent of the transitional area "which is a most valuable compromise" in which a sense of the real is possible? Could this be a root to connect his idea of the real as, on the one hand, only the outcome of the True Self communicating with subjective objects and, on the other, aggression up against the resistance of the external world? He qualifies the role of cultural life with the notion that it is only for some that it provides a sense of the real, not for all, and yet all children do establish eating as part of the relationship to objects. The comment about cultural life seems to suggest that only the privileged, or the educated, or those of a particular personal bent have the feeling of the real as it relates to the world at large. Out of this could come an idea of the aristocracy of the real. This would be a strange introduction of social and/or cultural class into considerations so far focused solely on the development of all individuals.

Under the heading "Psycho-Somatic Disorder," the discussion is broken down into "1. Psycho-Somatic Illness in Its Positive and Negative Aspects,"[12] and "2. Additional Note on Psycho-Somatic Disorder." This discussion addresses his experience with the patient who committed suicide at the Cassel Hospital. The dissociation at the heart of Winnicott's thesis expresses itself, as he tells us, in divisions among doctors trying to help, which is what happened with the "special patients." He includes a review of his work to date on psyche and soma, and he asks: "Am I beginning to convey my meaning that *in practice* there does exist a real and insuperable difficulty, the dissociation in the patient which, as an organised defence, keeps separate the somatic dysfunction and the conflict in the psyche? Given time and favourable circumstances the patient will tend to recover from the dissociation. Integrative forces in the patient tend to make the patient abandon the defence."[13]

He goes on: "In the practice of psycho-somatics what the psychotherapist needs is the co-operation of a *not too scientific* doctor. This sounds very bad, and I expect opposition when I make this claim. Yet I must state what I feel. When doing the analysis of a psycho-somatic case I would like my opposite number to be a *scientist on holiday from science*. What is needed is science-fiction rather than a rigid and compulsive application of medical theory on the basis of perception of objective reality." He declares, "The essential psycho-somatic dissociation . . . is the subject of this paper."

His range and grasp of the interconnectedness of psyche and soma, or their essential unity, is reflected in scattered examples he gives of psychosomatic disorders:

> A severe disintegration threat can be hidden in a cricked neck; an insignificant skin rash may hide a depersonalisation; blushing may be all that shows of an infantile failure to establish a human relationship through the passing of water, perhaps because no-one would look and admire in the phase of micturition potency. Moreover suicide may be gathered into a hard patch on the inner maleolus [a bony obtrusion in the ankle], produced and maintained by constant kicking; delusions of persecution may be confined clinically to the wearing of dark glasses or a screwing up of the eyes; an antisocial tendency belonging to serious deprivation may show as simple bed-wetting; indifference to crippling or painful disease may be a relief from a sado-masochistic sexual organisation; chronic hypertension may be the clinical equivalent of a psycho-neurotic anxiety state or of a long-continued traumatic factor, such as a parent who is loved but who is a psychiatric casualty. And so one might go on, but all this is familiar ground.

To Winnicott perhaps, but the assembly of examples enforces a newly emphatic awareness of the ubiquity of serious conflict in everyday physical manifestations. He has shone high-intensity lights on the small details of daily existence. This sort of commentary enforces our impression of Winnicott the physician, always grounded in the body, no matter that he never had training in adult psychiatry.

The patient with psychosomatic disease has defenses "against the dangers that arise out of integration and out of the achievement of a unified personality. These patients need us to be split up (yet essentially united in the far background that they cannot allow themselves to know about)." He goes on:

> Psycho-somatic illness implies a split in the individual's personality, with weakness of the linkage between psyche and soma, or a split organised in the mind in defense against generalised persecution from the repudiated world. There remains in the individual ill person, however, a tendency *not* altogether to lose the psycho-somatic linkage. Here, then is *the positive value of somatic involvement.* The individual values the potential psycho-somatic linkage. To understand this one must remember that defence is organised not only in terms of splitting, which protects against annihilation, but also in terms of protection of the psyche-soma from a flight into an intellectualised or a spiritual existence, or into compulsive sexual exploits which would ignore the claims of a psyche that is built and maintained on a basis of somatic functioning.

He declares, "Our difficult job is to take a unified view of the patient and of the illness *without seeming to do so in a way that goes ahead of the patient's ability to achieve integration to a unit.*" The defense comes "against a threat of annihilation at the moment of integration."

He spoke about childhood neurosis to a Scandinavian orthopsychiatric congress in Helsinki, where he spent the month of September 1964 for the World Health Organization.[14] His presentation, primarily a fine review of all psychopathology, includes this offhanded comment about the toddler stage, when neurosis begins: "At this stage of development the child is in process of working out a relationship between the dream potential or the total imaginative life with the available environmental reliability. For instance, if father will be there at breakfast (I refer to England) then it is safe to dream that father got run over, or to have a dream in which in symbolic form the burglar shoots the rich lady's husband in order to get at her jewel box. If father is not present such a dream is too frightening, and leads to a guilt feeling or a depressed mood. And so on." This speech is notable because the father is mentioned, and it adds to his total stock of observations about the role of the environment.

Winnicott's defense of his own theoretical accomplishment is evident in an exchange with John Wisdom, a follower of Klein in the academic world. On October 26, 1964, Winnicott wrote:

When *you write about* Bion I do not easily allow your failure to relate Bion's work to that of his colleagues, though I consider he himself has full right to go ahead without even knowing what others of us are writing, let alone putting in references. . . . It is important to me that Bion states (obscurely of course) what I have been trying to state for 2 1/2 decades but against the terrific opposition of Melanie. Bion uses the word reverie to cover the idea that I have stated in the complex way that it deserves that the infant is ready to create something, and in good-enough mothering *the mother lets the baby know what is being created*—of Sechehaye's[15] term symbolic realisation, i.e. in therapy. Bion says . . . "What happens will depend . . ." Melanie Klein absolutely would not allow this, and my relation to her was (though always warm and good) impaired by her adamant objection to "what happens depends. . . ." . . . I like Bion's treatment of this subject, and I can learn something from it. But if you (not he) are talking about it you ought to say: this is what D.W.W. has been trying to get us to see for two or three decades. In a way, all that Bion has done is to divert our attention from the main issue to alpha and beta functions. . . . Bion talks about the needed objects that tantalise. Now anyone can use the English word tantalise, but it is I who have used it in this context. I have spoken of the worst kind of mothering, in which the mother, at the very early stage, must tantalise—that is, be unpredictable, so that she cannot even be relied on to fail to adapt to need. From this, I have said, it is to be doubted whether a baby can recover, and in treatment this is, in my experience, the most difficult type of case. . . . I don't mind being shown to be wrong, or criticised or banged about. But I have done some important work out of the sweat of my psycho-analytic brow (i.e. clinically) and I refuse to be scotomised.

In his reply (November 12, 1964), Wisdom tells Winnicott, "To me you are a poet, that is to say a clinical poet. . . . [C]linical poetry initiates into understanding of basic mental activity, but does not deal with basic structure + function required as machinery for operating that mental activity. Bion does." As Winnicott well knows, calling someone a poet—or an artist—can be a way to depreciate an analyst who strives, in the spirit of science, to find and express what is truthful. In any case, the fact that Winnicott is indeed a poet and an artist does not cast a suspicious light on his vast oeuvre as a psychoanalyst who adheres to scientific principles. What he is, is not identical to what he writes. Thus, Wisdom's reply is an insult that continues to elevate Bion at the direct expense of one who originated some of the ideas Bion presents as entirely his own.

Anna Freud did not wish her seventieth birthday (December 3) to be celebrated by the British Society, and Winnicott felt that same way about his own. What he wanted as a present to himself was the opportunity to give twenty lectures on the contribution of child psychiatry to psychoanalysis.

He was elected president of the society, for the term 1965–68. On January 3, 1965, he gave a very interesting presentation to teachers, "New Light on Children's Thinking." It had to do with the variety of thinking styles or types: "Misunderstanding may occur in debate through the fact that one person talking belongs to the thinking and verbalising kind, while another belongs to the kind that hallucinates in the visual or auditory field instead of expressing the self in words. Somehow the word people tend to claim sanity, and those who see visions do not know how to defend their position when accused of insanity. Logical argument really belongs to the verbalisers. Feeling or a feeling of certainty or truth or 'real' belongs to the others." His use of the word "vision"[16] implies that he is a hallucinator rather than a word person. This paper closes: "In a positive way thinking is a part of the creative impulse, but there are alternatives to thinking and these alternatives have some advantages over thinking. For instance, logical thinking takes a long time and may never get there, but the flash of intuition takes no time and it gets there immediately. Science needs both of these ways of going along. Here we are reaching out for words, thinking, and trying to be logical, and including a study of the unconscious which affords a vast extension of the range of logic. But at the same time we need to be able to reach out for symbols and to create imaginatively and in preverbal language; we need to be able to think hallucinatorily."

His paper implies the question: What is the relationship of hallucinatory thinking and "gestures"? Gestures are a way of showing. They can be visual or auditory, unaccompanied by words or accompanied. They would seem to be closer to concrete demonstrations than the more abstract words. Words can be sorted according to their closeness to abstraction or concreteness, as in onomatopoeia. Rhyming and rhythmic arrangements of words appeal to body rhythms and are closer to gesture. They are combined with words that may appeal to abstract thinking as well. Are not all communications subject to classification along these lines?

In addition, the paper calls our attention to the possibility that Winnicott the visualizer finds himself in a professional group that is largely composed of verbalizers, and is therefore not understood.[17] This idea may contribute to the quizzical expressions often seen when psychoanalysts are trying to comprehend his papers.[18]

His defense of his own work is expressed again on February 15, 1965, in a scolding reply to the Cuban analyst Humberto Nagera, an associate of Anna Freud at that time who had written a monograph on early childhood disturbances. Winnicott charged that what Nagera had quoted of Klein could have come from reading a single page of her work, and implied that his own work had been essentially ignored. He reminded Nagera that he wouldn't have a place if it weren't for Klein and himself, among others, chiding, "I hope you accept this broad comment from an older man."

On June 24, 1965, he wrote to Michael Fordham about a meeting the night before, where the discussion was about autism. Referring back to a case he had presented a few months before, he writes:

> I wanted to say something more about repetition. . . . [W]hat happened in the pencil case has to be understood in terms of the dynamics of that place into which the withdrawn child mentally withdraws. In this place dynamics is to be looked at in terms of pendulum movement. Even in stillness there is a potential pendulum movement, so that stillness alternates, as it were, from being relative to right or left. If there is no pendulum movement then there is death. I think that this patient in the course of her recovery was able to make a relationship with me on the basis that I accepted one half of the pendulum, so that she could accept the other and the game had to do with establishing a relationship to the world on this basis. The normal equivalent of this from my point of view is the rocking of infant-care, and in psycho-pathology there are all the clinical rhythms of autistic children and the rocking of deprived children to be remembered.

The depth of the insights Winnicott drew from the details of a single case can be seen again in comments he made on the case of "Frankie" at the Amsterdam Congress in 1965, in which he remarks that "the best that can happen is that for the time being the obsessional person has arranged a kind of order in the place of the idea of confusion." He notes in detail in the case having to do with the child sitting on a chair placed in an elevated position: "He was held by a thing, a contraption, or whatever one might wish to call it. The thing is a split-off function of the mother, not part of her attitude." And further, "there is nothing that a child can do about being held by a split-off function except to think of the mechanics of its working well or badly. There would be an alternation between elation (or some equivalent) and being dropped. . . . [The] cure of this man cannot be reached unless this first detail of his analysis at the age of 5 1/2 can be met and his helplessness in respect of his being cared for by a split-off maternal function instead of by a mother [is] reached in the transference setting." The word "contraption" reminds us of a previous comment about autism, undoubtedly related to a view of the mother as not fully devoted to the child.

"The Psychology of Madness: A Contribution from Psycho-Analysis"[19] elaborates on the subject matter of "Fear of Breakdown," with significant fine-tuning and deepening. He writes: "The individual is forever caught up in a conflict, nicely balanced between the fear of madness and the need to be mad. In some cases it is a relief when the tragic thing happens and the patient goes mad, because if a natural recovery is allowed for, the patient has to some extent 'remembered' the original madness. This is, however, never quite true, but it may be true enough so that clinical relief is obtained by the fact of the breakdown. It will be seen that if in such a case the breakdown is met by a psychiatric urge to cure then the whole point of the breakdown is lost because in breaking down the patient had a positive aim and the breakdown is not so much an illness as a first step toward health."

He goes on to make a link to fundamental theory: "At this point it is necessary to remember the basic assumption that belongs to the psychoanalytic theory that defences are organized around anxiety. What we see clinically when we meet an ill person is the organisation of defences and we know that we cannot cure our patient by the analysis of defences although much of our work is engaged in precisely doing this. The cure only comes if the patient can reach to the anxiety around which the defences were organised. There may be many subsequent versions of this, and the patient reaches one after another, but cure only comes if the patient reaches to the original state of breakdown."

The complexity of his attempt at a summary leads him to elaborate, addressing the condition of patients who have been in analysis "for a long time, or who have become by some means or other, perhaps through the passage of time and the process of growth, able to tolerate and cope with anxieties which were unthinkable in their original setting." In other words, the time element and processes of growth must be taken into account in understanding how unthinkable anxieties may become manageable. For any student of this subject, including psychoanalysts, engaging the issues of this paper would seem to take a good deal of time and acquaintance with mental function. "In the simplest possible case there was therefore a split second in which the threat of madness was experienced, but anxiety at this level is unthinkable. Its intensity is beyond description and new defences are organised immediately so that in fact madness was not experienced. Yet on the other hand madness was potentially a fact." He is speaking of potential madness from which immediate flight is taken, making for a kind of lifelong impending madness progress toward which is activated in the good-enough psychoanalytic setting, so that the patient's impulse toward health will lead him or her toward facing the moment that was not allowed to occur. Thus, "the core of madness has to be taken to be something so much worse because of the fact that it cannot be experienced by the individual who by definition has not the ego-organisation to hold it and so to experience it."

Winnicott verbalizes how difficult it is for an analyst to provide the ego support in the transference which makes it possible for the patient to get closer and closer to the unrememberable:

> It requires a considerable experience and courage to know where one is in the circumstances and to see the value to the patient when the patient reaches nearer and nearer to the X that belongs to that particular patient. Nevertheless if the analyst is not able to look at it in this way, but out of fear or out of ignorance or out of the inconvenience of having so ill a patient on his hands he tends to waste these things that happen in the treatment, he cannot cure the patient. Constantly he finds himself correcting the delusional transference or in some way or other bringing the patient round to sanity instead of allowing the madness to become a manageable experience from which the patient can make spontaneous recovery. . . . [T]here is a great deal of fear of breakdown, and if it could seep through that the breakdown

that is feared is a breakdown that has already done its worst, there is at least the possibility that the edge of the fear of breakdown could be dulled.

The main clinical wisdom here is Winnicott's recognition of the need for forbearance in the analysis of regressing and regressed patients, whose demands are so great and who threaten to move back toward less and less sanity, more and more dependency. The analyst, he says, must have faith that such movement will reach a limit, from which spontaneous recovery and renewed health will follow. He is the explorer who has been there and knows.

A paper on the concept of trauma, written in 1965 ("Trauma in Relation to the Development of the Individual within the Family"), is full of clinical examples illustrating the main point that "trauma is a failure relative to dependence. Trauma is that which breaks up an idealisation of an object by the individual's hate, reactive to that object's failure to perform its function." He continues:

Trauma in the more popular sense of the term implies a breaking of faith. The infant or child has built up a capacity to "believe in," and environmental provision first fits into this and then fails. In this way the environment persecutes by getting through the defences. The infant's or the child's reactive hate breaks up the idealised object, and this is liable to be experienced in terms of a delusion of persecution by good objects. Where the reaction is one of appropriate anger or hatred the term trauma is not apposite. In other words, where there is appropriate anger the environmental failure has not been beyond the individual's capacity to cope with his or her reaction. . . . In the end, trauma is the destruction of the purity of individual experience by a too sudden or unpredictable intrusion of actual fact, and by the generation of hate in the individual, hate of the good object, experienced not as hate but delusionally as being hated.

This may be relevant to an experience he describes (see below) in which, in pursuit of a piece of theoretical understanding, he arrives at a moment of what seems to be terror, and cannot continue.

"Notes on Withdrawal and Regression"[20] is one of a Winnicottian genre: condensed bits of brilliant clinical description with accompanying

new insights. He mentions, for instance, "the extreme reaction of a delusional transference and the need to just put up with it. I think that one
does need a great deal of confidence in oneself to just take all this without
saying anything out loud in self-defence." There is a brief discussion of
the acceptance of gifts from patients, in which he notes that he generally
is reluctant to do so with neurotic patients "because I know that I will
have to pay for it in inflated currency." With the psychotic, however, "I
find that presents have to do with damage already done."

"Absence and Presence of a Sense of Guilt Illustrated in Two Patients"[21] is another of his brilliant, brief clinical descriptions, with startling comments here and there, such as: "There is no doubt that the
pattern of the failure of the analyst if he is free from a set pattern of his
own belongs to the pattern according to which the patient's own environment failed at a significant stage." Describing one of his failures, he says
that he was "in a state of longing to have somebody to talk to about myself," in response to which he "made one or two references to [his] alternative preoccupations." For anyone who practices analysis, this is a
touching remark about what the analyst must forgo. "This patient went
into a state in which she felt she must be loathsome. No-one could possibly do this sort of thing except in reaction to some awful quality about
her which makes everybody do the worst." In fact, however, "what she
really cannot stand is that I may have made a mistake or failed her not
because she is loathsome but because of something about me." He continues: "My failure . . . was something that she had to try to bring within
the area of her own omnipotence, and she could only do this by knowing
very well about her own horrible ideas and impulses and feeling guilty
and so explaining what I had done in terms of retribution." Thus, "what
my failure had done was to sidetrack the patient from this main issue so
that she now wanted to kill me not as part of loving but in reaction to my
having broken up the processes of her growth." She had undergone "a
lifetime of trying to feel guilty but never succeeding."

This first portion of the paper closes with: "From here it is possible
to see what a patient meant who came to me about fifteen years ago
and whose first words were: 'I want you to help me find my own nastiness.' This patient had had a very terrible environment from the beginning and it took years of analysis for her to be able to reach to the place
where she knew about the nastiness which she would find in herself in
a good environment."

Part two concerns a woman whose sense of guilt—and it is of a horrendous order—arises only if she thinks she has betrayed herself. There is no guilt over the usual matters. She has a powerful aesthetic sense. The implications of this condition are not elaborated upon. I am reminded of Joan Riviere, one of those with an aesthetic preoccupation, the intent of which is often to maintain and improve one's *inner* condition, which threatens to be or actually is chaotic. There is a link as well to the sense of receiving life as a precious gift that requires the greatest care as a built-in responsibility. Failure of that care is a betrayal of the giftedness of life itself, a kind of a sin. This focus is not inconsistent with Riviere's notion that patients who show a negative therapeutic reaction are preoccupied with saving their destroyed internal objects. This condition is more widespread than generally recognized and often takes the form of the belief that one has ruined one's life, or is on the brink of doing so, or as a preoccupation with those who seem to have known from the beginning how to lead a successful and productive life, in contrast to one's own bumbling and naïve self.

During 1965, Winnicott was treating the little girl described in his posthumously published book *The Piggle*. In July he had to ask the girl's mother to tell her that he could not see her again until September, because, as he explains to the reader in a footnote, "the summer of 1965 was an exceptionally demanding time and included a period of illness." From the descriptions of his work in that book we see a nearly exhausted master of psychoanalysis at work. He was in fact much more than a master of psychoanalysis. He had become a superordinate figure taking his place in the history of Western thought, even as his physical powers were sorely tried.

At the very end of the year,[22] in response to a note from me, he sent a list of seven books he had written. He was justifiably proud of the seven titles. This is a prolific output for a psychoanalyst, but, as the world would learn in the years to come, only a fraction of his writings. The insights enclosed in his vast eventual oeuvre represent the maximum expenditure of his deep wellsprings of intellectual strength—this in a man seen by others as a fragile presence in frequent need of support. At this point he was expending all of his substance in the treatment of especially needy patients and at the same time attempting to put into words the full force of his dazzling insights.

— 21 —

Female/Male; Being/Doing

In the period from 1966 on, the aging Winnicott took ever greater risks in his theorizing effort to understand himself and others. His brilliant forays into the unknown were accompanied by moments of instability, and very possibly physical effects as well.

A group of writings around "The Split-Off Male and Female Elements to Be Found in Men and Women"[1] is valuable not only for its insights, but also for several statements[2] that describe his state of mind as he pursued the implications of these insights. The paper is built around a case in which Winnicott came to see himself as mad because he was seeing the patient as a woman rather than as the man he knew the patient to be. This led to the idea that when the patient was born, his mother saw him as a girl rather than a boy, and this affected his development profoundly. (The subject here has nothing to do with sexual preference.) He writes:

> I said: "It was not that *you* told this to anyone; it is *I* who see the girl and hear a girl talking, when actually there is a man on my couch. The mad person is *myself.*"
>
> I did not have to elaborate this point because it went home. The patient said that he now felt sane in a mad environment. In other

Masud Khan. *Photo by Zoe Dominc*

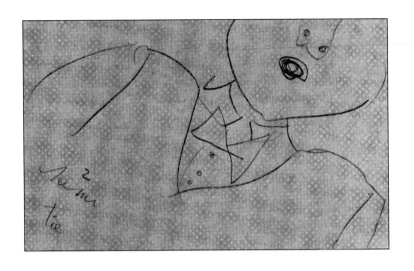

Squiggles

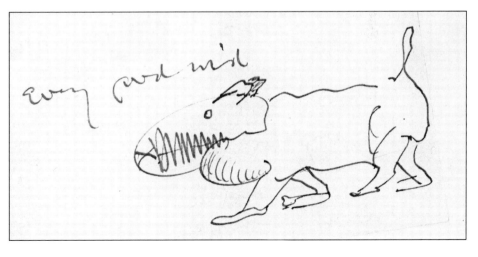

Squiggles

Collage of Christmas cards, drawn and colored by Donald.

Portrait by Lotte Meitner-Graf, late 1960s.

Donald, Clare, and Roger Money-Kyrle, 1960s.

Donald and Anna Freud at the banquet marking the completion of James Strachey's translation into English of the *Complete Psychological Works of Sigmund Freud*, August 10, 1966.

Donald and Oscar Nemon with Freud statue in the studio of Oscar Nemon, 1968.

Portrait by Lotte Meitner-Graf, late 1960s.

words he was now released from a dilemma. As he said, subsequently, "I myself could never say (knowing myself to be a man) 'I am a girl.' I am not mad that way. But you said it, and you have spoken to both parts of me."

This madness which was mine enabled him to see himself as a girl *from my position*. He knows himself to be a man, and never doubts that he is a man.

Further on Winnicott observes:

My interpretation continued along the line started up on the Friday. I said: "You feel as if you ought to be pleased that here was an interpretation of mine that had released masculine behaviour. *The girl that I was talking to, however, does not want the man released*, and indeed she is not interested in him. What she wants is full acknowledgement of herself and her own rights over your body. Her penis envy especially includes envy of you as a male." I went on: "The feeling ill is a protest from the female self, this girl, because she has always hoped that the analysis would in fact find out that this man, yourself, is and always has been a girl (and 'being ill' is a pregenital pregnancy). The only end to the analysis that this girl can look for is the discovery that in fact you are a girl." Out of this one could begin to understand his conviction that the analysis could never end.

We feel the excitement of discovery in this passage: "I and my patient had been over this ground before. Yet we had here something new, new in my own attitude and new in his capacity to make use of my interpretative work. I decided to surrender myself to whatever this might mean in myself, and the result is to be found in this paper that I am presenting." And a little further on: "The first thing I noticed was that I had never before fully accepted the complete dissociation between the man (or woman) and the aspect of the personality that has the opposite sex."

From this case Winnicott moves into diverse territory, including an original dichotomy between *being* (female) and *doing* (male), with speculations about the earliest origins of these two elements. Among his observations are: "A patient will always cling to the full exploitation of personal and *internal* factors, which give him or her a measure of omnipotent control, rather than allow the idea of a crude reaction to an environmental factor, whether distortion or failure. Environmental influence, bad or even good, comes into our work as a traumatic idea, intolerable because not operating within the area of the patient's omnipotence. Compare the melancholic's claim to be responsible for *all* evil." Also: "The split-off other-sex part of the personality tends to remain of one age, or to grow but slowly." And further: "It is interesting that the existence of this split-off female element actually prevents homosexual practice." His patient fled from homosexual experience because this "would establish his maleness which (from the split-off female element self) he never wanted to know for certain."

Under the rubric of "speculation," he goes on: "However complex the psychology of the sense of self and of the establishment of an identity eventually becomes as a baby grows, no sense of self emerges except on the basis of this relating in the sense of BEING. This sense of being is something that antedates the idea of being-at-one-with, because there has not yet been anything else except identity. Two separate persons can *feel* at one, but here at the place that I am examining the baby and the object *are* one. The term 'primary identification' has perhaps been used for just this that I am describing, and I am trying to show how vitally important this first experience is for the initiation of all subsequent experiences of identification."

He observes that

> the object-relating of the male element to the object presupposes separateness. . . . The male element *does* while the female element (in males and females) *is*. . . .It seems that frustration belongs to satisfaction-seeking. To the experience of being belongs something else, not frustration, but maiming. . . . object-relating backed by instinct drive belongs to the male element in the personality uncontaminated by the female element. . . . The study of the pure distilled uncontaminated female element leads us to BEING, and this forms the only basis for self-discovery and a sense of existing (and then on to the capacity to develop an inside, to be a container, to have a capacity to use the mechanisms of projection and introjection and to relate to the world in terms of introjection and projection). . . . When the girl element in the boy or girl baby or patient finds the breast it is the self that has been found.

He notes that "Hamlet . . . was searching for a way to state the dissociation that had taken place in his personality between his male and female elements, elements which had up to the time of the death of his father lived together in harmony, being but aspects of his richly endowed person. Yes, inevitably I write as if writing of a person, not a stage character."

About the patient he says: "This was exactly what the patient needed but it took me the whole hour to get there and in the course of that time I had made many false interpretations, many of them very clever, each making me more ridiculous (mockery theme)."

Under "Answers to Comments" of 1968–69, three years after the original paper and in the aftermath of the illness in New York that foreshadowed his death, he tells us, "It could be said that the patient was in search of the right kind of mad analyst and that in order to meet his needs I had to assume that role." He goes on:

> At the extreme I discovered myself looking at an essential conflict of human beings, one which must be operative at a very early day; that between being the object which also has the property of being, and by contrast a confrontation with the object which involves activity and object-relating that is backed by instinct or drive. This turned out to be a new statement of what I have tried to describe before in terms of the subjective object and the object that is objectively perceived, and I was able to re-examine for my own benefit the tremendous effect here on the immature human baby of the attitude of the mother and then of the parents in terms of adaptation to need. In other words, I found myself re-examining the movement of the reality principle from . . . what? I have never been satisfied with the use of the word "narcissistic" in this connection because the whole concept of narcissism leaves out the tremendous differences that result from the general attitude and behaviour of the mother. I was therefore left with an attempt to state in extreme form the contrast between being and doing.

And here, possibly as a direct result of his close encounter with death in New York, he allows himself statements of a different, self-referential order:

> What I want to do is to explore further. I want to get right behind all the crossed-sex sophistications, cross-identifications, and even cross-

expectations (where a baby or child can only contribute to a parent in terms of the other than biological sex), and I want to go where I find myself both drawn and driven. I want to reach in a new way a concept that no doubt has roots in the writings of other analysts.[3]

I want to get to a statement of a basic dilemma in relatedness:

a. The baby *is* the breast (or object, or mother, etc.); the breast is the baby. This is at the extreme end of the baby's initial lack of establishment of an object as not-me, at the place where the object is 100 percent subjective, where (if the mother adapts well enough, but not otherwise) the baby *experiences* omnipotence.

b. The baby is confronted by an object (breast etc.) and needs to come to terms with it, with limited (immature) powers of the kind that are based on the mental mechanisms of projective and introjective identifications. Here we need to note that again each child's experience is dependent on the environmental factor (mother's attitude, behaviour, etc.).

In the framework of this concept, which deals with a universal human problem, one can only see that baby = breast is a matter of being, not of doing, while in terms of confrontation baby and breast meeting involves doing.

In psychopathology some of the greatest blocks to instinctual— or drive—involvement come when patient = object violently changes into patient confronts and is confronted by object, involving a change from a cosy defence to a position of anxiety of high degree and a sudden awareness of immaturity. I cannot avoid it, but just at this stage I seem to have abandoned the ladder (male and female elements) by which I climbed to the place where I experienced this vision. [The vision of a seer? The ladder as the contraption of a split-off aspect of mother?]

What does he mean? He has gone to the place where he was drawn and driven, has experienced "this vision" but now he "cannot avoid it," he has "abandoned the ladder ([a theory of] male and female elements) by which [he] climbed to [this] place." This is the end of his note, as if he has lost touch with continuity and is unable to continue. Is this impotence of a sort? Is he overwhelmed by anxiety? Is this a trauma now, which he was reliving in his theoretical adventure, in which (as he describes in other places as well) the subjective object suddenly knows too much and there is a "sudden awareness of immaturity"? He had recently written, "Trauma is the destruction of the purity of individual experience by a too sudden or unpredictable intrusion of actual fact." Perhaps he has gone too far at this point, knows too much, has entered a sacred realm where he is "confronted by the object." (Did he have a cardiac event at this point in his writing. . . . is that what caused him to cease?)

It seems likely to me that he has been driven by his illness to realize that time is short and, under the influence of his newfound insights into the split-off male and female elements, which arose from his capacity to stand being insane in the countertransference, he has embarked on his journey into the uncharted interior. Classifying and theorizing as he goes, like a good Darwinian naturalist, he finally comes upon a terrifying presence, the object objectively perceived and himself found out.[4] He feels hopelessly immature and loses touch with the ladder up which he had climbed, like Jack losing his grip on the beanstalk when the ogre senses his presence. This marks the limit of his analytic adventure.

I find these quotations pertinent to his experience. From Valéry: "No doubt there is nothing more morbid in itself, more inimical to nature, than *to see things as they are*. . . . The real, in its pure state, stops the heart instantaneously. . . . O Socrates, the universe cannot for one instant endure to be only what it is."[5] And from *A New Path to the Waterfall* by Raymond Carver: "We look with fluorescent starkness into the unrelenting, obsessive magnetism of 'the real,' its traps and violences."[6]

In this regard, there is a footnote in Ilse Grubrich-Simitis's book on Freud, in which she comments on a letter he has written to a childhood friend: "Beneath the humorous surface . . . we may already discern here the rejected, threatening theme of dependence on a cold, demanding object."[7] This would seem to be the author's inference about Freud's early experience. Can this be the primal response to the object, the one Winnicott experienced as he pursued his thinking to the point of interruption? And if so, is this then the root of the urge to destroy the object, that possessor of the omnipotence suddenly nonexistent or lost? Is there behind this a feeling of guilt at having felt a sense of omnipotence, as if, in the light of the encounter with a terrifying object newly perceived, it had been stolen from elsewhere? Or is this attributing too much psychic capacity to the infant? Photographs of big game hunters like Ernest Hemingway with a slaughtered lion suggest extreme efforts to triumph over the object objectively perceived.

I am reminded of the lure of art to the scientist, drawn, under stress, to the mitigating indulgence of the mother and, contrapuntally, to the father as one who can restore the capacity to be whole, to face the stresses with strength: the father, that is, the figure behind science, demanding, aggressive, concerned with nothing less than wholeness and coherence.[8]

This late-life meditation on split-off male and female elements suggests to me that he had found a way to present his own case, or to integrate his own case into that of someone else, in the concept of the man seen as a woman. He would have realized that in the beginning he had been seen by his mother as a girl, and that he had been dealing with this throughout his life without having been able to identify it as such. His determination to find his way to the ultimate nature of babyhood (to which he was "drawn and driven"), and the element of alarm that brought his meditation to a halt, suggest the depth and personal importance of his reflection. He had an urgent need to complete his own analysis.

The shift he describes from union with the object to confrontation supports the notion that he had emerged from the state of subjective object (under the sway of his mother's confusion about his gender) into the world in which the separated object can be objectively perceived. He has, in effect, finally been able to separate from his mother and feels himself to be the immature baby helplessly seen. He is traumatized by a fact. This line of thinking, with its speculative element, adds a new dimension of understanding to Winnicott's lifelong struggle to emerge as his own person as an individual being and his own person as a pyschoanalyst.

Landmarks in his quest for the "doing" element of maleness can be identified in his smashing of the little doll "Rosie" about which his father teased him, his revolt against being too "nice" at age nine, his use of the word "drat," which resulted in his father's sending him to boarding school (for which he was grateful—the father was there to kill and be killed), and his cultivation of the word "hate" throughout his life. His mother's possibly erotic response to breast-feeding, resulting in her interruption of it, may be a referent of the case material on the subject of split-off elements, as in "Nothing at the Centre" in which the male child is wrapped in such a way as to demonstrate the mother's wish to suppress his penis. Throughout the paper itself and its associated writings, there is rich material for the biographer trying to understand Winnicott's earliest conflicts. In the light of this material, his marriage to Alice may be seen as the marriage of two females. Clare, with her "toughness" lent support to his masculine side.

One may also better understand his unwillingness to submit to Klein's views. He was, of course, drawn to Klein and at the same time frightened that her theories might submerge his own. Going along with her powerful views would have been the equivalent of submitting to his mother's idea that he was actually a girl.

In the paper on split-off elements, he refers to Hamlet, who was "searching for a way to state the dissociation that had taken place in his personality between his male and female elements, elements which had up to the time of the death of his father lived together in harmony." A bit further on he writes: "It seems possible to use Hamlet's altered attitude to Ophelia and his cruelty to her as a picture of his ruthless rejection of his own female element, now split off and handed over to her, with his unwelcome male element threatening to take over his whole personality." I am reminded of the fact that his separation from Alice took place only after his father had died. This was the moment at which his inner struggle came to the surface, when he could be cruel to Alice, showing a ruthless rejection of his female element. As with Hamlet and Ophelia, he was at the same time reluctant to abandon it.

I find this material pivotal to the effort to understand Winnicott's struggle.[9]

On March 15, 1966, Winnicott sent Walter Joffe a list of some fifty invitees to his seventieth birthday party on April 7. The list does not include his sisters, nor Clare's sister Elizabeth, nor Clare's older brother Karl. These relatives were apparently not part of their social circle.

To David Holbrook he wrote on April 15: "I think that the study of man's identification with woman has been very much complicated by a persistent attempt on the part of psycho-analysts to call everything that is not male in a man homosexuality, whereas in fact homosexuality is a secondary matter or less fundamental and rather a nuisance when one is trying to get at a man's woman identification." His paper on "Split-Off Elements" had been given in February.

James Home wrote on April 27 that "your use of the term Psyche-Soma usually infuriates me (intellectually, I mean). To me it is impossibly vague and emotive. By emotive I mean that you are really using it to describe your feeling as you contemplate a given set of facts and not to describe the facts or the pattern you discern in the facts. The term is then poetical [this word again among the Kleinians] and not useful for discursive thought. I become furious because in your thinking about the mother-child situation, you have, in my opinion, laid bare the true and proper matrix for a psychoanalytical theory of behaviour. It pains me that you have never pushed your theoretical thinking firmly through the caul of instinct theory and ego-iddery."

Speaking on October 8, 1966, at the banquet held upon the completion of the *Standard Edition*, Winnicott noted:

> The British Psycho-analytical Society is celebrating something. Not Id: though it is hoped that you have enjoyed both food and wine. Not Ego: which I would think, as a pure concept, cannot really have much of a time, being in a state of constant vigilance against encroachment by the other concept, the Self. Not Super-Ego. Indeed, Strachey would not like us to honour him out of a sense of duty. We are celebrating a cultural achievement, this time not so much that of Freud as of James Strachey.
>
> I believe Freud did not have a place in his topography of the mind for the experience of things cultural. He gave new value to inner psychic reality, and from this came a new value for things that are actual and truly external. Freud used the word "sublimation" to point the way to a place where cultural experience is meaningful, but perhaps he did not get so far as to tell us where in the mind cultural experience is. Whether we know, or do not know, where we are in terms of topography of the mind, we are together at this time to congratulate ourselves that the Standard Edition of Freud, now completed, is an erudite work.
>
> . . . In my own reading I am proud to have reached Volume 2. (Laughter) I think you are laughing because there is no Volume 1. (Laughter) But, of course, I began at the end. I like to learn that in 1896, just as I was being born, Freud was first using the term "angst," pointing out the implication in the word of the straight and narrow path by which we are precipitated into the brief world of our personal existence. . . .
>
> We are grateful to find that psycho-analysis has caught hold of the tail of the Bloomsbury set, and just in time to swing itself up on to the high shelf where the Standard Edition may now stand alongside

the works of Leslie Stephen, Virginian Woolf, Lytton Strachey, May-
nard Keynes, and why not add Geoffrey Keynes, Duncan Grant,
Vanessa Bell, and so on and so on. . . .

Would we rather Freud be known as a scientist or as a man of
stature and erudition? A man with a sense of eternal values? We can
have both.

In a letter dated January 2, 1967, from Lucie Freud, the wife of Ernst
Freud (one of Sigmund Freud's sons), she discusses her son Lucian, the
celebrated painter, and writes, "It warms my heart to think of your own
mother sharing my rare experience." This comparison between her son
and Donald may imply her perception that Donald was in some sense an
artist.

Strachey, on January 17, mentions looking down from his veranda in
Tobago at people snorkeling and adds: "But that doesn't prevent my ap-
plauding you and continuing to watch with admiration, alarm and envy
as you schnorkle [his spelling] in the depths of the bay down below."
This was probably the last letter Winnicott would receive from him.

From Stanford, also on January 17, he received an invitation to
spend a year in residence at the Center for Advanced Behavioral Study,
which he turned down, saying, "If I were to accept this wonderful opportunity for meeting others in the behavioural field and for thinking and
writing, I would run a very great risk of cutting myself off for ever from
the source of my inspiration, which is the constant impingement of private cases."

We learn from Douglas Kirsner's book *Unfree Associations* that Wilfred Bion visited Los Angeles in the spring of 1967 to lecture. He was invited by Bernard Brandchaft to come work in Los Angeles, and he
responded favorably. Winnicott wrote him on July 10: "I have been told,
of course, about your proposal to leave England in the new year and to
spend a few years in Los Angeles. This will be very good for Los Angeles
and I think you may do a really good job there. The trouble is, however,
that we shall miss you a very great deal in this country. Your position
here and your personality in what you stand for in the work is of the very
greatest importance to us and we can ill afford to lose you." Bion replied
on the eighteenth: "Dear Winnicott, many thanks for your kind letter and
generous remarks. Francesca and I both look forward, with some trepida-
tion. . . . Naturally we hope good will come of it; what it costs to uproot

from all our friends and associates here is painfully obvious but we shall have to wait to see what the compensating . . . may be—and hope. With all good wishes to Clare and yourself from Francesca and me." They moved in January 1968.

Bion had been analyzed by Klein and believed that many of his contributions derived from her work. But he was an original, widely admired thinker in his own right. The ostensible point of coming to Los Angeles was to be able to work without the administrative burden he had in London.[10] He wanted to give himself over to writing and to deal with patients. He remained separate from the Los Angeles Psychoanalytic Society, to which Brandchaft belonged, and avoided becoming entangled in the conflicts with which psychoanalysis in Los Angeles was afflicted. Kirsner writes: "He felt that many of the attributions made about him in Los Angeles were, as he put it, 'wide of the mark.' In Los Angeles Bion feared being inappropriately 'thrust into the role of being a sort of messiah or deity' and did not want to be involved in disputes as to whether or not he was Kleinian or crazy. Although he was often revered, Bion did not seek a following. Bernard Bail, an analyst of Kleinian persuasion, found him 'always a modest man to the point of self-deprecation.' In 1969 Bion said that he planned to stay 'for a short space of time, I thought perhaps five years' but remained in Los Angeles until a few months before his death in 1980."[11]

Bion's reception frequently rose to a pitch of adoration, based to some extent, it seems, on the vagueness with which he presented his ideas. Many enrolled for periods of analysis with him and have since used their experiences as badges proving them genuine Bionians. He could sometimes be seen pacing the streets of Beverly Hills, his large head tilted back at the angle of an Easter Island monolith, lost in thought. He was a kindly person, devoted to his wife, Francesca, and his daughters, born to them late in his life. He had more books than he could house and so put two rows on each shelf. He periodically renewed the bindings by the application of a formula he obtained from the British Museum. He once said to me,[12] "I told Melanie that I did not want to be a Kleinian," and of his interpretive approach he said that his first attempts were, in naval parlance, "sighting shots" (Albert Mason's recent brief memoir of Bion agrees),[13] that is, unlikely to hit the mark, but they could then be revised so that they could come closer. This spirit was not that of the Kleinian in total possession of the truth, as Klein's followers so often presented themselves. Winnicott wrote to him (October 5, 1967) about his recommendation that analysts eschew "memory and desire,"[14] a precept often misinterpreted, it seems to me. The value of his idea is that it liberates the analyst from being preoccupied with remembering what was discussed the day before, or with worrying about what is coming next. It frees him to pay attention to the here-and-now. I have often remembered this little idea, and it has helped me to give myself over to what is right there, in the moment. As Kirsner says, Bion was not a political person, but all around him there was a raging battle for possession, for association, and for disassociation. The context was the Los Angeles world of psychoanalysis, fraught with conflict and celebrity-oriented. It was the leading edge of a spreading tension between the ego psychology of traditional American analysis and the challenge first of Klein, then of Kohut and of others, which produced a multiplicity of schools at this time. Those who were drawn to Winnicott's work never formed into a coterie. This was the consequence of Winnicott's own attitude. Their interest continued in the face of the fracturing of psychoanalysis in Los Angeles.

On October 4, Paula Heimann wrote to invite the Winnicotts to have dinner with herself and a Dr. and Mrs. Birdsall. The next day Donald replied that he might come, but he could not promise that Clare would. Actually, he wanted "to hear your disagreements with Klein, and can't if the Birdsalls are there." Winnicott also did not like to socialize with professionals, and he had recently consulted Dr. Birdsall about himself.

In reply on October 24 to a letter from a doctor inquiring about physical contact with patients, he answered: " I have lectured a great deal on the subject of physical contact between patient and therapist. If one writes these things down one gets very easily misunderstood, and I am afraid that there is no way of referring you to what I have written on this subject except to ask the reader to get a general inference from going through my writings."

"The Concept of Clinical Regression Compared with That of Defence Organisation," presented on October 27 at McLean Hospital in Massachusetts, is a review of his ideas notable only for the strength of two statements. The first is: "I have to confess that I did at one time think of schizophrenia and schizoid types of clinical disorder as regressions, so that I joined in the hunt for fixation points. This was a carry-over from the corresponding witch-hunt in the attempt to state the aetiology of psycho-neurosis in its various manifestations." The second is: "In other words, I found that in my study of schizoid phenomena I was using the word 'regression' to mean *regression to dependence*. I did not any longer care whether the patient had stepped back in terms of erotogenic zones." To give due credit, he has abandoned his prior efforts to hedge, to soften his unique contribution. He was by now, of course, seventy-one years old.

On November 13, 1967, he wrote to the playwright Arthur Miller, via Miller's publisher, inquiring about a book of Miller's called *Jane's Blanket*, which is about transitional objects. He wanted to know if Miller came to the observations himself or if, perhaps, he had derived them from reading Winnicott. He writes: "I often wonder whether Schultz [i.e., Charles Schulz] with his Peanuts character who had a transitional object had also read what I wrote.[15] Obviously both he and you are inspired by what you observed in the children around just as I was, but it is rather interesting that we have all started drawing attention to these things at about the same time." The letter ends: "You might conceivably have heard of me through Marian Kriss [sic] and her late husband with whom I believe you had contact over Marilyn [Monroe]. I am thinking of this as a private and confidential correspondence. It is simply that I feel curious and also that I want to let you know how much I like the book." He misspells "Kris," as well as "Schulz," an uncharacteristic lapse, and he uses the unadorned name "Marilyn" where he would be expected to refer more graciously to Miller's late former wife, if he chose at all to deal with such a matter. His narcissism is in evidence here: he wants some measure of the extent to which he has altered people's perceptions with his contributions.

Miller replied (November 26):

> The central inspiration for *Jane's Blanket* came from observing my own daughter as a child. (She is now 23 years old but the occasion for writing a children's book only came up two or three years ago.) In fact, however, I believe this habit of clinging to certain comforting objects is quite common in children, although I had never heard them called Transitional Objects, which indeed they are.
>
> I never knew Marian Kris very well. As Marilyn's doctor her relationship to me was restrained by that formality. I imagine you are aware that she was not treating Marilyn in her last few years.

I should like to thank you for letting me know that you found the book interesting.

On November 28, 1967, Lady Allen of Hurtwood writes: "I have read '[Notes on the] Preparation of Young Men for War' [an unpublished paper of mine that Winnicott had sent to her] with fascinated nausea." It is signed Marjorie Allen. Her husband, a socialist, was imprisoned for eighteen months in solitary confinement. The paper was written as a stark statement of what was being done to adolescent boys to change them, in a matter of weeks, into soldiers willing to kill.

"The Location of Cultural Experience," written around this time, is a short piece in which he states in deceptively simple terms that give the reader pause— his thesis that the location of cultural experience is the potential space between the individual and the external world. That is the space that begins as transitional, and it is sacred. In this way he connects the beginnings of personal life with the vast inherited culture into which an individual may contribute and from which he may draw. The bodily experience with which life begins thus becomes linked to the accumulation of other people's creative discovery. His "Addendum to 'The Location of Cultural Experience,'" dated December 18, includes a reference to his dreams of being at what he calls "the club," a location that is the setting for many of his dreams, which he puts on the dream side of awakening but not in the fully dreaming state. He gives some detail about this club, this community, mentioning its continuity, but saying as well that it is a bit like fantasying and is subject to some sort of manipulation. Dreams that cluster in a particular location, revisited again and again, the identical place or a contiguous place through which an elaborate setting is exposed over time, are not the same as a dream that repeats itself again and again, he says. This is the only instance, to my knowledge, in which such dreams have been noted, and Winnicott's notation is incidental. He points us, however, toward a new variation on the dream.

A long diatribe, dated December 10, from a psychoanalyst who is enraged about conditions in the Canadian Society is an attempt to arouse Winnicott to some sort of action. The patent nature of the man's provocations probably guaranteed that he would not succeed, but this handwritten and quite lengthy letter subjected the elderly Winnicott to an onslaught of accusations just at the point that his health was deteriorating.

Winnicott's instructions (February 9, 1968) to a Dr. Hunter-Smith about arrangements for a lecture to the Folkestone Medical Society, the first ever by a psychoanalyst, are interesting. His request is for "an overnight room and to do nothing, i.e. no dinner, before the lecture," though perhaps a drink afterwards. This makes perfect sense, allowing the speaker to think about what he will say without distraction; but the group to which a lecture will be given usually feels compelled to provide hospitality just at the point when solitude is most useful. Who besides Winnicott would have had the temerity to make this explicit request? He does indicate that his request comes from finding that he is getting older, and of course he had recently been ill.

On February 13, Masud Khan (not Winnicott's analysand since 1966) sent a lengthy note linking Winnicott's 1935 manic defense paper to his transitional object theory. Winnicott had not made the connection and was interested, though nothing seems to have come of it. Khan comments on the virtues of Oscar Nemon's monumental statue of Freud. Winnicott was fostering a project to erect this statue in Swiss Cottage; it would become one of the great quests of the final years of his life.[16] This letter expresses goodwill between the two, not the kind of estrangement that prevents communication.

In "Interpretation in Psycho-Analysis" (February 19, 1968), Winnicott notes that "a great deal of communication takes place from patient to analyst that is not verbalised." Furthermore, "there is also the vast subject which can be explored of the analyst's communications that are not conveyed in direct verbalisation or even in errors of verbalisation. . . . [There is] the analyst's tone of voice and the way in which, for instance, a moralistic attitude may or may not show in a statement." His fundamental comment here is that "in the simplest form the analyst gives back to the patient what the patient has communicated." Speaking of the different states of mind in the patient between the time of providing information through associations and the time of listening to the analyst's interpretation, he says that "the interpretation may even be given to the whole person, whereas the material for the interpretation was derived from only a part of the whole person. As a whole person the patient would not have been able to have given the material for the interpretation." This raises the question of what state the patient is in when giving material. Is the patient not communicating then as a whole person? Evidently not, according to Winnicott. In the matter of answers to the analyst's questions, he writes, "What the analyst knew . . . was that the whole material came from a question and that it would not have come if the analyst had not invited the material, perhaps simply out of feeling that he was getting out of touch with the patient. The material therefore was not material for interpretation." He does not include the word "impingement," which he coined for the disturbance that an infant can undergo when prompted to react by people in the environment or the environment itself. Yet his discourse on questions could easily include that term. Questions can be impingements in analysis, eliciting responses not voluntarily given and thus not material for interpretation.

The paper ends: "It cannot be too strongly emphasized, however, that in the teaching of students, that it is better to stick to the principle of the reflecting back of material presented rather than to go to the other extreme of clever interpretations which, even if accurate, may nevertheless take the patient further than the transference confidence allows, so that when the patient leaves the analyst the almost miraculous revelation that the interpretation represents suddenly becomes a threat because it is in touch with a stage of emotional development that the patient has not yet reached, at least as a total personality." This is reminiscent of Winnicott's statements at the end of the papers on split-off elements.

In a letter of February 28 to Ernst Freud, he mentions, "I got pleurisy after a fall in which I hit my chest badly. O.K. now." This event takes on retrospective meaning in the light of the illness to come the following November.

Still willing to seek new responsibilities in spite of his often acknowledged heavy workload, he asked Joseph Sandler on February 27 about becoming chairman of the Publications Committee. Though Sandler had often been angry with him, he replied that Donald would be welcome.

In his March 12 talk, "Playing and Culture," he raises the question "What do you live for?" He mentions the "potential space between baby and mother figure which is the location of play." Play, he says, "is always exciting. It is exciting *not* because of the background of instinct, but because of the precariousness that is inherent in it, since it always deals with the knife-edge between the subjective and that which is objectively perceived."

Winnicott's awareness of politics among the French is evident in his response to requests for presentations by Maud Mannoni (an associate of

Lacan). He tells her that he has to watch which meetings he attends lest he seem pro-Lacan. He had been part of the committee of the International Association which, in 1953, started a chain of events that led to the expulsion of Lacan from the IPA.

"Thinking and Symbol-Formation," probably written in 1968, ends with a new way of looking at failure:

> This case gives rise to the general consideration that success in analysis must include the delusion of failure, the patient's reaction to the analysis as a failure. This paradox needs to be allowed. The analyst must be able to accept this role of failing analyst as he accepts all other roles that arise out of the patient's transference neuroses and psychoses. Many an analysis has failed at the end because the analyst could not allow a delusional failure, due to his personal need to prove the truth of psycho-analytic theory through the cure of the patient. Psycho-analysis does not cure, though it is true that a patient may make use of psycho-analysis, and may achieve with adjunctive process a degree of integration and socialisation and self-discovery which he would not or could not have achieved without it.

On September 9 he reported to Hanna Segal that "Clare and I had a rather complicated holiday and this is one of the reasons why I am not continuing to ask for an opportunity to read a paper this term." In November she would write from New York that Donald had been having trouble with his health since August. As we know now, he had contracted pleurisy in late January or February, so there were difficulties with his health at more than one juncture before his major illness in New York.

In the midst of this late period a letter to Adam Limentani (September 27, 1968) describes his situation as a teacher in the British Society:

> I know that my three talks every year to the students are likely to produce a certain amount of upheaval. I would like to make a comment. Firstly, as I believe you understand, I am not trying to cause an upheaval; but I do find the students remarkably frightened into conformity. This year this was less true than usual. There is hardly any reaction during the discussion when I talk to students that is comparable at all to the reactions that the analysts of these students get during the next week. I suppose all this is inevitable. I do worry,

however, on the score that students seem to be taught that psycho-analysis of what is called orthodox variety is something that can be counted on to be successful in the end if you plod on. On the whole the students do not seem to have been told that all analysts fail and that they all have difficult cases and that they all want new developments in theory which will widen the scope and make possible the treatment of less carefully chosen cases.

The other thing I want to say is this. It is not really a good idea for someone with my experience to talk three times to a group of students. What can I do? I can hide all my discontent and I can add a little bit more to the complacency which I find around me, or alternatively I can let the students know some of the difficulties which will arise in their practices quite soon inevitably. There is nothing in between these two extremes because in three times one cannot develop gradually the exposition of a point of view. I do realise very well indeed from having been Training Secretary that there is not enough student-time for you to be able to ask senior analysts to give long courses of either lectures or seminars. This is part of the facts of life. Nevertheless I do feel that Dr. Balint was right when he said that he would not speak to students three times. The only reason why I continue to consent when invited is that I am afraid that otherwise I will never see the students at all.

I could add an historical detail. For a long time, as you know, I was not asked to do any teaching of psycho-analysis because neither Miss Freud nor Mrs. Klein would use me or allow their students to come to me for regular teaching even in child analysis. I therefore missed at a critical time in my life the stimulus which would have made me work. When later on I became acceptable and was invited to do some teaching, I had already had some original ideas and naturally these came to mind when I was planning to talk to the students. This accounts to some extent for the way things are. I am not complaining, only I think that these matters of history are sometimes interesting.

There is a letter to his sisters on October 7, 1968, giving them formal permission to sell some land across from Rockville, so long as no tall building—which would obscure the view—was built. There are very few other letters to his sisters in the archive he kept.

This period, the initial phase of the last five years of his life, finds Winnicott driven to come to terms with the nature of reality and the "contrast between being and doing." "I want to get to a statement of a basic dilemma in relatedness," he writes. And "I want to go where I find myself both drawn and driven." He was determined not to fail out of faintheartedness, as it were. And what other people think is entirely irrelevant when a person such as Winnicott sees death rising up just ahead of him. We see him becoming ever more expressive, without fear of criticism. This effort would continue all the way to his final days.

— 22 —

"The Use of an Object"

In October 1968, Winnicott sent Anna Freud a copy of "The Use of an Object." On the thirtieth she responded: "Thank you very much for sending me the paper which you are going to read to the New York Society. I was very interested to read it and I shall be very interested to know whether you get a good reaction and discussion of it. As concerns your remark about me, I do not think that our New York colleagues will find this justified. They know your work very well and they will feel that they do not need me to draw their attention to you. I think that your 'transitional object' has conquered the analytic world."

The paper was given in New York on November 12. He had spoken by then to the William Alanson White group. The invitation was extended with the idea that by inviting Winnicott to speak, the New York Psychoanalytic Society was opening itself up to a Kleinian. This society was the bastion of ego psychology in the United States, the universally recognized center of a point of view about psychoanalysis as a rigorously pursued form of research and treatment, deriving from the work of Freud. While admired in many circles, it was also regarded as rigid, doctrinaire, and insufficiently open to new ideas.

In the paper, so new, probably bewildering, Winnicott comments, not uncharacteristically, "I am now ready to go straight to the statement of my thesis. It seems I am afraid to get there, as if I fear that once the thesis is stated the purpose of my communication is at an end, because it is so very simple." This sort of talk from Winnicott was familiar in London, but it had never been encountered in New York. This strangeness, together with his illness, may account for the idea that he had been savaged in the discussions.[1] Of course, others had always been concerned with his vulnerability, to some extent equally because of his cardiac condition and his uniqueness, but also because of the impression he gave of a mind pulsing with new insight that could easily be destroyed. He was subsequently seen as having ventured into hostile New York, fallen ill, and died. He had been seeking wider recognition and had offered up the farthest reach of his speculations, the thinking goes. The New Yorkers must have delivered the fatal blow. But an examination of the events fails to support this thesis. Donald had been ill since at least the previous August, or perhaps as far back as February. He was ill at the time of the presentation. Hong Kong flu was striking everyone. He had a long pulmonary and cardiac history. He developed pulmonary edema on top of a weak heart. Probably he had another heart attack while in Lenox Hill Hospital. But the events were, in any case, dramatic and easily remembered.

The theme of his paper is one he had been developing for years. In "Notes Made on a Train, Part 2," written in April 1965, he states, "It is only the perfect object that is worthy of destruction," so that the "rendering down of the object from perfection toward some kind of badness" (denigration, dirtying, tearing, etc.) "protects the object." He then considers "the practical issue [that arises] out of the distinction between 1. spoiling the good object to render it less good and so less under attack, and 2. the destruction that is at the root of object-relating and that becomes (in health) channelled off into destruction that takes place in the unconscious, in the individual's inner psychic reality, in the individual's dream life and play activities, and in creative expression."

In "The Use of the Word 'Use'" dated February 5, 1968, he writes: "Is it not so that before the change-over into usage the patient (subject) protects the analyst (object) from being used? In the extreme the subject is left with an ideal object, or an object idealised, perfect, and unattainable." The changeover in a patient from successful analysis of the problem, leading to a capacity to use and to be used, "can be a reward for the years of blind groping which analysis can seem to be." Here, as usual, he supports the struggle of any analyst to come to grips with a patient. An analyst thinking in these terms is watching for a phenomenon entirely differ-ent from the usual occurrence of transference and resistance. Such an an-alyst is ready to think in terms of whether the patient is protecting himself or herself, or is free in a way that corresponds to the unprotected freedom of the analyst, a state that allows for aggressive feelings and statements that differ in quality from all others.

The paper itself focuses on what was then a new concept in psycho-analysis, the "use" of an object, which Winnicott differentiates from ob-ject-relating. He writes that he would not have been able to come to the conclusions he presents in the paper if he had not learned not to inter-pret so much, but to wait "for the natural evolution of the transference arising out of the patient's growing trust in the psycho-analytic tech-nique and setting." He goes on: "This interpreting by the analyst, if it is to have effect, must be related to the patient's ability *to place the analyst outside the area of subjective phenomena.* What is then involved is the pa-tient's ability to use the analyst, which is the subject of this paper." Par-enthetically he adds: "(In this context I deliberately omit reference to the aspect of relating that is an exercise in cross-identifications. This must be omitted here because it belongs to a phase of development that is subse-quent to and not prior to the phase of development with which I am concerned in this paper, that is to say, the move away from self-contain-ment and relating to subjective objects into the realm of object-usage.)" This subject needs study in view of his later formulation of the original division of being and doing, female and male, at the very beginning of life. He continues:

> Psycho-analysis always likes to be able to eliminate all factors that are environmental, except in so far as the environment can be thought of in terms of projective mechanisms. But in examining usage there is no escape: the analyst must take into account the na-ture of the object, not as a projection, but as a thing in itself.
>
> For the time being may I leave it at that, that relating can be de-scribed in terms of the individual subject, and that usage cannot be described except in terms of acceptance of the object's independent existence, its property of having been there all the time.
>
> This thing that there is between relating and use is the subject's placing of the object outside the area of the subject's omnipotent con-trol; that is, the subject's perception of the object as an external phe-

nomenon, not as a projective entity, in fact recognition of it as an entity in its own right.

The subject is continuously destroying the object once it is perceived to be outside omnipotent control:

> The price has to be paid in acceptance of the ongoing destruction in unconscious fantasy relative to object-relating.
>
> Let me repeat. This is a position that can be arrived at by the individual in early stages of emotional growth only through the actual survival of cathected objects that are in time in process of becoming destroyed because real, becoming real because destroyed (being destructible and expendable).
>
> From now on, this stage having been reached, projective mechanisms assist in the act of *noticing what is there*, but they are not *the reason why the object is there*. In my opinion this is a departure from theory which tends to a conception of external reality only in terms of the individual's projective mechanisms.

This is a reference to Klein's views especially, and tells us that in this paper, with its emphasis on an external world that exists outside the distortions of the mind, he is extending his original emphasis on the characteristics of the mother herself as indispensable to an understanding of the infant. That "there is no such thing as a baby" leads all the way to the notion of object usage:

> The central postulate in this thesis is that, whereas the subject does not destroy the subjective object (projection material), destruction turns up and becomes a central feature so far as the object is objectively perceived, has autonomy, and belongs to "shared" reality. This is the difficult part of my thesis, at least for me.
>
> This destructive activity is the patient's attempt to place the analyst outside the area of omnipotent control, that is, out in the world. Without the experience of maximum destructiveness (object not protected) the subject never places the analyst outside and therefore can never do more than experience a kind of self-analysis, using the analyst as a projection of a part of the self. In terms of feeding, the patient, then, can feed only on the self and cannot use the breast for

getting fat. The patient may even enjoy the analytic experience but will not fundamentally change.

Here Winnicott examines the ultimate nature of reality. This conception of reality as the result of a process of purification through destructiveness that does not succeed may be set against another source of a sense of reality—one that comes from the isolated individual communing with internal objects, which reaches its zenith in the case of schizophrenics. This latter conception emphasizes what is totally inside, while the former emphasizes what is totally outside.

He continues: "In psycho-analytic practice the positive changes that come about in this area can be profound. They do not depend on interpretive work. They depend on the analyst's survival of the attacks, which involves and includes the idea of the absence of a quality change to retaliation. These attacks may be very difficult for the analyst to stand, especially when they are expressed in terms of delusion, or through manipulation which makes the analyst actually do things that are technically bad. (I refer to such a thing as being unreliable at moments when reliability is all that matters, as well as to survival in terms of keeping alive and of absence of the quality of retaliation.)" The suicide of his patient during his New York illness illustrates what he regarded as his unreliability.

He then writes:

> At whatever age a baby begins to allow the breast an external position (outside the area of projection), then this means that destruction of the breast has become a feature. I mean the actual impulse to destroy.
>
> Undoubtedly inborn aggression must be variable in a quantitative sense in the same way that everything else that is inherited is variable as between individuals. By contrast, the variations are great that arise out of the differences in the experiences of various newborn babies according to whether they are or are not carried through this very difficult phase. Such variations in the field of experience are indeed immense. Moreover, the babies that have been seen through this phase well are likely to be more aggressive *clinically* than the ones who have not been seen through this phase well, and for whom aggression is something that cannot be encompassed, or

something that can be retained only in the form of a liability to be an object of attack.

This involves a rewriting of the theory of the roots of aggression, since most of that which has already been written by analysts has been formulated without reference to that which is being discussed in this chapter. . . . The assumption is always there, in orthodox theory, that aggression is a reaction to the encounter with the reality principle, whereas here it is the destructive drive that creates the quality of externality. This is central to the structure of my argument.

This quality of "always being destroyed" makes the reality of the surviving object felt as such, strengthens the feeling tone, and contributes to object-constancy. The object can now be used.

This sequence can be observed: (1) Subject *relates* to object. (2) Object is in process of being found instead of placed by the subject in the world. (3) Subject *destroys* object. (4) Object survives destruction. (5) Subject can *use* object.

The copy of the paper in the files of the New York Psychoanalytic Society[2] includes a footnote not found in the published version: "I am influenced here by my second analyst Joan Riviere who pointed out to me that the mother's failures are of prime importance—at the same time she did not seem to me to be adequately stating the basic fact of the mother's initial success (100% initial adaptation associated with the concept of primary maternal preoccupation)." A summary by David Milrod includes discussions of the paper by Edith Jacobson, Bernard Fine, and Samuel Ritvo, and a description of Winnicott's reaction:

In a charming and whimsical fashion Dr. Winnicott responded, saying that his concept was torn to pieces and that he would be happy to give it up.[3] He had been trying to say something but had not succeeded, he felt. There are patients, not ordinary patients, for whom arriving at a point where they can use him as an analyst is more important than his interpretations to them. For these patients the trouble in the transference is that "they never take the risk of something and they protect the analyst from something." The crucial change occurs, when they are able to take the risk and the analyst survives. It produces in the process a new phenomenon in the patient's life. What is it the analyst is protected from, he wondered? It is not merely anger, but it is destructive. On this note he ended, leaving no doubt that his interest in his topic had been revitalized and that we would be hearing from him further about it.

The role of the father is central in the clinical illustration provided along with the paper. The patient is a fifty-year old man who, though accomplished, is not as successful as he knows he could be, and who also has a compulsive urge to blaspheme. He had a weak father and a strong mother. Winnicott writes:

> The control of aggression was not forthcoming from his father, and the mother had to supply it and he had to use his mother's fierceness but with the result that he was cut off from using his mother as a refuge. The symptom of that in the present day is sleeplessness.... He could ... never come to terms with the father that he had hated.... [H]e always protects the mother because he must preserve her in order to be able to have any rest or relaxation at all. He therefore has no knowledge that his mother might survive his impulsive act. A strong father enables the child to take the risk because father stands in the way or is there to mend matters or to prevent by his fierceness.
>
> The result in my patient ... was that he had to adopt self-control of impulse at a very early stage before he was ready to do so on the basis of an introjected father-figure. This meant that he became inhibited. The inhibition had to be of all spontaneity and impulse in case some particle of the impulse might be destructive. The massive inhibition necessarily involved his creative gesture, so that he was left inhibited, unaggressive, and uncreative.

The final part of Winnicott's description of the case involves the importance of the survival of the monarchy in this man's dream. This is a theme to which Winnicott would devote one of his last papers.

Rather than limiting his speculations to the role of the mother, who, by surviving, fosters the child's aggressiveness, he has here, via his case, added the role of the father as a necessary ally of the child of a fierce mother in the quest for license to express his destructiveness. Left out is any information as to whether the mother's fierceness is thought to represent her own fear that she would not survive without it. This would make sense of the patient's corresponding fear.

Winnicott was not feeling well during the presentation. As we have seen, he had not been in good health since August when there was evidence of lung congestion. And he had written to Ernst Freud in February that he had suffered an attack of pleurisy connected with a fall "in which I hit my chest badly." These were the preconditions for the Hong Kong flu that he contracted in New York. Clare caught it from him and was seriously compromised herself. This was a particularly severe form of influenza and Winnicott, seventy-two years old, a smoker for long periods prior to that time, and who had suffered several heart attacks, was quite vulnerable. As a result of the flu, his heart was overtaxed and began to fail. His lungs filled up with fluid, pneumonia supervened, and there was evidence of a mild coronary as well.

He was taken to the intensive care unit of Lenox Hill Hospital. His condition was precarious.[4] There he stayed until the end of the following month, when he returned to London.[5] Clare saved a number of letters from that period. Louise Carpenter, a friend who lived in New York, was a great help.[6] During this siege, Clare stayed with her.

The myth among those who recall this episode—that Winnicott fell ill as a result of extreme criticism of his paper in New York—is understandable from the sequence of events. Winnicott himself expressed an element of fear in his letter to Anna Freud before he left London. He seems to have been seeking some sort of protection from her. Her reply, including the comment that his transitional object idea "has conquered the psychoanalytic world," brings together the two extremes of his New York experience: his fear and his triumph. Perhaps triumph itself, though, is not without its psychosomatic dangers. I have heard it said that in New York circles, he was regarded as a Kleinian, which, if true, would show how out of touch with the conditions in the British Society the New Yorkers were. Even today, all the so-called object relations analysts tend to be lumped together in the minds of the ego psychologists who have been the traditional center of American psychoanalysis. This would account for Klein's being put together with Winnicott, among others.

An examination of the transcripts of the meeting shows the discussants to have had a great deal of difficulty understanding the paper (as has been the case for new readers ever since), but there is no savagery in their comments. Bernard Fine spoke for so long that there was hardly any time for Winnicott to deal with what he had said. An overflow crowd attended, with television monitors in an adjoining room for those who could not be seated. In sum, there is no evidence that Winnicott's illness was the result of intense attacks on his paper.

Clare wrote to Joyce Coles, Donald's secretary, on November 18:

> Things are the same—some improvement in his [Donald's] condition. I brought our friends the Zetzels[7] from Boston in on it last night, and they went into the whole thing thoroughly with the Doctors & assure me that nothing more can be done i.e. he is having the best possible treatment & care.... [C]ould you start thinking about our medical insurance policy & whether or not it applies to treatment received in other countries? ... I should think that the special unit D. is in is about the most expensive in the world—I haven't dared to ask yet.
>
> ... I can't think how Violet & Kathleen [his sisters] are taking this. We'd just had a letter to say how much better Kathleen is— which is a good thing. Elizabeth [Clare's sister] will take it hard I'm afraid—please keep her informed—it's better that you do this than I under the circs.[8] Thank you for keeping our world to-gether for us, while we wrestle with this strange one. With love,
>
> Clare
>
> Could you ring my brother James . . . and ask him to let my other brother know. Also ask him if he and/—my sister in law (called Robert) would keep in touch with my aunt at Thorpe Bay. She relies on a contact with me so much. I have written her and will be writing to V & K this evening.

She wrote again at this time (although the letter wasn't dated):

Dear Joyce,

It is difficult to know how to report on things this end. The heart condition has st*a*bilised[9] and D. is better in himself, although up & down. He has a lung infection which still needs careful watching & treatment. He said yesterday that he knows he still needs hospital care. So it looks as though he will be here for a bit. It all seems like a nightmare as you can imagine. I go to the hospital each day at 1:30 and stay till about 6 when Louise comes to bring me home. She is being wonderful & is even talking about travelling back to England with us when the time comes. I am still pretty groggy myself from this ghastly 'flu. It's a form of Asian flu called "Hong Kong" & seems to be travelling round the world according to the papers.

I think the answer to enquiries about D is that he is making satisfactory progress but is still needing hospital care.

Now I must get ready to go & see him.

Yours, with love, Clare

A letter to Karl Britton and his wife, postmarked November 25, 1968, from Lenox Hill Hospital's Coronary Care unit, reads:

Dear Karl and Sheila:

Thank you for the odd warm expression of the positive, which I value tremendously. I do hope your book will come soon, and I love to think of the uncle King's nice ackn[owledgement] of Sheila's courtesy.[10] You must know that the strain on Clare is tremendous. She's quite marvellous. The trouble is that I have had a serious heart complication, and Clare & both have to face up to the idea of my possible death. We can both do this. You know what I mean, and we are not morbid about it. And we can so much enjoy some more years together if I get well and get home. The chances are that I shall get home with Clare in December, and of course the consequences of all this for her life and important job (important for me) are very real & big. I think this is all I can manage just now.

Very much love,
Donald

P.S. For the record: we would have had a fine time here had it not been for this Asian flu with [sic] I got, and Clare got from me & then we both had which made us both descend to the bottom—so that even Clare couldn't look after me when my heart went wonky. This bit of bad luck made the difference. I think Clare is nearly over her plague now, but not really so. She has to take time for recovery from this too, as well as from the shock of losing my moral and physical support.

Donald

Clare wrote to Joyce Coles again on November 25:

> I have posted a letter to you today from Donald. From it you will see
> that we have our ups & downs, and yesterday and to-day are *downs*.
> Certainly the next 4 or 5 days will be critical, because it looks as
> though he had another slight coronary, probably about the time he
> came in here. Anyway they are working on that theory at the mo-
> ment and taking every precaution, & I can only wait and hope.
>
> The Zetzels from Boston (Cambridge) are coming here on Thurs-
> day & will see him & although they are both rather difficult people it
> will be a relief to see them.
>
> Sometime we may be very glad to have Arthur's [Coles's hus-
> band] help about arranging currency, but that can wait for the time
> being. We must be running up a vast bill here. With love, Clare. Glad
> you had [a few words] with Elizabeth—it was nice of you.
>
> . . . It looks as though our Private Patients Plan will not cover
> Donald's illness but when I get a chance I will ask the doctor.[11] I
> should love to be able to give you a reassuring message to pass
> round, but at present I just can't. Every day that he holds his own is a
> gain, but it is going to be a long job. After great difficulty he has
> given in to the doctors and is leaving things in their hands. This has
> not been easy, as you could imagine I am sure. [J. N., a patient] has
> come to NY to see him today, but we have put her off. . . . Sometime I
> shall try to write Elizabeth—& V & K.
>
> With love, Clare

J. N. (not the correct initials) was a suicidal patient who had regressed to dependency. Her reaction to Winnicott's illness could be
compared to that of the patient who killed herself at the Cassel Hospital
in 1950, both in his category of patients who are an actual physical
threat to the survival of the analyst. He suffered a coronary after the
first suicide, and in the case of J. N. there was a conscious effort on her
part to retaliate for his illness by destroying him. She wished him to die.
In 1981, Clare told me that the patient had written to say she was coming from England to see Donald, to which Clare had sent a wire telling
her not to. The patient then wrote to Donald, "I hope you die." Clare
opened that letter.

On November 26, Clare reported to Joyce Coles:

I have already posted one letter to you to-day—this morning—but since my visit to the hospital I feel I want to write again to say that there is some improvement to-day in D's condition. The doctors say so, and what is very much more important is that *he* says he feels more confidence in himself about his general state. He is, of course, having a great number of drugs, but they seem to be strengthening his heart, & the lung condition which has been a major complication, seems to be clearing up gradually. Actually he has had this thing ever since the summer holiday, on & off, & hasn't really been well since August. There is still a long way to go, of course (& there may be set backs) – but to-day there is an improvement, & I wanted you to know as soon as possible. . . .

Love from Clare

On the thirtieth she wrote:

Dear Joyce,

. . . Again it is difficult to say how things are going. Yesterday they said that his heart was less jumpy than it has been for the last few days. He is a better colour, and his lung condition seems to be clearing up—one side clear & the other improving—*but this may never clear completely*. In other words we are not through the wood yet, although there is improvement in some areas. He is so pleased that you are coping with the Rover and taking care of it for him. It must have been quite a job to get it moved without the key. I can't think how you did!

Yesterday we talked about coming home. There will have to be an ambulance to meet him at London Airport but I think that the Doctor here can arrange this—but we may need your help. Also I think he will have to sleep in the consulting room to begin with. But we have plenty of time to work all this out. I'll write again about it. The slightest thing going wrong, or unexpected, at the hospital affects his heart at the moment. So the journey home is a long way off. . . .

With love, Clare

And again on December 2:

Dear Joyce,

The doctors say Donald is *not* to be told about J. N. yet. This really seems the last straw in our turn of bad luck. On Sat 30th Nov: I got a cable from her saying "I shall be in N.Y. on my way to [Vancouver] on Tuesday Nov. 26th between 1:30 & 5 pm & it is essential for me to see Dr. W. even for 5 mins. Is this possible." I told D. & said this mustn't happen without permission from your doctors, to which he agreed, but said that he couldn't see her anyhow so no need to ask the Dr. & cabled back at once saying "Dr. W. is not well enough to fit in with this plan although he would like to be able to." Then he wrote to her, the letter which he sent you to forward. On Friday Nov. 29th a letter came here addressed to him which I opened & which contained a sealed letter which said on it "Not to be opened by Mrs. W, please. If Dr. W. is not well enough to receive mail, please leave until he is." From the postmark . . . I concluded that it was from her. And I still have it—unopened. But I may open it in case it is too upsetting. I can't decide yet. The whole thing is like a horrible threat hanging over us.

Meantime D. is progressing & was moved yesterday from the special unit to another part of the hospital & although he felt some apprehension at the move, he was also pleased. He is next to a big window & can watch all that goes on in the street & feels as if he is in the world again./ I'm sure you won't tell anyone about J. N. in case the news gets to D. What about Masud? Might he know, & write & sympathize?[12]

The visit of the Zetzels went off O.K. but I think they were shocked at how ill he was, & this of course was difficult for me. However there *is* improvement & we now talk of coming home. Louise has decided to come with us which is wonderful. Your letter in response to his letter sent in case he did not recover, was exactly right— bless you—he was pleased with it. He wrote Elizabeth yesterday but it is a relief to me if you keep in touch with her, although I don't think she is suicidal. I will also tell my brother to keep in touch with her. It is a lovely sunny day here—& warm too & I am going out to tea to-day with someone who lives near the hospital—he is well enough to let me!

With love, Clare

Wrote this am—now at hospital where news is that if all goes well D. may be able to come and stay with Louise at end of next week before coming home. *So* that's good but the doctor reserves the right to change his mind–

Given Clare's history of drawing a line that kept Masud Khan at a certain distance from Donald, her suggestion about getting in touch with him, though tentative, is surprising. It demonstrates how extreme was the situation that Donald was facing, and it indicates that of all his colleagues and friends, Khan was seen as especially supportive. I have no knowledge of a connection between Khan and J. N. Khan's entry in his diary (note 4) shows his sincere and deep concern with Winnicott's fate.[13]

On December 7, Clare wrote to Coles:

Yesterday D. had two walks along the corridor at the hospital—the second one with me in the evening & he managed it without any effect on his heart. It seemed like a miracle to me, & to him too, I think. He is still reading Shakespeare, & has not asked about [J.].

Now the other points in your letter.

(1) He will not be well enough to lecture to the Mental Health Students this term and next. An alternative lecturer should be found, but he hopes to be well enough to lecture to the Applied Social Studies students, if LSE want him to do so. (Summer term I think?)

(2) New consultations should find someone else—you are quite right, & he agrees. He hopes to keep "old" consultations going when he gets back.

(3) re letting Dr. [Peter] Tizard know about his illness—he doesn't want this yet. I know he's [i.e., Donald is] terrified of a whole lot of new consultations starting up, so let's leave this for the moment.

Thank you for protecting him from more correspondence by dealing with it yourself. I'm sure this is important, because he isn't really interested yet in hearing more. He's very much involved in coping with the present.

All for now, & love from Clare.

Two days later she wrote:

Dear Joyce,

Your "extra" letter about [J.N.], written on Dec. 6th came yesterday (10th) so that wasn't too bad. Thank you for taking so much trouble to prevent the news getting to him. You have succeeded. The doctor thinks I could tell him now, but that there's no need to hurry it. So I may do it any time but shall *not* mention the letter unless he asks. I did open it, and it was a horrible shock somehow, being D's *wife*—but if I can *make* myself think of it from the point of view of a psycho-analyst—it makes sense I suppose. [It contains one long curse of him and hopes he will die too,[14] etc.] So I may keep the letter from him as long as I can, and only you and I know of its existence & Elizabeth Zetzel with whom I discussed it all. (By the way I think you are right in what you say, that he may really feel relieved from having to go on helping her.)

The patient, in a state of regression to dependence, enraged that Winnicott was unavailable, wrote that she hoped he would die and then inflicted what damage she could upon him for having disappointed her by killing herself. Her letter shows a complete absence of feeling for the involuntary nature of his plight, although we might ask whether he had disappointed her in the past, perhaps because of a previous absence from London, with this climactic illness the last of a list of failures. Her wish for private access to him, that is, to bypass his wife with her note, hints at a sense that he has been taken from her, perhaps not just by illness but by another person, Clare. His caretaking of her has been replaced by Clare's caretaking of him. These dynamics, as she saw them, led to her death, leaving us to ponder the emotional weather that exacted such an outcome.

The letter from Clare continues:

Well now for something more cheerful. We hope to come home *next week* depending on when we can get a plane i.e Dec. 18th 19th or 20th. But we shall be ringing you about this so by the time you get this it will be stale news. D. is coming here to Louise on Sunday the 15th & he is simply longing to get home.

Do you think you could possibly ring Joan———for me (my hairdresser) . . . & ask if she could possibly get me in on the 23rd or 24th—am home either day—or, if not, as soon after Xmas as she can. That would save the having to write a letter to her, & I have much to do this end to clear up things.

Thank you again for your helpful letter—I am *longing* to forget about [J.N.] but will only be able to do so when I've told D. With love, Clare.

On Wednesday, Donald wrote to Coles:

That was just what I wanted you to do about the Christmas Card. The drawing could be called premonitory. I am in a phase of sleeping a great deal, because in the ordinary part of the hospital with only one personal doctor, I am no longer in fear of decisions made in conference by a dozen doctors in the next room. So I breathe a dime a time, and feel fortunate. This is my news. Perhaps you could tell Enid Balint that I was glad to get her letter, so I needn't write immediately. I have urgent projects for when I get back so I believe this time WE SHALL OVERCOME, i.e. get the writings done without everything getting lost in clinical involvement. I am making a nest for the pelicans should they decide to migrate, but they will find it is raining here just now. I have so many roses to watch die that I know I ought to be proud & happy. Have been visited by the Hartmanns, Phyllis Greenacre, Dr. & Mrs. Malev, The Zetzels, Dr. & Mrs. Bernard Fine. I am due to walk out of the room & down the passage probably tomorrow. Sorry this is all about DWW.

Then again, in undated letters from the hospital:

Still playing the waiting game though I can really claim to feel new confidence in self over the last 3 days. Perhaps I'll be staying with Louise, as Clare is, within a week. But who can predict? (which is the disturbing thing). So really all's well for the moment. The nights have a length to them which I had forgotten. You probably know what I mean.

When I leave this frantically expensive establishment (?£80 a day) Dr. Milton Malev will settle my account & I shall gradually pay him off as and when. Its funny but I had no choice—found myself in there with no discussion of cost, & its difficult to get any indication of ultimate cost.

It is important that you find a way of getting your salary from my bank and of your getting reimbursed for so much you have had to spend. It must make Philip [his accountant?] laugh, thinking of his advice to us to not earn so much.

I now think of myself as likely to come home like Cathy,[15] and restart in chosen ways the life I love at 87. . . .

> Yours gratefully,
> DWWWWWWWWW

. . . Send me [G. G.'s] address [16]

And again on Sunday:

We sent all the signed cheques back, but we are not sure about the stamps we put on—so they *may* travel surface mail. Let me know who sent the enormous cheque—I couldn't read it.

Improvement seems to continue, but the slightest setback upsets me inordinately. I'm even getting fed up with Shakespeare, but not to worry. It's very good to see daylight in the shape of a possible date for leaving here.

You may get a note from Pauline Taylor about the extra money I have to send for Alice's care.[17] I've written Pauline.

. . . I guess you got some paper from me about the USE OF etc. Writing that calmed me down & gave me a night's sleep. I've had some marvellous nightmares and other quality dreams to keep me going.

> Yours
> Donald W. and to Arthur

Any reply from Hendy? . . . or Art Israel?

On Saturday, an improving Donald wrote to Karl Britton:

I have just finished the John Dover Wilson, which was exactly right for my mood. Its amazingly good—tho' no one is perfect for another, & I had a job when I read: . . . the *comparative emptiness of Coriolanus*, point to weariness and reaction, a refusal of the over-driven spirit to respond to the spur. You see I had just finished Coriolanus & was still under its spell, and I do feel this play is completely satisfactory and a sort of preview of Winston can be got out of it.[18] But I do so much like the Dover Wilson view of Shakespeare, so thank you indeed, (and the Penguin poems that I have not read yet). Also your letter gave me happiness.

My doctor has been in and for the first time is thinking in terms of . . . Clare is, & thence to J. F. Kennedy airport & we hope across,

and so to Heathrow and Chester Square with its newly painted yellow door.[19] I *might* leave here (hospital) in a week's time. That gives
us something to work on, and I am happy.

Clare seems to me to be well now in herself. She is as always absolutely marvellous from my angle. My love to Sheila & to yourself.
Wasn't the 10/- stamp exciting, one of the 3 you put on the parcel,
which I did so like getting.

Donald

On Saturday, he wrote:

Dear Karl & Sheila

Thank you for the lovely stamps, much in demand here. Won't it
be awful when the world just francs letters & stamps are out. The
books were RIGHT. Penguin Book of English Verse has given me
much pleasure, though I haven't read it through. I got through the essential Shakespeare in (one?); quite fascinated. Yesterday I ate up
Forster's Hill of Dive [sic][20], and the evening before when I was anxious about something I read right through Georgian Poetry (R——)
So you see your efforts were not wasted.

Its wonderful to be actually leaving tomorrow, & going to London Fri. 20th Dec. 1968.

And now—much love and gratefulness
Donald

To Joyce Coles he sent this perhaps incomplete letter:

Every little sneeze makes me think of Louise.* Hope to reach her flat
tomorrow.

Sunday

Louise has fixed up everything with the help of BOAC . . . Mid-
land Bank (London & NY) the British Consul and The Queen. Send
£10 my Xmas present to Norma [Williams, Donald's deeply respected
assistant at Paddington Green]. We shall have phoned you ere you get
this. You read such a lot. Louise is coming with us and so I don't know
how we will manage re car, & 3 luggages—must leave you & Clare to
sort this out. Louise could go by coach perhaps. She's amenable. . . . I
know all about [J.N.] now. Actually I should have been surprised if

not. When I got ill I knew I was killing her. Had dealt with it but Clare
& you were right to keep it from me while I was hypersensitive. Now
I can include relief with my deep grief. Clare went thro' a great deal in
not telling me about [J.N.] till the right moment. What upsets me is
rather of a different order, something that plucks at my paranoia potential. Like USA Warships in the Black Sea.

    *I mean, if I sneeze I think—O dear! more viruses, and perhaps
not get out to Louise's.

Winnicott's concern with further assaults on his physical being is evident
here, though expressed lightly, and this fear—likened to "USA Warships
in the Black Sea"—transcends his relief and grief about the fate of J. B. In
the hierarchy of preoccupations, his survival heads the list.

    Clare wrote a brief note to Coles on Saturday, December 14: "The
'use' paper has just arrived & D is very pleased to have it. All going well
here—I've just brought his clothes to the hospital in preparation for leaving tomorrow!" and then a longer letter the next day:

Dear Joyce,

    We got here to [Louise's] flat at about 12 PM to-day, and about
an hour ago I put through a call to you to say that we are coming
home on Friday, Dec. 20th. The seats are booked, and with the help of
the British Consul here & BOAC, arrangements are made for him to
be met at London Airport by a nurse or medical attendant of some
sort, with a wheel chair, & we hope that you can meet us & bring us
home. Louise will cope with the baggage & the customs & come on
in the bus to Cromwell Rd. & will get a taxi to Chester Sq. In other
words, 2 operations are planned—one for us, and one for Louise.

    We are coming on Flight 530—leaving Kennedy Airport at 10 am
and arriving London Airport at 10:30 pm. So they say, but I guess you
will check it at your end, and I only hope that we shan't keep you
waiting too long, because it will be so late for you, but not for us.

    Donald has to be kept very quiet & steady, & is really unable to
cope with any fuss, so I hope you will be able to impress this on people that end. He is coming home for a month's convalescence at least.
At the moment he is covered in a horrible rash which is hot & irritating (probably due to all the drugs) & I hope this will have cleared up
by Friday.

I simply can't believe that this time next week we shall be in Chester Square. It seems too good to be true.

So—will be *seeing you*! We shall not write again, because you won't get it anyhow before we're back. D. coped with the suicide [of his patient] very well. I've told him there is a letter, but he has not yet asked to see it.

So many people have said in their letters how wonderfully well you have held things together, & how much they have appreciated the way you have kept them informed about D's progress. My brother said how much your contacts had meant to them all. And *we* felt tremendously reassured that you were there, & coping. Love from us both,

Clare

Masud Khan recorded Winnicott's return home in his Workbook:

Saturday, December 21st, 1968. D. W. W. has returned home safely from New York—triumph of will to live.

Sunday, January 5th, 1968. 4:00 p.m.

Visited Winnicott at his home—first time since his return from New York after his heart attack. . . . He is now so faded physically—only the omnipotence of his will persists and his mind is clear and lucid and restless to have all its say said.

How wise D. W. W. is, and yet how *blind* about himself. He cannot accept that anyone else can *treat* a case. This is a malignant bias of most analysts. And incapacity to believe he can be *damaged* by others. Hence his incapacity for gratitude! And yet his is the truest and most profound devotion to his patients and his self-questioning vis a vis them most incisive and austere. But as a *man* he has not questioned his malice, envy and hate!

Khan's devotion is evident, as is his literary self-discipline in the form of compact, unadorned sentences. Yet we know that Winnicott had spent much of his life finding, expressing, and making use of his awareness of his own hate. Perhaps Khan was giving voice to his own bitter frustration at being held at a distance by Winnicott, not given what he considers his due. What with Winnicott's efforts to gain access to his hate, and to express it, he may not have felt guilty about doing so.

In the face of such dislocation in his pattern of living, Winnicott's conscience bothers him enough for him to write, on December 30, 1968, to a recent guest in London, the psychoanalyst Maud Mannoni: "When I look back on the evening that you spent in London I am sorry that I spoiled the happy relationship which I felt we had with each other at dinner by my irritation that I manifested during the scientific meeting. Certainly you did speak at too great a length for our type of meeting, so that discussion was not possible, but also I consider I was rude. I would like to feel that I was already not well and therefore excessively tired. Certainly when I got to New York I knew that I was ill and after three or four of the meetings I had arranged there I actually had to go to hospital for a month with acute pulmonary oedema and heart failure."

Winnicott's active correspondence continued without a break. On January 3 he wrote to his New York physician, Dr. M. Rosenbluth, summarizing his condition:

It was a great relief to be convalescent in England and this alone has been of tremendous therapeutic importance. I have come to know how to use the house and the stairs, doing as much as seems good and yet being ready to take a sleep whenever necessary. There is no doubt that in a general way I am making very steady physical progress. Moreover I have managed to get myself completely free of drugs so as to know what I am like basically, as it seemed necessary to be able to get to this state in order to know how to make a plan for the future. I have not yet been out, but the weather has been cold, and I shall not take any risks about cold air.

The complication, I would say, is that although I have a basically sound heart rhythm, somewhere about 60, I do have extra-systoles and dropped beats. This is extremely variable and I think I can say that they are least in evidence when I am interested in something or active. They are most in evidence somewhere in the night when I am fully relaxed or alternatively when I have a dream in which there is a little more than the ordinary kind of excitement or anxiety, usually the former. In the night I often have to get up and deal with one at least of these times when the heart beat is chaotic but it is easily dealt with by free breathing, and in the course of a few minutes I am able to go to sleep again.

As I explained to you, I find 1/2 gr. of phenobarbitone tablets suits me extremely well and one of these is usually enough to quieten everything down.

It would be hypochondriacal of me to go into all these details were it not for the fact that you have interested yourself in my physical condition and that you have been my doctor in U.S.A. I am not asking you to continue your responsibility for me or to prescribe medicines but I am simply writing to keep you informed. My General Practitioner, Dr. David Tizard, is gently standing by, and I have a heart specialist in mind whom I may consult, but you would be surprised if you knew to what extent I have become allergic to heart specialists. I realise how subjective all this must be, but I would do almost anything, including taking a great risk of dying at home, rather than go once more into a cardiac care unit. These feelings are not affected at all by the knowledge that I have that the Lenox Hill Cardiac Care Unit saved my life.

This is the present state of affairs and I hope you will not have found the account boring. I try to avoid salt as you have told me this might be important, and there is no sign of oedema anywhere. The main thing seems to be that in regard to the lung condition I am sure from various signs and symptoms that I am steadily recovering.

I am not asking you to reply to this descriptive letter. Please remember myself and my wife to your secretary who, in spite of having flu herself, did give us very great help in a time of trouble.

Masud Khan's correspondence with the French analyst Victor Smirnoff preserves his impressions of Winnicott at this point. On January 5 he writes: "He looked much better than I had expected and was battlesomely vigorous from his very meager physical resources now, and (he was) lithe, restless & searching in the creative ferment of his mind, trying to get shape & definition to his latest thoughts about his work. How enviable to keep alive & creative right to the last dregs of physicality in one." Khan's view of Winnicott took quite a different form at two o'clock the following morning:

Somewhere the meeting with Winnicott has left me very anguished. . . . How militantly lonely & refusing some humans are, and can never be truly related to Winnicott is one such. Perhaps

Lacan is another. Nothing is valid for them which is outside the creative omnipotence and munificence of their mind and being. And what terrible pain of isolation it must create in them. And yet they also so insistently evoke deep emotions and loyalties in others which they then merely nibble at and waste. Winnicott was so physically frail & spent today & yet he was as willful and unyielding as ever. It is so excruciatingly frustrating and depriving—one could almost say castrating—to have to tolerate their refusal and adapt to it.

Naturally, one who reads these words has to ask what he wanted from Winnicott and why the pain was so great, and, more pointedly, whether what he wanted was possible or a transference wish, forever frustrated, with Winnicott as the ongoing refuser and frustrator.

Being in a vastly different position, I found that the letter I received from Winnicott a few days later evoked no such emotions. On January 10 he wrote a four-page response[21] to my paper, "Accidental Technical Lapses as Therapy." This paper, written during the first flush of my renewed analytic training after discharge from the army, must have been largely inspired and perhaps unconsciously copied from material in Winnicott's published work, even if it had roots as well in the work of Harold Searles and Sidney Tarachow. I can see that possibility now but doubt I could have allowed myself to recognize it at the time. I remember that there had always been some sort of pressure within me to give therapeutic credit to what bursts out of the analyst, whether it be the overriding characteristics of his natural being, or some thought or wish or conflict that has to do in some way with the patient, even if its power originates in the personal life of the analyst. This, of course, is countertransference, but perhaps there is a larger category to describe such moments.

Winnicott wrote: "In the extreme of a borderline case everything boils down in the end to what I have tried to describe as the survival of the analyst, only it may take years for the patient to take the risk of a relationship in which the analyst is absolutely unprotected. I have just read a paper on this to the New York Psychoanalytic Society but my ideas are not well formulated in this paper. The idea is there, however, that when the patient gets towards this very serious state of affairs [when the analyst is not protected from the patient's destructive fantasies] then almost anything can happen and it is irrelevant. The only thing is arriving at the point at which the risk is taken and the analyst survives or does not survive." Later on he speaks of the tremendous strain on the analyst of having to adapt for long periods to patients who regress to dependence. His own tendency is to misbehave, to act as if the patient were suddenly well, by talking about all sorts of things.

This letter from Winnicott represented a new element in my life, a sort of welcome into what I considered to be the farther reaches of psychoanalytic study. I was thirty-four years old and knew next to nothing, and yet he took me seriously. And I did not know until a good deal later how much he meant when, continuing the theme of the consequences of "misbehavior," he wrote: "The awful thing when a patient commits suicide at this stage is that this leaves the analyst for ever holding the strain and never able to misbehave just a little. I think that this is an inherent part of the revenge that suicide of this kind contains, and I must say that the analyst always deserves what he gets here. I say this having just lost a patient through being ill. I could not help being ill, but if I am going to be ill then I must not take on this kind of patient." I had no idea how ill he had been—and still was.

Winnicott's ability, despite personal suffering, to maintain a kind of complete attention that was in itself therapeutic is shown in a review of *Psycho-Analytic Explorations* by Alan Stone,[22] which included the following reminiscence:

> I met D. W. Winnicott one time, and it was an experience I shall never forget; it lends to everything he wrote a special context for me. He had just given a paper at a conference, and afterward I went up to him to describe an idea of my own related to what he had been saying. He suggested we walk back together to his hotel so that we could continue our discussion. During all of our ensuing conversation he held me in the center of his attention (or so it seemed to me) in a way that I have never experienced with any other human being. It was not that he made constant eye contact, or that he interjected the traditional psychoanalytic hum of empathy, or that he was selflessly accepting. As we walked he spoke of his own ideas, he reacted and responded with dignity and originality, yet all the time I felt recognized and encouraged—I was in a "facilitating environment." Quite unexpectedly he said to me, "Dr. Stone, we will have to stop for a moment. I have terrible angina." His face was white with the pain, but then with amazing equanimity he continued as before.

On January 14, Winnicott wrote to a man in a small Oklahoma town, using the word "taproot" to stand for the deep source of aggressive energy that the man must at the moment do without. This troubled person had sought out Winnicott for help, through the mails, and Winnicott wrote in reply:

> May I refer to the places [in my writings] where I speak of the *unthinkable anxiety* that some people have to carry round with them all their lives. My use of the word "unthinkable" might provide a link with your disappearing mind which you closely associate with the core of yourself. (. . . You are talking about a loss of your capacity to be a whole integrated human being, containing and able to stand (tolerate) whatever anxieties (and good things) may be in your total make-up.). It could be if you are "all there" then sooner or later this anxiety beyond what you can tolerate comes over you, and you cannot hold it long enough to look at it and see what is the content of the anxiety. If you could do this you would find it contains—at root—the deepest source of your own psychic energy, so when you have to blot it out (or it happens to you that it gets blotted out) you lose the taproot, so to speak.

It is a three-page letter. Even in the shadow of death, he was moved to give all he had. This letter, Alan Stone's reminiscence, and perhaps the letter to me are examples of the lengths to which he went, throughout his career, to provide comfort for patients and for other analysts. His article on the necessity that certain patients retain the delusion that their successful analysis had actually failed is a kind of ultimate example. In such instances, the analyst must accept this delusion or risk damaging the analytic work. But there is a great deal more. He knew that analysts who try to treat those with early damage require more resources with which to comfort their patients and themselves than those who limit their work to the more classically neurotic cases. He knew it because of his own pioneering suffering, and he delivered this aid and comfort himself. It is visible, it is palpable, on the page. We are allowed to regress slightly toward dependency as readers, as we sense how capable are the hands into which we have put ourselves, and this sort of learning experience is a model of what we are then better prepared to offer our patients. Winnicott is at these times not so much offering up his findings to an objective audience as reaching across the gap through a relationship to his readers.

On January 20, Michael Balint wrote him, "I was very sorry to hear from Enid that you had a bad night on Saturday and that your state does not improve as fast as all of us in the Society would wish." On the same day, Winnicott wrote to Anna Freud. "If you were to ask me what about my paper, The Use of an Object, I would say that the answer is complex. I read the paper and got considerable personal benefit from the reaction of the three discussants, so that I am now in process of rewriting it in a quite different language. The unfortunate thing was that the three said discussants occupied the whole of the time so that there could be no response from the very large audience which collected for some reason unspecified. There was an internal TV arranged so that the overflow in the library could watch me, which I thought rather amusing. Actually I was already ill but I think this was not noticed."

23

Endings and Beginnings

In the astounding interval of less than four weeks after his return to London, Winnicott wrote "The Use of an Object in the Context of *Moses and Monotheism*." He praises the book but says that Freud overreached himself "in the formulation of monotheism as important because of the universal truth of the loved father and the repression of this in its original and stark (id) form. . . . It is not that Freud is wrong about the father and the libidinal tie that becomes repressed." But a certain proportion of people never do reach the Oedipus complex, Winnicott says, so repression of the libidinized father figure has little relevance. Monotheistic tenets are not limited to those who have reached the Oedipal phase. "A great deal of religion is tied up with near-psychosis and with the personal problems that stem from the big area of baby life that is important before the attainment of a three-body relationship as between whole persons."

As Winnicott notes, "Freud did not know in the framework of his own well-disciplined mental functioning that we now have to deal with such a problem as this: what is there in the actual presence of the father, and the part he plays in the experience of the relationship between him and the child and between the child and him? For there is a difference according to whether the father is there or not, is able to make a relationship or not, is sane or insane, is free or rigid in personality." Here he emphasizes the actual father along with the father as an object of fantasy, in parallel with his approach to the mother: "If the father dies this is significant, and when exactly in the baby's life he dies, and there is a great deal to be taken into account that has to do with the imago of the father in the mother's inner reality and its fate there."

He continues:

> As the baby moves from ego strengthening due to its being reinforced by mother's ego to having an identity of his or her own—that is, the inherited tendency to integration carries the baby forward in the good-enough or average expectable environment—the third person plays or seems to me to play a big part. The father may or may not have been a mother-substitute, but at some time he begins to be felt to be there in a different role, and it is here I suggest that the baby is likely to make use of the father as a blue-print for his or her own integration when just becoming at times a unit.
>
> In this way one can see that the father can be the first glimpse for the child of integration and of personal wholeness. It is easy to go from this interplay between introjection and projection to the important concept of the world's history of a one god, a monotheism, not a one god for me and another one god for you.
>
> It is easy to make the assumption that because the mother starts as a part object or as a conglomeration of part objects the father comes into ego-grasp in the same way. But I suggest that in a favourable case the father starts off whole (i. e. as father, not as mother surrogate) and later becomes endowed with a significant part object, that he starts off as an integrate in the ego's organisation and in the mental conceptualisation of the baby.
>
> Could it not be said that "poetically" Freud was ready for this idea, not that monotheism had its root in the repressed idea of the father but that the two ideas of having a father and of monotheism represented the world's first attempts to recognise the individuality of man, of woman, of every individual?

Winnicott adds, "I feel that Freud would welcome new work." He clearly needs to be welcomed by the father figure he is now in the process of correcting, and not that this is the first time, though with respect to the father this *is* the first time. This may give a hint as to why the father has been left out until now; that is, as long as it was the mother to whom he attended, he was supplementing the father figure's work ("I must be about my father's business," he writes in "The Tree"), adding to it, while revision in the area of the father is a more direct challenge, and one that he was unconsciously reluctant to make. Anna Freud's remark about his having "conquered the psychoanalytic world" was the closest he could possibly come to a confirmation of his successor status to Freud himself.

In his revision of basic instinct theory, Winnicott explains that "the crux of my argument is that the first drive is itself *one* thing, something that I call "destruction," but it could have been called a combined love-strife drive. The unity is primary. This is what turns up in the baby by the natural maturational process:

> The fate of this unity of drive cannot be stated without reference to the environment. The drive is potentially "destructive" but whether it *is* destructive or not depends on what the object is like; does the object *survive*, that is, does it retain its character, or does it *react*? If the former, then there is no destruction, or not much, and there is a next moment when the baby can become and does gradually become aware of a cathected object plus the *fantasy* of having destroyed, hurt, damaged, or provoked the object. The baby in this extreme of environmental provision goes on in a pattern of developing personal aggressiveness that provides the backcloth of a continuous (unconscious) fantasy of destruction. Here we may use Klein's reparation concept, which links constructive play and work with this (unconscious) *fantasy backcloth* of destruction or provocation (perhaps the right word has not been found). But destruction of an object that survives, has not reacted or disappeared, leads on to use.

He continues: "Could it be said that the mother can be dismantled, whereas the father must be murdered, with dismantling a reversal of the building-up from part-objects as opposed to reversing an original wholeness into its opposite?"

Under the pressure of illness, and in the deep meditations that he had been pursuing for many years, now on the nature of reality and the use of an object, he comes finally to the father, as if to achieve a kind of completeness of thinking. This meditation occurred during his recuperation, with the memory of his near-demise fresh and the possibility of sudden death ever-present.

In "The Use of an Object," the continuous backdrop of destructiveness in relationships (one question being how to determine which relationships elicit this phenomenon and which do not) integrates Melanie Klein's emphasis on early, primitive aggressive fantasy into "ordinary" life. Does "love" accompany the awareness of the survival of the object? ("I haven't killed you. I love you for that"?) Does this survival encourage greater outpourings of unconscious destructiveness in an atmosphere of safety? This would make for a sense of the fullest reception for instinctual life, which might thereby encourage a sense of wholeness within the context of such a relationship. The overall attitude toward the other would be that "he or she receives everything I am or could become." Psychoanalysis provides this, at its best, if the patient is capable of the destructive element. Winnicott taught this to us.

In the "Use" papers, *Moses and Monotheism*[1] makes an appearance in connection with the idea of the father as the first person who is whole from the start. This unprecedented appearance of the father occurred, for Winnicott, in the shadow of death. It is easy to wonder whether, under threat of loss of integration, he turned to an example of one who was a model of integration. Ilse Grubrich-Simitis's discussion of Freud's late work on Moses[2] adds tremendous interest here. Freud is identified with Moses himself and values independence above all. He has not been able to deal with the early trauma of his little brother's death and his mother's reaction to it. Winnicott's interest and Freud's bring them together. Grubrich-Simitis also mentions Jung, the Joshua to Freud's Moses, thus providing a speculative link to Winnicott's interest in Jung, his twin, as well. In a way, Winnicott's "Use" papers are a climax to his work, the interest in the father bursting from him under extreme duress, a final acknowledgment which he has succeeded in avoiding all his life. Both men shared an interest in splitting (Freud's papers on constructions in analysis and fetishism; Winnicott's male and female elements) at the end of their lives, a manifestation of their own struggle to remain whole against forces that were tearing them apart. And Moses was the bulwark to which each turned for support.

Moses and Monotheism, Grubrich-Simitis writes, "could be productively read as a daydream under extreme duress." The threats to existence are the advance of the Nazis, cancer of the jaw, and old age. In

Winnicott's formulation, concentration on the father, the first whole object, fosters the reassuring notion that wholeness may survive. For Freud it was also a final attempt to link trauma and drive models of neurosis, to unify these two dissociated viewpoints. "Towards the end of his life, now that he himself was under the distressing pressure of a traumatic political reality, he perhaps felt a need, in his study of Moses, to restore the *external* aetiological factors to the foreground of his theorization, in order to fill what might upon superficial examination appear to be a gap in his teaching," writes Grubrich-Simitis. She cites "'early injuries to the ego (narcisisstic mortifications),'" and notes that "the central pathogenic factor" might even be "only an early emotional relationship" whose adverse eventual consequences include "permanent alteration of the ego." She continues: "These formulations are at any rate perfectly consistent with more modern psychoanalytic theories of the traumatic genesis of the narcissistic and perverse, borderline and psychotic disturbances." Here again is a link to Winnicott.

Romain Rolland suggested that the oceanic feeling was the source of religious faith, but Freud did not accept this. Instead, she writes, "he ascribed [religious faith] to the universal helplessness of human beings during childhood and to a correspondingly pressing, but structured, longing for the father." Rolland was probably referring to his own turn to Moses, and, as we see, Winnicott does the same. Is the father's strength based solely on his original wholeness, or are other elements part of it, such as actual physical attributes of strength, and the psychology of the male facing outward toward the world? The father, as a whole person, counteracts the threat of disintegration. Here we think of Anna Freud's comment to Winnicott that she never saw her father in a depression.

Grubrich-Simitis continues: "Monotheism is harsh on the human craving for visual expression.[3] By its ban on images—that is, the exclusion of seeing—Mosaic monotheism enforced a higher development of intellectuality and directed the gaze inwards; and one of the consequences of this withdrawal of attention from the periphery of perception—in effect a shift from sensory stimuli to those of the drives—was the discovery of the mind, which opened up the invisible field that is the province of psychoanalysis." Winnicott was a visual person, one who drew squiggles, and he was concerned with the role of the external, the mother first of all, and all he saw as a pediatrician. He insisted on a current of thinking that ran in a direction different from the purely intrapsy-

chic interpretation of the origin of neurosis, though, in the end, capable
of blending with it.

In a letter Freud wrote to Jung in 1909[4] he says, "If I am Moses, then
you are Joshua and will take possession of the promised land of psychiatry, which I shall only be able to glimpse from afar." Winnicott identified
with Jung, also had a depressed mother, and was allowed to take possession of the Promised Land. A small footnote to this is his paper on classification, in which psychoanalysis makes its contribution to psychiatry.

Freud is quoted as having written: "Some rationalistic, or perhaps
analytic, turn of mind in me rebels against being moved by a thing without knowing why I am thus affected and what it is that affects me." This
stands in contrast to Winnicott, who writes about discussing horses with
a patient without knowing where it will lead. Or in his idea that it is important to enjoy first and analyze later.[5] Or from a Marion Milner's book
on painting, "Creativity can be destroyed by too great insistence that in
acting one must know beforehand what one is doing."[6]

Summarizing the place of Moses in Freud's later thought, Grubrich-
Simitis writes: "Mental wounds sustained through his [Freud's] own experiences of loss while at the developmental stage of profound infantile
dependence had made their presence felt in him in adulthood at times of
acute anguish—already during the crisis with Jung, but particularly
under the Nazi threat—and had on both occasions compelled his obsessive preoccupation with the figure of Moses, the representation of his
ego-ideal that was precisely then so highly cathected because it was supposed to guarantee immunity from dependence."

Thus, Winnicott's late life condition, intensified by his New York illness, extended his preoccupation with object use to Freud's work on
Moses, to which he added his own idea of the father as the first whole object. His views illuminate the role of Moses in Freud's psyche, protector
against dependence, rooted in early trauma, and a constant threat. Undoubtedly Winnicott's commentary on the father, unprecedented in his
work, manifests his own fear of death.

On March 19, 1969, the British Society held a symposium on the subject
of envy and jealousy, as originally suggested by Winnicott. His contribution was read by Enid Balint. Here again, as he had made ever clearer
over time, he posed the criticism that Klein's theory left out the individual's environment. Envy, he maintained, could not be understood with-

out taking the mother into account. In related notes, more fully developed, he deals with the effect of the tantalizing mother, the originator of conditions that give rise to envy, that is, the good breast that is not available.

In "Development of the Theme of the Mother's Unconscious as Discovered in Psycho-Analytic Practice" (June 1969), he refers to his 1948 paper "Reparation in Respect of Mother's Organised Defence against Depression." The children he discussed in the earlier paper

> were often highly creative [but] this tended to fizzle out in the course of the child's development and did not form the root for adolescent ambition and adult career or achievement. . . . Achievement for these children is the achievement of mending something wrong in the mother and achievement therefore leaves them always without any personal advancement. . . . [O]ne of the factors may be that all effort towards recovery is being made to deal with someone else's hate, notably the mother's. . . . What they cannot ever satisfactorily use in their emotional development is the mother's repressed unconscious hate which they only meet in their living experiences in the form of reaction formations. At the moment that the mother hates she shows special tenderness. There is no way a child can deal with this phenomenon.

The last sentence is conclusive and is probably a function of age and the impending end of a career.

Also in 1969 he wrote "The Mother-Infant Experience of Mutuality." There is, he says, a resistance to the study of very early mutual influences, as if "a sacred area is being encroached upon. It is as if a work of art were being subjected to an analytic process." Under the heading "Communication," he notes that "whereas all babies take in food, there does not exist a communication between the baby and the mother except in so far as there develops a mutual feeding situation. The baby feeds and the baby's experience includes the idea that the mother knows what it is like to be fed."

He goes on: "I wish to keep open the bridges that lead from older theory to newer theory. Nevertheless, I am obviously near to Fairbairn's statement made in 1944 that psycho-analytic theory was emphasising drive-satisfaction at the expense of what Fairbairn called 'object-seeking.'[7] And Fairbairn was working, as I am here, on the ways in which psycho-analytic theory needed to be developed or modified if the analyst could hope to become able to cope with schizoid phenomena in the treatment of patients."

He continues: "Analysts with a rigid analytic morality that does not allow touch miss a great deal of that which is now being described. One thing they never know, for instance, is that the analyst makes a little twitch whenever he or she goes to sleep for a moment or even wanders over in the mind (as may well happen) to some fantasy of his or her own. This twitch is the equivalent of a failure to hold in terms of mother and baby. The mind has dropped the patient." One may wonder whether Winnicott now found himself dropping off, the result of age and illness, or whether this was always the case.[8]

A handwritten letter of April 20, 1969, to Clare's brother Karl Britton (which must have been saved and returned to Clare after Donald's death) describes a large conference in Manchester of a group of social workers, now 2,500 strong, initiated by ten of Clare's first-year students at the London School of Economics: "Clare spoke at the dinner. She looked splendid and had a lovely frock on which we got at Peter Jones. She said exactly all the right things and everyone was pleased, and I like you to know these things." This is more of Winnicott giving his all, making sure that people heard whatever he could tell them that was good, knowing that the end was in sight. Madeleine Davis wrote[9] of his last two years: "I visited him then: he came to Manchester twice to give talks and stayed with us. He was working, analysing, supervising all the time. He *did* get very exhausted, and had to be careful. He couldn't have managed what he did without Clare."

Dr. Agnes Wilkinson had commented on an article on Strachey he had written, perhaps an obituary. His reply, dated June 9, 1969, is the occasion for two comments in particular: "I thought to myself 'really it is only in the split-off intellect that one can be 100% honest; as soon as living processes come in, then there is self-deception and deception and compromise and ambivalence.'" And "there are problems of management which belong to the here and now, and that are separate from matters of eternal truth." Here we see an aspect of the balance in him between the uncompromising and the practical.

On June 24 he wrote a scathing letter (perhaps his last scathing letter) to the organic psychiatrist William Sargant, author of an article titled

"The Physiology of Faith," and who always depreciated psychoanalysis: "There seems to be no playing in what you write, and therefore a lack of creativity. Perhaps you reserve your creativity for some other part of your life, in friendships for instance, or in painting. I don't know. The result, however, as comes over rather well in this shortened version of your Maudsley Lecture, is a materialism of a gross kind, and the only good thing that I can see from it is that it gives us a close view of the way the next dictator will work, and maybe it is we who will be the victims and for whom the dictator will make life not worth living because of the destruction of personal creative living at its root." He could still unleash the full force of his venom, the operative word being "full," just as he could be generous. Sargant replied at length, and not without tolerance, in an attempt to explain his position more fully and less provocatively, ending "Cannot we meet together on the urgent need to help patients by one means or another, and agree to differ on the importance of the brain in the creation of the soul?" Winnicott, on July 23, sent a conciliatory reply. He agreed with Sargant's comment, adding, "I would like to feel that I had not said that about your work lacking creativity." Here we see another typical sequence: initial rage tempered by a response into apology. He demands and gets "a reception" and then subsides.

In June 1969, Winnicott agreed to be supervised in his work with a little girl by Ishak Ramzy for the forthcoming Rome Pre-Congress, with the Congress to be held in London. He had no student's work to supervise, and so suggested that he be the one to present the case. A more complete account of that work was published in 1977 as a book, called *The Piggle*, edited by Ramzy. The material had been in the hands of Clare Winnicott after Donald's death, and she made it available as part of the extensive publication program of the Winnicott editors. (Shortly after Winnicott's death, Masud Khan wrote to Ramzy: "It is my moral responsibility and my debt of love to him to see to it that all his works get published in the way he would have liked them to be." Khan's correspondence took on an authoritative tone when Winnicott's work was the subject, as if putting himself forward to take over for him and do the job he imagined he was best fitted to do. Clare Winnicott, it turned out, had other ideas.)

The Piggle deals with a little girl who came to Winnicott at two years, four months, and saw him thereafter "on demand" for sixteen consultations. Her final contact took place when she was five years, two months old. The parents were apparently mental health professionals sophisticated in matters psychoanalytic. The little girl was having difficulty sleeping, and, after the birth of a sibling was easily bored and depressed. She expressed a good deal of fear of a "black mummy and daddy" and a "babacar." The book is a detailed account of the hours, with the addition of letters from the parents and, occasionally, the Piggle herself, a fantasy figure who became designated by the child's name, Gabrielle. Winnicott took notes during the sessions, the only way so much detail about their exchanges could have been saved.

The material exhibits constantly shifting associations, with confusion and diversion ever present. Out of that mass of data gradually emerge the themes that form into a deep understanding of the nature of Gabrielle's fantasy life and symptomatology. Her moods clarified during the nearly three-year period of the work. At the end of each session Winnicott reviews the significant themes and observations by way of keeping himself and his readers au courant. What the book gives us is an opportunity to experience some of the treatment ourselves through a kind of immersion. We share in both the confusion and the clarification and develop strong feelings for both participants.

Many pages contain the usual striking phrases of insight: "Importance of my not *understanding* what she had not yet been able to give me clues for. Only she knew the answers, and when she could encompass the meaning of the fears she would make it possible for me to understand too." This is his warning to "analysts who know too much," a theme that appears also in *Playing and Reality*. There is no attempt to gloss over irregularities or to produce a rounded narrative. "My notes are relatively obscure because of the heat and my sleepiness," he writes at one point. "An analyst in supervision with me had asked for a three-year-old child just at this time, and I thought of referring Gabrielle to him. This warped me, made me feel guilty, and so I became muddled when I raised the issue with her father. However, in my considered opinion the fact that the sessions were 'on demand' did not alter the fact that the child was having an analysis."

The analytic experience leads to observations such as:

> There is now a recollection of an actual mother, orgiastically eaten and also shot in ambivalence, replacing the more primitive split into good mother and black mother related to each other because of the split between the subjective and that which is objectively observed. . . . Black

mummy as a split-off version of mother, one that does not understand babies, or one who understands them so well that her absence or loss makes everything black. . . . If it's the mother's breast, you get the stuff out to get fat and to grow, but when it's a wee-wee you really want to have stuff to make into babies. . . . Black as denial of absence (looking as denial of not seeing), covering up the memory of the absent object. . . . As a matter of principle, the analyst always allows the enjoyment to become established before the content of the play is used for interpretation. . . . The climax of this [game] was getting in touch with the mother's need to be rid of the baby when it is too big. Associated with this is sadness about getting bigger and older, and finding it more difficult to play this game of being inside mother and getting born. . . . There was not much hostility in the game, and I referred to breathing, the essential element in being alive and something which could not be enjoyed before birth.

As we come near the end: "I felt that she had now brought everything into the transference and had in this way reorganized her entire life in terms of the experience of a positive relationship to the subjective figure of the analyst, and his inside. . . . In the middle of all this I said: 'So the Winnicott you invented was all yours and he's now finished with, and no one else can ever have him.'" In the final consultation he says to Gabrielle, "I know when you are really shy, and that is when you want to tell me that you love me."

This account is one of the most poignant documents ever to appear in the literature of psychoanalysis.

Alix Strachey wrote to Winnicott on June 27 about a matter having to do with the preparation of the index to the *Standard Edition*. She writes (to "Douglas," a slip): "I saw, and much appreciated, your obituary of James, tho' it was rather upsetting as it brought him back to me so vividly.[10] He *was* a wonderful person—so sensible, so kind, so witty & 'unstuffy'—& I was happy all the time I was with him. Well, I think he's left me enough of himself to make do for the rest of my life." She then refers to "Mr. Khan (or should I say 'Mr. Masud')," one of many ironic references to Khan throughout the Winnicott correspondence.

On July 20, 1969, two American astronauts landed on the moon, and Winnicott was moved to write a poem[11] that evaluated the achievement as of a lesser magnitude juxtaposed with the moon itself as "symbol of cold purity," "tide-master," "phase-determinant of women's bodies," and "The lamp fickle yet predictable to the /Shepherd astronomer that variably lights up /The dark night or generates bats and ghosts / And witches and things that go bump." He refuses to have his moon reduced to an object masterable by man. Some of the ideas in the poem suggest a subtext that portrays the astronauts as having had a kind of intercourse with the female moon, without any underlying content to their act.

On September 15, Ralph Greenson of Los Angeles wrote, in the British fashion, "Dear Winnicot [sic]," sending a check for time involved in a recent discussion. According to Douglas Kirsner,[12] Greenson had been in London studying the Kleinians. The check may well have been drawn from a research fund provided by a former patient who was an heir to the fortune of Walter Annenberg. The arrival in Los Angeles of Wilfred Bion and Albert Mason had been received in certain circles with great enthusiasm. Greenson was studying failures in psychoanalysis and would, not long after this period, challenge the Kleinian presence in Los Angeles in a most vituperative fashion. I was witness to some of this contention. It seemed clear that his close alliance with Anna Freud contributed to the ferocity of his assault on Klein. It was a version of the conflict in England, without the civility. On September 22, Winnicott replied to "Dear Ralph Greenson" with thanks.

Anna Freud wrote on October 21 to thank Winnicott "for writing about the 'dead loss' of Max Schur. In the end, one feels it is presumptuous to be alive still." Then, on November 14, Oscar Nemon, the sculptor of the Freud statue to which Winnicott gave so much of the final energy of his life, wrote to say: "My dear patient friend, I just came out of hell where I was hounded by wild machines and the thunder of beaten metal. I have survived the first round of my torment. We have amputated one leg of the statue in the hope that the great man will help to grow another next week. This Sunday I shall be in my studio and hope to see you as well as Sir Martin and Lady Charteril (spelling) who is looking forward to meeting you. I am sure you have spent yourself too lavishly on your patients, but I hope that there is something left for me of you. Your irritant demon, Nemon." Clare told me in 1979 that Donald enjoyed spending time on Saturday mornings in Nemon's studio, which was located in St. James's Palace, playing with clay.

On the last day of 1969, the Reverend Vernon Sproxton, writing as a producer of religious programs for the BBC, asked Winnicott to help with a series on the nature of evil. He requested a very brief contribution, adding that he was "a very old friend of Harry Guntrip. Sometime in the spring we shall be mounting a whole programme on his life and work."

Winnicott replies on January 12, 1970, "There has been a delay because of my uncertainty about my physical health." He was interested, he said, but not hopeful that one or two minutes of self-expression could do justice to such a big subject. "[I] am not at the moment able to plan for the future. Maybe in a week or two I shall be well enough to plan to visit the studio," he wrote, adding, "I am glad to hear that you are a friend of Harry Guntrip for whom I have the greatest possible respect and affection."

Jeanne Lampl-de Groot wrote in March to express support for the Nemon statue of Freud to be erected in Hampstead, and told him that Anna Freud supported it too. Winnicott gave freely of his limited energies to make sure the statue would be created and installed in a public place, a tribute to Freud which expressed his deep sense of gratitude and admiration for the founder of psychoanalysis. On September 11, 1970, he wrote a detailed letter to Anna Freud about the ceremony scheduled for October 2. He was trying at that time to get W. H. Auden ("whose poem on Freud I like") to come over from the United States to speak.[13]

On March 26, 1970, Masud Khan, about to leave for Pakistan, offered his addresses there, with the hope that there would be no need to use them. "I need hardly say," he wrote, "how grateful I am to you for what you have done for Svetlana [Beriosova, his wife]," whom Winnicott did not treat. By July 30, Dr. William Sargant, of whom he had been so scathingly critical, was writing about Beriosova, whom Winnicott had referred to him. Sargant had decided that he could not treat her as long as she was drinking. She did well as an inpatient in St. Thomas' Hospital, but once on the outside had resumed her drinking. "Certainly my treating Mrs. Khan has not interfered with our personal relationship. I am only sorry for the failure," Sargant wrote. Winnicott's genius for friendship allowed him to be genuinely cutting and then not merely to be forgiven but to be held dear. He must have evoked a kind of respect from those who realized that in Winnicott they had a really honest friend, one who did not resort to the usual misrepresentations in the interest of harmony. His ongoing friendships were affected by sharp disagreements, for Winnicott could probably not help but put the warm feelings to the test at critical moments.

After Ernst Freud's death, Winnicott suggested to Michael Balint that he and Khan write something about him for the British Society's news bulletin: "Perhaps we could have a short Winnicottism followed by a more detailed piece of Masudery." Here the inveterate humor surfaces even in discussing an obituary, probably with additional irony because of his own state of health. By July 20, however, he was having trouble writing the article: "I think the matter is made more difficult by the fact that Lucy (Ernst's widow, the mother of the painter Lucian Freud) seems to be cracking up. I have looked at Martin Freud's book for items of interest, and if we go on with the project I think I ought to see Miss Freud. If I go to see Anna, however, I would like to see her about more important and interesting matters." Balint wrote on April 20 of everyone's indebtedness to Ernst Freud, adding, "The two people who worked closest to him are, of course, you and Masud."

Beginning on May 11 there was an exchange with Melanie Klein's daughter, Melitta Schmideberg, about an article she had written for the *British Journal of Psychiatry*. Winnicott wrote on June 8 that he would like to write in support of her, but he was ill and trying to do so much. He mentions a "high-powered project on cases that failed in spite of the fact that the analyst thought he or she was doing well, sponsored by Ralph Greenson of Los Angeles. Also there is to be a weekend meeting of our Society on this same subject in the autumn." She reported on June 10 that his was "the first fair letter I have received from an analyst" and wanted it published in her support. She was most interested in Greenson's project and the society meeting, and wished to be invited to participate. "I would also suggest that you ask Dr. Glover," she added, her former analyst and ally against her mother. In addition, she wanted him to invite the well-known psychiatrist David Stafford-Clark to the forthcoming meeting to show that the society was inclusive and interested in the opinions of non-analysts. Winnicott, however, feared that he might exploit the controversy for his own purposes, and finally decided against writing a letter in support of Schmideberg as well, since the correspondence had played itself out and the important thing was the paper anyway.

He wrote to the neurologist and author Jonathan Miller on August 10 about the death of Miller's father, Emanuel Miller, a psychiatrist and child psychiatrist: "When I came on the scene in the early twenties your father was already established. One could not help seeing immediately on meeting him that he had erudition, and that he could have succeeded in many different ways if he had chosen alternative routes for self-expression and for contributing in to society." As a child, Jonathan Miller had a period of analysis with Winnicott. He went on to succeed in many different fields himself, as a physician, director, opera impresario, author, and humorist.

On September 7, Phyllis Greenacre wrote from Garrison, New York:

My dear Donald—I have had it very much in mind for months to write you a letter after you wrote me concerning my paper. I somehow did not find it as difficult as I judge you did—to reconcile our points of view. My feeling was that the T. O. and the Fetish are interrelated—or perhaps exist in a kind of spectrum of manifestations—in which the more than favorite blanket and the fetish are at opposite ends of the rainbow. As soon as one gets into the "manifestations" or "phenomena," then the two blend very much together. I have been impressed with the differences, I suppose, because I came to the whole problem through the need to understand adult fetishists,—in which the use of the fetish was clearly and stubbornly pathological.

I shall always be grateful to you for your work which opened the door to me to the essentially normal nucleus of fetishistic developments even though what I dealt with *were* the bizarre pathological symptoms as well as/or other ideas.

This has been a difficult year for me and I have seemed to go from one thing to another without having time to catch my breath. Just now I am here in the country, where it is really delightful. It is one of the few places—less than 60 miles from N.Y.C. where there are still dirt roads and wild life. I stare down three fawns who come up each morning to get apples from the small tree in the orchard. So far I have been able to out-stare them, for in the end, they break down, toss their white tails and run for the woods. We used to have red fox around but I have not seen one for some time, —and vols? too seem to have left us. But there are beavers, racoons, and a great variety of small animals. After years of absence, squirrels have returned,—to my horror one got into the house through the chimney and did a good job of vandalism.

I have just finished an article on *Youth, Growth and Violence* (associated with squirrels I guess) which presumably will come out in the

Psa Study of the Child. I found myself developing some ideas in it which I think have some merit, though I am not quite sure where they are going.

I had hoped to go to England this fall and had looked forward to it additionally as my 20 year old grandson had announced his wish to go with me. But I have had to have my mouth "done over"—rearranged and redecorated as it were,—and it isn't yet in the best working order,—so I shall delay the trip—probably until Spring.

I do wish you and Clare might be here right now. It is a really beautiful September—just at the end of Summer. In another three weeks we will have a gaudy display of autumn foliage,—but this in-between time is peaceful and not quite so riotous in color.

Best wishes to you both
Phyllis—

My . . . address is the same—501 East 87th St. N. Y. C. I go back today.

This lovely handwritten letter, one of the last he received, tells of the relatedness of their concepts and is redolent of the harmony of nature. She sees the humor in the condition of her teeth, and somehow we know that this would have appealed to Donald. And she longs for him and Clare to be with her in the "in-between" time, between summer and autumn, the transitional time.

Harold Searles wrote on September 27 to ask for the names of London physicians for his daughter. He looked forward to visiting Dr. Winnicott, he said. Searles's writings, which reach across to the reader rather than displaying learning as an objective object, do bear similarities to Winnicott's. They knew of each other, of course, but there was never any intense friendship between them.

Evidence of Winnicott's continuing ability to reach deep into his imagination for explanatory ideas comes from an excerpt from the Workbooks of Masud Khan, in which Khan writes about a conversation with Winnicott that took place on Sunday, June 7, 1970. "He was recounting recent material from a session of a female patient who for years had suffered from an acute spider phobia. She had asked D. W. for the meaning of her spider phobia, and suddenly he had an idea to offer. He interpreted that somewhere in her early development, while she hadn't quite personalized into her separate identity, she had hallucinated the subjective object (breasts or whatever), expecting to be met, and she wasn't. There was a gap. This dark back [lack?] now she quickly *dealt with*, in terms of her nascent ego-capacities, by putting legs around the dark spot which was *the absence of the subjective object* and then it became a spider and she is afraid of it."[14]

"On the Basis for Self in Body" (published in *Nouvelle revue de Psychanalyse* shortly after his death) was written sometime during the last year of Winnicott's life. The word "disintegration" is misused, a lapse not ordinarily allowed by the scrupulous Winnicott.; he carefully differentiates between "unintegrate" and "disintegrate" in other places. He writes "Forward development is in all respects frightening to the individual concerned if there is not left open the way back to total dependence." He gives further detail on various stages where this pathway is required or not. The period from twelve to fourteen, for example, is one with that need.

Much of the paper consists of case material on children who are physically compromised. The father's death is a prominent theme. There is a long definition of the word "self":

> For me the self, which is not the ego, is the person who is me, who is only me, who has a totality based on the operation of the maturational process. At the same time the self has parts, and in fact is constituted of these parts. These parts agglutinate from a direction interior-exterior in the course of the operation of the maturational process, aided as it must be (maximally at the beginning) by the human environment which holds and handles and in a live way facilitates. The self finds itself naturally placed in the body, but may in certain circumstances become dissociated from the body or the body from it. The self essentially recognises itself in the eyes and facial expression of the mother and in the mirror which can come to represent the mother's face. Eventually the self arrives at a significant relationship between the child and the sum of the identifications which (after enough of incorporation and introjection of mental representations) become organised in the shape of an internal psychic living reality. The relationship between the boy or girl and his or her own internal psychic organisation becomes modified according to the expectations

that are displayed by the father and mother and those who have become significant in the external life of the individual. It is the self and
the life of the self that alone makes sense of action or of living from
the point of view of the individual who has grown so far and who is
continuing to grow from dependence and immaturity towards independence, and the capacity to identify with mature love objects without loss of individual identity.

In his last two years, Winnicott was trying to preserve what was left
of his physical health as he continued to write and consult. His hair grew
ever thinner and his false teeth became ill fitting, but his mind was vigorous and clear. We find great generosity, and the persisting capacity for
vitriolic attack where he deems it warranted. He had always sought a capacity for ruthlessness in order to reconstruct and reinspire the damaged
impulses of his infancy and thereby realize a certain kind of productive
and fulfilling destiny. The ruthlessness of infancy, and even of adulthood,
is closely associated with instinctual aggression and hate. In his own
search for effectiveness (or potency, sexual and otherwise) in human relations, he pursued the idea that ruthlessness is indispensable to human
happiness, beginning in its pure form as the infant sucks at the breast.
That state of mind in which the object is of no interest and only personal
satisfaction matters was said to be succeeded by the stage of concern, in
which the object does matter and the child is concerned with making
reparation to the person whom he or she depletes of nourishment in moments of instinctually driven feeding. Winnicott, however—or so it
seems to me—finally affirmed that the ruthlessness of infancy is never altered in its basic form, which is to say that in spite of any concern that
does develop and that protects the object from exploitation, there is another level, another, deeper layer, of the original urgency, the destructive
aspect which is activated whenever an intense relationship develops. It is
precisely this continuous destructiveness, to which he refers in "The Use
of an Object," which is indispensable as background for the "use" to
which the surviving object may be put. This is to say that the nourishment of an external reality that survives its fantasized destruction stands
in parallel relation to the substantive nourishment provided by the
mother at the beginning of life.

This capacity for destructiveness must not be "civilized" out of the
child by the parents, or there is a risk that life will lose its meaning. That is,

the quality of reality which is attained through the survival of the external will not occur. Life will be gray. The father is an important figure in seeing to it that this does not happen. Winnicott failed spectacularly to speak adequately of the role of the father—except at the very end of his life—and it seems likely that this is a reflection of his disappointment in his own father.

In the end, it seemed up to himself alone to find the masculine ruthlessness with which to pursue his life. Melanie Klein was a sort of heroine, with Freud looming behind her. She was probably the model of a phallic woman with whom he could identify, the one who contained the grandfatherly backbone which represented structure. If it was true, as Marion Milner believed, that his mother's pleasure in breast-feeding was interdicted by her own father's attitudes, then his long-standing struggle with Klein to get her to acknowledge that mothers really matter was probably the adult equivalent of the struggle to get milk out of his own mother.

He took hold of the word "hate" at a certain period and repeated it as if he had found an avenue by which he could cultivate what had received insufficient support. His letters—forthright, unsentimental, powerful at times in their critical content—show the stature to which he aspired and which he attained. But it was not until the climactic "Use" paper that he was able to verbalize the essential features of what he regarded as necessary for an effective, potent, reality-nourished life, and the lack of enthusiastic understanding which he suffered in New York may well have represented the final obstacle, the final failure of that good reception he pleaded for from Klein, on his own behalf and on behalf of others. Of course, the paper itself practically begged for *mis*understanding in those days (it still causes confusion), and may be viewed as an ultimate statement of his separateness, of his unique and incommunicado self.

That permission should be required for ruthlessness undercuts the independence of mind required for ruthlessness. And yet, for an infant, and perhaps the infant's successors at all stages, a receptive mother may be necessary, or the expression of ruthlessness will be aborted and stymied. The need is for one who will not retaliate, thereby fostering the sense of a world ready to receive one's instinctually based outpourings. Or, more likely, there is a range of needs, resulting from early experience and inherent temperament, which allows some to bypass permission-seeking and come forth with what presses for expression, while at the other end there are those who are on the brink of perishing for lack of a sign that self-expression is welcome.

Some years after his New York paper, I was told by someone who had been at that meeting that Winnicott was undoubtedly a brilliant thinker, but, I was asked, "Why is it that he insists on talking about space? Why couldn't he put his ideas into the accepted language?" I believe that this sort of comment tells us what we need to know: that there would be no quarter given, because a tradition had been erected over a long period of time which did not make room for the likes of this renegade. There is, of course, room for criticism. It is not unfair to say that Winnicott reified his concepts and that it is therefore necessary for those who find value in them and who wish for a consistently unreified psychoanalytic theory to do the work of translation. But one can hardly demand of a contributor that his special talents be harnessed to preexisting conceptual frameworks if that would mean the destruction of the impulse to put forward authentic and valuable notions in whatever form they emerge.

Clare, interviewed by Michael Neve in June 1983, said of Donald that

> he'd had about six coronaries, and recovered from them and kept himself going. And didn't stop himself doing a thing! He'd be up— When we went down to his home in Devon, he'd be up at the top of a tree, in the last year of his life. A few months before he died. He was at the top of a tree, cutting the top off. I said, "What the *hell* are you doing up there?"
>
> He said, "Well, I've always wanted to top this tree off. It spoils the view from our window." Which it did! And he got it off.
>
> And I thought, "I must get him down! He's absolutely crazy." And I thought, "No, it's his life and he's got to live it. If he *dies* after this, he dies."
>
> But this was him. He wanted to *live*. He said—He'd started his autobiography, you see. And it was going to be called *Not Less Than Everything*. And he quotes Eliot. And then he's, he's put at the bottom. "Prayer: Oh, God, may I be alive when I die." And he was, really.

It had been clear for a long time that Winnicott might die at any moment. As Pearl King told me: "We got used to it." When Donald, who always watered the office plants, told Joyce Coles how to care for them, it was clear that he knew he would soon die.

The usual Christmas cards were not sent out in 1970 because Donald had the flu. On January 22, Clare called Joyce Coles at 7 A.M. to tell her that Donald had died during the night. She said that he went to the loo in the middle of the night and collapsed. She called out for one of the two doctors who were living in their basement flat to come help him, but he was dead. At his funeral Madeleine Davis asked Clare what happened. She told her, too, that he had got up to go to loo, which he needed to do every night.[15] He was gone a long time. When Clare went to look for him, she found him on the floor, leaning on a chair. He was already dead. He seemed to have been resting his head against the side of the chair, she said. "Often in the office he used to kneel on the floor and rest his head on a chair. He was a great one for getting down on the floor. It was a method of easing his back by leaning against a chair, backward."

Although Clare told both Joyce Coles and Madeleine Davis that he was "in the loo" when he died, she told a different and rather touching story in a 1978 interview: "We'd looked at a film. It was a very comic film of old cars, a very amusing film. I'd spotted that it was on, and I said, 'I think you'll like this.' We looked at this, and he said, 'What a happy-making film!' and went to sleep. And I woke up and he was already dead, on the floor."

On January 29 at 3 P.M. a memorial service was held in the chapel at Golders Green Crematorium, after Winnicott's body had been cremated. It was a very cold, dry day.[16] Bach selections were played on the piano. A large gathering heard eulogies delivered by Peter Tizard, Winnicott's old and dear pediatrician friend, and the deeply respected psychoanalyst W. H. Gillespie. Gillespie spoke for all the mourners when he said that they felt "a very special anguish at having to part in the end with Donald Winnicott, for he held a unique place in the hearts of all who knew him. I say 'in the end' because the threat of his loss has been with us for many years." Even though everyone had known that he could die at any time, the fact of death was not the same as death anticipated, and the shock of Winnicott's passing resounded throughout the world of psychoanalysis.

Alice Winnicott had died on November 19, 1969, a little over a year before Donald. Alice's letters portray a forlorn person with whom Donald communicated by mail and to whom he sent reading material, but very likely never visited.[17]

Donald's sister Kathleen would live on until January 15, 1979, age eighty-seven. Violet was ninety-five when she died on December 9, 1984, only months after Clare. Valerie A. Brown of Mannamead, Plymouth, wrote me at some length on April 11, 1993: "Violet I loved, she was the naughtier one! Kathleen was very quiet with her glorious colour hair which she wore in coils around her ears. I thought Violet would crack up after her death but she was wonderful about it all, and one day she said to me (in her 90's) 'Valerie, it takes 12 staff to look after one old lady!' She was totally blind of course. Violet used to thank me for going to see her always. . . . Once she asked me if I could get her the music of "Lord of The Dance" for her as it was so happy and gay, and she thought she might have it for her funeral! So I did! One day I was at home and the telephone rang. I picked it up, no voice, sound of music only, Lord of the Dance played by Violet in her 90's totally blind—*wot guts*!!! Later she came off that idea and settled for 'All Things Bright and Beautiful.' I know I was at her funeral, and it brought a lump to my throat—faith they all had in plenty, both for nature, and mankind in general—wonderful people—sometimes a lost Race I feel in this very violent age."

Hannah Henry wrote in 1993: "I missed Donald so much and then Clare. Clare too came and stayed, anxious to know more about the early Donald. I liked her and was so sad at her passing, she was so ill, and had to deal with the move from Chester Square. The lease ran out, her sister was helpful and shared her last days with her, and then she too died." Clare died on April 15, 1984, of melanoma, for which she endured many painful operations in the 1970s and early 1980s. Hannah enclosed an unidentified newspaper obituary which read, "This lovely and much moved woman enriched the lives of all who knew her—and beyond them those countless children she never met but who were helped by her unique professional achievements."

On July 15, 1971, at a memorial meeting for Donald Winnicott held at the Royal College of Physicians, organized by the National Association for Mental Health, Renata Gaddini submitted the following description: "When I gave the announcement of his death, at the grand round in our Department on the Friday following the official announcement, in that very amphitheater where everyone had seen him so alive and revolutionary, the whole staff stood up in silence, with deep reverence in remembrance of the Man and of the Scientist. May I add that I have never before witnessed such an authentic tribute to a man, and that I felt it to be the natural response to his respect for authenticity and search for the real self."[18]

Among the comments from former LSE students and psychoanalytic supervisees were these: "The enormous audiences that always came to hear him speak were sufficient indication of how greatly he was valued and those of us who were fortunate enough to be taught by him will never forget the experience."

"Donald's death is a light going out of psychoanalysis. I know no one of his calibre, originality and freshness, with his breadth of mind and vision, his integrity and stature."

"As fragile as Donald looked, his face seemed chiseled out of rock and this gave him the appearance of timelessness."

A number of colleagues spoke at the commemorative meeting held by the British Psycho-Analytical Society and the Institute of Psycho-Analysis on January 19, 1972, a year after his death. The chairman, W. H. Gillespie, spoke of Winnicott's courage, as well as his ruthlessness, referring to Winnicott's stand against bed rest for rheumatic children. So sure of himself was Winnicott that he was willing to risk his own reputation and, further, to place the children's lives in danger had he been wrong. He was that sure of himself. As noted in chapter 6, Gillespie added: "I have also heard him say that children would have been better off bombed than evacuated; and his attitude about a patient's right to take his own life, with the implication that no one should try too hard to stop him, is well known. This is what I mean by Winnicott's occasional ruthlessness, and I believe that without it he would have made a great deal less impact than he did. Nevertheless 'his life was gentle, and the elements so mixed in him' that this very quality was turned to noble ends, for he was a man full of love and tenderness as well."

Marion Milner's contribution, the one in which she compares him to a Catherine wheel, speaks of "his capacity for saint-like devotion to those he thought he could help; but also a certain capacity for ruthlessness. I even heard someone say that what they most appreciated in him was what they called his 'puckish maliciousness'; and of course, his wit."

Masud Khan said that "he wrote as he spoke: simply and to relate. Not to incite conviction or to indoctrinate. Some of us, and I am one of those, think he let the side down by his special stance of humility, which is larger than arrogance and authority. He made his idiom so much that of the ordinary cultured and common usage that everyone was illusioned into the make-believe that they have always known what he was saying."

Barbara Woodhead gave a vivid description of his clinic at Paddington Green. She captured the phenomenon of Winnicott attending to so many individuals so fully, and yet able to proceed from case to case, taking account of everyone's needs.

Margaret Little said, "If we think of him as an 'isolated phenomenon,' as he once called himself, we have to recognise his claim to both 'the use and enjoyment of modes of communication' and to 'the personal core of the self that is a true isolate, the individual's non-communicating self,' and know him in both aspects."[19]

Michael Fordham said that he "defined the false self but left [the True Self undefined] because he recognised it as a state that could be known but not put into abstractions or directly described." He said further that he understood Winnicott's impression of the meaning of Jung's childhood memories as close to his own impression, that he had discussed this with Jung himself, who did not disagree. "I believe he went a long way towards 'coming to terms' with Jung in his views on the relation between transitional objects, play and cultural experience."

Also at the commemorative meeting, Oscar Nemon told an anecdote about Freud. He had done a sculpture of his head in wood. Freud asked him, "Has anybody approached you to obtain a copy of the head you did of me?" "I was taken aback by that unexpected question," said Nemon, "because the idea of multiplication had not appealed to my romantic dedication some 40 years ago. I answered uneasily to the searching question, 'Nobody expressed such a desire, except your own brother, Alexander, who wished to obtain a bronze.'" At that Freud said, "Have no illusions; you will have to wait three generations before such a request can be expected from my followers." Nemon said as well: "I must say in tribute to Donald that he had a passion for rescuing which was fully applied to me. But what mattered most for him was that a debt of honour should be paid from him and his colleagues to Freud, from whom they had received so much encouragement to enable them to persevere in their endeavours."

Pearl King recalled that he had supervised her work with a small child. "What I did not expect was that I would learn so much about classical psycho-analysis from him, in spite of his reputation as an innovator. I realised that it was only when the usual interpretations did not seem to help the patient that he felt it as his task to explore beyond the usual limits of accepted psycho-analytic theory and technique and discover how else to help a particular patient but still within a psychoanalytic context." It was King who told me, in 1988, that Donald was "like the knight in chess." His moves were unique, unpredictable, oblique. Those who mourned Winnicott were moved to find unique words to describe their sense of the impact he had on their lives. Their praise was in no way routine or stereotyped, proof, though none was needed, that Winnicott had been sui generis and was irreplaceable.

Epilogue:
Not Less Than Everything

Winnicott held more or less dual viewpoints on many subjects, starting with his oft-repeated comment that Freud did the pioneering work of psychoanalysis, which could be taken for granted, and from which we, his successors, could proceed into new territory. An alternative was that Freud gave us a method and it was up to us to use it. He was free of slavish imitation of the founder while according him the utmost respect. His own Darwinian-medical background put traditional science in the forefront of his thinking, and his personal expressive propensities led him into the area of illusion. He combined the old-fashioned attitude of objectivizing science, in which it was possible to study what was "out there," with science that was based on a combination of what was "out there" and what was within the observer. Central as well, as he progressed, was the pairing of an incommunicado element in everyone with the spontaneous gesture as the expression in action of the True Self. Here we have perpetual isolation and continuous relatedness. Paradox was his wisdom, the acceptance, as he urged, of the simultaneity of opposites. Out of it comes an impression of human beings as wholes: while unitary, they are always also divided. This is the freedom that bewildered others. In the face of the striving toward unification, in life as well as in the psychoanalytic endeavor, how could one make room for its opposite? Yet, without a kind of human disarray, there could be no life as we know it. Without unintegration, the earliest stage of that disarray, there could be no moment of integration, followed by other moments of renewed unintegration, as in sleep, for example, leading to new integrations.

Winnicott's cultural ancestors were the English Romantic poets, who embraced the role of the imagination in the construction of reality.[1] He himself had an ebullience, a natural, inspiring freedom that was evident from his early years. He came up against violent opposition to his theories and natural proclivities in the person of Melanie Klein and her followers. The Kleinians, strict adherents to the old science, saw Winnicott's views as outside analysis as they knew it, and in this they were correct. Winnicott's sense of reality was of a profoundly different sort, including as it did, however, his Freudian inheritance. While preoccupied with elucidating the place of illusion, he also affirmed the not-me, a reality that exists apart from human views. This was clear very early, when he studied infants' reactions to tongue depressors ("Observations of Infants in a Set Situation," 1941). Later, in the treatment of patients with early damage, he allowed a regression in search of the recovery of the moment at which an original discontinuity in development occurred, or a breakdown that could not be encompassed at the time. This was a search for a moment that had actually occurred rather than been invented.

Freud had turned from the conviction that his patients had been seduced as children to a belief that it is the fantasy life of the child that usually gives rise to the seduction idea. This was the famous turn that led him to the concept of the Oedipus complex. But always in Freud there is the same duality we find in Winnicott, though some of his descendants have tended to obliterate the role of the actual event in favor of the fantasy. His struggle with these two etiological realities is evident in the late meditations embodied in *Moses and Monotheism*.

Winnicott's elucidation of the ubiquity of illusion in the encounter with reality seems to me to have given rise to a quite human frustration, an urgent desire to affirm the outside world as a thing apart from the imagination, the not-me. It seems to me that in his formulation, illusion is being smashed in the unconscious destruction of the object.[2] The requirement that a person find something in the world that stands opposed to the impulse to move, mobility leading to resistance and consequent aggression, was transformed in his "use" theory into a human event: he moved from inanimate to animate opposition. If this urgency arose from within, then it was parallel to the explicit comment in his paper on communicating: "I soon came . . . to staking a claim, to my surprise, to the right not to communicate. This was a protest from the core of me to the frightening fantasy of being infinitely exploited." Limiting his reflections to the role of relationships, he was able to generate the notion of the continuous destruction of (relational) reality, a condition through which what survives attains a new status: that of being "of use." Characteristically, the word "use," which ordinarily implies a demeaned status (as in the idea of "using" someone), is now elevated to a special role, exceeding in significance and value the ordinary role of another person. Those who are "of use" are distinguished by the fact that they contribute the genuinely new to the life of the subject, nutriment that is not the result of projection, not self-manufactured. In redefining "use," he created a primal word, with antithetical meanings, yet another paradox. The implications of his theory have never been expounded, neither the conditions under which a particular individual is chosen for this trial by destruction, nor the potential role of continuous destructiveness as a background for all perception. Nor do we know the natural history of "use."

In contrast to Freud, Winnicott was able to appreciate the human and hopeful elements in the idea of illusion. In his papers on this subject, John Turner cites the work of Edmund Burke,[3] who argued against what might be called the tyrannical use of reason in the French Revolution. Burke's essay contributed to a recognition of the role of the emotions in the apprehension of reality, a theme much explored by William Wordsworth. Burke suggests that nations are "large-scale groups held together (if at all) by the similarity of their common illusory experiences." Winnicott wrote that "it becomes the hallmark of madness when an adult puts too powerful a claim on the credulity of others, forcing them to acknowledge a sharing of an illusion that is not their own. We can share a respect for illusory experience, and if we wish we may collect together and form a group on the basis of the similarity of our illusory experiences. This is a natural root of groupings among human beings."[4] This idea, applicable to divisions within the British Society, relativized them, that is, it took away objective truth (truth, that is, with no component of illusion) as a backing for their theories. This posed a threat, particularly to the Kleinian group, with its fanatic convictions about its priveleged access to human truths, and its accompanying personal loyalties and animosities.

Man's isolation as embedded in Winnicott's incommunicado condition, the locus of creation/destruction which is never to be known, was for him an existential fact.[5] This element in Winnicott's thought, besides describing the outer reaches of psychoanalytic inquiry, places limits on the degree to which "relating" holds continuous sway in life. It puts limits on his object-relating theories and it defies schools of thought, starting with Klein and including the intersubjective, self-psychological, and interpersonal viewpoint of human life as a condition of relatedness in toto. It reinforces the idea of a primary narcissism—the baby at the start incapable of relatedness to objects—an idea inherited from Freud and supported by Winnicott's pediatric observations. Amidst all the optimism so characteristic of the works and speeches of a man capable of extending the range of human awareness so very far, there is the suggestion that we are together, yet we are alone. And this is probably an aloneness that persists from the beginning, underneath and in parallel to the relatedness he studied so assiduously.

The Freudian theory that the instincts in the beginning have no object is the predecessor to Winnicott's idea of permanent incommunicado status. We see the derivatives of both ideas at work in the course of life, and psychoanalysts make interpretations that are intended to expose the underlying truthful aims of those derivatives over the long course of analytic work. Patients come gradually to acknowledge their underlying motives, so to speak, with a resulting sense of responsibility for actions and consequences. This was one of the greatest of Freud's revisions, to show us how much more responsible we are for our fate than we could otherwise acknowledge. In addition to his concern with the intrinsic morality in human development, Winnicott identified a further dimension which enabled him to deal with patients who lack the fundamental capacity for ruthlessness in certain crucial life situations. For them, an emphasis on guilt and responsibility, on owning up to one's instinctual aims and deeds, may undermine the capacity for acting in the moment, when ruthlessness is all that matters. This may come in the moment of sexual ecstasy, or it may come when an issue of deep import to the True Self calls for a response. Winnicott himself struggled to liberate this capability in his own life, and through his own hard-won knowledge he helped others see the extent to which such issues affect countless lives.

Whereas Freud viewed man as bestial and in need of taming, Winnicott had faith that in the natural course of events—that is, with good-enough mothering and a stable family structure—the individual becomes a moral being, and in fact runs the opposite risk of being so severely tamed that he loses the animal capacity for celebrating his existence. Man becomes too sane. And "we are poor indeed if we are only sane."[6]

People who respond to Winnicott's work with immediate recognition of a liberating spirit are seized, I think, by the perception of coruscating thought that slips between and among gestures of self-interest and celebration, on the one hand, and serious and extended focus, on the other. He could not help but invest his writing with his own personal existence, unlike the usual scientific writing which seeks to establish the anonymity of the author in order to maintain the objectivity of science. Winnicott, like, in a vastly different field, the physicist Werner Heisenberg, taught that the observer cannot be separated ultimately from the observed. This may be said in spite of the considerable work of many others in the area of countertransference, and the common knowledge of all analysts that they navigate treacherous waters with all patients, the awareness that part of what distinguishes good work is the capacity of the analyst to re-achieve repeatedly an objective point of view. Winnicott, to put it simply, could not help but be himself, this being the basis of his efforts to help those who had difficulty taking so personal and unshakable a stand.

Near the end of his life Winnicott wrote: "I have this need to talk as though no one had ever examined the subject before, and of course this can make my words ridiculous. But I think you can see in this my own need to make sure I am not buried by my theme. It would kill me to work out the concordance of creativity references. Evidently I must be always fighting to *feel* creative, and this has the disadvantage that if I am describing a simple word like 'love,' I must start from scratch. (Perhaps that's the right place to start from.)"[7]

Shortly after Winnicott's death in 1971, two important books appeared: his *Playing and Reality*, a collection of related papers, and *Therapeutic Consultations in Child Psychiatry*, which contains twenty-one short cases of children seen once or a few times. These were two very different books, *Playing and Reality* rehearsed already published work in combination with a few pieces never before released in book form; the volume deepened and made more comprehensive many of his fundamental ideas. The transitional object paper at the beginning and "The Use of an Object" at the end were the bookends for a theory that had preoccupied him for twenty-five years, still not complete, but setting a framework for those to follow.

Therapeutic Consultations illustrated Winnicott's extraordinarily developed analytic skills. He was able to communicate, very often through squiggles, as what he called a subjective object. It is as if he were within the child's mind during this initial, time-limited period, after which he became, for the child, something else, an object objectively perceived (as he put it), just an ordinary person. Throughout *Consultations* we see the vast reach of his ever so simple method. "The only companion that I have in exploring the unknown territory of the new case," he wrote, "is the theory that I carry around with me and has become part of me and that I do not even have to think about in a deliberate way." Part of our pleasure in exploring this substantial psychoanalytic gift to readers of the inner lives of children derives from the pleasure he himself took in the work he did: "The test of these case descriptions will hang on the word enjoyment."

A Winnicott board of editors, appointed by his widow, Clare, took charge of compiling, editing, and publishing the large archive of book material he left behind. Out of this came a long series of volumes,[8] which fueled a mounting interest in Winnicott throughout the world and brought people back to his earlier works as well. Those earlier works show him to have been a powerful writer and undermine the claim that it was Masud Khan who made his writing accessible after 1951.

Many of Winnicott's ideas seem fresh and timely in the context of subsequent events and intellectual trends. It has been noted that "Do your own thing," one of the mottos of the 1960s, was typical of Winnicott long before it became a worldwide slogan of youth. And certainly he did write that parents owed support to their adolescents, even for being depreciated by them. His emphasis on the individual development of the psychoanalyst, with maximum freedom to achieve that development, and his unwillingness to associate himself with a single school of thought, gave him an appeal within the American culture, where he was embraced. Within psychoanalysis and related disciplines, the profusion of new titles kept adding to the growing interest in his work. While the Freud-bashing industry advanced and Kleinian contempt continued, Winnicott's papers were more often cited in bibliographies than those of any other author except Freud. There is, of course, no school of Winnicott, no courses in his methods. The complete absence of religious dogma in his work is, I think, most appealing, but would not be so were it not for the vast range of penetrating questions and complex intellectual struggles which he posed for himself and for others.

Both the idealization and depreciation of any great thinker are inevitable. Winnicott's influence as seen in voluminous citations, the continuing audience for his dozens of books, and the gatherings that focus on his work and call forth large numbers show that he has remained in the forefront of psychoanalytic thought. There is at the moment a questioning of his virtues in some circles, based on the notoriety attached to Masud Khan. The posthumous exposure of Khan's inadequacies and destructiveness, extending beyond what had already been known about him, threatens to tarnish Winnicott with the taint of Khan's ignominious behavior. The case of Masud Khan is an interesting one, and to the extent that Winnicott had a role to play in it, as he surely did, a great deal of scrutiny will be generated. Further understanding of Winnicott's complex mind will very likely come to light. And to the extent that he emerges as a person in conflict who expressed his genius, and also went awry, in manifold ways, his humanity will be seen more clearly and anew.

One's perception of a life is subject to continuous revision. Anyone who produced such a volume of insightful work as Winnicott will be considered and reconsidered indefinitely. At this writing, more than thirty years since he died, he has been greatly understood and misunderstood, appreciated and vilified. The fact that so many people keep trying to understand his contributions is proof that he spoke to fundamental human dilemmas in a way that aroused the imagination and promised the liberation of insight. His work is done. It continues to be the work of the living to make of it what they can and will.

Notes

Chapter 1

1. Psychotic patients who are "notoriously and maddenly oblivious" require, as he would tell us over time, extraordinary adaptation by the analyst, something reminiscent of the mother's with an infant.

2. I. e., students.

3. *The Complete Correspondence of Sigmund Freud and Ernest Jones, 1908–1939,* ed. R. Andrew Paskauskas, intro. Riccardo Steiner (Cambridge, Mass.: Harvard University Press, 1993).

4. Eric Rayner, *The Independent Mind in British Psychoanalysis* (London: Free Association Books, 1990).

5. Phyllis Grosskurth, *Melanie Klein: Her World and Her Work* (New York: Knopf, 1986).

6. Riccardo Steiner, *It's a New Kind of Diaspora: Explorations in the Sociopolitical and Cultural Context of Psychoanalysis* (London: Karnac, 2001).

7. Steiner's 2001 (ibid.) study provides a close look at conditions in Europe through the period of Nazi acquisition of power. Early in 1937, Anna Freud wrote to Jones about the new nursery that she and Dorothy Burlingham had opened in Vienna, the Jackson Nursery, and of her anticipated pleasure in being able to observe directly these twelve children, ranging in age from six months to two and a half years. She would be in a position to learn a great deal. She writes to Jones: "Federn told me that Frau Klein will come to Vienna in the spring. I hope she will be interested in the new *Kinderheim.* In any case I would be happy to show it to her." Anna Freud may have been anticipating her move to London, Klein's territory, so to speak, with a wish for amity between them. We see here something of the pleasure she took in observing children outside the analytic setting. I recall, in 1963, when I was a visiting student at the Hampstead Clinic, that she continued to exhibit a deep joy when discussing observations made in the Normal Nursery. This attitude was rather different from Klein's interventionist proclivity. Incidentally, this wish for a friendly tie to Klein may be what Winnicott meant when he referred much later to the idea that the two women "had a relationship in the Vienna days."

8. Pearl King and Riccardo Steiner, eds., *The Freud-Klein Controversies, 1941–45* (London: Routledge, 1991).

9. In a discussion of the letters between Sigmund Freud and Jones, the historian Paul Roazen quotes a 1927 letter from Freud: "Mrs. Klein's view of the ego-ideal in children

seems quite impossible to me and is in contradiction to all my postulates." When Jones wrote to inquire what Freud found so "heretical" in Klein, Freud replied: "Naturally I criticize her for denying half the facts, while the other—what you call 'the phantastic part'—is alone proclaimed, in an excellent way. This makes her viewpoint 'heretical,' contains an unfortunate similarity to Jung's, and, like his, is an important step toward making analysis unreal and impersonal. . . . All our apostates always grasped part of the truth and wanted to declare it as the whole truth." The words "unreal and impersonal" are prescient. Paul Roazen, *The Historiography of Psychoanalysis* (London: Transaction Publishing, 2001), p. 119.

10. Pearl King, "Activities of British Psychoanalysts during the Second World War and the Influence of Their Inter-disciplinary Collaboration on the Development of Psychoanalysis in Great Britain," *Internatonal Review of Psychoanalysis* 16 (1989): pt. 1: 15–34.

11. As we shall see later on, Winnicott's attacks on Klein and Kleinians were responses to an arrogant attitude that implied a privileged access to the truth. Central here was Klein's assertion that she always included the actual behavior of the mother in her formulations about the mental life of the child. This was self-evidently false. Schmideberg was pursuing a personal agenda, based primarily on her firsthand experience with a mother who "pushed ideas into her."

12. In 1988, the play *Mrs. Klein* by Nicholas Wright (London: Nick Hern Books, 1988), was staged in London and, later on, in New York. Margaret Little, who had been a patient of Winnicott's and later an analyst and colleague, sent me a program and a letter: "Marion Milner and I saw it a fortnight ago. . . . I think the play very clever and amusing, though it's a not too kind caricature of three persons, all mourning. It's closely based on Grosskurth's book (which isn't too accurate in places), but it brings out more strongly the just-unconscious use of the splitting mechanism. Mrs. K. splits her daughter into Melitta and Dr. Schmideberg, and Melitta from Paula [Heimann, a close follower and analysand of Klein's]. Her own marriage and Paula's are already split; she tries to split Melitta's marriage and Melitta from Glover [Melitta's analyst], and her son from his girl friend. Eventually, of course, in fact, she all but split the British Ps. Anal. Society, which has even now not fully recovered."

13. See Winnicott's paper "The Depressive Position in Emotional Development" (1954–55).

14. See Joseph Aguayo, "When Differences Matter: Clinical Affinities and Divergences between D. W. Winnicott, Melanie Klein and the Kleinians at the British Psychoanalytic Institute, 1935–1951," lecture delivered to audiences in San Francisco and Seattle, 1999, for a detailed description of the early development of their differences.

15. See David Locke, *Science as Writing* (New Haven, Conn.: Yale University Press, 1992).

16. Alexander Newman's 1995 book is titled *Non-compliance in Winnicott's Words* (London: Free Association Books).

17. See his 1967 talk to the 1952 Club in *Psycho-Analytic Explorations*.

18. Milner's remarks, from the commemorative meeting for Donald Winnicott, January 19, 1972, appear in *The British Psycho-Analytical Society and The Institute of Psycho-Analysis Scientific Bulletin*, no. 57 (1972).

Chapter 2

1. *Babies and Their Mothers* (1987).

2. Clare Britton Winnicott, "DWW: A Reflection," in *Between Reality and Fantasy*, ed. Simon. A. Grolnick and Leonard Barkin, in collaboration with Werner Muensterberger. (Northvale, N.J.: Aronson, 1978), p. 19.

3. Personal communication, Clare Winnicott, 1979.

4. Interview, Peter Woolland, 1988.

5. Edmund Gosse, *Father and Son: A Study of Two Temperaments* (1907), ed. Peter Abbs (London: Penguin Books, 1986).

6. Especially *The Origin of Species* (1859).

7. Typescript of taped interview of Clare Winnicott by Michael Neve, June 1983.

8. An advertisement, made available to me through the research of Barry S. Poland, styled his company, W. Woods & Son, as "Sole Proprietors of Woods' Areca Nut Tooth Paste, Woods' hair Grower, Quinine, Cantbar, & Rosemary, With or Without Grease, as preferred, Woods' far-famed Cough Linctus, &c., &c., &c., &c."

9. François Bedarida, *A Social History of England* (1967; reprint, London: Routledge, 1990).

10. Ibid., p. 12.

11. See frontispiece, kindly provided by Peter Woolland.

12. The house was built about 1850 (letter from Crispin Gill, March 18, 1993).

13. Interview with Stanley Ede, Edinburgh, 1988, by Madeleine Davis and Robert Rodman.

14. Madeleine Davis thought that this gesture might have been a way of stimulating herself out of depressive feelings.

15. Interview with Joyce Coles, 1988.

16. Copy in files of author. Winnicott sent the poem to Jim Taylor, brother of his first wife, Alice, which indicates the degree to which Jim remained Winnicott's confidant.

17. Newspaper clippings kindly provided by Victor Barton.

18. Interview with Marion Milner, 1996.

19. "The Tree" (see chap. 20), written in 1963, tells of his mother's depression and the effect of his conviction that it was up to him to bring her back to life, an image juxtaposing the weaning idea and the resurrection idea. That is, he was placed in the position of being too stimulating, and yet was required to be stimulating enough to induce liveliness in his depressed mother.

20. This information is the product of assiduous research conducted by Victor Barton and Barry Poland, residents of the Plymouth area who responded to my request for information with extraordinary devotion and kindness. A good deal of data came from the scrutiny of street directories for Plymouth in the nineteenth century.

21. *Western Morning News*, September 15, 1946.

22. Ibid.

23. He was elected a member of the Plymouth Town Council and afterward alderman, and was twice mayor, once of the town of Plymouth, in 1906–7, and again of Greater Plymouth, in 1921–22. Also in 1910, during the mayoralty of Thomas Greek Wills, he held the office of deputy mayor. He was also appointed a justice of the peace, in which capacity he acted as a judge for minor offenses. Both in his municipal capacity and in other ways he did much to promote the public welfare of Plymouth. He was actively associated with the inauguration of the Plymouth Civic Guide of Help, later the Council of Social Service, and of the Dunford Street Nursing Association, and gave his full support to the Church Extension Movement in the Church of England, which has led to the building of so many places of worship in the suburban parts of Plymouth. It was he who presented the Mayflower memorial on the Barbican. For his many public services he was knighted in 1924 and received the Freedom of the City of Plymouth in 1934.

24. *Western Morning News* interview.

25. C. Winnicott, "DWW," p. 23.

26. According to Madeleine Davis.

27. "He early became identified with the King Street Wesleyan Church, where he taught Sunday School, and in 1876 became Honorary Secretary to the Class for Biblical Instruction. In 1879–80 the Wesleyan Church on Mutley Plain was built, and he was one of the founders and a constant member, doing much in obtaining and contributing funds for improvements, and he acted as one of the Stewards for the rest of his life. He also held the offices of Circuit Steward and of Honorary Treasurer for the Theological Colleges of the district, and was a member of the Wesleyan Synod." Obituary notice in *Transactions of the Plymouth Institution* 21 (1947–49).

28. Donald said as much in a talk he gave late in life. Address to 1952 Club, 1967, in *Psycho-Analytic Explorations*.

29. Research of Victor Barton.

30. Perhaps they were already there at Christmas 1898, when, Donald later recalled, he received a gift from Switzerland, which his parents had visited.

31. Marie Winnicott, who married John Woolland (I met both of them in 1988) and had two children, Cynthia (Sandilands), who lived in Vancouver, British Columbia, and Peter; and Dorothy, who married a man named Rhodes and had three children.

32. Victor Winnicott, who married Evelyn Balkwill, became a beloved Boy Scout leader and was in charge of the family business for some years. S. Brown writes (February 24, 1993) that "he led a very varied life and was somewhat eccentric to say the least, although a real gentleman, very distinguished in looks and manners. . . . He met an untimely end by drowning off his yacht in the 1950's." Stewart Watts-Wills wrote (February 28, 1993) that "the loss of the business affected Victor Winnicott and he became somewhat isolated from society and lived on his yacht just cruising around Plymouth Sound or local places. . . . [H]e was found drowned in the Sound." Victor had no children. His surviving brother Harold, who had helped run the business, died in 1969. He had a son, Robert, who died in the British retreat at Dieppe in 1942. Russell, the third brother, died in the Great War in 1917. C. May wrote on March 8, 1993, to say that he had bought a house in Harley, and that "among rubbish in the garage, I found a medallion, as issued for war dead, in the name of Russell Winnicott."

33. Ede interview, 1988.

34. Another side of his goodness may be glimpsed in the recollection by a former employee, not inconsistent with other such reports, to the effect that in the 1930s, the pay was £1 per month, with no annual increment. Employees "had to ask Sir Frederick individually, Oliver Twist style, for any increase." The pay was low, even for that era, but "the Winnicotts had their choice of staff" (letter from P. M. Sharp, February 28, 1993). There is another bitter letter from a member of the staff who recalled being obliged to walk home and back the following morning, in heavy rain, when Sir Frederick, and Donald as well, failed to offer her a ride.

35. Personal communication, Clare Winnicott, 1979.

36. Letter from Mary Gamble, 1994.

37. Newspaper clipping from the *Western Evening Herald*, Herald Property advertisement, undated, supplied by Hannah Henry.

38. Letter from Mary Gamble, 1994.

39. Material supplied by Victor Barton and Barry Poland.

40. Guy Fleming, *Plymouth Bygones* (Exeter: Devon Books, 1991).

41. Research of Victor Barton.

42. Kenneth Grahame, *The Wind In The Willows* (New York: Charles Scribner's Sons, 1908).

43. According to Clare, he rode a bicycle "with his feet on the handlebars. Till *very* late in life. And a policeman stopped him and said, 'Fancy an old man like you setting an example for everybody!' Coming down Haverstock Hill with his feet on the handlebars." Interview with Clare by Michael Neve, 1983.

44. Fleming, *Plymouth Bygones*, p. 38.

45. "From this point he started coming bottom of the class. Blotting everything, blotting his copybook, shoving things around, torturing flies, pulling their wings off. . . . He wanted to find this other dimension of himself." Neve interview with Clare Winnicott, 1983.

46. Paul Roazen, *The Historiography of Psychoanalysis*, p. 175.

47. This was about the time his maternal grandfather died. In the chain of speculation that emerges from Winnicott's disclosure to Marion Milner, this grandfather looms large.

48. "Mother, sisters, nanny, sometimes a governess, mother's sister Aunt Delia often present." Neve interview with Clare Winnicott, 1983.

49. Address to the 1952 Club, in *Psycho-Analytic Explorations*.

50. The work of Donald Kuspit, historian of art who is psychoanalytically trained, throws a brilliant light on situations that, in my view, reflect Winnicott's, with special emphasis on the role of the spontaneous gesture in the psychology he would eventually promulgate. Kuspit writes in *The Cult of the Avant-Garde Artist* (Cambridge: Cambridge University Press, 1993) p. 62: "To express unconscious desire spontaneously is to defy the world's denial of spontaneity as a threat to consciousness. This is another manifestation of the world's indifference to the inner life of the individual. The world cannot imagine any-

thing beyond the small field of consciousness that it systematically cultivates. It brings desire itself into the field, conventionalizing it into a system of meaning, believing that it has thereby diminished or domesticated it. The world can accept spontaneity only in stylized form (not just in a strictly controlled situation). Like a Prometheus throwing off his chains, the spontaneous eruption of desire destroys the world's systems of meaning, rebelliously replacing them with madness—the 'meaninglessness'—of unconscious desire." In this densely packed meditation on the modern and the postmodern, Kuspit gives a proper context for the struggle that Winnicott faced from within psychoanalysis, a struggle that undoubtedly began in the context of his experiences in early life.

51. His father wrote him on August 8, 1940: "I cannot think however you got the idea that I ever had any desire to question your charitable or other gifts but you do know I have strong views in regard to Bank overdrafts and expenditures in excess of income. . . . Am afraid I am not interested in the suggested '£500 a year scheme.'" (Donald had suggested that his father provide that amount without specifiying particular expenses. Sir Frederick was continuously interested in what his son was spending and frequently offered to defray certain expenses, such as those incurred for dental work.) Donald was forty-four years of age, earning a living, in possession of private investments, yet he continued to show financial dependence on his father. On July 9, 1941, in a letter addressed to "My dearly beloved son," Frederick asked: "Would you like me to post you a cheque for £100 (and to which address?) If so I would love to do so." The fifty-eight letters from Sir Frederick that Donald kept are loving, appreciative, and supportive.

52. Interview with Martin James, 1988.

53. A recording of Winnicott's 1962 talk to the candidates of the Los Angeles Psychoanalytic Institute, provided to me by the late Dr. William Brunie, gives a strong impression that the speaker is an elegant and thoughtful professional woman.

54. See chap. 22.

55. General social conditions during Donald's childhood were undoubtedly reflected in his own home. "The Rev. Hugh Price Hughes, the 'conscience of Wesleyanism,' could congratulate himself in the first years of the twentieth century that the strictness of Protestantism had imprinted on British feminism a moral austerity that would protect it against the more dangerous aspects of Continental feminism." At the time, "the middle class ideal . . . was 'the blushing young maiden.' Woman was transformed into a sexless figure, and there was a lot of truth in the joke about Dickens' heroines—'angels without legs.' There was also widespread ignorance of the facts of life, from Dr. Acton, a reputable scientist, who remarked, 'Happily for them the majority of women are not much troubled by sexual desire: the best mothers, spouses and housewives know little or nothing of the pleasures of the senses; their strongest feelings are devoted to home life, children, and their domestic duties'—down to another learned doctor who, just before 1914, told his students at Oxford: 'Speaking as a doctor, I can tell you that nine out of ten women are indifferent to sex or actively dislike it; the tenth, who enjoys it, will always be a harlot.'" Bedarida, *A Social History of England*, p. 117.

56. Winnicott makes a passing reference to the sexuality of the mother in *The Child, the Family, and the Outside World*. The unelaborated comment is similar to another, elsewhere, in which he says that he never left out the father.

Chapter 3

1. Derek Baker, *Partnership in Excellence* (Cambridge: Cambridge University Press, 1975), p. 8.

2. Ibid. Donald became an Anglican convert. Clare (Neve interview, 1983) said that he was confirmed in his mid-twenties, just prior to his first marriage.

3. James Hilton, *Goodbye Mr. Chips* (Boston: Little, Brown, 1934).

4. Derek Baker, *Partnership in Excellence* (Cambridge: Cambridge University Press, 1975).

5. *St. Mary's Gazette*, 67, no. 5 (July-August 1961), pp. 137–38.

6. Brett Kahr, *D. W. Winnicott: A Biographical Portrait* (London: Karnac, 1996).

7. Roazen, *Historiography*.

8. Dr. Judith Issroff has written: "Once he told me he had restrained his impulse to throw himself into the dirty, cold, river Cam." From "John Bowlby and Donald Woods Winnicott: Personal Encounters with Two Great British Child Psychiatrists and Psychoanalysts," presentation given in Birmingham and Barcelona, November 2001, sent to me by Dr. Issroff via E-mail.

9. Strachey obituary (1969).

10. Letter to the author.

11. This book was sent to me by Hannah Henry, an old friend of Donald's. The swastika originated in India and Central Asia and was a widely displayed good luck symbol throughout Europe. Kipling combined a swastika with his signature in a circle as a personal logo (article by Sarah Boxer, *New York Times*)..

12. This material is adapted with the kind consent of Brett Kahr from his *Biographical Portrait*.

13. Masud Khan, of whom more later, told Clare Winnicott's interviewer Michael Neve (1978) that Donald had been a member of the Plymouth Brethren, a fundamentalist sect, which she hotly denied and for which there is no evidence. It does seem that bicycling was to be a long-standing pleasure for Donald. Khan's foreword to *Winnicott and Paradox* (first published in French in 1984) contains other errors, starting with his calling Winnicott's father Sir George Winnicott, and stating with authority that Donald damaged his hip at school, that in the First World War he became an orderly for the St. John's Ambulance Service, and that his first wife was an opera singer who went mad. See foreword to Anne Clancier and Jeannine Kalmanovitch, *Winnicott and Paradox: From Birth to Creation*, trans. Alan Sheridan (London: Tavistock, 1987). Khan, whose relationship with Winnicott was intensely ambivalent, was given to misstatements that combined disrespect for truth with a privileged authoritative tenor. One of his analysands told me, "In plain English he was just a plain goddamn liar!!"

14. Copies in author's file.

15. C. Winnicott, "DWW."

16. Letter from Frederick Winnicott, July 4, 1938. "Your cheery letter posted at midnight on Sunday reached us in time to flavour our cold mutton lunch this morning—which speaks well for our inland past."

17. Interview with Rosa Taylor, 1988, by Madeleine Davis and Robert Rodman.

Chapter 4

1. *St. Mary's Gazette* 67, no. 5 (July–August 1961): 137–38.

2. Anna Freud, *The Ego and the Mechanisms of Defense* (New York: International Universities Press, 1936).

3. Interview, 1988.

4. Speech at St. Paul's School, 1945, quoted in Madeleine Davis and David Wallbridge, *Boundary and Space: An Introduction to the Work of D.W. Winnicott* (Harmondsworth: Penguin Books, 1983).

5. Kahr, *Biographical Portrait*.

6. In author's file.

7. C. Winnicott, 1983 interview and "DWW."

8. Clare Winnicott, "DWW," p. 26.

9. *St. Mary's Gazette* 67, no. 5 (July–August 1961).

Chapter 5

1. The only record of his presence that remains is his signature on the student register on November 2, 1917 (letter from registrar, April 27, 1993).

2. *St. Mary's Gazette* 67, no. 5 (July–August 1961). op. cit.

3. The Pfister book was undoubtedly *The Psychoanalytic Method* (1913), trans. C. R. Payne (London: Kegan Paul, 1917).

4. Roazen, *Historiography.*

5. Kahr, *Biographical Portrait*, p. 37.

6. Letters to and from Arthur Rosenthal, 1958.

7. J. P. M. Tizard, "Donald W. Winnicott," *International Journal Of Psycho-Analysis* 52 (1971): 225–28. Tizard wrote in "Donald Winnicott: The President's View of a Past President," *Journal of the Royal Society of Medicine* (April 24, 1981): "When I went to Paddington Green in 1949 Winnicott was seeing run-of-the-mill outpatients. In the passage outside his large consultung room was a row of chairs occupied by mothers and children. Those who had arrived earlier were on chairs around his consulting room and he conducted his interviews in their presence and in that of observers, including occasionally mine. [Tizard was a good friend.] The presence of others would be regarded by most doctors as prohibitively disturbing, but the fact was that within a few minutes of a child sitting down by the desk both the child and Dr. Winnicott were oblivious to the presence of anyone else. A good example of his acceptance by, and communication with, children is a story told me by Mrs. Winnicott about what happened when he was to visit a Danish family for the second time after an interval of a few years. The children remembered his playing with them very well and were delighted at the prospect of again meeting an Englishman who could speak Danish. When their father pointed out that Dr. Winnicott could not speak a word of their difficult language his children simply did not believe him. . . . I recollect that Dr. Winnicott sat at a large desk in the middle of the room. But there were little tables around the room so that children could sit up and play or draw. This was an important part of the consultation."

8. His father had been instrumental in getting Nancy Astor elected to Parliament. Neve interview with Clare Winnicott.

9. He describes the theft of the "Bart's gun," doubtless a treasure symbolic of the school and hospital, by students of University College Hospital. After initial defeat, outnumbered as he and his compatriots were, "a mass meeting was held and it was decided to recapture that gun that very night at whatever cost. U.C.H. was at the Coliseum enjoying itself, and at the gate we found 20 policemen who had been summoned by the Provost to prevent mischief. We demanded our gun and since we were 200 to the police 20 a party was allowed in without a fight to loosen the gun from its rather secure moorings. After an hour we were on the road rejoicing. With the gun in our midst we marched down Charing + road, Trafalgar Sq., along the Strand up King's way, home, singing 'Who's got the gun? Bart's!' and 'Bart's patients never die, They simply fade away.'" He gets excitedly into his description of the adventure, as he does in other letters about other adventures, evidence of the deep love for life and the urge to communicate that were characteristic of Winnicott throughout his life.

10. This two-word sentence could be thought to imply that at the time he was himself a patient. There is no collateral evidence for this. Subsequently, when a medical student friend was already in analysis, Winnicott decided that this was what he wanted to do as well.

Chapter 6

1. *St. Mary's Hospital Gazette* 67, no. 5 (July-August 1961) .

2. Clare Winnicott, "DWW."

3. *St. Mary's Hospital Gazette*, 67, no. 5 (July-August 1961). This continuous awareness of the unity of mind and body, physical pediatrics and the life of the child's imagination and emotions, gave support to others who followed, notably Benjamin Spock and T. Berry Brazelton in the United States, against the strains of professional medicine that tore pediatrics away from child development. Winnicott tried all his life to foster openness in this area but felt in the end that he had not succeeded. Child psychiatry (part of the title of a posthumous book in which he demonstrates how a psychoanalyst may help children within the brief span of an hour or two) became alien territory to the pediatrician. The unification of

fields of thought also echoes his spiritual origins among the Romantic poets, for whom art and science had not yet become divided. Objective pediatrics should, he felt, have been indissolubly linked with subjective comprehension of the inner life of the child under care. Furthermore, the action of the human imagination upon the "not-me" external world was also a preoccupation, which reveals Winnicott's intrinsic belief in the unavoidably subjective nature of human experience.

4. Typescript of an article intended for the *St. Mary's Hospital Gazette*, sent to Clare Winnicott on June 15, 1971.

5. *British Journal of Children's Diseases* (1932).

6. Letter to Esther Bick, 1953, in *The Spontaneous Gesture*.

7. Talk to 1952 Club, 1967, in *Psycho-Analytic Explorations*.

8. In a talk to a group of doctors and nurses at St. Luke's Church, Hatfield, October 18, 1970, published in "Cure," in *Home Is Where We Start From: Essays by a Psychoanalyst* (New York: Norton, 1986).

9. Letter to Robert Tod, 1969, in *The Spontaneous Gesture*. When he was offered the opportunity to have inpatients, however, he rejected it out of concern that he would become too hardened to the children's pain. He wanted to preserve his sensitivity. On September 5, 1967, he wrote to Mrs. Alfred Torrie (author's file) quoting a paper by Thomas Main ("The Ailment") on the necessity for objectivity in the doctor and an anecdote about "not taking beds."

10. Lady Fleming showed me the culture, preserved as an icon of scientific discovery, in 1958, when for a month I was a visiting student at St. Mary's myself.

11. C. Winnicott, "DWW."

12. *St. Mary's Hospital Gazette* 67, no. 5 (July-August, 1961).

13. Letter to John Rawlings Rees, 1963, and other sources.

14. This volume was Winnicott's only attempt to systematize his psychoanalytic views, and is notable also for containing a lengthy consideration of libido theory. Dr. Judith Issroff, who was supervised by Winnicott for five years and was close to his widow, told me (October 28, 2001) that Clare asked her to edit "The Primer" (later known as *Human Nature*), but when it was published seventeen years later, most of her editorial work had been removed.

15. Tizard, "Donald W. Winnicott."

16. See *Julius Caesar* 5.5.73. The memorial meeting took place on January 19, 1972.

Chapter 7

1. C. Winnicott, "DWW"; letter from Barry Poland, March 31, 1993.

2. Hannah Henry gave me her copy of a book called *The Doorkeeper, and Other Poems*, by John W. Taylor, "with a memoir by his wife," 3d ed. (London: Longmans, Green, 1932). It is inscribed, "Queen from Alice, Feb. 28th 1936."

3. Hannah ("Queen") Henry wrote to me after a friend informed her of an advertisement I had placed in a Plymouth newspaper seeking information about the Winnicott family and business. She sent me many letters, pictures, and memorabilia relating to Donald and Alice. She was already in her nineties and was, to my knowledge, the only survivor from the early days of Winnicott's first marriage. Her recollections are invaluable.

4. In 1928 Jim Ede and his wife also bought a house in Hampstead, at 1 Elm Road. Obituary, *Daily Telegraph*, probably 1989.

5. Dr. Taylor was actually a gynecologist.

6. Kahr, *Biographical Portrait*.

7. C. Winnicott, "DWW."

8. Winnicott's address at birth had been Gordon Terrace, Plymouth.

9. Personal communication, 1979.

10. Letter, February 10, 1993.

11. "I was so pleased he had such happiness with Clare, and fulfilled with real love, I know that it was consummated Lilian Bently told me." Letter from Hannah Henry, May 14, 1993.

12. In 1993 I consulted with an astute neurologist friend about Alice's disorder, who wrote, "I can only say that it *sounds* 'organic.'" It would certainly be consonant with a sleep-disorder (of the narcolepsy type) but also with the effects of chronic sleep-deprivation, but perhaps even more with an organic lethargy (most likely, at the time, of encephalitis lethargica sort). The 'never looking as if she had washed or bathed'—the *indifference* implied—could be 'psychiatric,' but again could go along with an organic lethargy and indifference."

13. Personal communication, 1988.

14. Letters and interview, 1996.

15. Interview with Martin James, 1988.

16. Interview with Madeleine Davis and Robert Rodman, 1988.

17. Alice Winnicott wrote to Hannah Henry on March 26, 1936, thanking her for the flowers: "1/3 of the primroses went to Monique who is recovering from appendicitis. 1/3 went to St. Paul's and we kept the rest ourselves. So you see we all enjoyed them—also the little just-born violets. Mine are only now withering. That is the one snag of putting flowers in water—in town worse than the country. Accanal (spelling) flowers being so scarce one tends to hang onto them, after really they have had their day and should have gone. Lawrence's mother asked the [. . .] at St. Paul if he knew where the flowers came from, so I sent word that the snowdrops had come from Doughty's old home where he was born. I wonder if she had the message. It is raining here 'hen wraig a ffyn' as they say in N. Wales —(meaning 'old women + sticks') after being dry for so long. Fortunately we had a bee-eautiful bonfire on Saturday last + burnt up most of the garden rubbish. Just going to town about a picture. Wish you could come with me. Lots of love from Alice."

18. A threshold memory. Others too have recollected Donald standing in a threshold, a place of transition, of hellos and good-byes.

19. It was located at Benton End, Hadleigh, Suffolk. Letter from Marion Milner, May 16, 1993.

20. Milner says that this "Jeeves" had been living with Sir Cedric since the 1920s.

21. This must have been spring or summer 1949, when Donald and Alice's visit to Suffolk is documented in a letter to his friend the Jungian analyst Michael Fordham. The patient in question was undoubtedly Margaret Little. Marion Milner met Donald there, heard about his heart attack, and advised him to leave Alice. In her letter of May 16, 1993, however, Milner says that Donald did not have a patient there at the time she talked with him about leaving Alice. Either she was unaware that Little was in analysis with Winnicott, or I have conflated at least two occasions into one.

22. Where Madeleine Davis and I interviewed them.

23. Interview, 1988.

24. Interview, 1988. They had met in August, when Donald and Alice were going to their cottage in New Quay, Gloucestershire.

25. Here we see Winnicott's unattractive willingness to make use of an employee for personal purposes, although the mixture of professional and personal seems to have been characteristic of his relationship to Coles, who was pressed into service o behalf of patients as well, and who felt that Winnicott had a genius for inducing guilt.

26. Interview with Madeleine Davis and me, 1988.

27. See his article on psychosomatic aspects of coronary thrombosis in *Psycho-Analytic Explorations*, in which he speaks of the subject of cooling.

28. Kahr, *Biographical Portrait*.

29. Introduction to *The Spontaneous Gesture*.

30. See undated letter from Clare Britton to Winnicott quoted in chapter 10.

Chapter 8

1. Roazen, *Historiography*. He described himself as "originally . . . an inhibited young Englishman, with few outlets in fantasy, except music." This phrase, included in a type-script "A Meeting with Donald Winnicott in 1964" was not included in Roazen's published account in *Historiography*.

2. "Well do I remember my first meeting with [Jones], in 1923, when I went as a rather inhibited young man asking whether anything could be done about it. He alarmed me by giving me an advance list of my symptoms. That Dr. Jones was able to refer me to an analyst was entirely due to the fact that he had himself gone out to Vienna in 1905, and subsequently, and had brought Freud's work back, and had established it here in London. I forgot to pay my consultation fee, and now at a rather late date I wish to thank him, not only for myself, but on behalf of all of us in this country who have had a chance to make use of psycho-analysis in the search for personal health." This was Winnicott's introduction to the eighth Ernest Jones lecture, at which Margaret Mead gave a speech about "Changing Patterns of Parent-Child Relations in an Urban World."

3. Roazen, *Historiography*, p. 178.

4. *Bloomsbury/Freud: The Letters of James and Alix Strachey, 1924–1925.* Ed. Perry Meisel and Walter Kendrick. (New York: Basic Books, 1985).

5. As late as the 1960s Joseph Sandler, already deeply respected as a theoretician and clinician at the Hampstead Clinic under its director Anna Freud, felt it necessary to acquire a medical degree from the University of Leiden. He already had a Ph.D.

6. *Bloomsbury/Freud*, p. 166.

7. *Friends and Apostles: The Correspondence of Rupert Brooke and James Strachey*, ed. Keith Hale (New Haven, Conn.: Yale University Press, 1998).

8. Ibid.

9. *Bloomsbury/Freud*, p. 256.

10. The idea being that the bank would not recognize the handwriting and therefore would not render cash.

11. Interview with Joyce Coles by Madeleine Davis and Robert Rodman, 1988.

12. We should take seriously this view of Donald's state of mind, for it helps to explain his behavior over the remainder of his life. He had little to say about fathers and much to say about mothers. He was impotent. (Would the "bare" woman castrate him?) Was it the difficulty he had expressing rage at his father that prevented him from having a more masculine identity? Or was it his mother's inhibitions against excitement with her baby at the breast that imposed an early limit on his instinctual expressiveness, setting the stage for a later problem with his father? This would be the bottling up of aggressiveness required for intercourse. (Boys need a father to kill.) He cultivated his capacity to feel and express hatred as a means of transcending his difficulty. Thus, he worked to transcend the sense of detachment (see chapter 1). Rage at father was expressed as scotomatizing (creating a blind spot) fathers, which was accompanied by a scotomatization of himself as a father. That is, he never became one, though there were, throughout his life, substitute children, in the form of members of scout troops, child patients, foster children, and the children of his friend Jimmy Ede.

13. Strachey later had a heterosexual affair while Alix had a homosexual one. Robert Graves, one of Winnicott's correspondents, made a distinction between false and true homosexuals. As discussed by Paul Fussell in his book *The Great War and Modern Memory* (London: Oxford, 1975), Graves thought that their experiences in public schools pressured many young men in a homosexual direction which eventually gave way to rooted heterosexuality. Perhaps that was the case with James Strachey.

14. In a second version of his obituary, he writes: "In addition to the technical lessons that this relationship taught me, it was also very enjoyable in other ways. The Strachey household in Gordon Square was, of course, one of the principal survivors of the great Bloomsbury literary and artistic tradition, and one felt able to make some sort of peripheral contact with it in these supervisory sessions. On pleasant summer days we would go into Gordon Square gardens and conduct our discussion sitting on the grass and trying to avoid the offerings of the birds; this was really supervision without tears—in spite of my having been a patient on whom Strachey once commented that no one would have ever discovered the Oedipus complex from a man like this. [Repressed anti-Dad impulses?] Once he advised me that the best thing would be to make a *deep* interpretation. [The pa-

tient said] 'That's the *last* thing I would have thought of, Doctor,' which Strachey found as amusing as I did. Another occasion I remember with pleasure was when my wife and I were invited to dinner at Gordon Square; this was followed by an evening of Mozart quartets reproduced on what was then a very advanced form of record player. On the other hand, I have cause to regret another time, when Strachey offered me a couple of tickets for Glyndebourne, an institution which he always supported with great enthusiasm and expert knowledge. Unfortunately, it would have involved canceling my patient's session, so on super-ego grounds I regretfully declined the very generous offer. I am still not sure if this was dictated by a real super-ego, or whether I thought to please Strachey by this demonstration of my devotion to duty. I have little doubt now that he must have thought me a frightful prig."

15. The 1952 letter to Klein and the 1954 letter to Riviere are in *The Spontaneous Gesture.*

16. "Short Communication on Enuresis (1930).

17. This may be hyperbole.

18. In a discussion of a paper by Sandler in *Psycho-Analytic Explorations.*

19. According to her obituary in *Psycho-Analytic Explorations*, Isaacs joined the British Psycho-Analytic Society in 1921 and, "was among the earliest to sense the further sources of knowledge which were . . . opening up" with Melanie Klein's ideas. When they were fellow candidates, Isaacs was going through her second round of training, including a new training analysis, undertaken because of her wish to learn more.

20. See his letter to Klein November, 1952 in *The Spontaneous Gesture.*

21. For Klein's paper, see chap. 9, n. 15. Glover resigned from the British Society in 1944 and obtained a membership in the Swiss Society in order to continue as a member of the International. He responded to criticism of his resignation by Franz Alexander in a letter to LeRoy Maeder of the American Psychoanalytic Association, the relevant portion of which: "I wish to state as briefly as possible the decisive reason for my resignation. It was that the training of psycho-analysis in Britain was being organized on a tendentious, non-scientific basis which whether those responsible realized it or not (only a few did not realize it) meant that psycho-analytic training in Britain would be determined by factors of political (i. e. numerical) power rather than by appreciation of the basic principles of psycho-analysis." (Paul Roazen. *Oedipus in Britain: Edward Glover and the Struggle over Klein* (New York: Other Press, 2000), p. 159.

Chapter 9

1. According to Grosskurth, *Melanie Klein*; and Joseph Aguayo,"Interview with Hanna Segal," *Fort da: The Journal of the Northern California Society for Psychoanalytic Psychology* (Spring 1999).

2. Perhaps the deflection from direct contact with the sought-after nourishment of analysis from Klein was, for Donald, an echo of his deflection from the breast of his overexcited mother.

3. Athol Hughes, "Personal Experiences—Professional Interests: Joan Riviere and Femininity," *International Journal of Psychoanalysis* 78 (1997), p. 899.

4. See Riccardo Steiner's Introduction to the *Freud-Jones Correspondence.*

5. Ibid., p. 475, Freud to Jones, May 11, 1922.

6. Grosskurth, *Melanie Klein*, p. 206.

7. *The Inner World and Joan Riviere: Collected Papers, 1920–1958*, ed. Athol Hughes (London: Karnac, 1991).

8. Her theory is based on Melanie Klein's conception that the baby experiences "depressive anxiety" when realizing that the frustrating "bad" mother is also the gratifying and loving "good" mother. Riviere's idea is that patients who respond to what others would experience as analytic progress by getting worse are so preoccupied with saving their internal objects (which have been destroyed by hate and are in dire need of ongoing, reparative

love), that they cannot allow themselves to be diverted by receiving the help of the analyst. These "internal objects" derive from objects that were originally external, such as the mother above all, although in Klein's view, the fantasy life of the child is preeminent in creating these internal objects.

9. *Collected Papers*, p. 151.

10. Sigmund Freud, "Some Character Types Met with in Psycho-Analytic Work: II: Those Wrecked by Success" (1916) in *The Standard Edition of the Complete Psychological Works*, trans. James Strachey, 24 vols. (London: Hogarth Press, 1953–1974), 14:316.

11. Sigmund Freud, "Some Character Types Met with in Psycho-Analytic Work: I: The Exceptions" (1916), in *Standard Edition*: 14:312.

12. Anton Kris, "Freud's Treatment of a Narcissistic Patient," *International Journal of Psychoanalysis* 75 (1994): pt. 4, 649–64.

13. Athol Hughes, in *The Maturational Processes and the Facilitating Environment*, p. 32.

14. Leonard Shengold has written eloquently about the treatment of abused children, soul-murdered children, in *Soul Murder: The Effects of Childhood Abuse and Deprivation* (New Haven, Conn.: Yale University Press, 1989). He states: "We cure through love. Love for the analyst-therapist makes it possible for the patient to accept as his or her own the insight the analyst provides and evokes. If—it is a big, sometimes, alas, an impossible, if—the therapist or analyst can get the person prone to violence (too full of sadomasochism, conscious and unconscious) to care about him or her as a separate person, and to tolerate that caring, control over violence can at least be partially achieved or restored. The acquisition and toleration of love for another person are needed to temper the overload of murderous hatred and its associated terrors in those abused as children" (p. 273). Shengold has been driven by experience with severely traumatized patients to understand that they desperately require more than interpretations. He writes in a way that is entirely consistent with Winnicott's eventual commentary on the treatment of similar patients.

15. Melanie Klein, "A Contribution to the Psychogenesis of Manic-Depressive States" (1935), in *Contributions to Psycho-Analysis, 1921–1945: Developments in Child and Adolescent Psychology* (1948; reprint, New York: McGraw Hill, 1964).

16. Copies of all letters in author's file.

17. He would die in a few days; probably the analytic community was alerted to his failing condition.

18. Scott was seeing Alice for analysis.

19. Author's file.

Chapter 10

1. From which the Kleinian analyst Betty Joseph also graduated.

2. Joel Kanter, "The Untold Story of Clare and Donald Winnicott: How Social Work Influenced Modern Psychoanalysis," *Clinical Social Work Journal* 28, no. 3 (Fall 2000).

3. Remarks at memorial service, November 3, 1984, recalled by Kanter in an interview conducted by Alan Cohen, June 27, 1980.

4. Copies in author's file.

5. These were the Old Grammar School, Orchard Lea, Maitlands, Corner Cottage, and Lashbrook.

6. The article, "The Problem of Homeless Children," appeared in 1944.

7. On December 10, 1942, he wrote to a correspondent: "The way I manage my department is really not just a chance affair or a manifestation of pig-headed independence, but an expression of my conviction, now held for 20 years, that doctors should know psychological as well as physical medicine if they are to treat out-patients. Also I do not believe a team is ever so good as one person for treating one individual patient. . . . [A] very large number of patients are seen and 'treated,' and . . . there is only one person on the staff: i..e. myself, except when I happen to get hold of a good Psychiatric Social Worker. At present I have one and her name is Miss Norma Williams (paid by the hospital)."

8. Norma Williams had worked at the Tegel clinic in Berlin, where, on being assigned to work with an alcoholic at night, so that he wouldn't drink, came in drunk herself. She had lived with two autistic children in succession and had helped them. Winnicott heard about her and hired her to work at Paddington Green. After work at the clinic, they would "foregather" at her apartment near Regent's Park. She prided herself on how well she could live on next to nothing, though the clinic probably paid her.

9. Quoted in Daniel Berg, "Why Winnicott? A Personal Reflection," by Daniel Berg, manuscript, 1994.

10. Published in 1937 by Hogarth Press, a book that contains the essay, "Love, Guilt, and Reparation."

11. In the movie, adapted from a Broadway musical, a woman is seeing a psychoanalyst because she is immobilized by fears and doubts going back to childhood. According to Bruce Weber, in a review of the play's revival (*New York Times*, October 16, 2001), "An emotionally shriveled woman blooms into a life-embracing passion-monger." The main character, Liza, 'has a dream version of herself as more glamorous and ready for love than anyone knew.' William Zinsser writes that "the cure hinges on recalling the words to a tune from her childhood" (*Easy to Remember: The Great American Songwriters and Their Songs* [Jaffrey, N.H.: David Godine, 2000], p. 175.)

12. Both of Donald's sisters were lifelong activists in Girls' Clubs in the Plymouth area.

13. David Lehman writes in *The Last Avant-Garde: The Making of the New York School of Poets* (New York: Doubleday, 1998), p. 159, "Ashbery's love poems omit the name of the beloved out of a certain reticence, a reverence for mystery, which Mallarmé said was essential to any holy thing wishing to retain its holiness."

14. Interview with Michael Neve, 1978.

15. Berg, "Why Winnicott?"

16. Clare Winnicott, "DWW."

17. Neve interview; Berg, "Why Winnicott?"p. 30.

18. A surviving poem which they wrote together "after C. O. Conference at Southport" shows this playful side:

CLERIHEWS / Sometimes Mr. Craig / May seem a little vague. / But Prof. SIMEY— / Gor-Blimey!! / Mr. Brown / Will never paint the town. / Perhaps Mr. Brill / Will. / Edwin AINSKOW / Will leave a gap when his brains go. / A gap which Kenneth BRILL / Could fill. / Miss WANSBOROUGH-JONES / Is all skin and bones. / With Jane Rowell it's a different issue; / More subcutaneous tissue. / Miss CULLEN, known to the world as MEG, / Puts her head under her wing and stands / On one leg; / Miss WATSON, better known as BERYL, / Stands on both legs; ignore her at your peril!

Another poem, written by Donald alone, is quoted by Dr. Judith Issroff (via E-mail) November 11, 2001, "John Bowlby and Donald Woods Winnicott: Personal encounters with Two Great British Child Psychiatrists and Psychoanalysts"on the subject of the rabble-rousing racist Enoch Powell. This poem was included in a letter to Donald's good friend, pediatrician Peter Tizard:

If I could make Enoch's / knees knock / or set off a howl / in the Powell bowel / I'd feel cleaner.

19. Berg, "Why Winnicott?"

20. Personal communications, 1979, 1981.

Chapter 11

1. "Postscript: D.W.W. on D.W.W." (1967) in *Psychoanalytic Explorations* (Cambridge, Mass.: Harvard University Press, 1989), pp. 569–82.

2. On Klein, see Joseph Aguayo, "Historicising the Origins of Kleinian Psychoanalysis: Klein's Analytic and Patronal Relationships with Ferenczi, Abraham, and Jones, 1914–1927," *International Journal of Psychoanalysis* 78 (1997): 1165–82.

3. Grosskurth, *Melanie Klein*.

4. Freud himself, who reported the case of Little Hans, an analysis conducted through the boy's father, is not included.

5. King and Steiner, *Freud-Klein Controversies*, p. 16.

6. Alix Strachey characterized Anna Freud as "that open or secret sentimentalist" (*Bloomsbury/Freud*, December 14, 1924, p. 146).

7. All quotations in this discussion ibid., pp. 198–291.

8. The original transcripts have been lost.

9. For reference to Isaacs's letter, see *Freud-Klein Controversies*. And see my essay "Winnicott's Laughter," in *Humor and Psyche*, ed. James Baron (Hillsdale, N.J.: Analytic Press, 1998).

10. King and Steiner, *Freud-Klein Controversies*.

11. That is, before the church as a power structure came into being and distorted the original teachings of Jesus for its own purposes.

12. This struggle took place in the shadow of his internal effort to differentiate himself from his mother.

13. Her other son, Hans, died in 1934 while mountaineering. Her daughter Melitta Schmideberg, who called his death a suicide, had begun the violent deprecation of her mother the year before.

14. Copies of all the Klein letters referred to are in the author's file.

15. She had left London during the war to avoid danger, according to the Los Angeles Kleinian analyst Albert Mason (personal communication, July 2001).

16. Klein's devotion to her work, which was, for better or worse, fanatical, is evident through the generations. In the British Institute, candidates belonging to a particular group always took their first cases under the supervision of a member of that group. In the twenty-year period preceding the year 2001, however, not a single Kleinian candidate sought supervision from anyone but a Kleinian. Fifty percent of Independents did so (for their second cases) and 30 percent of what are now called contemporary Freudians did so. Further, the Melanie Klein Trust was found to be supplementing the fees to Kleinian supervisors so that Kleinian candidates could afford to adhere strictly to Kleinian training. This is fanaticism, emanating from its fountainhead and transmitted by her followers. What relation it has to science must be teased out. Klein averred that her teaching would be lost unless supported by those who understand and value it.

17. This is an interesting phrase, "one sidedness in our presentation," and only speculation can speak to the question of whether it represents a revealing slip of the pen or another, consciously intended meaning, or both.

18. Margaret Little, who wrote extensively about her experiences as Winnicott's patient, as well as on other subjects, wrote to me on May 13, 1987: "The letter seems to me characteristic of her—demanding attention and support, and total agreement; she insisted on the use of a language, as dictatorships do. And the people whose names she suggests as valuable supporters are really very odd. Gwen Evans followed her, but although didactic she was ineffective. Ronald MacDonald was a very lovable person; he did some quite valuable psychotherapy of a superficial kind, but he hadn't *any* idea what psychoanalysis was about! Sylvia Payne (who was a terrible old gossip) treated Klein for a time. She told me that Klein could have been a medium. I remember hearing Donald say of someone (I think Margaret Mahler) that she 'lacked humility.' My feeling is that it could have been said of Klein. She had a way of looking down her nose at one, with the air of an offended camel. I hear that Hannah Segal is determined to 'demolish Winnicott.' I think she has her work cut out. [. . .] Of course, I stand to get demolished too."

19. Winnicott was not being paid by Eric. Klein may still have been paying him. Here are the makings of a failure.

20. Fax, February 23, 2001.

21. The paper was read before the British Pscyho-Analytic Society on April 23, 1941. Klein attended.

22. See his 1967 talk in *Psycho-Analytic Explorations.*

23. King and Steiner, *Freud-Klein Controversies*, pp. 32–33.

24. Grosskurth, *Melanie Klein*, p. 255. "Quite clearly, Melanie dreaded pregnancy and her mother used this fear to separate her from Arthur as much as possible. Melanie could not have been altogether blind to Libussa's machinations. Was her mother going to punish her through the instrument of Arthur's penis? By becoming pregnant, her nerves would disintegrate. Libussa's stomach complaints would return, and her guilt at robbing her mother of something that did not rightfully belong to her would be intensified." Grosskurth continues: "One remembers that when Melanie was a small girl, her mother had told her that she was a surprise—that is, unwanted. It is not at all unlikely that she was subtly emphasizing that no man could ever love her, either—not her father, her husband, or anyone else. Perhaps it was Libussa herself who had told her that Emilie was her father's favorite. Libussa had been in fierce competition with Melanie over Emmanuel [Melanie's brother]. According to Libussa, Arthur blossomed when she was away, the children were much better off without her, and her own mother needed the absence in order to achieve serenity. Melanie was a pampered object, not a loved daughter, but a lap dog who had been taught to sit up and beg and to lie down passively."

25. Freud had used the word "unreal." Grosskurth, *Melanie Klein*, p. 59.

26. In Marjorie Brierley's words ("Problems Connecting with the Work of Melanie Klein," in *Trends in Psychoanalysis*, Institute of Psycho-Analysis, 1951), "Generalizations tended to be expressed in perceptual rather than conceptual terms and the language of phantasy was mixed with abstract terminology" (see King and Steiner, *Freud-Klein Controversies*).

27. They are, however, not incompatible with the search for conceptual laws, as long as the disorderly reality, from which it is always possible to extract examples that impose conditions on "law," is constantly kept in mind.

28. Greenson administered a fund provided by a former patient, one of the heirs to the fortune of Walter Annenberg. He made grants to himself for research in, among other subjects, failures in psychoanalysis, and he aided the sometimes financially strapped Hampstead Clinic in major ways. There is a large file of his correspondence in the research archive of the UCLA library.

29. This may well be the first instance of what Thomas Kuhn, in his posthumously published book *The Road to Structure* (Chicago: University of Chicago Press, 2001), calls "speciation" in psychoanalysis. Prior deviations from Freudian theory were effectively nullified by Freud himself during his lifetime. Kuhn believed that what he had previously called paradigm change in science gave rise to new subcategories, as previously unified areas gave rise to fragmentation.

Chapter 12

1. From Milner's obituary by Michael Parsons, *International Journal of Psychoanalysis* 82 (2001): 609.

2. Interestingly, these needs are described by Riviere in her paper on the negative therapeutic reaction. Perhaps this was Donald's influence on her.

3. Marion Milner, *The Hands of the Living God* (New York: International University Press, 1969).

4. Judith M. Hughes, *Reshaping the Psycho-Analytic Domain: The Work of Melanie Klein, W. R. D. Fairbairn, and D. W. Winnicott* (Berkeley: University of California Press, 1989), p. 151.

5. "She said she had lost her background as well as her feelings but also her appreciation of music, which before had been the center of her life but now was nothing but a jangle of sound. Perhaps music is the nearest of all the arts to communicating what can't be communicated." Marion Milner, "A Discussion of Masud Khan's Paper, 'In Search of the Dreaming Experience,'" in *The Suppressed Madness of Sane Men: Forty-Four Years of Exploring Psychoanalysis* (London: Tavistock Publications, 1987), p. 277.

6. Letter to me, September 30, 1991.

7. Sir Frederick Winnicott wrote to Donald on January 15, 1942: "We shall be quite interested to know how you and Alice are getting on with your live wire rather a risky experiment and quite plucky of Alice to take on. I hope she will not find it too trying."

8. In *Psychoanalytic Explorations*.

9. But with what real life evidence? He certainly worked hard to prevent Margaret Little from killing herself, and he gave much of himself to stave off the suicide of his patient in the Cassel Hospital (to be discussed later in connection with Thomas Main's paper "The Ailment").

10. Interview with the mother, 1991.

11. Letter, September 30, 1991.

12. Excerpt from fax from Nina Farhi, January 3, 2001: "About Marion's analysis with DWW—I don't actually know when it started—but she was increasingly open about it, indeed, she often would compulsively repeat episodes—nearly always angrily or with great puzzlement. I once said to her—only half-laughingly—that her problem with analysis was that she caused each of her analysts to fall in love with her—thus remaining forever outside the experience—deeply lonely, but formidably independent. She both did and did not seek 'to be found.'"

13.Issroff, "Bowlby and Winnicott."

14. An alternate description of the end of the analysis has been provided by Linda Hopkins. It too is based on an interview with Mrs. Milner. She writes (in her "Annotated Table of Contents" for her biography of Masud Khan): "Winnicott's analysis of Milner ends because Milner is treating Susan . . . who lives with Winnicott and his first wife. When Susan starts to accuse Winnicott of being seductive toward her, Winnicott tells Milner she has to choose between him and Susan—and she chooses Susan." This explanation seems most unlikely to me.

15. Milner insisted to me that he had his first heart attack in 1947. There is no collateral evidence for this date, but in later years he did misrepresent the number of attacks he had had.

16. Marion Milner. *On Not Being Able to Paint* (1950), 2d ed., with preface by Anna Freud (London: Heinemann, 1957).

17. Marion Milner, *Eternity's Sunrise: A Way of Keeping a Diary* (London: Virago, 1986), p. 69–70.

18. Marion said that she herself used to get cold feelings at the base of her spine, and perhaps Donald's volunteering to treat her had something to do with this mention of her spine. The daughter of a father who had had a schizophrenic breakdown and a depressed mother, she had always had trouble with anger. She had experienced angina (in the jaw) after a dream of Blake's devil coming down, after someone told her she never wanted to see her again in a response to a religious comment of Marion's. Marion's remark that perhaps Donald treated her because of her spine, links her with his mother in the chain of speculation.

19. Madeleine Davis wrote to me (December 30, 1988): "*She* [Marion] has got that humility that you talk about, omnipotence tamed; the ability, in the words of one of D. W.'s patients, to 'use imagination with discretion.' How difficult to arrive at this place! I think this was one of Winnicott's struggles as well. You remember his hymn to humanism?

O! to be a cog / O! to stand collectively / O! to work harmoniously with others / O! to be married without losing / The *idea* of being the creator of the world.

Yet for Marion losing the idea of being the creator of the world seems to be quite important at times. She seems to have the feeling that the *self* needs to be destroyed at times, like it was with Job."

Chapter 13

1. Clare told me in 1981 that they were painting her flat when he had his first coronary.

2. Sir Frederick died on December 31, 1948. The causes of death were listed as "Lobar Pneumonia" and "Senility" (death and birth certificates provided by Victor Barton). Fifty-three letters from his father were collected in Donald's archive, starting with January 21, 1934. The last one is dated April 7, 1948, Donald's fifty-second birthday. It reads: "My dear Donald, Hope our Birthday Greetings reached you in good time before leaving New Quay this morning and I am now writing to express our loving wishes of affection and love. In these difficult days it is not easy to think of a more suitable token than to repeat last year's gift with the enclosed cheque which no doubt you will find useful. Hope to get good news of Alice's recovery very soon. Heaps of love from all at Rockville. Your Affectionate Dad, J. F. Winnicott."

3. Margaret I. Little, *Psychotic Anxieties and Containment: A Personal Record of an Analysis with Winnicott* (Northvale, N.J.: Aronson, 1985), p. 48.

4. It was at least his second, possibly even his third, though she thought it was his first.

5. In *Psycho-Analytic Explorations*.

6. See also his October 30, 1950, letter to Hannah Henry.

7. To Esther Bick, June 11, 1953.

8. There are several extant letters from the late 1930s that show how warmly and admiringly Jones responded to Winnicott. A letter sent the day after Winnicott's delivery of his membership paper (December 5, 1935) extols its virtues. And another dated only May 24, probably 1939 or 1940, contains this paragraph: "I have at present a patient whose analysis is quite outside my experience, and I wish I had the opportunity of discussing it with you since it bears on all the problems of your paper. All the material consists of complicated movements in the nose and mouth, evidently of the earliest infantile stage, with shifting of the sense of self from one place to another. Curiously enough he appears to be a neurotic and not, as one would expect, a psychotic." In the same period—on August 17, 1938, shortly after the Freuds arrived from Vienna—Anna Freud requested his help in finding a school for a delinquent boy.

9. See Locke, *Science as Writing*.

10. This may well have been his own early home situation: there was not enough hate to allow him to hate to an adequate degree, leading to his outburst at nine and his subsequent emphasis on hate.

11. Masud Khan attended, his first direct exposure to Winnicott.

12. Klein's "paranoid-schizoid position" precedes her "depressive position" in the development of the infant, and is characterized by psychotic-like fantasies, based on the impulse to attack the frustrating mother. Fragmentation of experience predominates, by contrast with the wholeness that characterizes the depressive position.

13. Phyllis Greenacre was a New York analyst and a prolific writer on subjects that overlapped with Winnicott's. They admired each other's work greatly.

14. That is, hate, fear, and suspicion of the analyst as mother figure, which is difficult to bear. The accusation is that he promotes an idealization of himself.

15. Athol Hughes, "Personal Experiences—Professional Interests: Joan Riviere and Femininity," *International Journal of Psychoanalysis* 78 (1997), pt. 5: 899–912.

16. This is an amazing statement, that she has felt nothing about the candidate or Winnicott (in the supervisory context) until now.

17. Perhaps here she is also speaking of Winnicott himself.

18. A highly addictive sleeping medication, secobarbital, known in the United States as Seconal.

19. In 1988, Marion Milner told me that Winnicott's concept of management originated with his treatment of a woman named Barbara Corke, who was suicidal. His secretary, Joyce Coles (interview, 1988), remembered having been asked by Winnicott to drive "Corkie" and her bicycle to a farm in Dorset and then back, during Winnicott's holiday. If, while he was treating her, Corke could not make it to his office, he would visit her at home. Coles would be asked to go as well, to make tea and to shop for her. "This is not

secretarial work, but would you mind?" Donald would ask. And since he had a phenom-
enal capacity to make her feel guilty, she would agree. On one occasion, Winnicott had to
go to Corke's flat and revive her. After each session at the office, she would spend an hour
in the waiting room. Coles would give her a hot water bottle and a cup of coffee. This
began when it was so cold in Queen Anne Street that she felt sorry for her, but "Corkie"
continuted to ask for these things over the course of many years. Cole also recalled that
"Corkie" had many abortions. Masud Khan took over her treatment and helped her, but
also seduced her (evidence that Winnicott had spotted his predilections early on). She
eventually led a happy life in Dorset.

20. His revision of Klein's view is based on the infant's growing awareness that the "environment mother" and the "object mother" are one and the same. The object mother is the
recipient of both libidinal and aggressive urges, while the environment mother is not noticeable when she provides seamless care.

21. In Little, *Psychotic Anxieties*, p. 36.

22. Winnicott became the analyst of one of Balint's wives, Enid. I interviewed her in
1988. She told me that she would not get on the couch for several months because she was
afraid she would break it. Later on they talked to each other with great freedom, with Winnicott sometimes asking which of them would talk on that day. Much as she respected Winnicott, she felt that the greatest contributor in the British Society was Wilfred Bion.

23. Kanter, "Untold Story," writes: "In August 1950, Donald approached Karl Britton,
Clare's brother, and initiated a discussion of his relationship with Clare and his difficulties
in obtaining a divorce (Diary entry by Karl Britton, August 25, 1950). The personal strain
was evident and less than two weeks later, on September 5, 1950, Donald suffered his second [sic] heart attack. But these obstacles were overcome and Donald's divorce was granted
on December 11, 1951. Several weeks later, on December 28, 1951, Donald and Clare were
married."

24. All the evidence points to a reading inhibition about Freud, but Clare told Michael
Neve in 1983 that Donald was always reading Freud. According to Madeleine Davis, he
read Freud's work over and over again during his life. (See "Some Thoughts on Winnicott
and Freud," *Bulletin of the British Association of Psychotherapists*, no. 16 (1985): 57–71.

25. Interestingly (to me at least) Stoller rejected the Winnicott papers for the library of
the UCLA Department of Psychiatry. I was consulted by Clare Winnicott at the time when a
decision was going to be made and discussed the matter with Stoller, who was acting chairman. The papers went to Cornell instead. Stoller and Masud Khan, Winnicott's analyst
from 1951 to 1966, were friends. Khan always stayed with the Stollers when he came to Los
Angeles and a copy of Khan's Workbooks was entrusted to the Stollers.

26. There was first a Baptist ceremony, not an actual wedding, and a civil wedding later in
the day. The home where they resided thereafter, at 87 Chester Square, belonged to Donald.

27. In *The Critical Writings of Adrian Stokes*, ed. Lawrence Gowing, vol. 2: 1937–1958 (London: Thames and Hudson, 1978). *Smooth and Rough* was first published in 1951.

28. D.W. Winnicott and M. Masud R. Khan, Review of *Psychoanalytic Studies of the Personality* by W.R.D. Fairbairn (1953); also in *Psycho-Analytic Explorations* (1989).

29. He wrote this many years before the relationship of Freud to Shakespeare was elaborated upon by the literary critic Harold Bloom.

30. "Toward an Objective Study of Human Nature," in *The Child in the Outside World*
(London: Tavistock, 1957), pp. 125–33.

31. That is, rediscovered by individuals from within, as compared to their acquiring
ideas strictly as taught by others.

32. His theme, and Margaret Little's, is the inseparable nature of destruction and creation.

33. "She [Melanie Klein] has in fact produced something new in psycho-analysis,
namely an *integrated* theory which, though still in outline, nevertheless takes account of all
psychical manifestations, normal and abnormal, from birth to death, and leaves no un-

bridgeable gulfs and no phenomena outstanding without intelligible relation to the rest." See "General Introduction" in Melanie Klein, Paula Heimann, Susan Isaacs, and Joan Riviere, *Developments in Psycho-Analysis* (London: Hogarth Press, 1952).

34. His vast and continuous preoccupation.

Chapter 14

1. He wrote to Charles Rycroft, February 5, 1954, that "although I am apparently well on the road to recovery and doing half-time work, I would very much like to be relieved of Training Committee matters." This implies an illness in January 1954 or perhaps even December 1953. A letter to Clifford Scott dated January 27, 1954, confirms that he was recovering.

2. I base this speculation on a letter to Winnicott from Sylvia Payne dated September 16, 1954, in which she discusses the request that she stand for president of the British Society in order to prevent discord. She says, "The year may give you time to establish your health if you do not undertake too much." I have no other evidence for a coronary at this time. She may be referring to his general condition, worsened by his February illness.

3. For example, a footnote in *The Piggle* (1977) refers to the summer of 1965 as a time of illness. What kind of illness is not made clear, but there is only one kind that ever received explicit description.

4. Roazen, *Historiography*, p. 177.

5. Interview, 1988.

6. Note that dullness is the result of the battering down of gestures. Reciprocally, liveliness would be more likely to result from welcoming those gestures.

7. See her letter on this subject of February 19, 1955.

8. In the theory of the depressive position, Klein shows that guilt is the natural outcome of infant development, arising very early, in the first year of life (she thought at about six months), in contradistinction to Freud's view that guilt, a function of conscience, arose only at the time the Oedipus complex was resolved. Freud placed the development of the superego (with its conscious and unconscious components) at four to six years of age, when, in the case of the boy, there is an identification with the father as a solution to the problem of wanting possession of the mother with the father excluded. The superego is therefore the result of the boy's assumption through identification of the father's rules. Klein pushed the inception of conscience back into the first year and, in Winnicott's elaboration, generated a sense of respect for the function of love as the motive for caring, so vastly different from Freud's theory of the external origin of precepts of self-control. The infant recognizes that the frustrating mother who elicits rage is the same mother who gratifies. An impulse to repair the damage thought to have been done arises out of this combination. This state of mind prompted Klein to call it "the depressive position." One implication is that depressive feelings are a feature of mature living. In Winnicott's revision of Klein's concept, which he named the "Phase of Concern," he theorizes that the infant has experience with two mothers. One is the "environment mother," who maintains the necessary conditions for the continuity of the infant's mental and physical state, and is undetectable if all goes well. The other, the "object mother," is the recipient of the child's instinctual desires (i.e., the one in Klein's formulation that receives both the loving and hating urges in the infant). It is the infant's grasp of the oneness of these two "mothers" that gives rise to depressive anxieties.

9. He had had time to calm down and was taken aback by Rosenfeld's reminder of his involvement, without entering the tangled web of his personal involvement via the lover common to Q and himself.

10. Esther Bick, "Anxiety Underlying Phobia of Sexual Intercourse in a Woman," October 1, 1953.

11. He is taking the position, and the tone that goes with it, that he understands psychosis better than a non-physician such as Bick. This was an ongoing matter, especially in England, where non-physicians could undertake the treatment of psychotic patients only under the supervision of a physician. This idea dated back to earlier times when psycho-

analysis was gaining respectability through the medical training of its practitioners. The medical qualification played a role in Winnicott's struggle with the Kleinians.

12. This is his explanation for mother's identical behavior. His need to affirm that in saying this, he "is using the clinical notes [Bick] gave," is his defensive disavowal of the deeper fact that he is revealing something fundamental to his own life.

13. Rycroft told an interviewer: "Winnicott was already having heart attacks in the 1950's, so I was Acting Training Secretary for a while, which meant I did all the work. I can't remember Winnicott doing any work at all." *Psychoanalytic Conversations: Interviews with Clinicians, Commentators, and Critics,* ed. Peter L. Rudnytsky (Hillsdale, N.J.: Analytic Press, 2001), p. 72.

14. To Hannah Ries he wrote on November 27, 1953: "I do not think it matters if Melanie Klein and particularly her followers have a phase in which they claim too much. I always remember the word 'atom' which means that it cannot be split up. The physicists were great men and one cannot say that their work is no good because they thought the atom was the final dissection. In some places the followers of Melanie Klein speak as if they knew everything, but in the course of time they will find out that they do not. I would like also to say that working with Mrs. Klein I have found that the work of Freud and the sort of work which you describe in your paper is not ignored, certainly by Mrs. Klein herself and people like Dr. Heimann. The trouble is that it is taken for granted in their writings and in their case descriptions, and people think that they are supplanting Klein's [a slip—he means Freud's] work by their own instead of enriching it. They are therefore to some extent responsible for the tremendous misunderstanding that exists at the present time in our Society. It is very easy to fall into this sort of error. [He has just made one.] I find myself that when I talk about regression and very early infantile problems people very easily think that I am unable to do an ordinary piece of analysis involving instincts and the ordinary work in the transference situation, which as a matter of fact I am all the time taking for granted, knowing that there is no point at all in going on to discover new things if one forgets the old things. All this needs saying in our Society over and over again. I try very hard to put this point of view across in the three contacts that I have with the students each summer. I think you will not mind my reminding you, because you know it already yourself, that the kind of analysis which you describe in your paper is applicable to the well-chosen neurotic case, the sort of case that Freud carefully chose to work on, although he sometimes got involved with psychotics almost against his will. This kind of analysis of interpersonal relationships does not cut any ice, as the saying is, in the analysis of psychotics or of the psychotic phases that can occur in normal people. You may disagree with this, and certainly there is plenty of room for argument, but the matter has great practical importance because there are fewer and fewer cases coming for analyses that are psychiatrically speaking neurotic cases. My own view is that it is the job of the medically qualified analysts on the whole to tackle the analysis of psychotics [the same view as that held by Edward Glover, and this point of view has a bearing on his defense of his work in the management of early problems], but of course non-medical analysts cannot avoid meeting from time to time psychotic phases in character analyses where there is no obvious psychotic label."

15. Anna Freud, related by blood, profession, and loyalty to her father and his theories; Melanie Klein, as he repeatedly stated, the best analyst of all, and an authoritarian woman, and phallic leader of great power and intellect. She presented her viewpoint as the natural outgrowth of Freudian principles.

16. But in the chapter on regression in her 1965 book, *Normality and Pathology of Childhood: Assessments of Development* (New York: International University Press, 1965), she makes no mention of Winnicott, or of regression to dependency.

17. This refers to the familiar sequence of oral, anal, phallic, and genital stages. Freud's theory emphasized that libido is invested in this sequence of physical locations over the course of the first few years of life, that successful experience at each stage allows for the flow forward of libido all the way to mature genital relations. Difficulties at a given stage,

however, owing to overindulgence or deprivation, result in a fixation of libido, which makes for weakness in later life. Thus a conflict might result in regression toward a stage of fixation, with symptoms relating to that particular stage. This is libidinal regression.

18. This applies to the everyday work of the psychoanalyst, who sometimes benefits from interpretations directed at patients.

19. Psychoanalysts as a group may be reminded by the concept of regression to dependence of the hypnotic trances that figured in Freud's initial work and from which a rigorous discipline was systematically differentiated. The importance of the caretaking analyst might be reminiscent of the all-powerful hypnotist. In addition, there is more generally a sense among some that human beings, originating in a state of dependency, might want to return to that state and never emerge from it, so that anything that fosters dependency may be viewed as potentially disastrous in effect. And still more generally, the complaint about psychoanalysis is often made that it fosters precisely that dependency, which is antithetical to the presumed aim of patients to lead a more independent life. Thus psychoanalysts might be suspected of practicing their profession as a way of gathering about them dependent people who support them emotionally and economically. Such considerations were and are to an incalculable extent part of the opposition to Winnicott's ideas about regression to dependency.

20. Included in *The Spontaneous Gesture*.

21. Margaret Little wrote to me on January 8, 1986, about this letter: "This could well refer to me, but the crucial thing is the actual date, for the 'bottom' of my regression was clearly reached during the time in hospital, 1st August—about 5th September 1953. If it is earlier than that it couldn't, but it seems to fit otherwise."

22. W. Ronald D. Fairbairn, "Endopsychic structure considered in terms of object-relationships" (1944), in *An Object-Relations Theory of the Personality* (New York: Basic Books, 1952).

23. Guntrip was a minister in Leeds who became a psychoanalyst on his own (as did Fairbairn) by organizing treatment and supervision from diverse sources. He was not a member of any society and had no formal training. Guntrip's letter of April 29, 1954, in response to the regression paper compares Winnicott's concepts to Fairbairn's and is very largely appreciative and supportive. The two men were obviously on the same page.

24. H. S. Guntrip, "My Experience of Analysis with Fairbairn and Winnicott," *International Review of Psychoanalysis*, pt. 2 (1975): pp. 145–56.

25. Jeremy Hazell, *H. J. S. Guntrip: A Psychoanalytical Biography* (London: Free Association Books, 1996).

26. Interview with Joyce Coles, 1988.

27. Margaret Little's phrase.

28. I met Guntrip during the period he spent in Los Angeles giving lectures, though only briefly. He was, unfortunately, exhausted by the demands made on him by a rigorous schedule.

Chapter 15

1. I saw Khan once at a meeting of the Los Angeles Psychoanalytic Society. He had given a paper and was standing alone on the platform, sweat streaming down his dark face. He was quite tall, about six foot four, and was looking nervously around, perhaps for his friend Robert Stoller, with whom he was staying. Mrs. Stoller told me many years later (2002) that he was "quite phobic."

2. This was not true.

3. The psychoanalyst Linda Hopkins told me that Khan started analysis with Winnicott in 1951, "soon after [John] Rickman died. Khan needed to be in analysis for training. The 1966 ending date comes from Khan's Workbooks, and also from his correspondence with Wladimir Granoff, a French analyst who was his friend." Out of her assiduous research, Hopkins, biographer of Masud Khan, has provided me with information about Khan and

Winnicott that would otherwise have escaped me. I am deeply grateful to her for that information, for her subtle and powerful reflections, and for her friendship.

4. Thus, Winnicott in 1952 had no compunction about analyzing husband and wife at the same time—and his colleague Masud Khan's wife at that—nor any compunction about displacing Khan in favor of his wife, for however long that might last. From the start, this was therefore a confused undertaking, fraught with ethical questions.

5. In a letter to Winnicott, the much-despised (by Winnicott) William Sargant, a psychiatrist who favored ECT and prefrontal lobotomy, wrote that she could not be helped unless she stopped drinking, which she did not do. She was not able to dance either, because of her drinking.

6. Protecting a patient's identity did not count as much as providing good material for discussion.

7. In a February 24, 2002, E-mail message to me.

8. Fairbairn, *Object-Relations Theory*.

9. Ernest Jones responded (August 3, no year) to a mention of Zilboorg by writing: "To tell you the truth I was very bored with Zilboorg's rubbish about science versus scientism. It is astonishing how a fine mind can deteriorate under the influence of religion. . . . I well remember the emptiness after God disappeared when I was about seventeen, but the vacant space soon filled up again and one gets the enormous advantage of being spared the enigma of evil and the bewilderment about suffering and misfortune."

10. M. Masud R. Khan, *When Spring Comes: Awakenings in Clinical Psychoanalysis* (London: Chatto and Windus, 1988). Published in the United States as *The Long Wait*.

11. Quoted in Rudnytsky, *Psychoanalytic Conversations*, p. 22.

12. Ibid.

13. Ibid.

14. I owe this definition to Joseph Delvey, Ph.D., a clinical psychologist in Philadelphia.

15. Personal communication, November 2000.

16. Adam Limentani, "Obituary: M. Masud R. Khan (1924–1989)," *International Journal of Psychoanalysis* 73 (1992): 155–59.

17. "Anna Freud was one of Khan's supervisors in the 1950's. She always called him 'Mr. Khan' but she really liked him and enjoyed his wit and charm. . . . Anna also liked Khan because Khan was always a big defender of Sigmund Freud—Khan had a real conservative streak. . . . When Khan had supposedly fatal lung cancer in 1976, he went into "analysis" (twice a week) with Anna Freud to deal with his depression. She didn't help him much however, because he was drinking a lot at the time and, even more, she couldn't have helped him because she was much too charmed by him" (E-mail, Linda Hopkins, March 17, 2001).

18. Wynne Godley, "Saving Masud Khan," *London Review of Books*, February 22, 2001, pp. 3–7.

19. Based on E-mail from Linda Hopkins, April 8, 2001.

20. Godley's wife was the daughter of the sculptor Jacob Epstein.

21. Khan to Anna Freud, June 18, 1974.

22. Quoted to me by Linda Hopkins from Khan's workbook, a private diary, February 7, 1971, under "Chapter 19. Ending of Analysis [1966]."

23. Linda Hopkins, "D.W. Winnicott's Analysis of Masud Khan: A Preliminary Study of Failures of Object Usage," *Contemporary Psychoanalysis* 34 (1998): 5–47.

24. Wladimir Granoff to Masud Khan, April 3, 1967.

25. Telephone conversation between Hopkins and Svetlana Beriosova, July 30, 1998.

26. By October 24, 1967, Winnicott was sensitive to misunderstandings of his occasional touching of a patient. In a letter to Charles Clay Dahlberg, M.D., he wrote: "I have lectured a great deal on the subject of physical contact between patient and therapist. If one writes these things down one gets very easily misunderstood, and I am afraid that there is no way of referring you to what I have written on this subject except to ask the reader to get a gen-

eral inference from going through my writings." See also A. K. Richards, "Sadomasochism in Psychotherapy: The Lady Is a Tiger," *Journal of Clinical Psychoanalysis*, in press.

27. Dodi Goldman, "The Outrageous Prince: Masud Khan's Rise to Oblivion," presentation to panel, "Winnicott and Masud Khan: A Study of Addiction and Self-Destruction," October 30, 1999, sponsored by the William Alanson White Institute, Mt. Sinai Medical Center, New York.

28. Held, according to Goldman, at 3 Hans Crescent in London, Masud Khan's apartment.

29. Quoting from Khan's workbook. "It was most typical of his type of omnipotence that he could never refuse those he knew would compel him to fail. . . . I know all this on my own pulse. . . . Yes, I have known all his failings and he never tried to hide them. . . . He knew and allowed for the margin of weakness and error in every human individual and worked with the 3 per cent that was creative and vital." Entry for February 4, 1971, quoted in Goldman, "Outrageous Prince."

30. Such an incident was also known to Ray Shepherd, one of the Winnicott board of editors, who died in 2002. I had asked Madeleine Davis if she knew of such an incident and she replied that she herself did not, but that Dr. Shepherd said he did. He had in his possession papers and documents that he would allow neither Madeleine nor me to examine.

31. Quoted by Nina Farhi in her eulogy for Madeleine Davis, one of the Winnicott board of editors, *Winnicott Studies: The Journal of the Squiggle Foundation*, no. 6 (1991): viii.

32. See chapter 21.

33. At Amherst, Massachusetts. In his *Winnicott* (Cambridge, Mass.: Harvard University Press, 1988), p. 23, Phillips writes: "It is a not uninteresting detail, in the light of his son's future interests, that he was by profession what was then still called a merchant, specializing in women's corsetry." There is no citation for this preposterous statement.

34. "Contributions to the Commemorative Meeting for Donald Winnicott, January 19th, 1972," *The British Psycho-Analytical Society and The Institute of Psycho-Analysis Scientific Bulletin*, no. 57 (1972): 11.

Chapter 16

1. She may have had good reason. Charles Rycroft recalled: "I remember Winnicott coming up to me, shaking me vigorously by the hand, and saying, 'Dr. Livingstone, I presume?' an anti-Semitic joke, I think. . . . [That's] what Stanley said when he met Livingstone in the middle of Africa. . . . The Society after the war was predominantly Jewish. It wasn't exactly a problem not to be, but you had to be careful. I think this is what he meant. It was a relief to meet a blonde Gentile in the woods. He was quite capable of making jokes, and some of them were in arguably bad taste" (Rudnytsky, *Psychoanalytic Conversations*, p. 72). See also my essay "Winnicott's Laughter," in *Humor and Psyche*, ed. James Barron (Northvale, N.J.: Analytic Press, 1999).

2. This was Margaret Little, who in a 1988 interview demonstrated to me how Winnicott enclosed her small hands, and who wrote (January 6, 1986) about her treatment: "I only once actually hit or attempted to hit Donald, in 1953, when he suggested hospital. Before that, when a danger situation threatened I used to rush out of the room and drive away, often going back just before the session was due to end. And here, I think, I unconsciously followed his example. When I smashed his vase he rushed away, and I know it was to deal with his own feelings. When, holding me, he dozed off ('dropping' me, 1970) and I felt as if I had been hit I re-lived the experience of having been hit by my older sister, as in my sleep, I disturbed hers. (We had to share a bed). This was one of the many things I never told Donald, but somewhere he was aware of such things having happened to me."

3. See her letter of February 26, 1954.

4. This is the struggle to which Joan Riviere refers in her paper on the negative therapeutic reaction: the preoccupation with dead internal objects (destroyed by hate), in dire need

of love. She believed that patients cannot turn their attention away from this life-giving task toward their own need to be loved.

5. A former student in the mental health course at LSE, Jill Ford, wrote in a tribute to Winnicott (manuscript, July 15, 1971) that she had learned from him "only when you could be depressed could you be truly ruthless, but only then, too, could you truly care for, care about, another person."

6. He wrote: Dear Miss Freud, Mrs. Klein:

"This letter follows on the remark that I made somewhat clumsily at the meeting on Monday when yourself, Mrs. Klein [was this letter intended for Miss Freud at first?] and Dr. Payne attended a Council meeting by invitation. I am writing because I feel rather strongly on the matter that I raised. I want to draw attention to the effect of the official grouping. I am thinking of the health of the British Psycho-Analytical Society and trying to look into the future.

My suggestion is that it is not only true to say that the A and B groupings were essential 10 years ago and that the adoption of these groupings saved the Society from splitting, but that it is also true that at the present time the reason for this arrangement has ceased, that is to say, there is no danger whatever of the expulsion of those who follow Miss Freud. Neither is it true that either group is likely to walk out; the Society has now settled down like any other society to the fact that there are scientific differences which automatically clear up in the course of time just as other and new differences appear.

There is a comment that I would like to make at this point which is there is a slight but interesting difference between the formation of the two groupings. In the case of Mrs. Klein's colleagues and friends it is true, whether by chance or otherwise, that inclusion in the group depends on the fact of having analysis from Mrs. Klein or an analysand of Mrs. Klein or an analysand of such an analysand. The only exception I know is Mrs. Riviere and I know of no analyst who has completed an analysis in the Klein group who is not included by Mrs. Klein as a Klein follower. In the case of Miss Freud's followers, the matter is more one of a type of education and it happens that this gives a less rigid boundary. One could say that whereas the followers of Mrs. Klein are all children and grandchildren, the followers of Miss Freud all went to the same school. I mention this difference in the formation of the two groups as I think it produces its own complications and contributes to the false view which the newcomer to psychoanalysis gets through being told of the two groups.

The idea that certain analysts are more likely than others to express Mrs. Klein's views accurately and that certain other analysts are more likely to express Miss Freud's views accurately can be accepted easily and it is to be hoped that this state of affairs will continue and that other members of the Society will also have those who are closely in touch with their individual point of view. Also that there will be overlap and no rigid line between those who accurately interpret and those who are not qualified to represent the analyst in question. There is no doubt that for some time to come there will be no-one of comparable importance in this respect to your two selves and I can see no reason why the abolition of the idea of named groupings that are officially recognized would alter procedure. The teaching programme would remain, balanced as at present, for some years, and we have no right to legislate for the future. Incidentally, if we in the present try to set up rigid patterns we thereby create iconoclasts or claustrophobics (perhaps I am one of them) who can no more stand the falsity of a rigid system in psychology than they can tolerate it in religion.

In writing this letter I am concerned with the future and with the fact that any one of us may die. I consider it to be of absolutely vital importance to the future of the Society that both of yourselves shall break up the official groupings insofar as they are official. No one can break them up except yourselves and you can only do this while you are alive. If it should happen that you should die, then the grouping which is officially recognized in the nomenclature will become absolutely rigid and it will be a generation or more before the Society can recover from this disaster which will be a clumping based not on science but on personalities or even I might say on politics since the original groupings were justifiable but defensive constructs.

I have no reason to think that I shall live longer than either of yourselves but I find the prospect of having to deal with the rigid groupings that would become automatically established at the death of either of yourselves one which appalls me.

This matter is so important that if there is something about my manner which is irritating I hope you will not let it stand in the way of an objective review of the whole situation. I am trying very hard not to let my own peculiarities confuse the issue. . . .

I am addressing this letter to yourselves and sending a copy to Dr. Sylvia Payne. Apart from this there is no-one who knows of this letter and I think this is of extreme importance because, should you decide to abolish the idea of official recognition of the two groups, this idea should come from yourselves."

7. This emphasis on harmony comports with her recommendations for starting the analysis of children with a period of preparation to enlist their help. This contrasts starkly with Klein's approach, in which she assumes intense conflict that requires immediate verbalization. According to Roy Schafer (interviewed in Rudnytsky, *Psychoanalytic Conversations*), Kleinian conditions in London have now changed in a way that allows for less controversy. The Kleinians are in the ascendancy and the Anna Freudians (now called "contemporary Freudians") in decline. The Hampstead Clinic (as of 2002) was in financial trouble. In the United States, the Kleinian Betty Joseph proselytizes successfully in San Francisco and Cleveland. Schafer outlines the ways in which the groups have altered their clinical methods. Some of Winnicott's objections have had an effect, yet he himself continues to be depreciated. It is an interesting tactic: to deny his effect as a way of maintaining the idea of a triumphant Klein. One example: a colleague of mine consulted a Kleinian about what to include of Winnicott in a course on object relations. "A page and a half should suffice," he was told.

8. Survival is a kind of opposition against which unconscious fantasy pushes, thereby defining the self in the resistant setting of the external world. As in "Keeping Things Whole," a poem by Mark Strand, one moves to avoid opposing the resistant environment— one is continuously getting out of the way—with an inflated fantasy belief that to oppose it is to do it damage, to mark it up. The background for this may be a depressed mother unable to receive such "damage," unable to be "eaten." In certain cases, the beauty that is engendered by a willingness to do "damage," for example, in the form of skating or carving ski turns in the snow, and all other forms of beauty that accompany movement, such as dancing, may be what compensates for the damage done to the mother. The obsession with beauty may be exactly this dynamic, whether it is beauty in action or in other forms.

9. He had previously expressed the view that only medical doctors should deal with psychotics. Klein's exposure to psychosis was limited to non-hospitalized patients. Thus her experience was narrower in scope than his own.

10. Here he uses the dread word that he has accused Anna Freud of using and that she denied using.

11. Athol Hughes writes: "Joan Riviere was always rather uneasy in groups, and as the Klein group grew, she withdrew. In the 1950's a coolness developed between her and Melanie Klein—it is not quite known why. Whatever the reason for the estrangement, Joan Riviere never wavered in her allegiance to Melanie Klein's ideas, and she sought to increase her knowledge of them in many ways, as she did by discussing with Herbert Rosenfeld, for instance, how she could develop her skills in work with very disturbed patients." (Athol Hughes, *The World of Joan Riviere*, p. 32.

12. Interview with Hanna Segal by Joseph Aguayo, *fort da, The Journal of the Northern California Society for Psychoanalytic Psychology* (Spring 1999).

13. In the 1950s, the work of Erik Erikson commanded widespread interest. The historian Paul Roazen (*Historiography*, p. 47) has made comparisons of Erikson and Winnicott, as well as Erikson and Klein. He writes: "I can remember once trying to talk to Erikson about Klein; it seemed to me, as an intellectual historian, that there were parallels to how Erikson and Klein were adopting a religious-seeming perspective on human psychology. Erikson, in an autobiographical piece, once mentioned that his use of play constructions

with children had appeared, within the Vienna Psychoanalytic Society, alarmingly similar to Klein, and that the response he got then, which amounted to being charged with betraying his own analyst, Anna Freud, was one of the reasons for him having decided it would be better to leave Vienna entirely. But when I spoke to Erikson about Klein, he wanted to hear nothing at all about her work. His view of children, and of the human condition in general, was so different from Klein that he simply brushed her aside. I certainly failed to get him to reconsider his views about her; I am inclined to think, based on my own limited contact with Kleinian doctrine, that Erikson, like Winnicott, was on the right track. But Erikson and Winnicott relied on others around them to place their work within the history of psychoanalytic concepts; neither had, I think, minds which were comfortable making conceptual distinctions. Winnicott, living in Britain, could not evade coming to terms with Klein's ideas, and felt stimulated by them; Erikson, on the other hand, could go his own way without having to pay attention to Klein's contributions." Roazen also reports that in his 1965 interview of Winnicott, it became clear that "Winnicott wished he were the author of Erikson's books—this was said with the utmost conviction." Also, "when Erikson had been over in London once, and saw patients at a children's clinic, he could spot something positive in each of them; 'he was not making it up either,'" said Winnicott. Erikson's life story (see Lawrence J. Friedman, *Identity's Architect: A Biography of Erik H. Erikson* [New York: Scribner, 1999]), with its concealment of the fact that he was Jewish, is reminiscent of the case of Heinz Kohut, who also concealed his Jewish identity, not to mention his homosexuality and the fact that the famous "Mr. Z." was Kohut himself (Charles B. Strozier, *Heinz Kohut: The Making of a Psychoanalyst* [New York: Farrar, Straus, Giroux, 2001]).

Chapter 17

1. In "The Development of the Capacity for Concern" he writes: "I would say that human beings cannot accept the destructive aim in their very early loving attempts. The idea of destruction of the object-mother in loving can be tolerated, however, if the individual who is getting towards it has evidence of a constructive aim already at hand, and an environment-mother ready to accept." Case material is used to illustrate the point that "[the patient's] capacity to have an idea of ultimately contributing . . . was making it possible for him to get into more intimate contact with his destructiveness. But constructive effort is false and meaningless unless . . . one has first reached to the destruction." He underscores what might be regarded as a counterintuitive idea: "The constructive and creative experiences were making it possible for the child to get to the experience of her destructiveness."

2. Paper delivered at the British Psycho-Analytical Society on June 20, 1956.

3. Delivered July 25, 1956, at the Congress of Pediatrics in Copenhagen.

4. Elisabeth Roudinesco, *Jacques Lacan* (New York: Columbia University Press, 1997).

5. Ibid., p. 249. The SFP was the Société française de psychanalyse.

6. Dr. Kulka, to whom he wrote on January 15, 1957, was a pediatrician and child psychiatrist, though not, I believe, a formally trained psychoanalyst. She had been born and raised in Vienna, the child of a professional family on close terms with the Freuds' pediatrician. She was acquainted with many of the pioneers of child analysis and consulted Freud herself when she was eighteen. Dr. Kulka supervised my work as a psychiatric resident, and we became friends. She was one of those respected senior people whose enthusiasm for the work of Winnicott helped me to look into it and feel similarly. Another was the great Austrian-born child psychiatrist Dr. Norbert Rieger, a devoted therapist of the most disturbed of children.

7. Thomas Main, "The Ailment," *British Journal of Medical Psychology* 30 (1957): pt. 3, 129–45.

8. Letter from Margaret Little, February 19, 1990.

9. "The Cure," unpublished.

10. See my "Winnicott's Laughter."

11. Ursula Bowlby, John's widow, wrote me (January 27, 1993): "I thought Winnicott really a poet at heart (John being a scientist at heart). I found him endearingly 'fey' and I remember being impressed when I heard him speak in public. He spoke cheerfully, smilingly, relaxedly—and often the things he said were fanciful to a degree. He didn't seem to care a bit. I admired this. He was rather an enfant terrible, but a nice one. When we met I found him extremely congenial, very easy to talk to—we seemed to be instantly compatible. I used to meet him at gatherings, but I think John and I never visited him in his own home, nor he here in our house. In this sense the Winnicotts and Bowlbys were not close friends."

12. As did I.

13. Presented to the Paris Congress in July 1957.

14. Delivered at the British Society, July 24, 1957. The use of the word "capacity" has been discussed with great scholarship and insight as part of a larger study by Brooke Hopkins, "Winnicott and the Capacity to Believe," *International Journal of Psycho-Analysis* 78 (1997): 485.

15. James Strachey responded to an early reading of the paper with a plea for clinical illustrations.

16. R. D. Laing, *The Divided Self: An Existential Study in Sanity and Madness* (London: Tavistock, 1959).

17. He writes: "Many an analysis has failed at the end because the analyst could not allow a delusional failure, due to his personal need to prove the truth of psycho-analytic theory through the cure of the patient."

Chapter 18

1. Quoted in Steiner, *Tradition, Change, Creativity,* p. 10.

2. Ibid., p. 27.

3. All the correspondence from Jones in Winnicott's archive is cordial and often laudatory. What was Klein's motive in comparing herself to Winnicott in Jones's eyes unless it be to assert priority over the person asked to write the obituary?

4. Linda Hopkins indicates (E-mail, 2001) that at this time Khan was still married to Jane Shore but had not been living with her for years, and that she was still in analysis with Winnicott. The question arises as to whether Khan is referring here to his wife or his mistress, Svetlana Beriosova.

5. As reported in 1967 to the 1952 Club, in *Psycho-Analytic Explorations.*

6. "Winnicott said openly that he didn't want to read Ferenczi, for instance, because he wanted to think it out for himself. So he didn't read. He'd read Freud when he was a student, I suppose. He knew Freud absolutely" (Enid Balint, in Rudnytsky, *Psychoanalytic Conversations.* But we know that he had an inhibition about reading Freud.

7. Hopkins (E-mail, 2001) speculates that this review of the literature was actually by Khan.

8. The theme of this dichotomy was developed earlier in chapter 11.

9. This remark also echoes sentences in his letter to Klein (March 7, 1957): "I am writing about one small detail. I would not like you to think that in asking about the use of the word internal I have forgotten all you taught me twenty years ago. I used the word as Dr. Segal used it constantly, and I could not be doing my work without always looking for the internal situation as represented in the material of the patient." Among his approaches to Klein and Riviere, reassurance figures prominently.

10. Melanie Klein, "On the Sense of Loneliness (1963),"in *Envy and Gratitude and Other Works, 1946–1963* (New York: Delacorte Press/Seymour Lawrence, 1975); originally published in England by The Hogarth Press and the Institute of Psychoanalysis.

11. June 12, 1959, to Dr. Paul Halmos about a proposed talk.

12. A psychiatry professor noted for his book *The Myth of Mental Illness,* published in 1962, in which he argued for punishment of offenders, no matter what their diagnosis, out of respect for their responsibility for their deeds.

13. Issroff, "Bowlby and Winnicott."

14. "It is possible for a serious person to maintain a professional standard even when undergoing very severe personal strains in the private life" (*Therapeutic Consultations in Child Psychiatry* [1971]).

15. Matters having to do with Lacan's children are discussed. The letter is published in translation in *Ornicar*, no. 33 (Summer 1985), and in Lacan's in *Television: A Challenge to the Psychoanalytic Establishment*, trans. Dennis Hollier, Rosalind Krauss, and Annette Michelson (New York: Norton, 1990).

16. G. T. de Racker, "Transference-Autism and the Interpretation as Transitional Object."

17. The first use of the word "autism" was in a 1943 paper by Leo Kanner.

18. Quotations throughout are from Grosskurth, *Melanie Klein*.

19. Supplied to her originally by Donald in their Oxfordshire period.

20. Munro was one of the Independents, not a Kleinian as Hanna Segal claimed. Segal also claimed that Clare had a major depressive breakdown when Scott left for Canada, but she is the only one to say so. Margaret Little told me that Segal wished to destroy Winnicott. This is consistent with more recent comments to that effect from the Kleinian camp. There is a vitriolic and vengeful attitude on the part of the Kleinians, as if Winnicott had either transgressed in some fatal way or presented an alternative to some Kleinian precepts that was all too appealing and/or all too effective. Yet there is no reason to doubt that they sincerely held Winnicott in contempt.

21. Rudnytsky, *Psychoanalytic Conversations*.

22. Personal communication, 2000.

Chapter 19

1. In *Psychoanalytic Explorations*.

2. In a 1963 talk in Philadelphia. Her concept is closely related to Winnicott's.

3. Letter to Mrs. Alfred Torrie, September 5, 1967: "I am reminded of a curious thing about myself right back in the twenties. After being an Out-patient Physician at Paddington Green I became entitled to beds. This was very exciting, because the doctor in charge of cases in the hospital has status. Having beds means one has arrived. Hardly knowing why, I refused to step up. I got permission to use beds where necessary but I handed the in-patients over to my junior. I knew at the time why I was doing this. I said to myself: the distress of babies and small children in a hospital ward, even a very nice one, adds up to something terrific. Going into the ward disturbs me very much. If I become an in-patient doctor I shall develop the capacity not to be disturbed by the distress of the children, otherwise I shall not be able to be an effective doctor. I will therefore concentrate on my O.P. work and avoid becoming callous in order to be efficient. So I lost the status symbol but that didn't matter somehow."

4. Copy in author's file.

5. "Your 'unit status' has a precursor and this is the self (original unity) as an unperceivable (by the infant) entity. This original unity then divides itself up and the bits are readinesses for experience. I call these bits deintegrates of the self. The deintegrates then fit the objects they are ready to fit, and so the infant has a 'good' experience. All this is at present a consequence of Jungian theory which needs an original integrate to start with. It is the precursor of your 'unintegrated state.' On this basis a 'whole self' experience is a reflection in consciousness of the original unity, i. e. it has behind it an archetype." Letter of April 29, 1954.

6. The paper's title is not given, and there is no explanation of his reference. The entire note reads as follows: "Concept of 'holding' in case work: Cf. Winnicott, Clare [1954]." The date is enclosed by one bracket and one parenthesis. Masud Khan probably edited the book in which this paper appears (*The Maturational Processes and the Facilitating Environment*), and this is Khan's grudging acknowledgment of the source of the concept of holding, which Winnicott could have expanded had he wanted to. The actual citation is Clare Winnicott, "Case Work Techniques in the Child Care Services" (1954) in *Child Care and Social Work* (London: Codicote Press, 1964), also published in *Social Casework* 36 (1955): 3–13.

7. The book is *The Leaven of Love* by I. De Forest.

8. See Leo Rangell, M.D., "A Unitary Theory at Century's End: Splits and Comings To-gether, A Life in Psychoanalysis," unpublished manuscript, 2002, for a detailed description of the conference which, "admitted this popular mechanism into the fold of Freudian and general explanatory theory."

9. Telephone conversation, August 2, 2001.

10. As cited by Genevieve de Racker in her paper ("Transference=Autism") linking tran-sitional objects to autistic objects and Leo Kanner's work. A patient recounting early memo-ries mentioned having a kaleidoscope in his crib, which prompted Winnicott to remark on how hard an object it was.

11. Hughes, *Riviere: Collected Papers*, p. 34.

12. In Riviere's introduction to the 1952 collection *Developments in Psychoanalysis* we read: "[Klein] has in fact produced something new in psychoanalysis: namely, an integrated theory which, though still in outline, nevertheless takes account of all psychical manifesta-tions, normal and abnormal, from birth to death, and leaves no unbridgeable gulfs and no phenomena outstanding without intelligible relation to the rest." In Winnicott's 1968 "Roots of Aggression" (not published until *Psycho-Analytic Explorations* [1989]), he quotes this statement and calls it "a sentence which Melanie would have disallowed had she been truly a scientist." There are in *Explorations* many other extended statements written toward the end of his life, which make as explicit as possible his objections to Klein's envy concept and his explanation for its appearance in 1955.

13. Kris, " Freud's Treatment of a Narcissistic Patient."

14. Hughes, Ed. *The Inner World and Joan Riviere: Collected Papers 1920–1958* (London and New York: Karnac, 1991).

15. The law of Talion dictates the terrifying punishment of "an eye for an eye, a tooth for a tooth."

16. Where I happened to be present, the only time I ever saw Winnicott. By now I cannot tell what is pure memory and what has been added by the study of his work and his vari-ous portraits. What I think I recall is a rather slightly built, tired, and aging but determined man who, speaking with great seriousness, gripped the lectern with both hands. (His friend Dr. Peter Tizard called him "a pale man with rather sunken cheeks.") Anna Freud was pres-ent on that occasion, as she was for many of his papers. He was, of course, no longer re-garded as a Kleinian by then, and their correspondence became increasingly cordial as she grew ever fonder of him in the decade after the death of Melanie Klein.

17. This puts the noncommunicating aspect of an individual beyond observation, essen-tially undiscussable, as compared with a True Self that makes itself known through sponta-neous gestures. I owe this observation to my daughter, Ingrid Rodman-Holmes. Marion Milner, in her presentation to the British Society's memorial meeting for Winnicott (January 9, 1972), addressed the subject as follows: "He claims that the sense of self comes from desul-tory formless activity or rudimentary play, and then only if reflected back, and he adds that it is only in being creative that one discovers onself. I have a difficulty here. I can understand him when he claims that the sense of self comes on the basis of the unintegrated state but when he adds later that this state is by definition not observable or communicable, I begin to wonder. Not communicable, yes. Not observable, I am not so sure. I think of the dark still center of the whirling Catherine Wheel [to which she had compared him] and feel pretty cer-tain that I can, in the right setting, be related to by the conscious ego discovering that it can turn in upon itself, make contact with the core of its own being, and find there a renewal, a re-birth. But in fact isn't Winnicott himself referring to this when he talks of 'quietude linked with stillness'? And this reminds me of T. S. Eliot's 'still point of the turning world' or 'words after speech reach into silence' in 'Burnt Norton.'" Eliot's "still point of the turning world" is where "the dance is, But neither arrest or movement. And do not call it fixity . . . Except for the point . . . there would be no dance, and there is only the dance." He describes the ulti-mate elusive point from which all else is exterior, even including the True Self.

18. See letter to Clifford Scott, March 18, 1953.

19. Given in May–June 1963 at the Congress of Child Psychiatry in Rome.

20. Her daughter Priscilla had sought a referral from him for a medical problem. Her husband, Dr. Bernard Brandchaft, had visited Winnicott during a stay in London. His growing interest in the work of Melanie Klein resulted in a major move by Wilfred Bion and Albert Mason to Los Angeles. They increased the enthusiasm for Klein which proved disruptive to the Los Angeles Psychoanalytic Society and Institute, and eventuated in the formation of a separate institute of Kleinian leanings.

21. Personal communication from Leo Rangell, 2001.

22. Masud Khan's Workbook notes that this took place on Sunday, April 26, 1970, at 5:00 P.M., though the Wolffheim letter reached Winnicott in 1963. I cannot explain this discrepancy. The entry reads: "Had called on D. W. W. after riding. He was in buoyant health [this supports the 1963 date—in 1970 he was dying], and we talked a lot about Melanie Klein because he wanted me to read Nelly Wolffheim's '*Melanie Klein as I knew her*: Autobiographical Notes.' According to D. W. W., he has not been able to get Klein's son to agree to its publication, largely because of Betty Joseph's nose in it—with whom he is at present under analysis. He threatened to sue for libel if this account was published. D. W. W. told me today what had chequered his relation with Melanie Klein. In the Thirties she had sent her son to him for analysis. At the same time, she had given him a reprint of her paper, 'The Development of a Child' [1921]. Evidently, the boy Fritz in that paper is her own son, Eric, and on him she had tried her analytic technique. D. W. W., of course, disregarded the paper because he could not see any of the argument and reported material in his clinical work with the youth. This had disconcerted her because she had hoped to supervise his analysis of her son, as she tried to do later with Milner, to whom she sent her grandchild. But the real crisis came in 1939. The son wanted to join the army and D. W. W. told her that this was the most positive and true thing that had crystallized from the boy's own initiative in his analysis. Klein was dead set against her son, Eric, going into the War-Service and wanted D. W. W. both to dissuade the boy from going and also to write to the War Office making out a case of psychiatric illness in order to avoid War-Service. She was terrified he would be killed or injured. D. W. W., however, refused to obey her, and from that time onwards she was estranged from him. The boy did join the army and survived. But Klein never let D. W. W. teach child-analysis at the Institute, and thus spoilt his chances of creating a group round his work!

What petty squabbles had set the character of the analytic movement have to be seen to be believed. It is always the private vulnerabilities, whether in Freud, Jones, Klein or Anna Freud, and not ideas that have dictated the progress of the movement."

Chapter 20

1. In my 1988 interview with him, Dr. James used the same word, "Teutonic," in describing the bewilderment of certain analysts in regard to Winnicott's way of thinking and writing. "Teutonic," referring to the racial or ethnic aspect of those who are German, is sometimes contrasted with "Celtic."

2. In a letter to Heinz Kohut, however, two years after Winnicott's death (dated July 2, 1973, included in *The Curve of Life: Correspondence of Heinz Kohut, 1923–1981*, edited by Geoffrey Cocks [Chicago: University of Chicago Press, 1994], Anna Freud recalls that Winnicott wrote "such a hostile and denigrating review of one of my books for an official journal that it was refused. And afterwards he said that he was sorry, he did not know why he had done it, he really liked the book." Here is the underside of his sometimes obsequious behavior toward Anna Freud. I do not know which book she refers to here, but her 1965 book *Normality and Pathology of Childhood* would seem a likely candidate. In that book she leaves out any reference to regression to dependence in her chapter on regression. In a September 23, 1965, letter to John Klauber, Winnicott mentioned that he was reviewing the book," *but* [my ital-

ics] there are some rather good things." Anna Freud cites this incident as a response to Kohut's anger that Martin James had written a review of his work that was very favorable, except for a comment that implied that much of Kohut's work was plagiarized. She thought that this was a reference to Winnicott, "to whom he [James] was very devoted."

3. In *Psycho-Analytic Explorations*.

4. That one can dream a dream for someone else is an unprecedented idea.

5. Freud had selected Jung to be his successor, partly because he believed that Jung's Christian background would spare psychoanalysis from being seen as a Jewish science. He also likened Jung to Joshua in the biblical story of the Exodus, wherein Moses leads his people out of slavery but is denied entry into the Promised Land. That privilege is to be reserved for his successor.

6. See my introduction to *The Spontaneous Gesture*.

7. April 28, 1954, letter from Michael Fordham to Winnicott.

8. I asked my friend Eric Korn to comment on this poem. He is a scholar of language and literature and a fine and generous critic. He wrote: "Eloi, Eloi, Lama Sabachthani is Aramaic, and the words of Jesus on the Cross [Matthew 24:36]; my God my God, why hast thou forsaken me? The Glastonbury thorn which invariably flowered at Easter was supposedly brought by Joseph of Arimathea to England in 32 A.D., a part of the True Cross, planted at Glastonbury when a monastery was founded. (There's a mass of legend about Celtic Christianity, supposedly truer, purer, and more magical than the Latin kind brought by St. Augustine.) 'The Tree' in old English poetry is always the True Cross. Mary in line seven is Magdalene, not the Blessed Virgin Mary. And it's always said that Jesus Christ spoke Aramaic, which was the current dialect of Hebrew. (The Kaddish prayer, likewise the Passover Hymn, *Only one kid* are Aramaic.), but these words seem to be identical with classical Hebrew. I assume that many analysts (at any rate most European analysts) identify with Christ, and ask that the cup be taken from them. (A psychiatric character in T. S. Eliot's 'The Cocktail Party' is explicitly Christ-like.) The virtue goes out of them, making even the direst thorns flower, even the dead wood (or rood) on which they suffer. Their personal affairs suffer ("no time for loving"). The notion that he has to be not only 'about his (heavenly) father's business,' but also his (earthly) mother's, is very *un*theological, and surely has to do with Winnicott. Paintings of the Virgin and child often show the Holy infant with arms outstretched, a proleptic reference to the crucifixion, so there's nothing personal about that. In fact except for the line 'to enliven her was my living' and the four lines following, it is strictly orthodox. There's a reference also to the Holman Hunt painting of Christ in his father's workshop, a scene of family joyousness and foreboding. The children are both the children who followed Christ at the sermons, but also his traditional brothers and sisters. Note that the last four lines form—clumsily—[a] crucifix."

9. Adam Phillips (Winnicott, p. 29) states that Donald sent this poem to his brother-in-law James Britton, "with the words: 'Do you mind seeing this that hurt coming out of me. I think it had some thorns sticking out somehow. It's not happened to me before & I hope it doesn't again.'"

10. The letter is dated April 28, 1964. She might have thought he meant clinical depression in the psychiatric sense, but she does not ask.

11. He seems never to have adopted the "ph—" spelling of the word, suggested by the Kleinians for unconcious fantasy.

12. The title of a lecture to the Society for Psycho-Somatic Research, May 21, 1964.

13. He seems to have focused on dissociation in the 1960s more than previously. I am reminded of Freud's late paper on fetishism, in which dissociation is important as opposed to repression. The fruit of Winnicott's lifelong study may be his coming finally to the idea of dissociation. The sense of personal disintegration probably contributed to such a preoccupation, or the preoccupation with death was formulated as a dissociative element.

14. June 1964, letter to John Rosen, *Symbolic Realization: A New Method of Psychotherapy Applied to a Case of Schizophrenia* (New York: International Universities Press, 1960).

15. Madame Sechehaye's book (*Symbolic Realization*) on the treatment of a schizophrenic girl was widely known in that era. In a climactic moment of treatment she presents the patient with an apple, which represents the proffered breast of the mother, the consumption of which completes the cycle of therapeutic change.

16. A concept described at the very end of his paper "Split-Off Male and Female Elements" (1966).

17. "Keats substitutes the discovery of beauty through the imagination for the discovery of facts through the reason, and asserts that it is a more satisfactory and more certain way of piercing to the heart of things, since inspired insight sees more than abstract ratiocination ever can. Keats' concern is with the imagination in a special sense, and he is not far from Coleridge in his view of it. For him it does much more than imagine in the ordinary sense; it is an insight so fine that it sees what is concealed from most and understands things in their full range and significance and character. The rationale of poetry is that through the imagination it finds something so compelling in its intensity that it is at once both beautiful and real. The theory which Keats puts forward piecemeal in his letters receives its final form in the last lines of 'Ode on a Grecian Urn.'" Maurice Bowra, *The Romantic Imagination* (1950; reprint, New York: Oxford University Press, 1961), pp. 147–48.

18. "I am one of those people Freud once mentioned, saying we must not forget that they exist; that is, people who think in pictures," said Marion Milner at the memorial meeting for Winnicott, British Psycho-Analytical Society, January 19, 1972. This quality, so unusual among psychoanalysts, must account to some extent for the special understanding between Winnicott and Milner. Also, Harry Guntrip's obituary of Winnicott calls him "a highly intelligent, intuitively gifted 'seer,' who saw far more deeply into human nature than our intellectual capacities enable us to do" (manuscript sent to Clare Winnicott, unpublished).

19. Prepared for the British Psycho-Analytic Society in October 1965.

20. Written for a seminar in December 1965.

21. Probably written in 1966.

22. December 2, 1965.

Chapter 21

1. Read to the British Society on February 2, 1966.

2. In Winnicott's "Answers to Comments," which dates from 1968–69.

3. In the throes of his quest for an utterly original viewpoint, he is still shadowed by possible predecessors.

4. Joseph Conrad's *Heart of Darkness* describes a parallel adventure.

5. Quoted in Frank Kermode, *Wallace Stevens* (1960; reprint, London: Faber & Faber, 1989).

6. Raymond Carver, *A New Path to the Waterfall* (New York: Atlantic Monthly Press, 1989).

7. Ilse Grubrich-Simitis, "Freud's Study of Moses as a Daydream: A Biographical Essay," in *Early Freud and Late Freud*, p. 82.

8. Someone I know, made anxious by the first subjects in medical school, allowed himself to read some favorite classic authors for a time and gained considerable relief.

9. It has been suggested to me by Linda Hopkins that Masud Khan was, in fact, the patient cited in the paper on split-off objects. In a letter to Winnicott, who was at the time ill in New York (December 1968), Khan wrote " [Guntrip] . . . discussed this paper solidly and most constructively, and in many ways my point of view and his are similar." (He is referring to Guntrip's recently published book *Schizoid Phenomena, Object Relations, and the Self* [London: The Hogarth Press and the Institute of Psycho-Analysis, 1968] pp. 245–71.) There was nothing in the content or tone of Khan's note to suggest that he was actually the patient cited by Winnicott.

10. Bion's early life had been spent in colonial India, and I have wondered whether the warm climate of his youth played a part in his decision to move to Los Angeles, or even

more simply, whether his personal history of emigration might have made such a move thinkable at the age of seventy.

11. Douglas Kirsner, *Unfree Associations: Inside Psychoanalytic Institutes* (London: Process Press, 2000), p. 173.

12. Personal communication, 1978.

13. Albert Mason, "Bion and Binocular Vision," *International Journal of Psychoanalysis* 81 (2000): 983–989.

14. "I am not quite settled up in my mind about the idea of memory and desire or intention. When I got home Clare reminded me again that the phrase memory and desire, which you have used before, is a quotation from T. S. Eliot, and she was able to give me the whole poem, and for some reason or other I accept memory and desire as naturally interrelated in the poem. At the same time in the application of the same idea to psycho-analytic work I cannot help finding myself using the word intention and not feeling desire to be correct. As you said, we each have to find the word that fits for oneself. For me, memory and desire is all right in a poem because it refers to an experience that is 100% subjective. In the application to psycho-analytic work I find I cannot allow that this is 100% subjective. The memory includes memories of phenomena from external reality and certainly what is likely to turn up tomorrow in my analytic work cannot be covered by what I have in my own mind to want, precisely because I have to be able to allow the patient to be a separate person, as the patient has to come to be able to allow me to be outside his or her omnipotent control.

So you see why it is that I find myself unhappy with your word desire in this context."

15. In 1955, a few years after the publication of his paper on the transitional object, he had written to "The artist, PEANUTS cartoon: I have been sent a cutting, unfortunately undated, in which you give a cartoon which exactly illustrates a point in a collection of my lectures to parents which I am about to publish. It is of the little boy whose mother had washed his blanket, and he is seen sucking his thumb and catching hold of the blanket on the line.

I have written to the editor of the New York Herald-Tribune asking for permission to include this cartoon as an illustration to the book, the importance of it being that it illustrates the general understanding of children which can be tapped with the aid of a sense of humour.

I am sorry that I am not more in touch with your cartoons and if they have been published in book form I would be glad to know."

16. At the memorial meeting for Winnicott, held at the British Society on January 19, 1972, W. H. Gillespie recounted the events leading to the commissioning of the Freud Statue. Ernst Federn had persisted in his attempt to get Freud to sit for such a work for twenty-five years. Oscar Nemon made a plaster bust which eventually arrived in England and was converted into a statue of heroic size through the support of Dr. and Mrs. Peter Glauber. By 1964, the model still uncast, Penelope Balogh (now Lady Balogh) approached Winnicott, who believed that the statue must be cast. By April 1968, when he was president of the society, he "took it upon himself" to appeal to all analysts in the International Association, and, with their help and that of his secretary, Joyce Coles, he raised considerable funds. A committee was formed. Further appeals were made to component societies and finally to individual psychiatrists. When Winnicott fell ill after his New York presentation, others stepped in to help; but after his recovery, he resumed his efforts and announced the completion of the project in September 1970. At the site provided by Camden Council, the statue was unveiled on October 2, 1970, by some of Freud's great grandchildren after it had been formally presented to the mayor by Winnicott. "It must have been a source of the greatest satisfaction to Donald Winnicott," said Gillespie, "to have lived to see this project realized; alas, he had little more than three months to live." At the memorial meeting Gillespie announced that Nemon had presented to the society a "sculpture of Donald Winnicott's head . . . now cast in permanent form."

Chapter 22

1. A member of the gathering recalled, in 2002, that as Winnicott spoke, the audience became as if paralyzed. There appeared to be a malaise spreading throughout. Certainly this group in New York had never encountered a speaker so far removed from familiar psychoanalytic theorizing, but it is also possible that they were responding to evidence that he was already ill.

2. Generously obtained for me by the late Robert Kabcenell, M.D.

3. He thus played the role of the not-me object that elicits destructive urges.

4. From Masud Khan's Workbook: "15th November 1968. 12:00 noon. D. W. W. is seriously ill in New York with heart failure. I pray he can return home and die peacefully in his own home. Amen!!"

5. Phyllis Greenacre visited Winnicott at the hospital in New York rather often, as well as the Hartmanns, but Clare could not recall anyone else. Personal communication, 1981.

6. From an interview with Jane Shore, Masud Khan's first wife, conducted on November 17, 1998, by Linda Hopkins: "One of my rescuers was an American woman named Louise Carpenter. She was a teacher at the Dalton School in New York City and she ran a summer camp for rich boys at Spotted Bear Lake in Kalispell, Montana. Winnicott met Louise through me—and he lived in her flat in NYC after he had that heart attack and couldn't return home in 1968. She had a flat up on the borders of Harlem. They were good friends—she used to stay with him in London." Louise Carpenter is no longer alive.

7. Louis Zetzel, a distinguished internist, and his wife, Elizabeth Zetzel, who had trained in London.

8. Why, one wonders, should Elizabeth take it so hard? There must have been a special relationship to Donald. Had he treated her?

9. The underlining of *a* in "st*a*bilized" is a reminder of the extent to which Clare underlined in the letters to Donald in the 1940s. She achieves an audible note with that one little mark. In fact, the word's meaning is now illustrated by the underlining. In this way the written word is transformed into a sort of spoken word, sight and sound combined and thus vividly expressive and alive. Donald's letters home from school include similarly animated notations and illustrations. Clare's love of poetry and of language is unself-consciously evident in her style in the writing of ordinary letters. In his introduction to a book of poems by George Herbert (*Herbert* [London: Penguin Books, 1973]), W. H. Auden writes: "The music of a poem is its meaning in sound as distinguished from word. . . . The sound of a verse is the harbinger of the truth contained in it. . . . Herein Herbert excels. It will be found impossible to separate the music of his words from the music of the thought which takes shape in their sound."

10. Reference unknown.

11. Clare told me in 1981 "I had to help him out," implying the separateness of their finances.

12. Winnicott wrote to Masud Khan, who replied gratefully on November 27: "I do not think one can use the concept 'failure' regarding your paper in New York. Of course, I do not know how it was received and have been too distressed to write to my friends and gather gossip from New York. Of one thing I am sure and that is that the paper on 'use of an object' breaks new ground, which of course is always discomfortable for the pundits in the beginning." Winnicott replied on November 29 and Khan wrote back on December 2, a four-page, single-spaced typewritten letter full of news and gossip.

13. Two notes from Masud Khan to Victor Smirnoff demonstrate his opinion of Klein at this late date. On August 21, 1967, he wrote: "Klein had neither the true feel of persons nor literature, but she did have a very compulsive insightfulness into the mental (phantasy) representations of primitive affects. Hence in Klein's world, there are no object (external) relations, only internal objects. . . . If Freud discovered the pervasive & vital presence of polymorph perverse infantile sensuality as a 'biologic' given, Klein really charted out its mental correlatives. But she also exaggerated it to become a closed system & hence antagonistic to life in reality. It is interesting to watch that whenever the inner reality has been made exclu-

sive & absolute, it has always led to a death cult: in religions, rituals and psychologies— even in literature, e.g. the dadaists & G. Bataille!. Klein knew of Grace but couldn't find it in life." He must be referring to the central role in Kleinian thought of the death instinct.

14. "Too" obviously indicates that the patient had threatened to kill herself.

15. He identifies with Catherine in *Wuthering Heights*, whose shared moments on Penniston Crag with Heathcliff were the best in her life. Or with the dead Catherine's ghost "coming home." At this point he is somewhere between a renewal of life and the prospect of death.

16. Acording to Margaret Little, this was an analyst who was treated by Winnicott in two-month periods, twice a day. He eventually committed suicide. She wrote me (February 19, 1990): "My understanding is that G. G. was essentially needing a greater degree of reliability in dealing with his psychotic anxieties than D. W. W. could, in fact, provide—hence failure—breakdown into madness and suicide. Comparable to what happened to Masud Khan." In a letter in early 1967 (January 2), Winnicott complained to G. G. about all the gifts he was sending, and of his reluctance to send him "messages on tapes." He was willing to see G. G. again in the summer, when "I hope I shall be more definitely useful than I was (in my opinion) last summer."

17. They had been divorced for eighteen years.

18. Winnicott refers to Shakespeare's last tragedy, in which the empty, self-centered hero, a Roman consul, is expelled by the citizenry, and to Winston Churchill, who was defeated in the election of 1945, just after the end of World War II, in which as prime minister he had led his country to victory. Harold Bloom writes of Coriolanus: "His authentic heroism is his hermetic endeavor to be the mortal god Coriolanus, and not the perpetually infantile Caius Martius. Barren inwardly, almost empty, he nevertheless possesses a desperately heroic will." (Harold Bloom, *Shakespeare: The Invention of the Human* [New York: Riverhead Books, 1998], pp. 582–86). Given Winnicott's struggle for survival at this point in his life, the "desperately heroic will" of Coriolanus might have resonated. There is also a great deal in the play that illustrates Winnicott's insights; for example, the description of Coriolanus, who "sups upon himself and so shall starve with feeding," may be studied for its relationship to ideas in the "Use" paper. People who survive destruction are "of use" and contribute nourishment, in contradistinction to those who provide only what has been projected onto them.

19. A threshold reference to go with the placement of Winnicott in thresholds in the memory of many who knew him.

20. E. M. Forster's *Hill of Devi*, published in 1953, was built on letters Forster wrote in the early 1920s from Dewas, in India, to describe "the bewilderment and pleasure at being plunged into an unknown world."

21. Reprinted in *The Spontaneous Gesture*.

22. *American Journal of Psychiatry* 148 (1991): 259–60.

Chapter 23

1. Sigmund Freud, *Moses and Monotheism*, in *Standard Edition*, vol. 23 (London: Hogarth, 1964).

2. Ilse Grubrich-Simitis, "Freud's Study of Moses as a Daydream: A Biographical Essay," in *Early Freud and Late Freud*, pp. 60, 63–4, 65, 70, 80.

3. In his introduction to *Herbert*, W. H. Auden writes: "Herbert is concerned with liturgical manners and styles of piety. In his day, Catholic piety was typically baroque, both in architecture and in poets like Crashaw. This was too unrestrained for his taste. On the other hand, he found the style of worship practiced by the Reformed Churches too severe, too 'inward.' He would have agreed with Launcelot Andrewes who said: 'If we worship God with our hearts only and not also with our hats, something is lacking.' The Reformers, for instance, disapproved of all religious images, but Herbert thought that, on occasions, a stained-glass window could be of more spiritual help than a sermon.

Doctrine and life, colours and light, in one / When they combine and mingle, bring / A strong regard and aw; but speech alone / Doth vanish like a flaring thing, / And in the care, not conscience ring.

Walton tells us that he took enormous pains to explain to his parishioners, most of whom were probably illiterate, the significance of every ritual act in the liturgy."

I quote this in an attempt to put forth the idea that Winnicott was a sort of Christianizing influence on psychoanalysis via his arguments in favor of the influence of external reality. Freud had not excluded external reality, but his revolutionary contribution had to do with the recognition of the role of the internal, the world of fantasy, as so much more determinative of our individual fate than had previously been recognized and identified. Following a long Jewish tradition, he tended away from the external and toward the internal. Harold Bloom has observed that the Second Commandment, against the worship of graven images, illustrates the interiorization that is closely associated with Judaism. By nudging us toward trust in the visual world, Winnicott tends to overcome a mistrust of appearances. The environment does count, he taught (in a way that elicited unrelenting opposition from Melanie Klein and her followers), on condition that it not displace the world of fantasy.

4. Letter 125F, January 17, 1909, In *The Freud-Jung Letters: The Correspondence between Sigmund Freud and C. G. Jung*, ed. William McGuire, trans. Ralph Mannheim and R. F. C. Hull, Bollingen Series 94 (Princeton: Princeton University Press, 1974).

5. "The test of these case descriptions [in *Therapeutic Consultations*] will hang on the word enjoyment. If they are a labour to read then I have been too clever; I have been engaging in displaying a technique and not playing music. I am of course aware that this actually does take place from time to time in case descriptions." The individual nature of the work is emphasized in his subsequent statement that "the work cannot be copied." An example of the way in which the spirit of the work may inspire others is evident in *Untying the Knot* by Abraham Brafman (London: Karnac 2001), a finely written book of cases that involve children and parents.

6. Marion Milner, *On Not Being Able to Paint*, p. 392.

7. I do not know whether Winnicott was aware of Fairbairn's 1944 work when it first appeared, and if so, whether he saw the significance of it right away, but the year itself, to which he refers more than once, is significant as the date when he shifted his views about patients' "wishes" to "needs." This change, I have speculated, was related to his affair with Clare Britton, seen in the "forgiving" overtone that accompanies the idea of needs as opposed to the potentially accusatory one that can go with wishes. The idea of object seeking as opposed to drive satisfaction is commensurate with a forgiving attitude as well, as if one were thinking in terms of the patient's need for contact with the object rather than the satisfaction of drive without respect to the object. Both sets of alterations point toward a less judgmental view of early (and undoubtedly late) human behavior.

8. See Little, *Psychotic Anxieties*, p. 44.

9. Letter, June 11, 1989. She also wrote to me (June 19, 1991) apropos this stage of his life, with its emphasis on his ideas around "use" that "he reports a patient as saying 'Perhaps (when I am better) I will be able to use imagination with discretion.' That is what seems to me to happen in the truly 'free' association; and I have for a long time thought that D.W. implied that this can only happen (i.e. free association) after the object has begun to be used (that is, has been destroyed + survived)."

10. How many could write, as Donald did, about a much-admired person that "he was not a great man, [but] . . . he was a man who was so infinitely enriched by what he had gathered in from the cultural inheritance that he did not depend on distractions for feeling glad to be alive."

11. I / They say / They reached the moon / Planted a flag / A flag stiffened of course / (no gods breathe there) / II / Clever devils I would fear / I would panic / I would doubt / I would make a mistake / I would faint / I would leap, scream, laugh, go to pieces / Not so they / III / What moon? / They made a moon out of their heads / In a computer box they devised / Near-infinite complexity and then / Explored its finiteness, And then / They stepped on to it, planted a stiffened flag, / And took some marbles home, but not for chil-

dren to play with. / IV / Has anything altered? / Is this the shape of man's triumph, / the mark of man's greatness / the climax of civilization / the growing point of man's cultural life? / Is this the moment for setting up a god / Who is pleased with his creative efforts? / V / No not for me / This is not my moon / This is not the symbol of cold purity / This is not the tide-master / Not the phase-determinant of women's bodies / The lamp fickle yet predictable to the / Shepherd astronomer that variably lights up / The dark night or generates bats and ghosts / And witches and things that go bump.

12. Douglas Kirsner, "Fear and Loathing in Los Angeles," in *Unfree Associations: Inside Psychoanalytic Institutes* (London: Process Press, 2000).

13. He did not come. Dr. Sheldon Bloch, an American psychiatrist, was among the few hundred present and saw what he described to me (conversation, November 12, 2001) as a "sparkling" Winnicott, enjoying the great occasion.

14. Khan's own brilliance is evident in his elaboration on this idea: "I was fascinated by this material and told him that here he is extending the concept of transitional object to include the 'unthinkable anxiety' that belongs to the absence of the subjective object at the critical point. This *anxiety* cannot be provided ego coverage by the infant-child. It can only be screened by something else. Elaborating this further I was able to postulate to D.W.W. that one could argue there are basically only two types of art: the one that derives from the positive area of the transitional object. I quoted Braque saying to an interviewer that he does not invent his shapes on the canvas: he merely removes the pigments that are hiding it to let the object reveal itself. Per contrast, there is the other type: where what is being dealt with is *the absence of the subjective object*. Picasso is its greatest exponent: such art is endlessly inventive, hallucinatory and myriad-faceted. Bacon is another example. But also Rouault. D.W.W. was very intrigued by this and urged me to write a paper on it. The Surrealist art is the manic denial of the absence of the subjective object: it is hence willfully hallucinatory and mental, not plastic."

15. Madeleine herself was supplied with a saucepan whenever she stayed with them.

16. According to Winnicott's old friend Harry Karnac (E-mail, August 5, 2001).

17. Dr. Judith Isroff, who knew the Winnicotts and many of their acquaintances, writes (letter, October 28, 2001) that "Clare actually burned a drawer full of letters from his first wife he'd kept locked and concealed from her." If true, this suggests an ongoing conflict. Dr. Issroff also told me that Clare kept everyone who had been close to Winnicott away from materials that would have allowed a biography to be written, more evidence of an assertion of ownership, and a jealousy of his legacy, perhaps, to be only in her possession. Though aware, as she told me early on, that no one would ever own all of her or all of him, she may have made a long-term effort to hold onto him, to the exclusion of others, to what extent she could. Winnicott's notation "When I see Alice" appears in a letter to the psychoanalyst Lawrence Kubie (September 12, 1957). After the divorce, according to research done by Brett Kahr (*Biographical Portrait*), Alice moved to Meadow Cottage, on Lodden Drive West, in Wargrave, Berkshire. By 1961 she had moved to Cardiganshire, Wales, probably with her sister Mary. She died in Bronglais Hospital in Aberystwyth of bronchopneumonia, hypothermia, and renal failure.

18. Manuscript, Clinica Pediatrica dell'Università di Roma. This spontaneous and silent tribute is, to me, the most moving of all.

19. She also wrote: "W. is as easy to diabolize as to idealize; being human, he erred; his clinical judgment was only too often unsound. Over-compensating perhaps for failing in some other area, while aware of lack of humility in others he became blindly over-confident and opposition strengthened this—acting as a spur throughout his professional life, and notably at its end, he failed grievously some who trusted him, for whom he cared deeply and sincerely." When I quoted this back to her she replied: "I'm glad you picked up that paragraph. It's important that I wrote it. *Reference* specific to Masud Khan and "G. G."—(and ?how many others). We *all* have failures. His stand out, therefore he is outstanding. His failure to have a child rankled" (March 3, 1991).

As her health grew more and more precarious, Margaret Little sent me a sheaf of materials to make of them what I could. Included were notes on the question of whether Winnicott was a genius. She had collected various definitions and settled on the "rather prosaic" definition of Ralph Vaughan Williams: "The right person in the right place at the right time." "For me personally," she wrote, "he was a genius" according to this definition. Little listed these characteristics: "Integrity, blend of depth and simplicity, toughness and sensitivity, omnipotence and humility, gentleness and firmness, kindness and generosity, courtesy, humour and fun, deep sense of responsibility, intellect, wide reading, knowledge of what he had learned, command of language, capacity for sheer hard work, absence of self-pity, a fighter, exaggerated self-respect (amour proper)." She also lists "physical courage, moral courage, patience and forbearance, will power and determination, reality sense, artistic faculties (music, drawing and painting, poetry), control and coordination, balance: physical and mental, judgment." She lists also, in the collection of notes: "difficulty in paying people who worked for him adequately"; "Recognition of importance of environment (1) in infancy (2) in analysis. Central, and later: importance of play for the development of creativity, also dependent on environment"; "DWW was one for whom 'truth is greater than consistency,' and yet he was consistent in his efforts to find and set forth truth"; "The basis of my claim to know anything about him is the depth of experience in being his analysand, and that subsequent limited friendship and being a colleague."

Epilogue

1. Bowra, *Romantic Imagination*: pp. 271, 273, 285. "The word 'Romantic'. . . is applied to a phase of English poetry which began in 1789 with Blake's *Songs of Innocence* and ended with the deaths of Keats and Shelley. . . . [The Romantic Movement] insisted passionately on the imagination, but demanded that it should be related to truth and reality. . . . The whole movement has been called the rebirth of wonder."

2. John Turner believes that Winnicott "was trying to identify four stages of illusion, primary; secondary, belonging to the transitional object; then a stage belonging to play; and finally to adult culture." As he sees it, "the 'Use of an Object' paper provides an account of one of the mechanisms whereby illusion is extended still further into the outer world." He attaches "importance to the way Winnicott puts 'shared' in inverted commas when talking of 'shared' reality in this paper." This seems to him "to confirm that there cannot be a world beyond illusion; but equally, of course, there is a significant difference between the different kinds of illusion belonging to different stages of development . . . that we may recognise the externality of the world, but that the quality of that recognition (the world as a good place, bad place, etc.) is what goes on belonging to illusion." In his studies of illusion in Winnicott, Turner describes "the gradual materialization within Winnicott's prose of a poetic spirit that animates the traditions of scientific inquiry" ("Illusion in the Work of Winnicott," 2001, unpublished manuscript).

3. Edmund Burke, "Reflections on the Late Revolution in France"(1790), Edmund Burke, in *The Portable Burke*, ed. Isaac Kramnick (New York: Penguin, 1999).

4. John Turner, "Wordsworth and Winnicott in the Area of Play," in *Transitional Objects and Potential Spaces: Literary Uses of D. W. Winncott*, ed. Peter L. Rudnytsky (New York: Columbia University Press, 1993); and John Turner, "Illusion in the Work of Winnicott" (2001), unpublished manuscript.

5. Harry Guntrip was critical of a theory that emphasized ultimate noncommunication, as if the schizoid core were regarded as normal. (Jeremy Hazell, *H.J.S. Guntrip, A Psychoanalytical Biography* [London: Free Association Books, 1996] pp. 217–18.)

6. "Primitive Emotional Development" (1945).

7. From "Living Creatively" (1970), an amalgamation of two drafts of a talk prepared for the Progressive League.

8. *Home Is Where We Start From, Human Nature, Deprivation and Delinquency, Babies and Their Mothers, Psychoanalytic Explorations, Thinking about Children*, a collection of letters, *The Spontaneous Gesture*, a new edition of his *Collected Papers*, and a new edition of a fragment of clinical material, *Holding and Interpretation*.

The Works of D. W. Winnicott

Compiled by Harry Karnac

W1   *Clinical Notes on Disorders of Childhood*. London: Heinemann, 1931.

W2   *Getting to Know Your Baby*. London: Heinemann, 1945.

W3   *The Ordinary Devoted Mother and Her Baby*. Privately published, 1949.

W4   *The Child and the Family*. London: Tavistock, 1957.

W5   *The Child and the Outside World*. London: Tavistock, 1957.

W6   *Collected Papers: Through Paediatrics to Psycho-Analysis*. London: Tavistock, 1958. New York: Basic Books, 1958. [Reprinted as *Through Paediatrics to Psycho-Analysis*. London: Hogarth Press & the Institute of Psycho-Analysis, 1975; reprinted London: Karnac Books, 1992].

W7   *The Child, the Family and the Outside World*. London: Penguin, 1964. Reading, MA: Addison-Wesley, 1987.

W8   *The Family and Individual Development*. London: Tavistock, 1965.

W9   *The Maturational Processes and the Facilitating Environment: Studies in the Theory of Emotional Development*. London: Hogarth Press & The Institute of Psycho-Analysis, 1965. New York: International Universities Press, 1965. [Reprinted London: Karnac Books, 1990.]

W10   *Playing and Reality*. London: Tavistock, 1971. New York: Methuen, 1982.

W11   *Therapeutic Consultations in Child Psychiatry*. London: Hogarth Press & The Institute of Psycho-Analysis, 1971. New York: Basic Books, 1971.

W12   *The Piggle: An Account of the Psychoanalytic Treatment of a Little Girl* (ed. Ishak Ramzy). London: Hogarth Press & The Institute of Psycho-Analysis, 1977. New York: International Universities Press, 1977.

W13   *Deprivation and Delinquency* (ed. C. Winnicott, R. Shepherd, & M. Davis). London: Tavistock, 1984. New York: Methuen, 1984.

W14   *Home Is Where We Start From* (ed. C. Winnicott, R. Shepherd, & M. Davis). London: Penguin, 1986. New York: W. W. Norton, 1986.

W15   *Holding and Interpretation: Fragment of an Analysis*. London: Hogarth Press & The Institute of Psycho-Analysis, 1986. New York: Grove Press, 1986. [Reprinted London: Karnac Books, 1989.]

W16   *Babies and Their Mothers* (ed. C. Winnicott, R. Shepherd, & M. Davis). London: Free
       Association Books, 1987. Reading, MA: Addison-Wesley, 1987.
W17   *The Spontaneous Gesture* (selected letters, ed. F. R. Rodman). Cambridge, MA: Har-
       vard University Press, 1987.
W18   *Human Nature.* London: Free Association Books, 1988. New York: Schocken Books,
       1988.
W19   *Psycho-Analytic Explorations* (ed. C. Winnicott, R. Shepherd, & M. Davis). London:
       Karnac Books, 1989. Cambridge, MA: Harvard University Press, 1989.
W20   *Talking to Parents* (ed. C. Winnicott, C. Bollas, M. Davis, & R. Shepherd). Reading,
       MA: Addison-Wesley, 1993.
W21   *Thinking About Children* (ed. R. Shepherd, J. Johns, & H. Taylor Robinson). London:
       Karnac Books, 1996. Reading, MA: Addison-Wesley, 1996.

Absence of a Sense of Guilt (The)	1966	W13:106–112
Absence and Presence of a Sense of Guilt		
Illustrated in Two Patients [probably 1966]	n.d.	
Absent by Max B. Clyne [review]	1966	***
New Society 29/9 and *Brit. Med. J.* 8/7/67		
Active Heart Disease	1931	W1:69–75
Adolescence: Struggling through the Doldrums	1961	W8:79–87
New Era in Home & School [1962]		
Also in an altered form entitled "Struggling through		
the Doldrums" *New Society* [1963]		
Adolescents and Morality by E. M. & M. Eppel [review]	1966	W21:48–50
New Society 15/9		
Adolescent Development and Their Implications for		
Higher Education (Contemporary Concepts of)		
[part of Symposium: British Student Health		
Association, 1968]	1971	W10:138–150
Adolescent Immaturity	1971	W14:150–166
Published earlier as "Contemporary Concepts		
of Adolescent Development and Their		
Implications for Higher Education"		W10:138–150
Adolescent Process and the Need for Personal		
Confrontation	1969	***
Pediatrics 44:5 part 1		
Adopted Children in Adolescence	1966	
In *Medical Aspects of Child Adoption*		W21:136–148
Originally published in *Report to Standing*		
Conference of Societies Registered for Adoption [1955]		
Adoption (On) [B.B.C. radio broadcast]	1955	W4:127–130
Adoption Policy and Practice by Iris Goodacre [review]	1966	***
New Society 24/11		
Advising Parents	1957	W8:114–120
Aetiology of Infantile Schizophrenia in Terms		
of Adaptive Failure (The) [paper prepared		
for a study day on Psychosis in Infancy,		
Paris]	1967	W21:218–223
Aggression	1939	W5:167–175
Aggression, Guilt and Reparation	1960	W13:136–144

*** Indicates that the entry does not appear in volumes W1 to W21.

Child Psychiatry, Social Work and Alternative Care
    [talk given to the A.C.P.P.]   1970   W21:277–281
Child Therapy: A Case of Anti-Social Behaviour   1965
    In *Perspectives on Child Psychiatry*
    ed. J. Howells Appears also as Case XV in: W11:270–295
Childhood and Society by E. H. Erikson, 1965
    (Review of)   1965   W19:493–494
    New Society [Sept.]
Childhood Schizophrenia by William Goldfarb, 1961
    [review]   1963   W21:193–194
    Brit. J. Psychiatric Social Work 7
Children and Their Mothers   1940   W13:14–21
    New Era in Home & School 21
Children in Distress by Alec Clegg &
    Barbara Megson [review]   1968   ***
    New Society 7/11
Children in the War   1940   W5:69–74
    New Era in Home & School 21/9:229
Children in the War   1940   W13:25–30
Children Learning   1968   W14:142–149
    In *The Family & God*, Christian Teamwork
    Inst. of Education
Children's Hostels in War and Peace   1948   W5:117–121
    Brit. J. Med. Psychol. 21/3:175
Children's Hostels in War and Peace   1948   W13:73–77
Child's Needs and the Role of the Mother in the
    Early Stages (The) [An excerpt]   1953   W5:13–23
    published in series *Problems in Education*
Classification: Is There a Psycho-Analytic Contribution
    to Psychiatric Classification? [postscript dated
    1964]   1959   W9:124–139
Clinical Approach to Family Problems (A): The Family
    [lecture at London School of Economics]   1959   W21:54–56
Clinical Example of Symptomatology Following
    the Birth of a Sibling (A)   1931ca   W21:97–101
Clinical Illustration of "The Use of an Object"   1968   W19:235–238
Clinical Regression Compared with That of Defence
    Organisation (The Concept of)   1967   W19:193–199
    In *Psychotherapy in the Designed Therapeutic Milieu*
    ed. Eldred & Vanderpol [1968]
Clinical Study of the Effect of a Failure of the Average
    Expectable Environment on a Child's Mental
    Functioning (A) 1965 *IJP* 46:81 Appears also as
    Case IV in: W11:64–88
Clinical Varieties of Transference   1955   W6:295–299
    IJP 37 [1956] :386
Close-Up of Mother Feeding Baby
    [B.B.C. radio broadcast]   1949   W3:27–31
Close-Up of Mother Feeding Baby   1949   W4:38–42
    Colleague (A): Letter to [Sept. 4th]   1967   W17:165
Collection of children's books reviewed
    under the title "Small Things for Small People"
    (A) 1967 *New Society* 7/12

Getting to Know Your Baby [B.B.C. radio broadcast]	1945	W2:1–5
New Era in Home & School 26/1:1		
Getting to Know Your Baby	1945	W4:7–12
Glover, Edward: Letter to [Oct. 23rd]	1951	W17:24–25
Gough, Donald: Letter to [March 6th]	1968	W17:176
Grief and Mourning in Infancy by J. Bowlby		
(Discussion on)	1953	W19:426–432
PSC 15 [1960]		
Group Influences and the Maladjusted Child:		
The School Aspect	1955	W8:146–154
Group Influences and the Maladjusted Child:		
The School Aspect	1955	W13:189–199
Growing Pains	1931	W1 :76-W
Growth and Development in Immaturity	1950	W8:21–29
Guntrip, Harry: Letter to [July 20th]	1954	W17:75–76
Guntrip, Harry: Letter to [Aug. 13th]	1954	W17:77–79
Hallucination and Dehallucination	1957	W19:39–42 I
Hate in the Countertransference	1947	W6:194–203
IJP 30[1949]:69		
Hazlehurst, R. S.: Letter to [Sept. 1st]	1949	W17:17
Haemoptysis: Case for Diagnosis	1931	***
Proceedings of the Royal Society of Medicine 24:855–856		
Health Education through Broadcasting	1957	W20:1–6
Mother and Child 28		
Healthy Individual (The Concept of a)	1967	W14:22–38
In *Towards Community Health* ed. J. D. Sutherland		
[1971]		
Heart (The), with Special Reference to		
Rheumatic Carditis	1931	W1:42–57
Henderson, Sir David K.: Letter to [May 10th]	1954	W17:63–65
Henderson, Sir David K.: Letter to [May 20th]	1954	W17:68–7i
History-Taking	1931	W1:7–21
Hobgoblins and Good Habits	1967	***
Parents 22:9		
Hodge, S. H.: Letter to [Sept. 1st]	1949	W17:i7–19
Hoffer, Will: Letter to [April 4th]	1952	W17:29–30
Holding and Interpretation: Fragment of an Analysis	1986	W15:1–202
An earlier version published in *Tactics and*		
Techniques in Psychoanalytic Therapy ed. P. L.		
Giovacchini [1972]		
Home Again [B.B.C. radio broadcast]	1945	W5:93–97
Home Again	1945	W13:49–53
Hospital Care Supplementing Intensive		
Psychotherapy in Adolescence	1963	W9:242–248
How a Baby Begins to Feel Sorry and to Make		
Amends	1967	***
Parents 22:7 I		
How to Survive Parenthood by Edna J. LeShan		
[review]	1967	***
New Society 26/10		
Human Aggression by Anthony Storr [review]	1968	***
New Statesman 5/7		
Human Nature	1988	W18:1–189

Psychogenesis of a Beating Fantasy	1958	W19:45–48
Psychology of Childhood and Adolescence by C. I. Sandstrom		
[review]	1968	***
National Marriage Guidance Council Journal 11:3		
Psychology of Juvenile Rheumatism (The)	1939	***
In A Survey of Child Psychiatry ed. R. G. Gordon: pp. 28		
Psychology of Madness (The): A Contribution		
from Psycho-Analysis	1965	W19:119–129
Psychology of Separation (The)	1958	W13:132–135
Psycho-Neurosis in Childhood	1961	W19:64–72
Psychoses and Child Care	1952	W6:219–228
Brit. J. Med. Psychol. 26 [1953]		
Psycho-Somatic Disorder (Additional Note on)	1969	W19:115–118
Psycho-Somatic Illness in Its Positive and		
Negative Aspects	1964	W19:103–114
IJP 47[1966]:510		
Psychotherapeutic Consultation in Child Psychiatry (A)	1970	
In The World Biennial of Psychiatry & Psychotherapy		
ed. S. Arieti.		
Also appears as Case XII in:		W1i:194–215
Psychotherapy of Character Disorders	1963	W9:203–216
Psychotherapy of Character Disorders	1963	W13:241–255
Punishment in Prisons and Borstals (Comments		
on the Report of the Committee on)	1961	W13:202–208
Raison, Timothy: Letter to [April 9th]	1963	W17:139–140
Rapaport, David: Letter to [Oct. 9th]	1953	W17:53–54 •
Regression as Therapy Brit. J. Med. Psychol. 36:1.:		
Appears as Case XIV in:	1963	W11:240–269
Relationship of a Mother to Her Baby at the		
Beginning (The) [rewritten 1964]	1960	W8:15–20
Reparation in Respect of Mother's Organized		
Defence against Depression [revised		
August 1954]	1948	W6:91–96
Residential Care as Therapy	1970	W13:220–228
Residential Management as Treatment for		
Difficult Children [with Claire Britton]	1947	W5:98–116
Human Relations 1/1:87		
Residential Management as Treatment for		
Difficult Children [with Claire Britton]	1947	W13:54–72
Return of the Evacuated Child (The) [B.B.C.		
radio broadcast]	1945	W5:88–92
Return of the Evacuated Child (The)	1945	W13:44–48
Rheumatic Clinic (The)	1931	W1:64–68
Rheumatic Fever	1931	W1:58–63
Ries, Hannah: Letter to [Nov. 27th]	1953	W17:54–55
Riviere, Joan: Letter to [Feb. 3rd]	1956	W17:94–97
Riviere, Joan: Letter to [June 13th]	1958	W17:118–119
Rodman, F. Robert: Letter to [Jan. 10th]	1969	W17:180–182
Rodrigue, Emilio: Letter to [March 17th]	1955	W17:86–87
Roots of Aggression	1964	W7:232–239
Roots of Aggression	1968	W19:458–461
Rosenfeld, Herbert: Letter to [Jan. 22nd]	1953	W17:43–46
Rosenfeld, Herbert: Letter to [Oct. 16th]	1958	W17:120

Spock, Benjamin: Letter to [April 9th]	1962	W17:133–138
Squiggle Game (The) [an amalgamation of		
two papers: one unpublished, written in 1964,		
the other published 1968]	1968	W19:299–317
Voices: The Art & Science of Psychotherapy 4/1		
Also appears as Case III in:		W11:42–63
Stealing and Telling Lies	1949	W4:117–120
Stierlin, Helm: Letter to [July 31st]	1969	W17:195–196
Stone, L. Joseph: Letter to [June 18th]	1968	W17:177–178
Stone, Marjorie: Letter to [Feb. 14th]	1949	W17:14–15
Storr, Charles Anthony: Letter to [Sept. 30th]	1965	W17:151
Strachey, James: Letter to [May 1st]	1951	W17:24 I
Strachey (James): Obituary	1969	W19:506–510
IJP 50 [1969]		
String: A Technique of Communication	1960	W9:153–157
Journal of Child Psychology & Psychiatry 4:85		
Struggling through the Doldrums	1963	W13:145–155
New Society [April]		
Study of Three Pairs of Identical Twins (A) by D.		
Burlingham (Review of)	1953	W19:408–412
New Era in Home & School [March]		
Successful Step-parent (The) by Helen Thomson		
[review]	1967	***
New Society 13/4		
Sum, I Am	1968	W14:55–64
Mathematics Teaching [March 1984]		
Support for Normal Parents [B.B.C. radio broadcast;		
published as "Postscript"]	1945	W2:25–27
New Era in Home & School 26/1:16		
Support for Normal Parents	1945	W4:137–140
Susan Isaacs by D. E. M. Gardner (Foreword to)	1969	W19:387–389
Susan Isaacs: Obituary	1948	W19:385–387
Nature [Dec.]		
Symptom Tolerance in Paediatrics: A Case History	1953	W6:101–117
Proceedings of the Royal Society of Medicine 46/8		
Szasz, Thomas: Letter to [Nov. 19th]	1959	W17:126–127
Teacher, the Parent, and the Doctor (The) [read		
before the Ideals in Education Conference]	1936	W21:77–93
Temperature and the Importance of Charts (A Note on)	1931	W1:32–37
Their Standards and Yours [B.B.C. radio broadcast]	1945	W2:21–24
New Era in Home & School 26/1:13		
Their Standards and Yours	1945	W4:87–91
Theme of the Mother's Unconscious as Discovered		
in Psycho-Analytic Practice (Development of the)	1969	W19:247–250
Theoretical Statement of the Field of Child Psychiatry	1958	W8:97–105
Modern Trends in Paediatrics [Second Series]		
Therapy in Child Care: Collected Papers by		
B. Docker-Drysdale (Foreword to)	1968	***
Longmans' Papers on Residential Work Vol. 3		
Thinking and Symbol-Formation [probably 1968]	n.d.	W19:213–216
Thinking and the Unconscious	1945	W14:169–171
The Liberal Magazine [March]		
This Feminism	1964	W14:183–194

Permissions

I acknowledge with gratitude permission granted to me to publish materials as follows:

Paterson Marsh Ltd. on behalf of The Winnicott Trust, for the words and drawings of Donald W. Winnicott.
Paterson Marsh Ltd. on behalf of their Estates for the words of Clare Winnicott, Sigmund Freud, Anna Freud, Lucie Freud, Marion Milner, James Strachey, Alix Strachey, Madeleine Davis, Margaret Little, Michael Balint, William Gillespie, and Wilfred Bion.
Paterson Marsh Ltd. for the words of Hanna Segal.
Eleanor Fairbairn Birtles for the words of W. R. D. Fairbairn.
Nina Farhi for her own words.
James Astor for the words of Michael Fordham.
Renata Gaddini for her own words.
Dodi Goldman for his own words.
Peter Richter for the words of Phyllis Greenacre.
Phyllis Grosskurth for her own words.
Ilse Grubrich-Simitis for her own words.
Hannah Henry for her own words.
Linda Hopkins for her own words.
Athol Hughes for her own words.
Oliver James for the words of Martin James.
Brett Kahr for portions of his *Biographical Portrait* of D. W. Winnicott.
Harry Karnac for his alphabetical list of the work of D. W. Winnicott.
Sybil Stoller for excerpts from the workbooks of Masud Khan.
Pearl King for her own words.

Ruth Petrie, acting for the Melanie Klein Trust, for the words of Melanie
    Klein and Joan Riviere.
Adrian Laing for the words of R. D. Laing.
Jennifer Johns for the words of Thomas Main.
International Creative Management, Inc., for the words of Arthur Miller.
Alice Nemon Stuart for the words of Oscar Nemon.
Angela Rosenfeld for the words of Herbert Rosenfeld.
Peter Schur for the words of Max Schur.

Index

About the Author

F. Robert Rodman, M.D., psychoanalyst and writer, is the author of *Not Dying: A Memoir* and *Keeping Hope Alive: On Becoming a Psychotherapist*, as well as a much-admired interpretive edition of Winnicott's letters, *The Spontaneous Gesture*. Dr. Rodman is a member of the Institute for Advanced Psychoanalytic Studies in Princeton, New Jersey. He practices in Beverly Hills, California.